NAZISM AS FASCISM

Offering a dynamic and wide-ranging examination of the key issues at the heart of the study of German fascism, *Nazism as Fascism* brings together a selection of Geoff Eley's most important writings on Nazism and the Third Reich.

Featuring a wealth of revised, updated and new material, *Nazism as Fascism* analyses the historiography of the Third Reich and its main interpretive approaches. Themes include:

- detailed reflection on the tenets and character of Nazi ideology and institutional practices;
- examination of the complicated processes that made Germans willing to think of themselves as Nazis;
- discussion of Nazism's presence in the everyday lives of the German people;
- consideration of the place of women under the Third Reich.

In addition, this book also looks at the larger questions of the historical legacy of fascist ideology and charts its influence and development from its origin in 1930s Germany through to its intellectual and spatial influence on a modern society in crisis.

In *Nazism as Fascism*, Geoff Eley engages with Germany's political past in order to evaluate the politics of the present day and to understand what happens when the basic principles of democracy and community are violated. This book is essential reading not only for students of German history, but for anyone with an interest in history and politics more generally.

Geoff Eley is the Karl Pohrt Distinguished University Professor at the University of Ann Arbor, Michigan. His previous work includes *A Crooked Line: From Cultural History to the History of Society* (2005) and *Forging Democracy: The History of the Left in Europe, 1885–2000* (2002).

NAZISM AS FASCISM

Violence, Ideology, and the Ground of Consent in Germany 1930–1945

Geoff Eley

Routledge
Taylor & Francis Group
LONDON AND NEW YORK

First published 2013
by Routledge
2 Park Square, Milton Park, Abingdon, Oxon OX14 4RN

Simultaneously published in the USA and Canada
by Routledge
711 Third Avenue, New York, NY 10017

Routledge is an imprint of the Taylor & Francis Group, an informa business

British Library Cataloguing in Publication Data
A catalogue record for this book is available from the British Library

Library of Congress Cataloging in Publication Data
Eley, Geoff, 1949-
Nazism as fascism : violence, ideology, and the ground of consent in Germany 1930-1945 / Geoff Eley.
pages cm
Includes bibliographical references and index.
1. Fascism--Germany--Historiography. 2. National socialism--Historiography.
3. Germany--History--1933-1945. I. Title.
JC481.E35 2013
320.53'3094309043--dc23
2012047899

ISBN: 978-0-415-81262-7 (hbk)
ISBN: 978-0-415-81263-4 (pbk)
ISBN: 978-0-203-69430-5 (ebk)

Typeset in Bembo
by Taylor and Francis Books

CONTENTS

Preface vi

1 Origins, Post-Conservatism, and 1933: Nazism as a Breach 1

2 Driving for Rule, Extracting Consent: Bases of Political Order under Fascism 13

3 The Return of Ideology: Everyday Life, the *Volksgemeinschaft*, and the Nazi Appeal 59

4 Missionaries of the *Volksgemeinschaft*: Ordinary Women, Nazification, and the Social 91

5 Empire, Ideology, and the East: Thoughts on Nazism's Spatial Imaginary 131

6 Putting the Holocaust into History: Genocide, Imperial Hubris, and the Racial State 156

7 Where Are We Now with Theories of Fascism? 198

Index 226

PREFACE

While the underlying concerns and commitments go back a lot further, this book brings together my thinking about Nazism from the past 10 to 15 years. It is meant, above all, to help with the urgency of our present discontents. By reflecting in detail on the historiography of the Third Reich and its main interpretive approaches, it seeks to draw out a number of overarching themes, including the character of Nazi ideology, the forms of its presence in everyday life, and the processes that enabled Germans to turn themselves into Nazis. These in their turn build to a larger argument about fascism. If we can once historicize fascism by understanding its early twentieth-century dynamics, I want to argue, we will grasp far better its possible manifestations now. By studying its earlier forms in this way, we not only give it a past, but enable a general concept to be abstracted, one usable for other settings and other times, including the present. The menacing qualities of our current political moment, country by country, make this task pressingly important. A layering of crisis – the brokenness of polities and the collapse of civility; neoliberal transformations of capitalism and the transnationalizing of labor markets; widening extremes of social inequality; social calamities and political disorders resulting from global environmental catastrophe; a climate of fear where "security" trumps any other consideration; international rivalries for resources – makes it imperative. Those of us who know about earlier, differing but comparable crises can help with the work of theorizing. Whether spatially or metaphorically, in the United States or elsewhere, there exist zones of exception already actualizing a politics that comes dangerously close to what happened before. A portable concept of fascism helps to make these dangers legible.

For anyone concerned about the resilience of democratic forms in the early twenty-first century, coming to terms with Nazism – with the ease of a society's descent toward violence and barbarism – has to retain its urgency. The pursuit of that question led me in my earliest work to study the political fallout from the social consequences of Germany's capitalist transformation between the 1880s and 1920s, as that seemed an excellent means of clarifying why Germany became so vulnerable to fascism later on, whether in the crisis years of 1929 to 1933 or the counter-revolutionary violence of ten years before. In contrast to those historians who stressed the baleful effects of longstanding pre-1914 continuities, the backwardness of authoritarian "pre-industrial traditions" that supposedly kept Germany from becoming "modern," I urged the nature of the "fascism-producing crises" themselves (1929 to 1933, 1918 to 1923) as the best place to begin.[1] That could allow us to bring the pre-1914 years into more helpful and realistic perspective. Rather than defining the *origins* of fascism *per se*, including its *essential* German characteristics, a pre-war crisis of right-wing radicalization in the early 1900s brought some key enabling potentials, what I called "a vital condition of future possibility for the emergence of a German fascism."[2] Having established in this way a better ground for judging the question of continuity as the relation between the 1920s and the 1900s, I could then go back to the immediacies of the fascism-producing crisis itself. An earlier generalizing essay was the result, laying some lasting foundations for the discussion that brings this book to a close.[3]

During 2001 to 2002 while on sabbatical in Irvine, California, I updated my knowledge of Third Reich historiography by reading my way through all of the burgeoning new scholarship.[4] It seemed to me then, as a German historian grappling with Nazism from outside of the immediate field, that I could do useful service by making that new wealth of historiography more widely available. Interest in Nazism has never ceased to excite public interest on the very broadest of fronts, after all, whether from varieties of ethical and political concern, from diverse grounds of empathic identification, or simply from dramatic and sometimes lurid curiosity. In whichever case, German historians have counsel to provide. For faculty and graduate students needing access to the more specialized scholarship, for teachers and students seeking the same kind of guidance, and for any reader wanting a way into these difficult and challenging questions – questions that sometimes require unfamiliar language and ideas – my interconnected treatments may be of some help.

There is a clear politics to this book. It considers what happens when democracy, the rule of law, and the rights of citizenship are all swept away. It explores primary aspects of what comes in their place. It asks after the kinds of community imagined and created for a society in which fascists had their way – where equalities under the law, respect for differences, protections for those without power or property, and the principles of fellow feeling and human kindness were all brutally discontinued. What happened when the democratic gains secured so painfully between the late nineteenth century and the early 1920s were violently taken back? How did the new regime set about building its own forms of exclusionary and coercively secured solidarity? How were Germans made into Nazis? Conversely, how far were people able to push back? Under circumstances of Nazi rule, how did the non-Nazis manage to go on making a life – not just the outright opponents and dissenters, but the many different categories of the apolitical, the pragmatic, and the indifferent, the thoughtlessly patriotic and conformist, and everyone who just "went along," all those described these days somewhat reductively as "bystanders"? "Coming to terms with the [Nazi] past" (*Vergangenheitsbewältigung*) requires putting the most basic of questions – those concerning democracy and citizenship, community and the nation, differences among populations, and the elementary decencies of living together in a society. Under the Third Reich, those values of decency became anathema. Revisiting this past helps to remind us just how essential, if demanding, they have to remain.

Early versions of Chapter 2 were presented in lectures and seminars at the Universities of Melbourne, Sydney, and New South Wales (March 2002), University of California, Irvine (April 2002), University of Nottingham (October 2003), Yale University (January 2006), the German Historical Institute in London (May 2007), and the Pembroke Center at Brown University (October 2011). Elements of Chapters 3 and 4 were first ventured in reviews published by *Signs* (14:3, spring 1989), *German Politics and Society* (24–25, Winter 1991–1992), *Gender and History* (17, 2005), and *WerkstattGeschichte* (40, 2005). A different version of Chapter 5 appeared in the proceedings of a conference on "Space, Identity, and National Socialism" at the University of Loughborough (May 2010), where it began as a closing comment.[5] It was also presented to the Eisenberg Institute of Historical Studies at the University of Michigan (January 2012), King's College London (May 2012), and the Triangle Intellectual History Seminar at the National Humanities Center in North Carolina (September 2012). Distantly related to an essay I wrote in 1983, Chapter 6 began as the Bernard Weiner Holocaust Memorial Lecture at Stetson University in April 2011.[6] Written originally for the School of Criticism and Theory in Ithaca, New York (June 2009), Chapter 7 was presented to audiences at Emory University (November 2009), Birkbeck College (May 2010), the Anthropology–History Symposium at the University of Michigan (October 2010), and the University of California, Irvine (March 2011). I am enormously grateful for each of these invitations and opportunities. The resulting discussions always moved my thinking crucially along.

I would like to thank Ken Garner, who helped invaluably in the final preparation of the manuscript. At Routledge, Vicky Peters helped guide my thinking over many years about this and an associated project. More recently, the support of Michael Strang and Laura Mothersole was also extraordinarily helpful.

As always I am hugely indebted to the ideas and inspiration of many colleagues and friends, whether on the occasions listed above, or in the form of discussions and running conversation, critical readings and other kinds of input, or simply the continuity of intellectual friendship and collaboration. To Lauren Berlant I owe the original urging to make my thinking about Nazism more widely available as an argument about fascism. Whatever clarity I have achieved on the subject owes an enormous amount to Jane Caplan in conversations covering most of an intellectual lifetime. By their invitations, Erica Carter, Vinayak Chaturvedi, Malachi Hacohen, Eric Kurlander, Suzanne Stewart-Steinberg, Katie Trumpener, Chris Szejnmann, and Maiken Umbach provided especially good occasions for venturing my ideas.

For the actual writing of the book, the following proved wonderful interlocutors, offering input of many different kinds, from recondite citations to challenging questions and thinking of the largest kind: Ruth Ben-Ghiat, Anne Berg, Donald Bloxham, Kathleen Canning, Rita Chin, Jessica Dubow, Atina Grossmann, Julia Hell, Jennifer Jenkins, Alf Lüdtke, Bertrand Metton, Bob Moeller, Bradley Naranch, Gina Morantz-Sanchez, Dirk Moses, Roberta Pergher, Mark Roseman, Scott Spector, Richard Steigmann-Gall, George Steinmetz, Dan Stone, Ron Suny, Dennis Sweeney, Julia Adeney Thomas, Adam Tooze, Michael Wildt, and Gerhard Wolf. At the very final stage, Donald Bloxham, Kathleen Canning, Dirk Moses, Dan Stone, and Julia Adeney Thomas gave me indispensable close readings. Julia Thomas deserves the greatest thanks of all. She challenged me to think more clearly about how fascism should be approached comparatively, particularly in its global dimensions with respect to Japan. She guided me through the complicated literatures for that purpose, while a Workshop on "Fascisms Then and Now: Italy, Japan, and Germany" that we organized together at Notre Dame (October 2012) gave shape and direction at a crucial last stage of my writing. By pushing me to think more searchingly about fascisms elsewhere, especially in relation to resources, empire, space, and environment, she made my German arguments more pointed and precise. The closing Chapter 7, with its thoughts on the present, gained hugely as a result. Finally, she read each of the chapters as they were written, with the very best of critical eyes. Whatever virtues my book might possess were made possible by all of this help. The faults are entirely my own.

Notes

1 Here I am alluding to the so-called *Sonderweg* thesis ("special path"), which explained Nazism by deep-historical developmental peculiarities separating Germany from "the West." For the critique, see D. Blackbourn and G. Eley, *The Peculiarities of German History: Bourgeois Society and Politics in Nineteenth-Century Germany*, Oxford: Oxford University Press, 1984.

2 G. Eley, *Reshaping the German Right: Radical Nationalism and Political Change after Bismarck*, Ann Arbor: University of Michigan Press, 1991; orig. edn. 1980, p361. This was the book's very last sentence. I am returning intensively to those questions in a new book called *Genealogies of Nazism: Conservatives, Radical Nationalists, Fascists in Germany, 1860–1930*, forthcoming.

3 G. Eley, "What Produces Fascism: Pre-Industrial Traditions or a Crisis of the Capitalist State?," in Eley, *From Unification to Nazism: Reinterpreting the German Past*, London: Allen and Unwin, 1986, orig. pub. 1983, pp254–82.

4 See G. Eley, "Hitler's Silent Majority? Conformity and Resistance under the Third Reich," *Michigan Quarterly Review*, 2003, vol. XLII, no. 2–3, 2003, pp389–425 and 550–83.

5 C.-C. W. Szejnmann and M. Umbach (eds) *Heimat, Region, and Empire: New Approaches to Spatial Identities in National Socialist Germany*, Houndmills: Palgrave Macmillan, 2012, pp256–79.

6 "Holocaust History," *London Review of Books*, 3–17 March 1983, pp6–9. Other parts of Chapter 6 were first tried out in "Ordinary Germans, Nazism, and Judeocide," in G. Eley (ed.) *The Goldhagen Effect. History, Memory, Nazism: Facing the German Past*, Ann Arbor: University of Michigan Press, 2000, pp1–32. See also G. Eley, "Nazism, Politics, and the Image of the Past: Thoughts on the West German *Historikerstreit*, 1986–87," *Past and Present*, 1988, vol. 121, pp171–208.

1

ORIGINS, POST-CONSERVATISM, AND 1933

Nazism as a Breach

In finding longer-term explanations for Nazism, historians remained fixated for many years on the search for origins, on the uncovering of some peculiarly German pattern of cultural and intellectual history that was, in turn, usually linked to a belief in the weakness of German liberalism and the failings of the German bourgeoisie. Associated during the 1960s most prominently with George Mosse and Fritz Stern, that approach drew gratefully on the comparative knowledge of the postwar social sciences, where key figures such as Ralf Dahrendorf and Barrington Moore, Jr., treated German history as a site of pathology or "misdevelopment," a case of normal history badly gone wrong. German vulnerability to Nazism became identified with certain deep-seated and long-lasting socio-cultural traits, which included the absence of civility, exaggerated respect for authority, commitment to a spiritual ideal of national belonging, and the affirming of nonpolitical values inside a general culture of "illiberalism."[1] The main thrust was to assert Germany's profound differences from "the West." From city elites down to petty hometown notables, the prevailing "apoliticism" signified an absence of civil courage and civic-mindedness, a culture of passivity and deference which worked disastrously against the chances for any vigorous liberalism on the model of what emerged in Britain. Such attitudes were imposed by the political system, sharpened by class antagonisms, stiffened by the revered army, and taught by schools and universities. The Germans of the *Kaiserreich* became stunted and disabled in their exercise of citizenship, looking instead to the state for guidance. Further grounded by the so-called "milieu thesis" propounded by the sociologist M. Rainer Lepsius in a couple of essays at the turn of the 1970s, and imposingly codified by the writings of Hans-Ulrich Wehler and his West German co-thinkers, this *Sonderweg* thesis stabilized for a while into a reigning orthodoxy among German historians.[2]

Although by now the intervening critiques have laid that approach to rest, parts of its appeal remain disconcertingly active. In particular, the underlying argument about political culture – that a fateful gap had opened between the German Bürger's social standing in his local domain and the lodgment of political authority in the state, which could then stifle the civic-mindedness necessary for liberalism – continues to appeal to many German historians. If the steady growth of ideals and practices of self-government characterized social and political history in "the West," such historians believe, then the citizen's relation to the state in Germany went unmediated by the liberalism of representative institutions or the public performance of civic duties. Instead, nationalism functioned as a kind of compensation, a flight forward and upward to the "supreme value of the nation-state," without any intermediary mechanisms of participatory citizenship in between. Works such as Fritz Stern's *The Politics of Cultural Despair* also presented this as an obsessive disavowal of the "modern world" *per se*. The political values of liberalism ("tolerance, dissent, debate, openness") became rejected in favor of an aggressively "Germanic" philosophy.[3] German differences from Britain and France became elaborated into a nationalism based on "racial thought, Germanic Christianity, and Volkish (*völkisch*) nature mysticism," which then doubled as a generalized "anti-modern" cultural critique, a posture of cultural pessimism that became increasingly appealing to widening circles of the educated public.[4] The same outlook also became rooted in romanticist celebrations of local identity, focused on landscape, folkways, and "blood and soil," yet simultaneously joined upward to hypertrophied love of nation.

This gesturing toward a deep cultural sociology of backwardness was always the least adequately theorized or documented part of the *Sonderweg* thesis; yet it remains for many writers as seductive as ever. Even as they disavow any such implication, for example, George Williamson, Dominic Boyer, Kevin Cramer, Isabel Hull, and Helmut Smith have all recently reached for a version of the argument.[5] The same is now true of Thomas Rohkrämer. His latest book sets out to ground an explanation for Nazism in what he thinks was the deeply embedded longing of the German people for national community, "the desire for a *single communal nationalist faith*" (his italics) stretching back to the early nineteenth century (p6).[6] Repeating this phrase throughout the book like a mantra, he argues that "the call for a nation united in a single faith" began with romanticism in the ideas of "individual artists and thinkers in the realm of high culture" before passing into a phase of "highly effective populist mass mobilization" toward the turn of the century (p249). As aversion against "the plurality of modern society" became more and more pronounced and widespread, "the desire for a second, spiritual unification gained unprecedented force in individuals and movements ranging from the veterans' and reservists' associations promoting social militarism as a unifying ideology, the many life-reform movements calling for an authentically German culture, and the Pan-Germans advocating an authoritarian regime which would lead the German people into a struggle for world power" (pp248, 249). As a result of World War I and the divisiveness of Weimar, such desires then underwent a disastrous radicalization in the form first of the Conservative Revolution and later of the more ruthlessly decisive Nazi Party (*Nationalsozialistische Deutsche Arbeiterpartei*, NSDAP). More than simply another authoritarian regime or one "primarily based on force and fear," Rohkrämer argues, the Nazi state finally realized the long-standing popular longings in a "totalitarian" form moved by powerful "utopian" elements. In those terms, the Third Reich seemed "a wholly new phenomenon: a populist right-wing or fascist rule providing at least symbolic forms of political participation and finding majority support through integrative visions of a powerful, rich, and harmonious national future" (p250). But more fundamentally, it was the monstrous apotheosis of that much deeper, historically formed longing for national wholeness.

Most of this is familiar fare. While, in general, Rohkrämer's book rehearses matter already available in the author's earlier works, the nineteenth-century chapters seem especially predictable, taking us from Friedrich Nietzsche, Houston Stewart Chamberlain, and Eugen Diederichs through Richard Wagner to Paul de Lagarde, Wilhelm Heinrich Riehl, Hermann Wagener, and Friedrich Julius Stahl. After dithering over the difficulties of distinguishing between "civic" and "ethnic or cultural" nationalism (pp10–11), moreover, Rohkrämer then hitches his assertions about the peculiar character of German nationalism to the most wooden version of the latter. That culturalist approach has always taken its cue from the counter-reaction of the German Romantics against the French Revolution and the Napoleonic occupation, leading into the patriotic upsurge surrounding the Wars of Liberation. The very process of casting off French domination – and of turning away from "French" ideals – already imparted an anti-democratic quality to German nationalism, it is commonly argued, enabling an ethnically centered and organicist conception of the nation to substitute for the strong associations with citizenship and popular sovereignty forged earlier in France. The belief that nations were defined each by a unique cultural individuality, made manifest in language, customs, religion, institutions, and history, could then serve the purpose of constituting the nation into the new subject of history, forcefully subsuming individual freedoms into the superordinate ideal of national self-realization. Continually invoking the "close emotional ties of communal solidarity," Rohkrämer serves up a slightly warmed-over version of this approach. Thus, the pioneer German nationalists constructed an idealized "picture of a communal past, of eternal ethnic traits, and of a common destiny for the German people or Volk" (p9). They also honed their understanding of what it meant to be German via passionately adversarial commentaries about the French.

It is unclear what might be new about any of this. The central argument remains fuzzy and confused. Having called the opposition between "civic" and "ethnic" nationalism into question, Rohkrämer implements it nonetheless. He doubts the usefulness of the concept of "political religion" only to adopt it anyway, merely substituting the coinage of "communal faith" (pp13–15). He criticizes Jeffrey Herf's concept of "reactionary modernism" while re-inscribing its terms into the body of his account (p12). The ideology of "a single communal faith" cannot be called "a utopia," Rohkrämer thinks, because "the traditional and pragmatic elements are too important in right-wing thought"; yet the Nazis achieved their unprecedented popular success "because they played on deeply engrained anxieties, desires, prejudices, and utopian dreams" (pp13, 3). So which is it to be? In the end, the fantasy structure of Nazi appeals to popular desires for wholeness can only be properly worked out by theorizing a term such as utopia rather than simply invoking the word. But Rohkrämer's ability to tackle that need is preemptively undermined by the deep narrative structure of his account. He concedes Nazism's shockingly decisive breach with the past, only to smooth the force of that difference continuously away. If the devastating novelty of the Nazis is given explanatory priority, then the overarching interpretation works to diminish the clarity of any such recognition. The same applies to Rohkrämer's emphasis on the crises of war and revolution and the vital populist mobilizations of the late *Kaiserreich*. The reader becomes drawn back ever deeper into the nineteenth century instead.

Most tellingly, Rohkrämer recurs time and again to those "deeply engrained" peculiarly German cultural traits that occupy privileged place in his narrative. It seems that something exceptional, a fateful difference from "the West" – namely, that baleful continuity of "fundamentalist desire for a single communal faith" (as the book's blurb describes it) – did provide the distinctive mark of German history after all. The *Sonderweg* thesis "has been rightly criticized for reducing the multifacetedness and openness of history," while demoting the importance of the immediate crises of World War I and Weimar. Yet, at the same time, "many important aspects of the Nazi appeal can be understood adequately only within the context of a longer-term national culture" (p3). Despite Rohkrämer's disclaimer, this straightforward privileging of "longer-term cultural trends and convictions for understanding the fatal attraction of National Socialism" can only be tantamount to bringing the *Sonderweg* back in (p3). In each of the preceding paragraphs' instances, it is less the paradoxes and aporias themselves – the abiding conundrum of the relations between change and continuity, contingency and structure, conjunctural impact and the cultural *longue durée* – that constitute the problem than Rohkrämer's facile manner of presenting them. He states difficulties only in order to roll them over.

To a degree, Rohkrämer offers a useful résumé of arguments about the bases of conformity and ideological cohesion under the Third Reich. The final chapter begins with Walter Benjamin's idea of the "aestheticization of politics" and a glancing reference to political religion, while moving into more detailed explication of the ideas of Alfred Rosenberg, Heinrich Himmler, Adolf Hitler himself, and Josef Goebbels. It continues with the Nazi use of rituals and the "reconciliation of nature and technology," before ending with the *Volksgemeinschaft* (*The Vision of a Harmonious Community of the People*), which for Rohkrämer forms the culmination of the desire for his "single communal faith." But as a general treatment of Nazi ideology, this leaves a huge amount out. The preceding discussions of the Right during Weimar and World War I likewise bring nothing to the given understanding. If potted accounts of the ideas of Oswald Spengler, Arthur Moeller van den Bruck, Carl Schmitt, Ernst Jünger, and Martin Heidegger carry the burden of the one, the latter rests on the usual account of the "ideas of 1914." It is here that the confusion becomes acute. If, as the chapter title suggests, the war was a "watershed," and "what happened in Germany after 1918 is unimaginable" without it (p141), then what exactly is the valency of the argument from deep-cultural continuity?

My point is not that the explanatory importance of the war and the cultural *longue durée* cannot be argued together, but that Rohkrämer makes no attempt seriously to do so. As the Grand Idea of the Single Communal Faith marches through history, any attentiveness to specific causalities or specific effects, to the practical realizing of ideas in particular contexts, or to the concretely contextualized efficacy of intellectual influences in politics falls entirely by the wayside. To gather all of the German Right's history into the terms of this single master-formula entails a truly massive amount of conflation. For one thing, it ignores Germany's well-known regional differences and the extraordinary convolutions of those intervening processes of nation-forming – both before and after the 1860s – which any generalizations about German culture under the *Kaiserreich* must surely have to presume. It also effaces the subtle and burgeoning diversity of philosophical traditions, political ideologies, cultural outlooks, intellectual networks, and circuits of thought that composed the world of ideas that the educated citizenry of the new national state would actually find themselves encountering after 1871. It flattens the heterogeneous and contradictory possibilities of the discursive landscape that enlivened the public culture in that rapidly expanding and transforming society that Germany became by the turn of the century. Still more, it homogenizes the entire nineteenth century extremely reductively into a single overarching narrative. Above all, Rohkrämer's exposition suggests that under the *Kaiserreich*, German society was always already the incubator for a set of cultural traits that, under conditions of crisis, would dispose its bourgeois citizenry toward irrationalist, mystical, authoritarian, anti-democratic, and other kinds of "illiberal" behavior less likely to be embraced in Britain, France, and other countries further to "the West." Against this relentless causal centering of "the single communal faith," any acknowledgment of either contested agency or historical contingency becomes merely rhetorical.

In welcome contrast, Stefan Breuer's study of the *völkisch* Right under the *Kaiserreich* and the Weimar Republic offers a carefully differentiated intellectual and political account of its subject. The latest of its author's many writings on the German Right, this book brings some much needed clarity and focus to a topic whose treatments have been notoriously diffuse.[7] German historians have never known quite what to do with the *völkisch* sector of right-wing politics and thought under the *Kaiserreich*. Most see it as an exotic and marginal fringe without influence on the mainstream of legitimate party politics and government policy, whose significance arrives only retrospectively in light of what happens after 1918. In those terms, historians from George Mosse to Roger Chickering have simultaneously dismissed the *völkisch* Right and valorized it, arguing its crankiness and marginality before 1914 while necessarily upholding its significance as an origin. Along with other extreme segments, such as the Pan-Germans and the various tendencies of anti-Semites, *völkisch* thinkers and activists become assimilated into an amorphously defined reservoir of dangerous right-wing ideas whose efficacy only the later radicalizations will eventually allow to be tapped. The young Adolf Hitler's relationship to this earlier *völkisch* heritage is presented in exactly this kind of way. In contrast, the more concrete relationship of *völkisch* ideology to the Right's transformations before 1914 seldom gets posed.

This is where Breuer makes a valuable contribution. He builds on the recent research of Uwe Puschner and his collaborators while going beyond their essentially compilatory methodology.[8] In keeping with his earlier works, Breuer concentrates on the drawing of ideological distinctions, taking pains to separate *völkisch* nationalism not only from the already formed conservative and liberal outlooks, but also from the subsequent nationalist departures associated in the 1920s with Jünger and the Conservative Revolution. He also distinguishes it from the various strands of race theory as they materialized between the 1890s and the aftermath of World War I. On the other hand, he draws a far stronger set of positive linkages to the political anti-Semitism of the late 1870s and 1880s than some of the latter's historians are now inclined to do, showing how the one feeds directly into the other. Indeed, the indifferent success of the anti-Semitic parties in electoral and parliamentary terms precisely encouraged a turn toward the associational networks, discussion circles, and intellectual societies, which for Breuer became the characteristic modalities of specifically *völkisch* political action, marking the passage "from discourse to movement." For Breuer – in contrast with Puschner's excessively eclectic definitional emphasis on religious and philosophical styles of thought – the distinctively *völkisch* politics inhered in a field of practice oriented toward the associational world of the pressure groups and parties enabled links, in particular, with the Pan-Germans and other radical nationalists, the colonial movement, the movement for "race hygiene," and many aspects of *Lebensreform* (life reform). Substantively speaking, a *völkisch* outlook implied belief in the social value of the *Mittelstand*, an emergent radical nationalist ideology, and a complex relationship to Germany's rapidly transforming urban-industrial modernity.

Breuer's exhaustive explication of right-wing thought in his earlier *Ordnungen der Ungleichheit* (*Orders of Inequality*) supplies a much fuller context for this argumentation. There he describes the various tendencies of the Right as inhabiting a common intellectual space defined by an elaborately differentiated array of themes. Ever the strict Weberian, he arranges the key conceptual distinctions around a set of ideal-typical standpoints, whose recurring combinations provided the trajectory that carried the Right forward from the Bismarckian period down to the Third Reich. The pertinent keywords were soil, blood, people/nation, political rule both in its domestic and imperialist guise, economy and the social, population and family, culture and civilization, religion, and anti-Semitism. On the basis of this schema, Breuer argues that the *Kaiserreich* brought a crucial historic break from an earlier traditionalist master discourse of conservatism, because, during the passage to industrial modernity, the values of family, religion, and rootedness that grounded that older conservatism decisively lost their purchase. Though recuperated into the new forms of right-wing politics, those ideas became necessarily infused with radically new content, thereby making the emergent repertoire of the

Right's thought specifically post-conservative. The motivating urgency for that post-conservatism came from an intensely ambivalent interaction with modernity.[9]

The new core was a commitment to inequality, whose particular meanings could be conceived in a variety of ways. The most salient version derived its principle of societal order from belief in the naturally unequal endowment of human populations, linked to a theory of elites and the attendant hierarchical ethic of social practice. That became combined more and more with a scientistic approach to the measurement and valuation of human capacities and entitlements, which likewise sustained a generalized philosophy of human nature commonly characterized as social Darwinist. Already a powerful explanation for the social topography of class, the distribution of wealth and attainment, and the perpetuation of poverty, such ideas were then worked into proposals for organizing access to power and participation in the polity, too. They also connected with theories of sovereignty, imperialism, and antagonistic relations among states. Given such thought, a range of more specific ideologies now coalesced, taking the master concept of inequality for common orientation. These included various types of nationalism, movements of the arts and aesthetics, bio-political and eugenicist programs, visions of prosperity linked to the national economy and its world-political expansion, geopolitical programs, diverse anti-Semitisms, and varieties of *völkisch* thought, all invariably revolving around ideas of race.

Of course, the unifying thread of this world of right-wing ideas, its political hardwiring, was the shared enmity against liberal and democratic calls for individual freedom and equality, not to speak of the still more radical hatred of socialism. It was against these progressivist ideals that the Right's redeployed hierarchical prescriptions for social and political order became so vehemently counter-posed. In the minds of many right-wing commentators, those hated ideals also inhered in the experience of the West, and to that extent the desire to validate a German *Sonderweg* – the idea that Germany could avoid the social divisiveness and class conflict accompanying the victory of liberalism in Britain and France – was certainly in play. But the German Right's hostility to democracy was not by that virtue antimodern in any analytically sensible use of the term. Its commitment to inequality implied no across-the-board or straightforward refusal of what by 1900 were understood to be the main features of the arriving social world of modernity.

Indeed, some of this emergent Right's most fervent beliefs – in the new technologies of industrial expansion and the imperialist entailments of a powerful economy, for instance, or in the challenges of the new conditions of mass-political action – now presumed that modernity had definitely arrived to stay.[10] As Breuer argues, it was the Right's unavoidable location inside the very processes of industrial society's creation before 1914 that made sense of its distinctive political outlook, whether ideologically in terms of its salient attitudes and commitments, or "objectively" in terms of its sociological profile. The Right's most vigorous organizers and activists as it emerged into the 1900s – including the Pan-German ideologues such as Alfred Hugenberg and Heinrich Claß, leading personalities of the nationalist pressure groups such as August Keim or Eduard von Liebert, *völkisch* impresarios such as Theodor Fritsch and Friedrich Lange, journalists and pamphleteers such as Heinrich Oberwinder and Ernst von Reventlow, and countless minor figures and functionaries – lived and worked inside the distinctively modern institutional worlds of the professions and the public sphere. Authentically "modern" forces, including the dynamism of the industrial economy, the romance of science and technology, the drive for imperialist expansion, and the harnessing of national resources, including all aspects of the available reservoir of human population, inspired them to grandiose projects of foreign and domestic policy. If superficially the national fantasy of harmonious community harked back to a chimerical lost age, moreover, that discourse was also necessarily shaped by the terms and consequences of Germany's unfolding societal transformation. The post-conservative Right's critique of modernity itself presumed the continuing and inescapable pervasiveness of "the modern." It subsisted on the given and unfolding actuality of modern times.

As intellectual history, *Ordnungen der Ungleichheit* offers a sophisticated and extraordinarily nuanced explication of the full range of right-wing ideas before 1914. It is hard to imagine a more exhaustive mapping of that ideological landscape. Yet, in the end, Breuer's approach displays two drawbacks, which become more visible in the more focused thematics of *Die Völkischen in Deutschland*. First, it shows too little interest in gauging the forms of practicable influence for this or that particular body of right-wing ideas. Indeed, no idea circulating in the most recondite corner of the Right's fringe publications seems outlandish enough to escape his gaze. It is very illuminating to have such ideas situated inside the various discursive fields Breuer sets out to distinguish, with all their complex overlappings and important inter-articulations. But he devotes scant attention to the problem of reception, to the place of those ideas inside the organized political histories of the pressure groups and parties, to their impact upon public debate, or to their meanings for the major episodes of advocacy and contestation through which the Right's politics moved forward. By concentrating specifically on the *völkisch* movement, the new book does more to focus the argument concretely in that regard, but a more extensive analysis of the practical impact of *völkisch* ideas in the polity is still badly needed.

The second drawback is a problematic account of the social tensions resulting from industrialization. To the extent that Breuer grounds his arguments in a particular social history, he resorts to a modernization-derived sociology of the status anxieties of those groups less able – structurally and statistically – to benefit from Germany's capitalist transformation or who experienced its goods mainly as a tense, ambiguous, and elusive set of prospective opportunities. These included small farmers and the traditional petty bourgeoisie of the towns (craftsmen, carters, merchants, shopkeepers, retailers, small independent producers, and traders of all kinds), but also the educated middling strata of teachers, clergy, journalists, white-collar personnel, and lower layers of the professions.[11] Interestingly, there is little trace here of Lepsius's old milieu thesis. Rather than any long-lasting persistence of traditional affiliations, Breuer finds mainly the instabilities resulting from the rapid mobility of the new social relations. He also highlights the "dissonance" between the new educational and professional opportunities offered to "the educated segment of the urban Mittelstand" and their actual experience of subordinated status, alienating bureaucracy, and rationalization of social life, which under the Empire's societal norms still compromised the benefits of upward mobility. Thwarted in the promise of the greatly vaunted "neo-humanist ideals," while denied the more traditional forms of cultural capital, this educated middle class, Breuer argues, reached for a wide variety of restorative philosophies – for the ideal of a reintegrated life, or "retotalization" in the search for "meaningful forms of wholeness" (*Ganzheiten*), as Breuer calls them – from *Lebensreform*, *Freikörperkultur* (nudism), natural therapies, environmentalism, theosophy, monism, and versions of the occult to the burgeoning repertoire of the new *völkisch* social and political outlook.[12]

This was a discomfort with modernity, a nervous disquiet attaching to the consequences of the *Kaiserreich*'s unfolding dynamism, rather than any anti-modernism *per se*.[13] Yet if Breuer takes some pains to situate this unease explicitly inside the structures of Germany's modernity, his argument is still constructed around an idea of the "winners and losers" of the modernization process.[14] The discursive shifts leading to a new politics of the Right before 1914 are still referred primarily to the destabilizing effects of changes occurring in the social structure. The translation from this sociology of occupational change to a narrative of political innovation then occurs by correspondence and correlation, with no mechanisms of concrete causality, no place for particular forms of agency, and no relationship to any particular events. We are back once again to a presumption of social determination based on a set of theoretical claims about the cultural proclivities of certain sections of the *Bildungsbürgertum*. His sociology may possess far more nuance, but no less than his predecessors, Breuer makes it into the underlying referent for his argument about the specificities of *völkisch* thought.[15]

Despite these difficulties, Breuer's account offers a sophisticated proposal for relating the emergence of new types of politics to the sociologies of German industrialization and the social histories of cultural modernity at the turn of the twentieth century – which, regardless of whether fully acknowledged, remains one of the abiding challenges for most German historians interested in this period. Breuer's specific analysis of the *völkisch* political presence is perhaps more valuable for the pre-1914 years than for the Weimar Republic, where the available historiography is both more extensive and more securely integrated within the overall political history of the period. While Breuer's account of the Wilhelmine *völkisch* groups succeeds by the very concreteness of the bearings it provides, much of that work for the later period has already been done. Instead, we need carefully constructed monographic explorations that show how the *völkisch* outlook was translated into political practices on the ground – in the kaleidoscopic local affiliations of the Right, in the everydayness of its political action, in the transactional dynamics of local coalition-building, and in the adversarial mobilizations that produced the coalescence of right-wing energies after 1930. In that regard, Breuer provides less of an advance on the much older literatures, for which Uwe Lohalm's superb account of the Deutsch *völkischer Schutz-und Trutz-Bund* still provides the gold standard.[16] Far more seriously, while Breuer upholds the vital enabling impact of World War I for the wider resonance of *völkisch* ideas, any substantive discussion of the war years themselves is omitted.

So these two books make an extremely revealing contrast. Breuer's *Die Völkischen in Deutschland* shows how an apparently well-worked topic can deliver valuable new knowledge about a particular sector of the German Right's development in the early twentieth century. While guided analytically by a larger conception of the Right's history in the period, its treatment of *völkisch* politics is linked theoretically in its turn to macro-historical arguments about Germany's capitalist transformation (or modernization, as Breuer prefers). Breuer also models the gains to be made by taking a controlled longer perspective that spans the conventional period break between *Kaiserreich* and Weimar Republic. Rohkrämer's *A Single Communal Faith?*, on the other hand, subordinates the particularities of periods and their processes of change to an overarching thesis about the dilemmas of modernity stretching across one and a half centuries. "How could the Right transform itself from a politics of the nobility to a fatally attractive option for people from all parts of society?" he asks. His answer, which sees "the fundamentalist desire for a single communal faith" as a constantly evolving dominant trope of German public life between 1800 and 1945, is so vague and malleable as to sacrifice any specificity of insight. The "searching for a sense of identity and belonging" *per se* has conventionally been taken to characterize the European experience of modernity more generally, after all. But Rohkrämer clearly thinks there was something peculiarly German about that need to satisfy "metaphysical security" by fashioning "a mental map for the modern world" out of nationalism. If that is so, then we are certainly back on the *Sonderweg*. Now more than ever, unfortunately, that leads only into a dead end.

Notes

1 See F. Stern, *The Politics of Cultural Despair: A Study in the Rise of the Germanic Ideology*, Berkeley: University of California Press, 1961; G. L. Mosse, *The Crisis of German Ideology: Intellectual Origins of the Third Reich*, New York: Howard Fertig, 1964; R. Dahrendorf, *Society and Democracy in Germany*, London: Weidenfeld and Nicholson, 1968, p404.

2 See M. R. Lepsius, "Parteiensystem und Sozialstruktur. Zum Problem der Demokratisierung der deutschen Gesellschaft," in G. A. Ritter (ed.) *Die deutschen Parteien vor 1918*, Cologne: Kiepenheuer und Witsch, 1973, pp56–80; and "Demokratie in Deutschland als historisch-soziologisches Problem," in T. W. Adorno (ed.) *Spatkapitalismus oder Industriegesellschaft. Im Auftrage der Deutschen Gesellschaft fur Soziologie*, Stuttgart: F. Enke, 1969, 197–213. Both essays were republished in M. R. Lepsius, *Demokratie in Deutschland. Soziologisch-historische Konstellationsanalysen. Ausgewahlte Aufsatze*, Göttingen: Vandenhoeck & Ruprecht, 1993, pp25–50, 11–24; H.-U. Wehler, *Das Deutsche Kaiserreich 1871–1918*, Göttingen: Vandenhoeck & Ruprecht, 1973, translated as *The German Empire 1871–1918*, Leamington Spa: Berg, 1985.

3 F. Stern, "Introduction," in *The Failure of Illiberalism: Essays on the Political Culture of Modern Germany*, London: George Allen and Unwin, 1972, px.

4 Mosse, *Crisis of German Ideology*, p1.

5 G. S. Williamson, *The Longing for Myth in Germany: Religion and Aesthetic Culture from Romanticism to Nietzsche*, Chicago: University of Chicago Press, 2004; D. Boyer, *Spirit and System: Media, Intellectuals, and the Dialectic in Modern German Culture*, Chicago: University of Chicago Press, 2005; K. Cramer, *The Thirty Years' War and German Memory in the Nineteenth Century*, Lincoln: University of Nebraska Press, 2007; I. V. Hull, *Absolute Destruction: Military Culture and the Practices of War in Imperial Germany*, Ithaca: Cornell University Press, 2005; H. W. Smith, *The Continuities of German History: Nation, Religion, and Race Across the Long Nineteenth Century*, Cambridge: Cambridge University Press, 2008. The same interpretive tradition certainly retains its life in Germany itself and elsewhere, too; but the discussion in the English-speaking world contains its own distinctive inflections. For a recent German text bizarrely indifferent to the critique of the Sonderweg thesis, see W. Lepenies, *The Seduction of Culture in German History*, Princeton: Princeton University Press, 2006.

6 T. Rohkrämer, *A Single Communal Faith? The German Right from Conservatism to National Socialism* (New York: Berghahn Books, 2007).

7 See S. Breuer, *Ordnungen der Ungleichheit. Die deutsche Rechte im Widerstreit ihrer Ideen 1871–1945*, Darmstadt: Wissenschaftliche Buchgesellschaft, 2001; Breuer, *Grundpositionen der deutschen Rechten 1871–1945*, Tübingen: Edition Diskord, 1999; Breuer, *Anatomie der konservativen Revolution*, Darmstadt: Wissenschaftliche Buchgesellschaft, 1993; Breuer, *Nationalismus und Faschismus. Frankreich, Italien und Deutschland im Vergleich*, Darmstadt: Wissenschaftliche Buchgesellschaft, 2005.

8 U. Puschner, *Die völkische Bewegung im wilhelminischen Kaiserreich. Sprache, Rasse, Religion*, Darmstadt: Wissenschaftliche Buchgesellschaft, 2001; U. Puschner, W. Schmiotz, and J. H. Ulbricht (eds) *Handbuch zur "Völkischen Bewegung" 1871–1918*, Munich: K. G. Saur, 1996.

9 As well as Breuer, *Ordnungen*, see S. Breuer, *Die Volkischen in Deutschland. Kaiserreich and Weimarer Republik* (Darmstadt: Wisserschaftliche Buchgesellschaft, 2008), pp12–22; *Anatomie*, pp9–25; and Breuer, "Der Neue Nationalismus in Weimar und seine Wurzel," in H. Berding (ed.) *Mythos und Nation. Studien zur Entwicklung des kollektiven Bewußtseins in der Neuzeit*, Frankfurt am Main: Suhrkamp, 1996, pp257–74.

10 Here Breuer observes his crucial distinction between conservative and post-conservative forms of thought, where the latter are taken to characterize the "Right" *per se*. In other words, the active embrace of technological modernity and mass political action was precisely what distinguished the early twentieth-century Right from those preceding traditionalist forms of conservatism.

11 Breuer, *Die Völkischen*, p14. This argument has affinities with an earlier literature linking the emergence of a new anti-Semitic and radical-right politics to changes occurring in those same parts of the social structure and small business sectors of the economy. See R. Gellately, *The Politics of Economic Despair: Shopkeepers and German Politics 1890–1914*, London: Sage Publications, 1974; S. Volkov, *The Rise of Popular Antisemitism: The Urban Master Artisans, 1873–1896*, Princeton: Princeton University Press, 1978; H. A. Winkler, *Mittelstand, Demokratie und Nationalsozialismus. Die politische Entwicklung von Handwerk und Kleinhandel in der Weimarer Republik*, Cologne: Kiepenheuer and Witsch, 1972.

12 Breuer, *Die Völkischen*, p14.

13 For an interesting and courageous attempt to explore this new cultural predicament, see J. Radkau, *Das Zeitalter der Nervosität. Deutschland zwischen Bismarck und Hitler*, Munich: Hanser, 1998; and A. D. Rabinbach, *The Human Motor: Energy, Fatigue, and the Origins of Modernity*, New York: Basic Books, 1990.

14 Breuer's approach is an adaptation of Ulrich Beck's concept of "reflexive modernization," which finds certain entailments of critique and dissatisfaction always already inscribed in the very processes of industrial society's unfolding. With subsequent twentieth-century restructurings of economy and society, such unease is then increasingly, explicitly, and elaborately realized across the many different fronts of social,

cultural, and intellectual life. For Beck this signifies the transition from a "first" to a "second modernity." Where the former may be characterized by the assertion of powerful ordering principles increasingly implemented through the agency of a state, accompanied by the dream of society's eventual cohesion and ultimately realized integration, the latter is predicated around growing uncertainty and skepticism about such things, involving instability, complexity, ambivalence, and necessary incompletion. Thus, a key manifestation of the advent of "reflexive modernity" at the turn of the twentieth century, according to Breuer, was the holistic desire for "re-integration," a "synthetic-harmonizing pattern of thought," through which its exponents hoped a lost wholeness might be regained. See Breuer, *Die Völkischen*, pp13, 14–20; and U. Beck, *The Risk Society: Towards a New Modernity*, London: Sage Publications, 1992.

15 For a similar determinism, see J. Z. Muller, *The Other God That Failed: Hans Freyer and the Deradicalization of German Conservatism*, Princeton: Princeton University Press, 1987, p38.

16 U. Lohalm, *Völkischer Radikalismus. Die Geschichte des Deutschvölkischen Schutz- und Trutz-Bundes 1919–1923*, Hamburg: Leibniz-Verlag, 1970.

2

DRIVING FOR RULE, EXTRACTING CONSENT

Bases of Political Order under Fascism

Changing approaches to the history of Nazism

Since 1980, scholarly approaches to the history of the Third Reich have been entirely transformed. Of course, some topics will never go away. The political dynamics of the collapse of Weimar always keep their fascination, as do biographies of leading Nazis and their opponents.[1] Studies of the Nazi economy, the Nazi state, and discrete policy areas, whether institutionally conceived or in their social effects, will still require the historian's careful attention.[2] But in other ways work on Nazism has moved with the historiographical barometer. Emerging from the 1970s, it showed all the strengths of the newly ascendant social history, including systematic sociologies of the Nazi Party (NSDAP) and its electorate, sophisticated analyses of its varying strength across regions and localities of different types, and accounts of its appeal to a wide variety of social groups.

Perhaps two types of study stood out. One was the local or regional account of Nazi social support, concentrating on the "movement" as against the "regime" phase of the history. The main arc of that research ran from, say, the classic accounts by William Sheridan Allen of Northeim and Jeremy Noakes of Lower Saxony published in 1965 and 1971 to, say, the six volumes of Martin Broszat's "Bavaria Project" appearing between 1977 and 1983.[3] Rather quickly, we acquired a comprehensive picture of Nazi sociology, including systematic studies of the Nazi Party and its electorate, similar studies of the SA (*Sturmabteilung*: Stormtroopers or Storm Divisions), the beginnings of work on the youth and women's auxiliaries, sophisticated analyses of the movement's varying strength across regions and localities of different types, and accounts of its appeal to a wide range of social categories. We had Michael Kater's book on the sociology of the party (1983), those of Mathilde Jamin (1984), Richard Bessel (1983), Eric Reiche (1986), and Conan Fischer (1983) on the SA, and that of Tom Childers on the Nazi electorate (1983), slightly preceded by Richard Hamilton (1982) and eventually followed by Jürgen Falter (1991). A very good cross-section through the scholarship of that time can be found in the Childers volume edited in 1986 on *The Formation of the Nazi Constituency 1919–1933*.[4] The culmination of this intensely accumulating monographic scholarship was Peter Fritzsche's 1990 study of northern Germany based on his earlier dissertation, *Rehearsals for Fascism: Populism and Political Mobilization in Weimar Germany*. From this apex of the social history of the rise of the Nazis there followed a definite hiatus. Yet, the lasting outcome has been a remarkably solid historiographical consensus about the grounding of the Third Reich's popular legitimacy, based on well-established claims regarding its pre-1933 eliciting of broadly based societal support. Fritzsche's 1998 synthesis, *Germans into Nazis*, provides the best access to this consensus.[5]

A second category of study focused on the Third Reich's institutional history, beginning with Hans Mommsen's classic account of the Nazi civil service and Martin Broszat's general dissection of the "Hitler state."[6] Both these approaches shared an extreme skepticism about ideology, as historians turned away from the intellectual history previously shaping the main Anglo-American historiography. Rather than explaining Nazism by its roots in Germany's peculiar cultural history or tracing its policies to Hitler's world view and the Nazis' public ideology, these new historians emphasized social forces and social determinations, foregrounding the social contexts that lent Nazi politics their sense. Likewise, Broszat and Mommsen discarded the simplified totalitarian model of the Nazi state with its stress on institutional cohesion and the successful top-down imposition of Nazi values onto German society. Instead of clearly held and consistent ideological designs driving Nazi policies, they saw a process of "cumulative radicalization" and the unevenly evolving consequences of the regime's institutional disorder. In this view, the brutal dynamism of the Nazis owed as much to initiatives from below and improvised aggression as to the logical unfolding of any detailed ideological plan.[7]

These approaches of the 1960s and early 1970s were guided by a politics. Once the explanatory sufficiency of Nazi ideology and Nazi totalitarianism had been questioned, in other words, it was possible to have a very different discussion of Nazism's relationship to German society, one less beholden to models of coercion and far more open to arguments about consent. If Nazi rule could rely less straightforwardly on a centrally directed machinery of police repression than we had previously thought, and if the Nazi state was less an efficient system of centralized authority than a veritable chaos of competing and overlapping jurisdictions, the new historians urged, then the way was clear for a more complex understanding of how the Third Reich worked. If the police state reached less completely into ordinary life than the totalitarian model claimed, and social conformity relied on more than violence, terror, and intimidation, then positive mechanisms of cooperation and complicity must surely have been present. In conceptualizing those bases of successful integration, accordingly, the new historians turned mainly to arguments about social interest and social function.

New research during the 1970s concentrated on the response to Nazism of the German élites, both before and after 1933, including heavy industry and other big business interests, large landowners, the civil service, the military, and eventually the professions. Whereas the earliest accounts of 1933 to 1934 had stressed the totalizing ruthlessness of Nazi actions after the seizure of power in the so-called *Gleichschaltung* (coordination and synchronization, the bringing of existing institution into line with Nazi rule), historians now found more complex negotiations and continuities to have been at work, leaving ample room for the self-regulated and willing adaptation of pre-Nazi interests to the emerging new order. A new concept, *Polykratie* (polycracy), was devised for the resulting system, implying the hybrid coexistence of multiple power centers within the superficially coordinated apparatus of the Nazi state, crystallizing willy-nilly to accommodate this collaborative regroupment. Rather than a rampant and criminal movement of fanatics simply ramming their ideology down respectable Germany's throat, as the earlier accounts often implied, a far more discomforting picture of broadly diffused societal complicity began to take shape.[8]

That approach proved highly contentious. So long as Nazism's crimes had been attached to easily demonized ringleaders and ideological fanatics (Hitler and his henchmen and their convinced Party and SS followers), accusations of guilt and responsibility also remained bounded; but once the compliance of wider social circles with Nazi policies was shown (civil servants, managers, businessmen, specialists and professionals of all kinds), the responsibility of supposedly non-Nazi élites inevitably came to the agenda, moved by a growing critique of fudged moral accounting after 1945. Against these political implications, advocates of the narrower conception of responsibility tightly drawn around Hitler, usually more traditional political or diplomatic historians, reacted with anger. Historians such as Mommsen and Broszat were seeking to tar post-1945 conservatives with the Nazi brush, they alleged, while sidestepping the depraved enormity of Hitler's personal agency and diffusing responsibility so widely through German society that it lost any relationship to specific authorship at all. The new historiography was thus politically disingenuous and morally evasive, they alleged. To understand Nazi military aggression and the genocide of the Jews, Hitler's own longstanding intentions were all that was needed. Nazi fanaticism supplied a perfectly sufficient explanation.

These disagreements erupted into reckless acrimony at a conference in Windsor organized by London's German Historical Institute in 1979, where "intentionalists" and "structuralists" fought each other to a polarized standstill. Controversy was most bitter around the "Final Solution," which was only then entering widespread West German public debate under the impact of the television film *Holocaust*. Thus, while reiterating Hitler's underlying authority for the Nazi drive against the Jews and the long-term impetus provided by Nazi ideology, on the one side, Mommsen and Broszat ("structuralists") argued that the turning to genocide as such was something new resulting from the years 1939 to 1941. The unprecedented wartime opportunities set off a complex dialectic between institutional chaos, logistical exigencies, and the new scope for extremist action. Only through the resulting "cumulative radicalization," they argued, could it become feasible to organize the complete genocide of the Jewish people. Against this view, on the opposing side, Klaus Hildebrand and Andreas Hillgruber ("intentionalists") insisted on Hitler's unique and direct authorship going back to the earliest years of his movement. In this understanding, the "Final Solution" unfolded with the force and logic of a "grand design," a "blueprint" originally laid out, with complete clarity, in *Mein Kampf*.[9]

Clearly, the search for complex explanations urged by social history was disturbing the established patterns of historical accounting for Nazism in West German political culture. Meanwhile, labor historians had been developing skepticism of their own about the usefulness of focusing on Nazi ideology. Both underrepresented in the Nazis' ranks before 1933 and solid in their own Communist and Social Democratic allegiances, such historians argued, German workers proved relatively resistant to the Nazi political message. Even after the labor movement's violent destruction, the regime only exercised its political control within certain practical limits, frustrated by the workers' strong residual and defensive class consciousness. In the thinking of many social historians, in fact, the potential for class conflict remained structural and endemic, a permanent and irreducible feature of social life under capitalism, giving working-class culture an imperviousness to certain kinds of ideological persuasion, which neither the Nazis' repression nor their propaganda offensives could ever completely penetrate or sweep away. This was the view of the Third Reich's premier social historian of the 1970s, Tim Mason, who made his case in a series of brilliant essays and an imposing volume of documentation and accompanying analysis, lending further weight to Mommen's and Broszat's critique of the totalitarian model.[10]

Mason took pains to distinguish between the political *resistance* of the labor movement's illegal underground (the surviving fragments of post-1933 Communist and Social Democratic organization), which was necessarily secretive, small scale, and isolated from wider support, and the slow resurfacing of class conflict in industry, which he termed the workers' *opposition*. Coerced into practical and self-protective conformity and deprived of their historic legal representation, the mass of ordinary workers pragmatically accepted the Third Reich's delivery of material improvements, he argued, while continuing to withhold their positive identification and political allegiance. This "opposition" thus remained essentially non-political. It amounted to a silent refusal of the regime's ideological message and a withholding of active consent, either by pulling back into the relative safety of private life or at most by holding to the ground of an economistically defined self-interest, obstinately akin to the trade unionism now no longer available. Thus, while the "workers' opposition" posed big problems for the regime during 1936 to 1940, in Mason's view, it could never graduate into any explicit political challenge: "It manifested itself through spontaneous strikes, through the exercise of collective pressure on employers and Nazi organizations, through the most various acts of defiance against workplace rules and government decrees, through slowdowns in production, absenteeism, the taking of sick-leave, demonstrations of discontent, etc."[11]

Most influential social histories of the 1970s followed some version of Mason's logic. In the Bavaria Project the analogue to Mason's "opposition" was Broszat's more qualified idea of *Resistenz*, for example. Broszat used this to capture not the forms of a translated or displaced authentic opposition whose actions thwarted the regime's fundamental goals, as Mason sought to suggest, but rather a category of behaviors that exercised only "a limiting effect" on its totalizing ambition.[12] But the implications reached no less far. The fine social histories published in the Bavaria Project's six volumes during 1977 to 1983 had the effect of shifting attention away from the failed assassination plot of July 1944, which had long monopolized perceptions of the German Resistance, refocusing instead on the contexts of everyday life. Broszat and his colleagues insisted that the efficacy of the Third Reich's governing system needed to be judged through the experiences of ordinary citizens, who lacked the conspiratorial resources, social privileges, languages of ethical heroism, and exceptional agency available to the élite participants in the July Plot, but faced no less acute moral and practical dilemmas in their working, social, and familial lives. A more complex concept of resistance as nonconformity or dissent would allow us to grasp those quotidian realities of social life far more effectively, Broszat and his colleagues now suggested. It could show us "how people behaved during the Nazi dictatorship, how they compromised with the regime but also where they drew the line – sometimes successfully – at the regime's attempts at interference, penetration, and control."[13]

Ian Kershaw's studies of popular opinion and the functioning of the "Hitler myth" in the Third Reich's popular culture were among the Bavaria Project's most important accomplishments. While providing ample evidence of the regime's broadly based popular acceptance in the mid 1930s, after the effective silencing of the old labor movement via the destruction of its institutions in the first year of power, Kershaw located the foundations of that acceptance in patterns of resignation and compliance rather than active enthusiasm or mobilized support, distinguishing carefully between day-to-day *popular quiescence* and actual *popularity*. Despite that pragmatics of ordinary living, he concluded, the 1940s saw the "complete bankruptcy of the Nazi social ideal," with widespread "disillusionment and discontent in almost all sections of the population." Among workers, the Third Reich failed to build spontaneous positive consent: "Deprived of political space in which to organize, the expression of injustice was mainly apathy, resignation, confusion, and despair."[14] Like Mason, and Mommsen/Broszat in their different ways, therefore, Kershaw found the same gap between appearance and reality – in this case, between the regime's public trumpeting of national solidarity in the image of the *Volksgemeinschaft* (the racialized community of the people-nation) and the general indifference of working-class culture, which remained unavailable for Nazi ideological appeals. Severed from the historic supports of their parties, unions, and subculture, workers nonetheless denied the regime the enthusiastic identification it so desperately sought. In this respect, too, despite its bluster and apparent pervasiveness, the ideology of the Nazi leadership lacked the effectiveness and specificity to explain the unique dynamism of the regime.

This recurring split between "ideology" and "social context" was what became most characteristic for the social history dominant in the 1970s. In both Mason's and Kershaw's work, the necessity of social context for understanding Nazism was eloquently upheld, especially with a view to the expanded notion of German societal responsibility for Nazism advocated by Mommsen and Broszat. But, in consequence, the power of Nazi ideology in any more specific sense became markedly downplayed. To put it another way, the practical complicity of the ordinary population in the regime's daily working was simultaneously acknowledged by the new social historians as a main theme of their work, only then to be counter-posed to German workers' apathy and practical indifference (their *Resistenz*) towards the Nazis' specific ideological claims. It was no accident that the main accent of this work was on the Left. In a complicated sense, that emerging argument about "non-permeability" seemed to become a way of honoring the integrity of the German working class and its ability to keep the Nazis at bay – in a subtle counterpoint to the celebratory anti-fascism of East German Marxist–Leninist historians, one might say, as a kind of fallback position once the beleaguered and isolated qualities of the actual Communist and Social Democratic resistance had been acknowledged. This was reflected in the trajectory of the other leading social historian produced by the 1970s, Detlev Peukert, who moved from major studies of the Communist Party of Germany (Kommunistische Partei Deutschlands, KPD) and workers' underground resistance in the Ruhr to a series of searching explorations of popular nonconformity beneath and behind the level of out-and-out opposition to the regime.[15]

But no sooner had these gains of understanding been recorded, interestingly, than a new set of historiographical departures supervened. During the 1980s, the ground of social history I have been describing – institutional histories, studies of particular occupations and professions and of whole social groups, interest-based accounts of political process, studies of popular opinion, the full repertoire of research associated with labor history – was first gradually and then decisively left behind. Again, like the earlier turning to social history, this change was shaped by broader trends of the discipline. One of these was the growth of women's history and the impact of gender analysis among German historians, for which the emblematic publication became the volume *When Biology Became Destiny* in 1984, bringing together scholars from both sides of the Atlantic who were later to publish their own major works.[16] A second trend during the same years was the upsurge of everyday life history – *Alltagsgeschichte* – partly presaged by the Bavaria Project but mainly borne by a remarkable grassroots movement, alongside which a vital scholarly network emerged. For our purposes, the most important practitioners included Alf Lüdtke, Lutz Niethammer, and Adelheid von Saldern.[17] A third strand concerned histories of medicalization and racialization in the social policy domain – "biological politics," as Tim Mason named this in 1988 at a conference in Philadelphia – which in the early twentieth century had permeated thinking about eugenics, population policy, welfare delivery, family policies, penal reform and criminology, elaborate projects of social engineering, rationalization of industry, and the general application of science for social goals.[18] The fourth and last of the fresh developments became the gathering recognition of the centrality of the Holocaust in how German historians were now thinking about their work.[19]

These developments brought *ideology* back to the very center of discussion. They were certainly influenced by the heterogeneous "culturalism" increasingly embraced by historians during the 1990s, most fervently in the United States, more haltingly in Germany. The particular forms of this sea change in the discipline varied – from the reception of Michel Foucault, the impact of cultural studies, and the echoes of Gramscian Marxism to the variegated influence of feminist theory and the consequences of the so-called "linguistic turn." How far historians of Nazism were directly drawn to such theory was perhaps unclear, but it certainly shaped the surrounding intellectual environment in which they found themselves thinking, and the changing subject matter of work on the Third Reich was soon plain to see.[20] In the course of the 1980s, historians stopped being mainly interested in Nazism's variable social context, which almost by definition encouraged them into relativizing or qualifying the efficacy of Nazi ideological appeals, and turned instead to the deeper, more elaborate, and often submerged genealogies of Nazism's operative thinking and big ideas. In so doing, though, they also built on one of social history's biggest gains. They shifted attention away from "Hitler's *Weltanschauung*" in the immediate sense to focus instead on much wider contexts of associated ideas. Following one of Broszat and Mommsen's key precepts, they asked after the broader societal settings where proto-Nazi thinking might be found.

One of the key moves this entailed was a radical deepening of perspective. Beginning in the late 1980s, a series of field-defining books began situating the origins of the Third Reich's racialized policy-making in climates of innovation that long predated the Nazi seizure of power. Decades in advance of the latter, these new studies showed, eugenicist, hereditarian, and equivalent ideologies of social engineering had captured the imagination of the medical, healthcare, criminological, and social policy professions, amply legitimized by the work of academics (ethnologists, statisticians, biologists, historians), backed by the agitation of public associations, and given powerful resonance via the press. From the early 1900s, society's health and cohesion became conceptualized increasingly in biologized terms. And within these expanding repertoires of racialist thinking, anti-Semitic idioms took their respectable place.

Indeed, the race policies of the Nazis were powerfully authorized by these longer traditions of thinking about "racial hygiene," where the primary fixation on the Jews figured among larger ambitions "to medicalize or biologize various forms of social, sexual, political, or racial deviance."[21] In this broad mode of thought, mooted and shaped during the late *Kaiserreich*, radicalized during World War I and the years of revolution, and then further diffused and codified during the Weimar Republic, social and political issues became systematically naturalized under the sign of "race." Science powerfully legitimized and enabled the Nazis' specific version of this emerging project, which envisaged nothing less than a root-and-branch remaking of the social order along racialized lines. As Robert Proctor, one of the leading pioneers of this analysis, argued, Nazism worked from an established eugenicist paradigm of normal science: so, far from perverting the purity and truth of scientific knowledge, Nazism's structure of thinking "was deeply embedded in the philosophy and institutional structure of German biomedical science."[22] Thus, the ground for the Nazis' "racial state" was discursively laid over many years by elaborate institutional machineries of knowledge production, which allowed "healthy" and "true" Germans to be distinguished from deviant or "less worthy" categories of people. Public discourse became reconfigured, producing a powerful set of default assumptions about how an effective social policy should be made.

In conjunction with cognate research across a wide variety of areas, this type of approach fundamentally reshaped our understanding of the Third Reich. Social historians of the 1970s had approached Nazism with an underlying master category of "society" as their guide: while the force of Mommsen's and Broszat's "structuralist" insistence on the enlarged social sustenance required by Nazi policies was certainly taken, historians such as Mason, Kershaw, and Peukert all accepted the continuing existence of "society" as a kind of intact and separable domain, a source of viable agency that, however limited and compromised, still allowed the impact of Nazi policies and propaganda to be hampered and contained. In Broszat's classic definition of *Resistenz*, society in this sense remained a damaged but recoverable resource: it allowed the "effective warding off, limiting, damming up of the NS rule or its claims," whatever the particular "motives, reasons or strengths."[23] For his part, Mason also proceeded from the continuing sovereignty of German capitalism and the primacy of class as determinants shaping and constraining the Nazis' ability to realize their goals, certainly in the years 1933 to 1939. Even during the war, when militarized expansion and the racialist frenzy of genocide overwhelmed everything else, the integrity of the "social context," however battered and reduced, could still be analytically upheld.

After some three decades of the new scholarship, this distinctive social historian's standpoint has now all but disappeared. Rather than continuing to explore the subtle and submerged ways under the Third Reich in which the autonomy of society was preserved, the new work sought to show how the very bases of the social order, whether in organized associational life, in cultural practices, or in the everydayness of social intercourse, became comprehensively disorganized and then *remade*. Different social groups may have kept some defenses against Nazism's formal ideological message, or protected some remaining privacy against Nazi intrusions, but their attitudes and behavior were influenced more insidiously by the diffusion of racialized discourse across all the shelters and crevices of ordinary life. In that case, cultural studies of German society's habituation to biological and racial modes of thinking were now advanced as historians' primary focus. The insidiously colonizing pervasiveness of racial thinking – across social groups, in multiple sites of policy-making and knowledge production, in state and non-state institutions, in academic and popular culture, in all manner of ways – became the new problematic, irrespective of the complexities of social differentiation in that older 1970s sense. To connect the progress of that hegemony to some underlying developmental dynamism, some alternative overarching framework was required. So instead of the "society" of the social historians, accordingly, "modernity" started to emerge as a new master category. In this new framework, "the spirit of science" became the new primary context for thinking about "the genesis of the 'Final Solution'."[24]

Two major shifts were entailed in this change. First, in contemporary historical writing the immunity against Nazi influences previously ascribed to the working class has definitively gone. Whether colluding in the exploitation of coerced foreign labor during the war, or wearing the uniforms of the genocidal army on the Eastern Front, or generally participating in the "good times" of the Nazi era from the mid 1930s to 1942–1943, it is now accepted, German workers could no more withdraw themselves from the consequences of Nazi rule than any other group, whether those consequences were structural (like the racialized labor market and its rewards), directly disciplinary (in the army and other coercively organized settings), social (as in the new patterns of discriminatory sociality), or cultural (in the new public mores and their sanctions).[25] Moreover, in regarding the working class as Nazism's principal antagonist, historians like Mason had used an overarching framework of fascism for understanding the Nazi regime, and this now too fell away: "Theories of fascism have been replaced by models of the racial state, in which biological rather than social categories are preeminent."[26] As the main organizing category of Third Reich historiography, "class" was now trumped by "race."

Similarly, the war years have replaced 1933 to 1939 as the Third Reich's defining context. For the social historians of the 1970s, the war was self-evidently an exceptional time, when the little remaining space for social negotiation was finally closed off. The atrocious violence of Nazism's horrendous self-realization during its drive for conquest and annihilation, and the final reduction of politics to coercion and terror, left small scope for the social historian's particular interests, it seemed. Yet, in contrast, the new historians have taken the wartime circumstances precisely as their starting point, where Nazism's most distinctive traits were to be found.[27]

At one level, all of the social historian's familiar emphases might then return, from studies of the home front through analysis of the war economy's coercive labor markets to research on the rank-and-file soldier's experience of the Eastern Front. But the machineries of genocide make these studies profoundly different from the equivalent historiography of World War I, where empathy for popular experience had always supplied the hardwiring of social-historical interest. Above all, the past decade's massive growth of scholarly research into the Holocaust now entirely overshadows the earlier social history concerns. In the wake of our currently accumulating knowledge of the shockingly generalized complicity of ordinary people in the killing and persecution of Jews and all the other excluded and criminalized groups attacked by the Third Reich, it has become uncommonly hard to find the place of empathic identification from which the best social history has always been written. As Mary Nolan observes, "to end the story in 1939 is to profoundly distort the histories of racism, rationalization, and *Resistenz*, and thus our understanding of work, workers, and the working class under National Socialism." Still more: "Auschwitz and the racial state and total war that produced it were the central facts of the Third Reich, and workers' complex involvement in them requires detailed analysis."[28]

Hitler's place in the Third Reich

The turn-of-the-century appearance of Ian Kershaw's magisterial biography of Adolf Hitler gave excellent occasion for judging these historiographical shifts. Aside from Alan Bullock's sober classic of 1952 and Joachim Fest's oddly enthralled study two decades later, few existing portraits escape sensationalism and superficiality.[29] But Kershaw's new account was splendidly successful. Eschewing psychological speculation while confidently threading his way through the self-serving memoirs of associates, old Nazis, and the plentiful ranks of the military and secretarial entourage, he cleaved consistently to the sureness of the archives with a peerless grasp of the scholarly literatures. In so doing, he built securely on his own earlier work in social history. The first volume of the biography published in 1998, which carried the story up to 1936, was already a triumph, but the completion of the project then confirmed Kershaw's standing as the Third Reich's preeminent English-speaking historian.

The first volume left Hitler savoring the triumph of reoccupying the Rhineland in March 1936, which reasserted Germany's territorial sovereignty against the restrictions imposed by the Treaty of Versailles. This act, which marked the transition in German foreign policy from a rhetoric of international injustice to straightforward aggression, displayed the familiar chemistry of Hitler's later diplomatic coups: the cautions and misgivings of the military leadership, which he successfully faced down; the failure of the British and French to resist; the surrounding popular acclaim; and the resulting absolute belief in his own program. On the last page of his first volume, Kershaw described Hitler's messianism in contemplating this success, as he moved "with the certainty of a sleepwalker along the path laid out for me by Providence." The German people were now united by fate with their Leader: "That you have found me … among so many millions is the miracle of our time! And that I have found you, that is Germany's fortune!"[30]

One of Kershaw's best achievements has been to manage so consummately the tension between the detailed centering of narrative around Hitler's person appropriate to a biography and the wider contexts of analysis needed by a political history. From 1936 Hitler grew obsessed by foreign policy to the practical exclusion of domestic affairs, making the view from the Reich Chancellery alone (and later the *Führer* headquarters) into a peculiarly partial one. To compensate, Kershaw moved back and forth in his second volume between Hitler's dictatorial isolation and the wider policy-making arenas. He did so in constant counterpoint, while pausing frequently for more extended treatments of the domestic scene, most crucially in separate chapters on anti-Jewish policies and the unfolding of the "genocidal mentality."[31] At other times the diplomatic and military narratives necessarily prevail, until by the book's end Hitler's role as supreme commander has entirely taken over. The chapter on the outbreak of war encapsulates Kershaw's method, in which the detailed narrative of events becomes vital to putting his own interpretation forward. The chapter then concludes by evaluating the decision-making process in the Third Reich, the centering of this around Hitler's own person, and the interplay between circumstances and personality. It is a masterful statement.

The links from Hitler's dominant agency to the wider decision-making patterns of the Nazi state were the biography's essential reference points. From September 1939, the regime's racialist and anti-Jewish policies dominate Kershaw's treatment of government actions beyond the military conduct of the war, reflecting both Hitler's own priorities and the Third Reich's larger political truth. In contrast, the weaker attention to "society" and the history of popular experience in the second volume made it easier to organize than the first. For the years before 1933 pluralism, political conflict, and the rule of law make it harder to capture a whole society's trajectory viewed from the governing center. But just as the centralizing of the dictatorship during 1933 to 1934 excised the room for public dissent, so the centering of the story around Hitler himself allows a more convincing narrative to be shaped. In his first volume Kershaw also departed perhaps less from existing historiography, whereas the originality of his synthesis is much greater after 1933. The sheer diversity of the scholarship now available has never been brought together so commandingly into a single account. If the second volume was more selective in its social history, it contains the best political history of the Third Reich we yet possess.

One powerful message of Kershaw's second volume was the shallowness of Hitler's personal life. As a site of complex introspection, reflectiveness, or self-doubt, even of serious internal conflicts, Hitler's personality became almost entirely vacated. Procrastination and indecisiveness were there in plenty, yet devoid of the ethical anguish and philosophical content or larger political dilemmas that give most major biographies their stature. Hitler seemed to lack complex interiority. This blankness grew ever more pronounced during the war, as he relapsed into silence and seclusion outside the daily briefings and associated routines of lunches, dinners, and tea parties. With Hitler there were no conversations, only monologues.

Hitler's *absence* from government emerged most strikingly from this account. That was true even of 1939: "Remarkably, for the best part of three months during this summer of high drama, with Europe teetering on the brink of war, Hitler was almost entirely absent from the seat of government in Berlin"; and for Kershaw this "illustrates how far the disintegration of anything resembling a conventional central government had gone" (pp197, 199). Göring's Ministerial Council formed on 30 August 1939 never worked as a war cabinet and rarely met.[32] A renewed initiative in January 1943 by Hans-Heinrich Lammers, head of the Reich Chancellery, to form a "Committee of Three" with Wilhelm Keitel (for the military) and Martin Bormann (for the Party), also foundered. Conceived as a central clearing mechanism for measures of "total war," it failed to deliver the needed liaison with Hitler and by September was defunct, succumbing easily to the endemic particularism in the upper echelons of the state. Efforts by Goebbels and Speer to produce greater direction, prompted by their own exclusion from the Lammers committee, too met defeat. As Kershaw says, under Nazism even the weakest "forms of collective government were doomed." It was impossible for "the arbitrary 'will of the Führer' ... to be expressed in ways conducive to the functioning of a modern state, let alone one operating under the crisis conditions of a major war. As a system of government, Hitler's dictatorship had no future."[33]

Hitler's disregard for the state's daily business contrasted with the obsessive involvement of a Churchill or a Stalin. Kershaw takes a strongly "polycratic" view of Nazi rule, providing numerous cases of its peculiarly disordered operation. He also accepts the pendant to that approach – namely, the structural complicity of pre-Nazi elites, indeed the Third Reich's dependence on their support, not least in the generals' craven endorsement of the "war of annihilation" in the East and the army's full-scale sharing in its atrocities. In Kershaw's account, "armed forces, Party, industry, [and] civil service" were "the pillars of the regime."[34] Wartime also heightened the capriciousness of Nazi administrative pragmatics. The new Ministry for the Occupied East formed in July 1941 compounded the existing conflicts among army, Goering's economic apparatus, and SS rather than smoothing their rivalry. As Kershaw tersely says, this projected "a 'New Order' in the East which belied the very name. Nothing resembled order. Everything resembled the war of all against all, built into the Nazi system in the Reich itself, massively extended in occupied Poland, and now taken to its logical denouement in the conquered lands of the Soviet Union."[35]

Yet, if the war turned the Third Reich "into a Führer state with an absentee Führer," Hitler's supreme military command set parameters that simply *could not* be questioned.[36] Kershaw combines his "structuralist" approach to the Nazi state with an equally forthright view of Hitler's personal power. Joining a highly "Mommsenesque" view of polycratic improvisation and the Third Reich's wider social supports to explicit insistence on Hitler's personal centrality and Nazism's ideological drive, he makes the old structuralist-intentionalist debate quite pointless. He can uphold the key structuralist tenet of "cumulative radicalization," while setting Mommsen's associated notion of the "weak dictator" firmly aside. In the first volume, he brought this to the formula of "working towards the Führer," with Hitler voicing the main purposes while subordinates managed the details, stoking mutual rivalries as they maximized influence and vied for favor.[37] Nothing showed this better than the drive against the Jews. If Hitler presided silently over the violence of "Crystal Night" in November 1938, he was still the instigator in chief. The outcome "had a profound impact upon Hitler," ratcheting his rhetoric forward. On 21 January 1939, he told the Czechoslovak Foreign Minister that "The Jews here will be annihilated." Nine days later, on the sixth anniversary of the seizure of power, he issued his infamous "prophecy," repeated intermittently during the war: "if international finance-Jewry inside and outside Europe should succeed in plunging the nations once more into a world war, the result will not be the bolshevization of the earth and thereby the victory of Jewry, but the annihilation of the Jewish race in Europe!"[38]

There are three nodal points in Kershaw's account of the unfolding of the "genocidal mentality." Each time, Hitler's guidance was the default inspiration, a kind of structuring principle of Nazi policy or its hidden hand. The first came amidst the immediate rush of the Polish campaign, which "recalled, in hugely magnified fashion, the wild and barbarous treatment of 'enemies of the Reich' in Germany in spring 1933."[39] In the massacres and deportations of the anti-Polish terror, viciously unleashed against Jews, Nazi intentions acquired institutional form – in the new administrative arrangements for the occupied territories, in the speedy handling of local tensions between military and SS, and in the latter's emerging primacy. As Kershaw says: "With the sanctioning of the liquidation program at the core of the barbaric 'ethnic cleansing' drive in Poland, Hitler – and the regime he headed – had crossed the Rubicon." This was not yet "the all-out genocide that was to emerge during the Russian campaign in the summer of 1941," but it provided "the training-ground for what was to follow."[40] Moreover, the final authorship was clear: "In a most literal sense, Goebbels, Himmler, Heydrich, and other leading Nazis were 'working towards the Führer,' whose authority allowed the realization of their own fantasies."[41]

Second, during summer 1940 the logistical nightmares resulting from the free-ranging "racial megalomania" in occupied Poland pushed Reinhard Heydrich and the SS planners into giving the "Jewish Question" a "final solution," a phrase first used by Adolf Eichmann in June 1940 for the so-called "Madagascar solution." Once schemes for deporting all of Europe's Jews to Madagascar had been dropped, the SS refocused its planning on the East, finding vital impetus from Hitler's decision to attack the Soviet Union before settling the war against Britain. Once again, Hitler played "little active role" as opposed to providing the "blanket approval."[42] "With scarcely any direct involvement by Hitler, racial policy unfolded its own dynamic," for which "the real crucible was Poland."[43] In consequence, "full-scale genocide was only one step away. Anti-Jewish policy had not followed a clear or straight line throughout 1940. But, particularly within the SS and Security Police leadership, the thinking and planning had moved in an implicitly genocidal direction."[44]

Finally, between June and December 1941 decisions were taken for the generalized murder of the Jews of Europe, further systematized at the Wannsee Conference in January 1942 and capped with the renewed deportation of the Reich's Jews in April. While historians differ over the exact timing of the most decisive step, the most judiciously persuasive approach is Christopher Browning's, who sees "an incremental, ongoing decision-making process that stretched from the spring of 1941 to the summer of 1942, with key turning-points in the midsummer and early fall of 1941 that corresponded to the peaks of German victory euphoria and sealed the fates of Soviet and European Jews, respectively."[45] This is Kershaw's view. At one level the gradations of Nazi policy were immaterial. Strategies of "population decimation, genocide, and Final Solution" had the same logic, Browning argues, borne by the same murderous intent and the same racialist ideology.[46] But in its terrible specificity, "shooting or gassing to death all the Jews of Europe" in a "full-scale industrialized killing program," the "Final Solution" *per se* still has to be distinguished.[47]

For Kershaw, the inexorable logic of the drift towards "genocidal war" formed the main truth of Hitler's aims.[48] His detailed accounting establishes beyond serious dispute the continuity of this commitment during 1939 to 1941 and its longer provenance from the formative years after World War I. Measured by this underlying drive, which ran sharply through all the key decision-making of the war, the exact timing and situational specifics of this or that particular act, including the inception of the "Final Solution" itself, become stunningly unimportant. The careful research of Browning and others remains indispensable, but Kershaw's lucidity makes debate over this or that particular dating far less material. His summary can hardly be bettered:

> In contrast to military affairs, where his repeated interference reflected his constant preoccupation with tactical minutiae and his distrust of the army professionals, Hitler's involvement in ideological matters was less frequent and direct. He laid down the guidelines in March 1941. He needed to do little more. Self-combustion would see to it that, once lit, the genocidal fires would rage into a mighty conflagration amid the barbarism of the war to destroy "Jewish-Bolshevism." When it came to ideological aims, in contrast to military matters, Hitler had no need to worry that the "professionals" would let him down. He could rest assured that Himmler and Heydrich, above all, would leave no stone unturned in eliminating the ideological enemy once and for all. And he could be equally certain that they would find their willing helpers at all levels among the masters of the new *Imperium* in the east, whether these belonged to the Party, the police, or the civilian bureaucracy.[49]

Kershaw expounds the role of "cumulative radicalization" while re-centering Hitler in the account. If he presents a polycratic view of the Nazi system with great subtlety, he also shifts this structuralist analysis decisively towards the driving agency of the SS. This emerges strongly from his chapter on "Crystal Night," which brought anti-Jewish policy directly under SS control. A year later, "an increasingly autonomous SS leadership" was unleashed on occupied Poland: "The planners and organizers, theoreticians of domination, and technocrats of power in the SS leadership saw Poland as an experimental playground. They were granted a *tabula rasa* to undertake more or less what they wanted."[50] Momentum increased throughout 1940 and early 1941, until Operation Barbarossa brought the grandiose plans for the New Order to fruition. By now, Heydrich and the Reich Security Head Office (RSHA) were "instrumental in gradually converting an ideological imperative into an extermination plan."[51] Through its control over settlement and population policy in the occupied East, the SS then duly exerted its superordinate power.[52] In Kershaw's account, this concentrated energy of the SS cut ruthlessly across the institutional anarchy of Nazi-occupying administration, making "governmental disorder and 'cumulative radicalization' [into] two sides of the same coin."[53]

Moreover, this energy was *ideological.* With this recognition of the SS as the vanguard of genocide, in fact, ideology reoccupies the analytical center ground. To the impressively accumulating scholarship on the SS and the "racial state", Kershaw added Hitler's own ideological contribution. His first volume had assembled a detailed picture of Hitler's political outlook up to the mid 1930s, and his second returns to the key elements again and again – the German nation's paramount need for living space, the demonizing of the Jews, and the inevitable "crusade against Bolshevism," all in an utterly racialized language of politics. Those obsessions fused into a terrifying unity by 1940 to 1941. The invasion of the Soviet Union was their passionately longed-for consummation. It showed Hitler's permanent fixation on the primacy of the anti-Bolshevik crusade, essentially intertwined with the war against the Jews; and it revealed the ideological drive supplied by Heydrich and Himmler, with their bizarre population plans and horrendous visions of a Europe reordered by colonialism and racial superiority. "Himmler and Heydrich, rapidly spotting a chance to extend their own empire and to create an entire new vast area for their racial experiments, had no difficulty in exploiting Hitler's long-established paranoia about 'Jewish-Bolshevism' to advance new schemes for solving 'the Jewish problem'." Drawing on the wealth of the recent scholarship, Kershaw makes the generalized popularity of the war against Bolshevism once and for all clear:

> The more ideologically committed pro-Nazis would entirely swallow the interpretation of the war as a preventive one to avoid the destruction of western culture by the Bolshevik hordes. They fervently believed that Europe would never be liberated before "Jewish-Bolshevism" was utterly and completely rooted out. The path to the Holocaust, intertwined with the showdown with Bolshevism, was prefigured in such notions. The legacy of over two decades of deeply rooted, often fanatically held, feelings of hatred towards Bolshevism, fully interlaced with antisemitism, was about to be revealed in its full ferocity.[54]

With this eloquent analysis, Kershaw accomplishes the goals he set for himself at the outset of the biography – namely, to see if someone trained as a "structuralist" historian could write a biography that escaped the polarized confrontationalism dominating histories of the Third Reich in the 1970s and 1980s; to deploy Max Weber's theory of "charismatic leadership" in analyzing Hitler's form of rule; and to revisit Hitler's biography in light of the vast expansion of knowledge of the Holocaust so strikingly missing from the framing and contents of the earlier biographies by Bullock and Fest. The results authoritatively ratified the movement of the Holocaust to the very center of German historians' necessary concerns. His idea of "working towards the Führer" brought discussion of the Nazi state onto a much better conceptual ground than before. And his account confirmed the growing irrelevance of the debates between "structuralists" and "intentionalists," however enabling they may once have been.

The need for a new general history

The profusion of new research drawn upon by Kershaw made the need for a new general history of the Third Reich abundantly clear. As its title suggests, Pierre Ayçoberry's *Social History of the Third Reich* eschews conventional political narratives or straightforward chronologies, recalling instead the social histories the first part of this chapter has discussed.[55] Its interpretive thrust frontloads the question of "Violence" by leading with the regime's peacetime agencies of coercion, from SA and SS to the early concentration camps. Next comes a chapter on the "Myth of the People's Community," followed by two on the response of social groups to the regime, and a brief bridging chapter on "Radicalization, 1938–1939" taking us up to the war. A picture emerges of a new and insatiable political force, whose aggressions overran German society and impoverished the space for autonomous expression – "a regime that sought to fuse private and public life into an ever more totalitarian community."[56]

The title of the book's first part, "The Invasion of Politics," clearly intimates this totalitarianism thesis, which the opening chapter on the war, "The Dissolution of Civil Society," then confirms.[57] This explores the disordering of the social landscape in its most elemental dimensions, from family and urban neighborhoods to town–country relations and work. A chapter on "The Nazi Party and the Social Authorities" then considers the interrelations among "the four powers that dominated society, namely the state bureaucracy, the Nazi Party, the business bosses, and the army."[58] The penultimate chapter, "Toward Utopia through Terror," resumes treatment of the "SS Empire," continuing into the forced movement and enslavement of subject populations, and ending with the "Final Solution." The final chapter deals with the army.

For Ayçoberry, the Third Reich began and ended in violence. On the foundations of repression and terror, which destroyed the labor movement and other key resources for democracy, the dictatorship became institutionalized with a ruthlessness that rapidly coopted the judiciary and dismantled the rule of law. Nazism's totalizing ambitions relentlessly reduced "society" to the regime's needs. Wartime then brought the expansion of the SS empire, with its horrendously generalized machinery of mass coercion, racialized exploitation, and government by terror, itself the brutal, systematized apotheosis of the wider violence of the regime, brought ever closer to home by the tightening military fronts, aerial bombardment, and states of emergency. Into the emptied societal arena, purged and bludgeoned into conformity during 1933 to 1934, came the new official agencies and mass apparatuses of the Party-state, purveyors of the organized myth of the *Volksgemeinschaft*.

In presenting the collaborationist accommodations of elites to the new regime, Ayçoberry followed the standard structuralist account while revealing once again the legacy of Franz Neumann's *Behemoth*.[59] In capturing working-class attitudes, he likewise observed the social-historical precepts of the 1970s, finding in the ambiguity of most workers' "refractory behavior" (his preferred term for Broszat's *Resistenz*) simply a self-protective desire "to limit the Nazification in their daily lives."[60] He thereby departed from classical usages of "totalitarianism" by acknowledging the *incompleteness* of the state's claims on society. In common with social historians like Mason and Broszat, he found the state's totalizing project imperfectly realized, however mean and compromised the surviving autonomies might have been. He understood the maximalism of Nazism's intentions, but even the extreme "atomization" produced by the war left some room for sociality's return. Society may have disintegrated – in the arresting image of a "kicked-in anthill" – but people could still "devot[e] all their cunning to minimizing its effects and repairing old ties."[61]

Thus, Ayçoberry drew astutely on the vast scholarly literatures to provide an introduction keyed to the main historiographical tendencies outlined above. The chapters on the reactions of élites and ordinary people to the regime drew successfully on the wealth of existing research, though more tenuously for the treatment of women than for workers and youth. The war was extremely well handled. But the "racial state," whose penetration of "the social" recent historians have so compellingly described, was very poorly addressed. The fundamental contributions of Burleigh, Friedlander, Schmuhl, Weindling, and others were shockingly absent. Their radical challenge to the older social histories went unnoticed. If Ayçoberry's desire to recuperate social history of the older kind was salutary, the harder task of integrating it with the new scholarship still remained.

In his imposing general history, Michael Burleigh went to an opposite extreme, omitting social history in the stronger sense almost entirely.[62] His book has an introduction and ten chapters, topically arranged in rough chronological sequence. The least successful are those closest to a usable narrative frame – namely, the first and the last. His approach to the Third Reich's pre-history oscillated between a rambling survey of the Weimar polity and a description of Hitler's own movement, in a selective rendition of the Republic's difficulties that stopped any coherent argument from forming. Likewise, the account of the Nazi regime's catastrophic dissolution fell unexpectedly flat, moving from the United States' entry into the war and the Red Army's advance through Eastern Europe through brief nods to the home front (life "beneath the bombs") and the final stage of the Judeocide to an inconclusive description of the transition to peace. This was a pity because the book's main core remains very impressive – robust, coherently argued, and well put together. Burleigh aggressively applied current perspectives in a very particular way, allowing their strengths and weaknesses to be fairly assessed.

Like Ayçoberry, Burleigh began with violence. His opening chapter on the Third Reich *per se* saw "the supersession of the rule of law by arbitrary police terror" as the key break with the past. It was the regime's defining specificity – "*the* most important departure from civilized values engineered by the Nazi government," "the crucial breach with the most fundamental characteristic of free societies."[63] The next chapter on the regime's official culture ("New Times, New Man") joined an acute treatment of the Nazi welfare system to surveys of family policies, the working class, and the churches, plus a brief coda on Nazi foreign policy. The chapter on the German Jews ("Living in a Land with No Future") moved into high gear, with a brilliantly composed conspectus of the regime's anti-Semitism and the public culture of salacious and self-satisfied bigotry it licensed, capped by a powerful section on *Reichskristallnacht.* The combination of ethical anger and rich historical knowledge moving this account was palpable. The events of November 1938 marked "the end, rather than a beginning, of a cycle and style of street violence, although it paradoxically paved the way for something more systematic and hence far worse. Hot violence, being driven by passion, was liable to peter out as moods changed; cold bureaucratic violence was a full-time career option."[64] Like Kershaw, he closed with Hitler's prophesy of Jewish annihilation in his Reichstag speech of 30 January 1939.

After "Crystal Night," as Burleigh showed, the totalizing implications of anti-Semitic violence were becoming plain. The isolating consequences of anti-Jewish laws, economic penalties, and vicious social discrimination had been steadily building during the 1930s, but the pogrom of November 1938 empowered the SS for a comprehensive bureaucratic assault, "with the ratchet of what was possible moving further up the scale of radicality."[65] On 9 November, Himmler himself voiced the apocalypse in his annual address to the SS leadership, affirming the universal primacy of the anti-Semitic struggle and the life-and-death quality of the choices Germany had to face. "[I]f we are the loser in the struggle which will decide this," he declared, in a chilling projection of the genocidal purposes the SS planners were about to pursue, "not even a reservation of Germans will remain, but rather everyone will be starved out and slaughtered." Participation would be racially determined: "This will affect everyone, whether or not he is now a very enthusiastic supporter of the Third Reich, it will suffice that he speaks German and that he has a German mother."[66]

The working through of this project, in a wild and grotesque dystopia of the "racial state," formed Burleigh's grand theme. The key chapter here, "'Extinguishing the Ideas of Yesterday': Eugenics and 'Euthanasia'," broadened the argument on anti-Semitism into a general thesis about the regime, carrying us into the war. After the oddly thin treatment of foreign policy in the 1930s, the war years stamped the book's overall shape.[67] These began with a nuanced account of Nazi occupation regimes and patterns of collaboration in Europe until 1943, matched by the ghastly saga of the anti-Soviet war. They continued through a 91-page treatment of the "racial war against the Jews," picking up threads on the German Jews and euthanasia. Burleigh carefully tracked anti-Jewish policies through the convoluted interactions of racial doctrine, planning fantasies, improvised local genocides, and rampaging ethno-imperialist savagery that brought SS policy-makers to the panoramic opportunities of the anti-Bolshevik crusade and thence to the infernal terminus of the "Final Solution."

Burleigh's expert distillation of the immense literatures and documentation remain beyond significant criticism. His relating of the Judeocide to Nazism's other racialist drives was admirably surefooted. Genocide's atrocious instrumental logic, only embraceable on the basis of an underlying fanaticism, was lucidly explained. Growing from the preposterously unrealistic vistas of ethnic resettlement unfolded by Himmler and Heydrich at the outset of the Polish war, with their massive relocation of ethnic Germans and associated deportations of Poles, that logic produced equally huge displacements of Jews as a deliberately expendable result. Here Burleigh's commentaries on the Madagascar Plan ("the nebulous background to a foreground of self-generated problems induced by the Nazis' own decisions") and the relationship of anti-Jewish planning to Operation Barbarossa can hardly be bettered.[68] The inception of the "Final Solution," in the passage from Barbarossa to Wannsee between October 1941 and January 1942, was equally acutely explained. Like Kershaw's account, the clarity of Burleigh's overview made some of the professional intricacies of Holocaust historiography seem arcane. His description of the *Einsatzkommandos* was wrenchingly powerful. His use of detail was devastating. Ethically impassioned, analytically controlled, authoritatively grounded, and eloquently written, Burleigh's summary of the "Final Solution" seemed the best short account we were likely to see.

How far did *The Third Reich* register current historiographical trends? Most obviously, it entirely replaced "class" with "race" as the main analytical term. The war also ruled the account. Indeed, the book's middle five chapters – dealing with the German Jews, euthanasia, occupation and collaboration, anti-Soviet war, and Judeocide – were its interconnected core. The earlier three chapters (on Weimar, the machinery of repression, and Nazi values) lacked the strong narrative thrust of those dealing specifically with race and the putative European New Order. Similarly, the closing two chapters on resistance and the final years were an anti-climax. By defining "resistance" primarily via loosely assembled thumbnail sketches of the aristocratic principals of the July Plot, Burleigh shelved all the most challenging discussions of "resistance and collaboration" of the preceding 20 years. Over some questions, Burleigh converged with Kershaw – above all, in analysis of the Judeocide and its unfolding. But his history lacked the overall narrative energizing Kershaw's biography. For a purported general history, foreign policy and government policy-making *tout court* were chronically neglected, while Hitler remained far too shadowy a figure. Burleigh sidelined social history of the classical kinds. Women's history was entirely missing.

At his best, Burleigh brought the disparate and hugely proliferating literatures on the Nazi "racial state" compellingly together, especially around the re-contextualized understanding of the Holocaust's centrality. As he said: "There is no 'normal' history somehow adjacent to, or detached from, the fact of the Holocaust," because the latter "breaks the bounds of whatever intellectual framework we variously impose upon it ... That is why the racially motivated criminality of the Nazi regime ... literally permeates this book, for no aspect of that past was untainted by it. Nothing can ultimately be detached from these horrors, neither

Nazi economic nor Nazi leisure policy, and certainly not the military history of the war."[69] Yet his view of the Nazi state was confused and indistinct. While polemically distancing himself from "structuralists" such as Broszat, Mommsen, and Hüttenberger, he took an approach that in practice seemed much the same. On the one hand, the "polycratic" view was reduced to a caricature, with scant resemblance to the sophisticated analyses it actually inspired. Burleigh dismissed features like "managerial Darwinism" and "the mutually radicalizing effects of competing agencies" as common to "many modern corporations and institutions," including "democratic governments," in which case (he argued) they could hardly differentiate the specific "singlemindedness" or "rare destructiveness" of Nazism. But on the other hand, whenever he came close to discussing the state himself, he repaired to exactly the same ideas, seeing (for example) the fundamental "nature of the Nazi regime" as "involving stalemate between irreconcilable positions, both of which were then pursued simultaneously," with all the outcomes Kershaw compellingly described.[70] Burleigh's account of anti-Jewish policies during 1939 to 1941 seemed a classic rendition of "cumulative radicalization," for Mommsen and Broszat always the corollary to polycracy.

Of course, while delivering vital insights into the Third Reich's peculiar institutional dynamics, Broszat and Mommsen dealt weakly with Nazism's hard ideological content. This remains the justified kernel of Burleigh's attacks. Burleigh's own solution here was to treat Nazism as a "political religion," involving the "sacralization of politics" or "the politics of faith."[71] By this means he set an ideal of critical reasoning against the calamitous results of a politics based on "belief." If the one requires a model of political decision-making based on "the sovereign judgment of separate individuals," then Nazism involved the unthinking pursuit of a collectivist myth and an irrationalist surrender "to group or herd emotions." A movement like Nazism could flourish because in the 1920s German society underwent a moral collapse. As a result of that collapse, "sections of the German elite and masses of ordinary people" abandoned pluralist tolerance for political differences to embrace "a politics based on faith, hope, hatred, and sentimental collective self-regard for their own race and nation." To succeed as a political religion in that way, Nazism required mass susceptibility to "ideological fantasy" from below, plus "the subtle, totalizing control of minds" from above. For Burleigh, the concept described "what can happen when desperate people turn to the politics of faith, purveyed by a mock-messiah … devoted … to permanent racial struggle." In such extreme crises, movements such as Nazism offer themselves "as pseudo- or substitute religions, with eclectic liturgies, ersatz theologies, vices and virtues." They offer "'quick-fix' leaps to happiness."[72]

The authors of this account cite certain homologies between the public symbolics, ritual practices, and formal beliefs of Nazism and those of German Protestantism, while ascribing a transmuted religiosity and distinctively Christian patterns of thought to ideologues such as Joseph Goebbels, Dietrich Eckart, and Alfred Rosenberg. Finding the Third Reich's public ceremonial and commemorative calendar "cult-like" or "quasi-religious" is hardly very original as such. But current analyses go beyond the functional and imitative similarities to postulate deeper forms of Nazi indebtedness to the apocalyptic and salvationist thinking unleashed by a crisis of German Protestantism in the early twentieth century. That crisis was partly institutional, they suggest, with a loss of centralized authority by the main churches and the associated spread of sectarian and liturgical alternatives; and it was partly societal, as secularization unevenly shifted the place of organized religion in social life. Still more, the traumas of World War I, military collapse, and revolutionary upheaval fed the apocalyptic predilections of many radical nationalists, who took ready recourse to religious tropes of spiritual endangerment, darkness, and catastrophe. Amid the resultant disorder of meanings, Nazis and other radicals offered a redemptive vision of political deliverance based on the leader's charismatic authority, the primacy of the *Volksgemeinschaft*, and a Manichean drive against the enemies of the race.[73]

This concept of political religion taps into a rich vein of affinities linking Nazism discursively to the angry right-wing Protestantism of the 1920s, often in very exact ways. Nazi rhetoric's mass appeal may easily be read for its displaced religiosity, whether viewed as consolation, chiliastic desire, or a broader search for collective spiritual and emotional solidarity, through which religious motifs, citations, and styles of thought became aggressively sutured to the movement's racialized and anti-Communist patriotism. By speaking to the religious disorientation of the 1920s, Nazism sought to capture for itself the primary faculty of faith in the divine – namely, the promise of transcendence, which could raise the movement above politics and sublimate worldly fears in the supreme postulate of the racial struggle for existence and its rewards.[74] These are certainly important arguments. They help to make sense of leading Nazis' salvationist language and the messianic aura imputed to Hitler, just as they illuminate the emotional landscape of the 1920s more generally in Germany, "where many felt so existentially threatened by a succession of crises that they preferred a leap of faith to rational understanding of their predicament."[75]

However, Burleigh's version was more diffuse than this. It seemed to require a highly problematic model of secularization in a grand-historical schema of unidirectional change, through which the place of religion in social life becomes reconfigured and diminished. In a "religious age", society lived beneath the tutelage of the institutional Church and its generalized culture of religiosity, he implied, but in a "secular age", religion becomes relegated into being one specialized practice among many, akin to enthusiasms or hobbies: by the later twentieth century, "religious emotion has been diffused into various compartments, one of which is organized religion itself, which becomes a private matter on a par with lifestyle options such as vegetarianism or knitting."[76] The passage between these two conditions is fraught with terrible dangers. To realize the generalized well-being promised by capitalist development and democratic constitutions, in Burleigh's view, the best chance lies with the attainable desideratum of a safe and satisfied personal life, secured by a politics of compromise and decent pluralism. But during the transition to this desirable state, which in early twentieth-century

Europe was accompanied by world war and political violence, emotional longings previously satisfied by religion can seek destructive outlets. People become susceptible to irrational surrogate movements in the shape of "political religions," which seduce them with "quick-fixes" or "utopian solutions."

There are various problems with this schema. While seeing Nazism's popularity as a mass defection from democracy, Burleigh defined the latter less by the Weimar Republic's specific arrangements than by a vague and generalized culture of "decency" that supposedly came before. Indeed, he seemed entirely uninterested in "democracy" as such (as a juridical system of voting rights, citizenship, and equality under the law, aimed at securing the sovereignty of the people), as opposed to some far less tangible quality of social stability, which under the newly achieved conditions of democracy in the 1920s the mass emotionalism of the electorate is then supposed to have destroyed. Burleigh's words evoke nothing so much as the elitist if high-minded liberalism of Cobden, Gladstone, and Mill: "A dreadful mass sentimentality, compounded by anger, fear, resentment, and self-pity, replaced the customary politics of decency, pragmatism, property, and reason."[77] But however appealing this may be to contemporary neoliberal sensibilities of the 1990s, for the specific political force field of the early twentieth century (or, for that matter, for the political imaginary of mid-Victorian liberalism) it provides a very poor guide.

To make sense in the context of the crisis of the 1920s, any talk of "decency" needs to be carefully calibrated by the concrete conditions that allowed democracy to be defended. Yet the supposedly "customary" values bequeathed by the late nineteenth century offered few resources to that end. By 1900, democratic principles had recorded only the meanest of gains across Europe as a whole. Politics before 1914, no less than in 1918 to 1923 or 1930 to 1933, was marked by the embittered resistance of governing élites and the political Right to democratic reform. Even by the 1920s democratic precepts claimed barely a foothold, and only then via the kind of determined militant action which Burleigh apparently abhors. Measured by the actually existing polities of the early twentieth century, in other words, Burleigh's idealized imagery of "the customary politics of decency" is pure construction. To have meaning, the "civilized, free, humane, and tolerant values that we [now] cherish" could only ever be established on the basis of constitutional guarantees, the franchise, civil liberties, and hard democratic struggle. But Burleigh clearly had something quite different in mind. The main embodiments of "decency" in his book were not the working-class defenders of democracy who fought the Nazis during 1930 to 1934 at all, but the aristocrats of the July Plot who supported the Nazis into power, pre-democratic to the core.

Burleigh's conception of political religion implied an underlying philosophical anthropology. He seemed to have in mind a structure of human psychology and emotional life beneath the level of organized religious practice and belief, which during the fraught transition to secularism provides a reservoir of baleful possibilities for unscrupulous, irrationalist politicians to exploit if the enabling conditions of socio-political crisis and moral collapse become sufficiently extreme. Unless the "core political or religious values" of a society can be preserved as a defense, these underlying or repressed emotional needs can become a dangerous source of instability: "For, as religion progressively accommodated itself to the secular world and politics, so politics not only plundered the property box, but tapped into the anthropological substrata." This was the power of political religion, in Burleigh's view: "Nazism did not merely hijack a few liturgical externals, all the better to win over a largely Christian country. It sank a drillhead into a deep-seated reservoir of existential anxiety, offering salvation from an ontological crisis."[78]

Apart from the historical vagueness of this argument, it re-describes Nazi ideology without managing to explain. Its approach to Hitler's charisma straddles a huge gap between the mass disorientation and resulting emotionalism imputed to the general populace, on the one hand, and the Nazi movement's manipulative choreographies, on the other. Yet to grasp more precisely how Nazi ideology worked on the conscious and unconscious motivations of ordinary Germans – whether via Hitler's speeches, the spectacular staging of the Party rallies, the barrage of daily propaganda, the practical presence of the mass organizations, or whatever – we need a different order of detail than the kind Burleigh offered. Whenever he focused on particular individuals or case studies via the book's many illuminating vignettes, ironically enough, he delivered the goods despite himself, pushing necessarily beyond the overgeneralized framework of political religion. Nor is it surprising to find the latter shadowed by the ghost of earlier totalitarianism theory because here "political religion" offers only a refurbishing of the old "mass society" thesis, whose fallacies were so damningly exposed by the social historians of the 1970s and 1980s, in critiques that certainly keep their pertinence today.[79] Similarly, Burleigh needlessly lards his account with facile allusions to Stalinism. By all means compare dictatorships, but not in this tiresomely polemical form. Suggesting that Nazis believed in "the utopian doctrine of the perfectibility of mankind" really goes too far.[80]

Rather than developing his comparisons carefully, Burleigh prefers scoring points. In fact, there are two Burleighs in this book. One is the careful analytical scholar, the Burleigh of the pioneering studies of *Ostforschung*, euthanasia, and the *The Racial State*.[81] But the other is an opinionated pundit, rarely missing a chance to vent a favorite prejudice in throwaway style. Pro-Nazi pastors were "happy-clappy" vicars "playing electric guitars in their churches"; the color-coded classification of concentration camp inmates into "anti-social, criminal, Gypsy, homosexual, Jehovah's Witness, Jew, or political" was the equivalent of "modern identity politics"; Hitler's rhetoric of *Volksgemeinschaft* was what Tony Blair calls "inclusivity"; as a student Nazi in the 1920s, the future Higher SS officer Franz Alfred Six was "a 1968er *avant la lettre*"; and so forth.[82] By annoying his left-wing readers, such remarks doubtless perform their purpose. But they also distract and demean the account.

How well do these two books discharge the tasks of a general history? Neither Ayçoberry nor Burleigh provides a strong enough narrative frame. To the former this probably seemed a defensible byproduct of the social history genre, although in the discipline at large "social history with the politics left out" has long been questioned. Burleigh also provides little help with the conventional chronologies of laws and decrees, institutional changes, policy developments, personnel shifts, and diplomatic maneuvers. He concentrated so firmly on the "racial state" that not only the politics but also the social history dropped out. Burleigh's book successfully recast the history of Nazism around the central facts of the Holocaust and racialization, but at the expense of all other social, cultural, and political complexities. Finally, for teaching purposes neither book will do. Ayçoberry provides no index and the bibliography is unusable: English titles are not provided when available; the citation method is barely comprehensible; the gaps are huge. Burleigh is much better, but both the notes and select bibliography are marred by opinionated and sometimes hidden partisanship. Most egregiously, he entirely ignores Mason and Peukert, by common agreement two of Nazism's key historians before their tragically early deaths.

Whether in their virtues or limitations, Ayçoberry and Burleigh reflect very much their own historiographical times. For a less time-bound critical synthesis, it is to Richard Evans's general history that we may now repair.[83] The more grandiose architecture of his imposing three-volume work (around 2,500 pages overall) allows Evans the scope for stronger interpretive and narrative lines, area by area.[84] Neither Kershaw nor Burleigh, the two other works that come closest in scale, provides anything like the same rounded treatments of the peacetime societal arenas – the former quite understandably due to his chosen biographical focus, the latter by dint of an aggressively idiosyncratic approach. In addition to Burleigh's stress on the ever-radicalizing projections of the "racial utopia," Evans offers carefully crafted analyses of the characteristic operations of the Nazi state and the associated intrusiveness of the *Volksgemeinschaft*, all bound together in the accelerating momentum toward *Lebensraum*, empire, and war.

The causal centrality of *war*, whether as preparation or practice, to Nazism's racialist social and political imaginary, indeed its entire *raison d'être*, as movement and regime – in its drive for rule – is one of those key themes. The pervasiveness of the morally coercive reach of the *Volksgemeinschaft*, both as "the mobilization of the spirit" and as the "social promise" of an egalitarian ethno-national solidarity, ordered around a gender regime of ascendant masculinity – the extraction of consent – is another.[85] A third is the vicious harmony between each of these purposes and the "*racial utopia*" of the sustained war against the Jews.[86] The *modernity* of National Socialism, or more exactly the harnessing of the resources of Germany's modernizing dynamism – in economics, productivity, science, technology – for its expansionist ambition, becomes a fourth theme. Finally, the *violence* of Nazism was always vital not just to its seizure of power and the erection of its rule, but to the movement's entire ethos, aimed aggressively against democracy, against Bolshevism, against civility, and against difference as such. This is the field of complexity my following chapters will seek to explore.

Judging the "Nazi consensus"

Burleigh's treatment of the German resistance is one of his book's weakest points. "Political religion" leaves little scope for collective agency between the determinative power of Hitler's demagogic messianism and the ideological prostration of the general populace. It concedes no space between the irrationalist and "herd-like" submissiveness of the vast majority of ordinary Germans and the pervasiveness of Hitler's impact as their pseudo-messiah. Because German society contained no organized bases after 1933 to 1934 from which the regime might be opposed, it then follows, opposition could only come via *personal* acts of ethical refusal, borne by exceptional individuals and the inspiration of a surviving pre-Nazi value system. Cultural capacities of that kind were sheltered mainly among certain circles of the aristocracy, Burleigh thinks, where family pedigrees and an ethos of military or bureaucratic service could fortify a few courageous personalities against the Nazi state's demands. The prime exemplars were the noble conspirators behind the July Plot who still lived "by simple codes of honor and sacrifice," by disdain for the vulgarity of the mob, by belief in the spiritual and cultivated life, and by possession of what Englishmen of Burleigh's persuasion used to call "breeding," a term which fortunately he prefers not to call upon here.[87]

Otherwise, Burleigh approaches resistance situationally via concrete instances taken from the case records of the various arms of the Nazi institutional complex. We encounter the dilemmas of collusion and complicity mainly through the vivid use of localized and everyday experiences – through the particular stories of the victims of the T-4 program, for example, or through the records of this or that psychiatric nurse or doctor enlisted in T-4's practical implementation. True to the dictates of the totalitarian model, the scope for non-compliance with Nazi policies becomes reduced to the existential choices faced by atomized individuals because once the protections of the rule of law had been destroyed during 1933 to 1934, and the parties and associations were banned, organized resources for dissenting acts had, by definition, gone. The perspective is also very much "top down," with little interest in the resistant qualities of popular culture or working-class community life. For Burleigh, all those potentials were washed away in a tidal wave of popular irrationalism and mass despair. All the subtleties and gradations of German society's response to the Nazi system found by social historians such as Broszat, Peukert, and Mason are now effaced. Measured against the power of political religion's totalizing drive, they lose any claim to efficacy.

Burleigh's dismissive indifference toward the possibilities for popular dissent was consistent with the new reading of Nazi rule gathering strength during the 1990s. As discussed earlier in this chapter, the social historians of the 1970s decisively dismantled an older dichotomous framework that pitted Nazi fanaticism against a cowed and terrorized general populace, alternately drilled into conformity by the Gestapo and whipped into enthusiasm by Goebbels. That earlier black-and-white contrast between the regime and its subjects gradually blurred into a new image of inconclusive and ambiguous complexity, in mottled blends of browns and grays, all deceptive angles and hidden depths. If "resistance" transmuted thereby into subtler repertoires of refusal and non-compliance, or "refractory behavior" and boundary drawing, sometimes consciously oppositional but as often not, then collaboration and accommodation acquired an equally ambivalent edge. If Broszat's Bavarian team pioneered this push toward ambiguity, moreover, they were hugely reinforced in the 1980s by the mushrooming of local history projects under the sign of *Alltagsgeschichte*.

But in the process the older problematic of "resistance" became all but eclipsed. Popular attitudes toward Nazism are now discussed mainly in the language of complicity, conformity, collaboration, and consent.[88] Earlier tales of coded and displaced opposition gave way to an encompassing story of popular inactivity and acquiescence. Few Germans were deemed any longer to have been immune from the values of the regime, rather than being insidiously coopted into them via the structures and modalities of everyday life. Christopher Browning's trope of "ordinary men" became emblematic for seeing Nazism's popular credentials in this way, with its stress on the situational logic of genocide's participatory roster. The resulting exigencies faced even rank-and-file auxiliary policemen of no particular Nazi background with the dailiness of mass murder and the normalizing of killing and abuse.[89] The presence of forced foreign labor in the war economy, the racialization of social policy, the connections between racial hygiene and women's reproductive health, the massive impact of the Eastern Front – all of these became paradigms for showing how Nazism took up residence in the lives of the ordinary German people.[90]

As interest in resistance ebbed, belief in the centrality of terror to Nazism's hold over the Germans has also declined. Long-needed studies of policing and Nazi judicial practice found the Third Reich far less reliant on surveillance, intimidation, and violent coercion than once thought, so that policing was seen to have functioned less by the depth of the Gestapo's penetration into average Germans' lives than by society's own collective self-regulation. As Eric Johnson summarized these findings, "the Gestapo often had less manpower, fewer spies, and less means at its disposal to control the population than had been assumed by nearly everyone since the Nazi period came to an end."[91] Indeed, the police state acquired much of its intelligence from the spontaneous input of a willing citizenry whose supply of political denunciations enabled the Gestapo to keep its ears to the ground. Moreover, motivations had little to do with Nazi ideology *per se*: "Angry neighbors, bitter in-laws, and disgruntled work colleagues frequently used the state's secret police apparatus to settle their personal and often petty scores."[92]

Two key books examined this societal interface between the police state's exercise of its powers and the mundane ways in which most Germans continued to live out their lives. Building on an earlier study of Würzburg, which persuasively outlined the more scaled-down version of the extent of the Nazi police state, Robert Gellately now painted these arguments onto the national canvas. In *Backing Hitler: Consent and Coercion in Nazi Germany*, he shifted the emphasis more markedly than ever toward a consensual view of the Third Reich's domestic stability, inflating his claims about the Gestapo's limitations into more elaborate claims about the regime's popularity. Organized into chapters on the various facets of Nazi repression – from the immediate assaults on Communists in 1933 through the new systems of "police justice" and concentration camps to the hardening wrought by the war, with its vicious targeting of "social outsiders," Jews, foreign workers, and "enemies in the ranks" – his book presented the regime as being securely founded in majoritarian German support.

But the meanings were very slippery here. Gellately continually pushed his evidence to deliver generalized interpretive readings of conformity and acquiescence, while often implying something far more – namely, positive endorsement for the regime's core values by "most Germans." This required marginalizing evidence of dissent and nonconformity, while flattening all those differences within German society that the social historians had chosen to emphasize. It also required playing down the extraordinary volatility and divisiveness on the eve of 1933 itself. It relegated anti-Nazi opposition of that time to negligible significance beside society's center ground, which Gellately argued the Nazis already decisively controlled. The absence of formal democratic mechanisms notwithstanding, he averred, Hitler spoke after 1933 for a majority of Germans. Nazi efforts at concentrating legitimacy in the *Volksgemeinschaft*, ordered around Hitler's charismatic authority, actually worked. Gellately acknowledged the "more openly terroristic" dictatorship of the war, but fundamentally affirmed the popular credentials: from 1933 to 1944, he asserted, the German people had the regime they really wanted.[93]

He cited two kinds of evidence, both requiring a type of inference. One was the fact of denunciations: *because* the Gestapo benefited from citizens' readiness to inform on their fellows, *ipso facto* the system had consent. Secondly, he used the press to show that knowledge of the coercive apparatus was easily acquired: so far from seeking concealment, the regime proudly displayed its effects. This was true of the camps, imprisonment of political opponents, attacks on the Jews, punitive application of the race laws, criminalizing of "social outsiders," wartime executions of criminals and "saboteurs," summary acts of police justice, the solution to the "Jewish problem," and so forth. Again, the absence of embarrassment around these policies, and the visibility of carceral and judicial violence – its transparency, we might say – was taken to imply generalized popular support: "the Germans generally turned out to be proud and pleased that Hitler and his henchmen were putting away certain kinds of people who did not fit in, or who were regarded as 'outsiders,' 'asocials,' 'useless eaters,' or 'criminals'." So, far from wanting "to cower the German people as a whole into submission," the Nazis sought "to win them over by building on popular images, cherished ideals, and long-held phobias in the country."[94]

A cognate work, Eric Johnson's *Nazi Terror: The Gestapo, Jews, and Ordinary Germans* used a rare set of extant Gestapo records to examine Nazi policing in one particular place, the city of Cologne and neighboring towns of Crefeld and Bergheim. Known previously as a social historian of crime, Johnson joined a quantitative analysis of some 1,100 Special Court and Gestapo case files to the telling deployment of individual stories and detailed portraits of the local Gestapo to produce a richly concrete account.[95] He agreed with Gellately that the drive against the Jews was widely known and understood: from the systematic stigmatizing of Jews after 1933 and their removal from the economy on through the violence of November 1938 to the deportations and killings, the public din of anti-Semitism was unavoidable. Non-Jewish Germans learned to live with it; many happily profited; and with the deportations, most realized what was happening, even if the killings remained hazy. Johnson also scaled back the Gestapo's everyday – "less than one percent of the ordinary Crefeld population had any brush with the Gestapo at all" during 1933 to 1939.[96] Thus, Nazi rule presumed popular acquiescence.

But Johnson outlined Nazi repression, too. Like Burleigh, he stressed the violent destruction of the rule of law, for in 1933 there was nothing modest or limited about the terror. It was wielded not by designated police organs alone, but via the collective violence of SA and party thugs, with a ferocity felt by Communists and Social Democrats above all. Once the Left had been smashed, the more modulated Gestapo surveillance became reattached to troublesome clergy and religious sects such as the Jehovah's Witnesses, while any surviving leftists remained under attack. Homosexuals were targeted, if less consistently than we might suppose. Meanwhile, discrimination was continuously tightened around the Jews, dramatically so with *Reichskristallnacht* and the war. Johnson likewise stressed denunciations, but mainly for cases where the victim's category was in the Gestapo's sights. Absent, such default vulnerability accusations were often set aside.

This is a key distinction. For Gellately, civilian denunciations made the Gestapo's practice mainly "reactive," as it trusted German society to police itself. For Johnson, it was "reactive" mainly "in cases of little consequence," often discarding denunciations that lacked connection to an already stigmatized identity. In pursuit of its primary agendas, in contrast, the Gestapo stayed proactively on message. It proceeded selectively, "which made the terror less than blanket perhaps, but all the more efficient."[97] This led to a baleful *modus vivendi*: while the regime silenced its opponents, extinguished "life unworthy of life," and dispossessed and murdered the Jews, the conformist majority kept their silence; and when the latter stepped out of line with petty infractions, the regime looked the other way. If, in consequence, terror became more precise, it was hardly less effective for that. Indeed, Johnson restored violence to its rightful centrality, which Gellately had badly occluded.[98]

In tackling Gestapo culpability as perpetrators, however, Johnson was far less successful. Wanting to see Gestapo officers as worse than "normal" men, he found the tropes of the "banality of evil" and the "ordinariness" of the functionaries unequal to the monstrousness of the misdeeds.[99] Yet, beyond an unsparing description of what Gestapo officers *did*, he failed to capture that criminal singularity. To illumine the latter, we need exactly that syndrome of amoral professionalism and expertise – rationalizing, efficiency driven, goal directed, project oriented, technocratic and scientistic, enthused by modernity – Johnson rejected as so unhelpful ("There is something wrong in this"). "Corrupted by a cold objectivity and emotional distance and fixated in an undoctrinaire fashion on the goals of the state," another pioneering historian of the Gestapo has argued, the typical Gestapo man "led security police operations without giving them much thought."[100] From Broszat through Peukert to the current arguments of Browning, Aly, and other specialists on the Holocaust, it was precisely this "normalizing" analytic that allows us to see the continuities between Nazism and the surrounding society. To push past it, a different discussion than Johnson's was required.

Johnson's disablement before the evil of Nazism came partly from the individualizing logic of his approach. One of *Nazi Terror*'s powerful strengths, his "flesh-and-blood narratives," showed the Nazi system being made via "the voluntary choices and local actions of individual Germans."[101] His use of case records and testimonies carried the arguments along throughout the book. But this aggregation of local transactions needed much stronger contextualizing. Apart from some commentaries on treatments of the Nazi state and its social underpinnings, the accounting led always back to the local settings and the individual lives. Johnson told us far more about "the role of individuals, such as Gestapo officers and ordinary citizens," than about "the role of the society in making terror work."[102] That bespoke nothing less than the prevailing commonsense of the 1990s, it might be said, with its ubiquitous logics of individuation, rhetorics of agency, and cultures of "choice." In this, Johnson had much in common with Gellately. Each approached "society" primarily via the use of case records, with some limiting effects.

Neither historian grasped the full import of the divisiveness in German society during 1930 to 1933. Johnson certainly described the viciousness of the terror against the Left. But from Gellately we would hardly know that Communists and Social Democrats recorded 1.5 million votes *more* than the Nazis in the last free elections of November 1932 (37.3 against 33.1 percent of the total), even keeping almost a third of the voting electorate in face of the intolerable intimidation of March 1933. Gellately shrank the meaning of these affiliations by his language, setting them against a bald category of "the Germans," as if 13 million voters were somehow a marginal minority beyond German society's core. In consigning such huge categories to the margins, *outside* the legitimate nation, Gellately came discomfortingly close to replicating the Nazis' own rhetorical violence. During early 1933, a massive onslaught was unleashed against the Left's strongholds in urban neighborhoods and working-class communities, an exclusionary rampage soon to be widened, reaching from the Jews to various categories of "asocials," like the 100,000 indigents arrested in the police sweep of September 1933 alone.[103] Later in the decade, the regime had clearly stabilized its dictatorship around the new normal of such exclusions. But to be first put into place, that system required its founding act of violence, laying down a powerful climate of fears for the future.

If the Gestapo could presume society's self-policing later in the 1930s, therefore, relying on ordinary complicity, this presupposed the massive wielding of coercive terror against broadly based dissidence earlier on. If Johnson and Gellately each neglected the traumatizing after-effects of this founding period, they also separated the Gestapo far too cleanly from the wider machinery of the Nazi state. Johnson considered only the Gestapo as an institution, neglecting the wider system of social discipline emanating from national and local government, including the welfare and youth agencies, health offices, hereditary health courts, Winter Aid, Labor Front, the mass organizations of women and youth, and so forth.[104] As the 1930s drew on, this reknitting of the social fabric became ever more ramified, radically reordering the boundaries of state and society. The populace was already caught in a fine net of surveillance and registration long *before* the Gestapo exercised its more brutal attentions. It was *this* that allowed terror's deployment to be so selective in the first place. Oddly enough, Gellately even saw this wider field of intervention, arguing that the state "encroached into ever more areas of social and intimate life," so that "the entire thrust of the new system was to expel or exclude ever wider categories of people who would not, or could not, fit in."[105] Yet, when he addressed the primary issue of coercion or consent, this faded from the account.

Imprecision about this central binary of "consent and coercion" vitiated Gellately's discussion. The consequences of the immediate violence of 1933 for the regime's permanent comportment were foundational, so that any consensual acceptance in the future was always already structured around this explicitly terroristic starting point. To the bloody example of 27 February 1933 (the savage repression of the Left surrounding the Reichstag fire) were then added the further demonstration effects of 30 June 1934 (the Night of the Long Knives against the SA) and 9 November 1938 (*Reichskristallnacht*). Given the spectacular quality of these events and their pervasive effects, Gellately and Johnson took a narrowly literal-minded view of Nazi repression. Subjects of the Third Reich hardly needed to be hauled off for Gestapo interrogation to feel the presence and efficacy of Nazi terror. If I know that on the next block several homes have been ransacked and the inhabitants beaten up and imprisoned, or that a sizeable contingent of my militant workmates have disappeared, and if I see political differences being settled by concentration camps and summary executions, or notice the plentiful evidence of bloodied sidewalks and broken glass, I might be forgiven for internalizing some fears. I might not want to express the resulting anxieties or discuss them with family or friends. I might certainly avoid voicing them in public.

To flatten this dialectic into "consensus" is the sound of one hand clapping. While Gellately never hid the coerciveness of Nazi rule – indeed, its horrendousness was vital to his case – he constantly downplayed its reach, making the victims into easily scapegoated marginals whose disappearance left the heartland of German society intact. But given the commonplace climate of terror, the violence could never be so easily contained. What Gellately called "a murderous game of pillorying, excluding, and eventually eliminating unwanted social 'elements' and 'race enemies'" was always more radically pervasive in its lessons.[106] During the first half of 1943, there were 982 convictions for treason, with 948 executions; 8,850 Germans were charged with left-wing activity, 8,727 with "resistance," and 11,075 with "opposition"; while 10,773 were arrested for fraternizing with prisoners of war and foreign slave laborers.[107] Huge by any standard, these figures trouble the meanings of "consent." In the continuing reappraisal of the Gestapo, Gellately's was a valuable voice. But when he concluded that "the Nazis did not need to use widespread terror against the population to establish the regime," something had gone seriously awry.[108]

Gellately showed that persecuting Jews, foreign workers, and "social outsiders" needed the active participation of the general populace, involving the desire for private gain, whether by denouncing personal enemies or plundering Jewish property.[109] He confirmed that knowledge of the concentration camps was inescapable: the system's wartime proliferation carried satellite camps, labor camps, and assignments of camp labor ubiquitously into German society, from industrial centers and factory sites to small villages and countless public places.[110] Open reportage in newspapers and magazines of the camps and the regime's racialist and anti-Semitic actions made these impossible for Germans to avoid. Yet that was *precisely* the place where "consent and coercion" became dialectically entwined. Parading the accomplishments of the camps might certainly have implied widespread popular endorsement of the Third Reich's "law and order" society, as Gellately claimed. But it was also a reminder to potential dissenters of what was in store. Public display of carceral zeal engendered fear, anxiety, and intimidation as often as the support and reassurance Gellately preferred to diagnose. Not to see these "coercive" dimensions is obtuse.[111]

Tackling each of these issues effectively – individual motivations, the extreme dividedness of German society in 1933, the enduring effects of the regime's founding act of violence, the place of coercion *in* consent – requires a more complex approach to ideology. As argued above, the social histories emerging from the 1970s tended to view "social context" and "ideology" dichotomously, giving the first clear analytical priority over the second. If the next scholarly wave of the 1980s took the social efficacy of ideas more seriously, it did so more by considering particular fields of knowledge or the prevailing philosophies in particular professions than by theorizing the penetration of Nazi values into everyday life. In the meantime, we also learned much about the extended ideological context of the Third Reich's policy-making from historians such as Götz Aly, Ulrich Herbert, Saul Friedländer, Henry Friedlander, and Michael Burleigh, whose studies of the "racial state" came much closer to the full scope of the Nazis' intended goals. Using a single career, for example, Herbert's biography of the SS leader Werner Best gave devastating insight into the ideological synergy forged by intellectual ambition, racialist philosophy, and technocratic reason in one particular Nazi life.[112]

We need to go still further to consider ideology inside the apparently "unpolitical" realm of *everyday transactions* that Gellately and Johnson found so vital to the vaunted breadth of the pro-Nazi societal consensus. If that consensus was less securely founded on "consent" than they thought, needing both constant attention to social divisions and palpable sanctions of violence, then the regime's ability to insinuate itself into ordinary life remained extremely impressive. *This* was where the broader repertoire of Nazi public intervention became so crucial – all those areas of state-directed action that Johnson and Gellately excluded from the narrowly drawn compass of Gestapo-organized terror, but that were nonetheless intimately linked to coercion, from the Hitler Youth, the League of German Maidens, and the National Socialist Womanhood to the People's Welfare and the increasingly elaborate regulations defining marriage, sexuality, child-raising, and reproduction.

To them may be added the Nazi public sphere of elaborately staged mass events. These aestheticized the exertion of the state's monopoly of violence through the regimented rallies, commemorations, festivals, associated monumental architecture, and spectacular ritualizing of public transactions.

These organized interventions filled up the space of public life while corroding previously tolerated private domains. The *Volksgemeinschaft* was an immensely coercive abstraction, concentrating all allowable affiliations into a single, exclusive, aggressively wielded loyalty. The mass voluntarism of Nazi public culture was actually its very opposite – a repressive and authoritarian coerciveness that belies the narrower definition of "Nazi terror." As Burleigh pointed out using the example of Winter Aid, participating or not participating in the state's obligatory charitable drive could bring either the warmth of patriotic sentimentalism or the opprobrium of exclusionary disgust: "Overt threats followed, for not fulfilling one's sacrificial duty implied a hostile attitude towards the collective educational goals of the National Socialist state. A choice had become a potential political crime."[113] Just beyond this moral coercion lay the brutality of the jackboot and the physical coercion of the camps.

Nazi rule on the ground: Coercing consent

Disputing the claims of Gellately and others about the generalized pro-Nazi consensus returns us to *Alltagsgeschichte*, or the history of everyday life. By questioning the breadth of the regime's popularity, pointing to the practical effects of Nazi violence and the coercive immediacies of Nazi rule as it played out on the ground, we quickly arrive at such an approach. The wider repertoire of the state's organized interventions and concrete institutional presence require our attention, especially its desire to occupy the leisure time and club-based arenas of social life, as well as the clamor of its massed spectacles and cultural intrusiveness. These point us urgently to the micro-political contexts where force and threats of reprisals would also be felt. In the process of making ordinary Germans into Nazi subjects, endangerment was essential too.

Readiness to go along with the regime's demands always presumed recognizing its capacity for violence. Living under the Third Reich, for anyone seeking to preserve some non-Nazi distance or personal integrity, involved not just the self-protections and stubborn self-assertiveness variously stressed by Broszat, Kershaw, Mason, and Peukert, but also the fears and anxieties engendered by the widely diffused, clearly perceived, and brutally instilled awareness of the new state's dangerous lack of inhibitions – its alacrity for discrimination and harassment, verbal and physical assaults, stigmas and taboos, ritual humiliations and social exclusions, arbitrary arrests and sanctioned killings, all held together by the *ultima ratio* of the camps. Where Broszat's idea of *Resistenz* sought to engage these complexities, Gellately's claims about popular consensus simply effaced them. Whereas the former required a subtle and complicated argument about the dangers, compromises, and pragmatics involved in trying to keep the regime's demands at bay, the argument for consensus builds mainly from a flawed methodology of inference – what the reliance on denunciations might be able to tell us about the system of policing; what the open reportage of the camps and deportations might say about popular endorsement.

In focusing on the everyday, the early writings of Detlev Peukert and Alf Lüdtke sought to rethink what the forming of a political outlook or the taking of a political action under Nazism might have entailed. Under the exceptional circumstances of the Third Reich, inside the brutally innovative social and political imaginary of the freshly ascendant German fascism, how might the categories of "agency" and "rule" (*Herrschaft*) be understood? Beneath and behind the public bluster and outward surfaces of the *Volksgemeinschaft*, how might the boundaries of the generalized complicity of ordinary Germans in the construction and effects of the Nazi new order best be gauged? Here, Peukert emphasized blurrings of the lines between "victims" and "perpetrators," probing instead "the multiple ambiguities of ordinary people making their choices among the various grays of active consent, accommodation, and nonconformity."[114] Surrounded by the regime's intrusions, which saturated the social environs with ideological advocacy and discursive noise, Nazism's opponents could never entirely escape either its ideas or its claws. Withdrawing to a personal redoubt of privacy helped only to consolidate the regime's public norms:

> The Third Reich cannot have failed to leave its mark on all members of society … Even the resistance fighters who did not conform were weighed down by the experience of persecution, by the sense of their own impotence, and of the petty compromises that were the imperative for survival. The system did its work on the anti-fascists too, and often enough it worked despite the shortcomings of the fascists themselves.[115]

In Lüdtke's earliest notations, *Alltagsgeschichte* was a way of getting "inside" the "structures, processes, and patterns" stressed by social historians in order to open up "the daily experiences of people in their concrete life-situations, which also stamp their needs," thereby allowing the intersections of *politics* and *social life*, or *politics* and *culture*, to be engaged.[116] "Micro-history," the careful construction of historical "miniatures," could in this way bring us closer to the ambiguities, conundrums, and contradictions through which people were perforce required to live out their lives. It examined the settings where the abstractions of domination and exploitation – or hope and possibility – could be directly encountered, processed into manageable meanings, and inscribed into the organizing commonsense needed for the conduct of individual and collective existence. Larger forces – the state and its exactions, publicness in all of its registers, as well as politics, economics, law, culture, beliefs – became imbricated together and embedded inside social relations where provisional unities of structure and action might then materialize.

By tracking larger effects into these mundane locations, in the constitutive concreteness of their encounters with individual wants and needs, in what Raymond

Williams called "specific and indissoluble real processes," we can best see people continuously negotiating and renegotiating questions of power, authority, and the capacity to define meanings in the world.[117] The point, though, is not to construct a new binary between the public sphere/politics/ideology, on the one hand, and the "real experience" of the everyday and its authenticities on the other. Rather, it is precisely here, "in the production and reproduction of immediate life" (in Engels's phrase), that politics may be found working complexly away. In Paul Steege's recent formulation:

> … historians still need to find ways to move back and forth between ideological visions articulated in Berlin; local, but mass, practices of violence, whether in the German capital or on the Eastern Front; and individuals' choices to watch, participate, muddle through, resist, or some combination of the above. *Alltagsgeschichte* embraces the shades of gray implicit in this mode of questioning for which there are more than two – black or white – answers … While acknowledging how structures of power, and the people who inhabit them, can limit the room for maneuver available to individual actors, it also leaves room for their mutual complicity in producing those same structures of power. This is why the historian of everyday life looks to stories of collaboration and resistance. The fact that they are often the same stories is precisely the point.[118]

I will return to *Alltagsgeschichte* as such in several other chapters.[119] Here I wish mainly to mark the importance of everydayness in enabling us to engage certain aspects of power under fascism (as authority, domination, rule) more searchingly than earlier forms of social, cultural, and political history have allowed. As Dennis Sweeney puts this, "analysis of the everyday experience of ordinary people and the mutually constitutive connections between the local, the quotidian, the public sphere, and the state might offer new ways of understanding wider systemic processes and political transformations from the perspective of the everyday."[120] Or, in Elissa Mailänder Koslov's words: "Ordinary moments of crystallization allow us to reconstruct the larger social relations and cultural meanings – I prefer the term resonances (*Sinnzusammenhänge*) – relating to power and violence that otherwise would be overlooked."[121] For Sweeney, "the formation of Nazi subjectivities" then becomes the key problem:

> This would involve taking seriously Nazism's capacity to enter into the various realms of everyday experience and private desires, including the domains of work, quotidian sociability, family life, and consumer entertainment and spectacle. It would also, however, involve the interpellative capacities of Nazi ideology as it [worked for the formation of] new fascist subjectivities, anchored in notions of ethno-racial purity and self-contained *Eigenart*, in response to competing notions of self, the proliferation of cultural difference, and the immediate presence of the other.[122]

"Taking seriously the ways in which ordinary people imagined themselves as coherent subjects in relation to Nazism" has made greatest strides perhaps in the recent growth of perpetrator (*Täter*) history, particularly regarding the genocidal and related policies of the Nazi imperium during the war. While much interest there has focused on the various official cadres, encompassing senior leadership and middle-rank bureaucracy, planners and desk-administrators, as well as killers in the field, new work is also attending to the massively ramified ground-level participation needed by the racial state for its day-to-day functioning. If Browning's study of Reserve Police Battalion 101 set one kind of standard in that regard, then the amassing of regional and local case studies of the Nazi-occupied east provides another.[123] Much of that work converges around key precepts of *Alltagsgeschichte*, stressing situational dynamics, emblematic careers and ethnographies, close readings of texts (such as soldiers' diaries and correspondence), symptomatic events, particularities of place, and micro-histories of all kinds. In their willingness to analyze aspects of the emotional and mental interiority of individuals caught up in the racial state's purposes and practices, Lüdtke's essays especially stand out, but everyday life perspectives are now integrated in some degree by a much wider range of historiography.[124] Such work aims to get inside the heads of the perpetrators, not just to interrogate the immediate and longer-standing motivations or examine the psychology, but also to reconstruct more complicated, far less transparent grounds of belief and action. One of the biggest priorities is now to push these approaches *back* into the peacetime years of the 1930s. For only then will we come closer to answering Sweeney's question about what was required to turn Weimar citizens into Nazi subjects.[125]

Unfortunately, these insights from "perpetrator research" (*Täterforschung*) feed back only unevenly into treatments of the Third Reich as a polity – as a system of political rule founded on the ruins of parliamentary democracy in 1933 to 1934. Having finally brought the histories of Nazism and the Holocaust *together*, German historians have now subsumed the one so entirely into the other, ironically enough, that studies of Nazi rule *distinct* from studies of the Holocaust seem hardly to exist at all. Conversely, not all the new approaches to Nazism have made it into Holocaust historiography. Most tellingly, for example, Lüdtke's essays figure nowhere in the comprehensive guides currently documenting the shape of that latter field. His name appears in none of the bibliographies attaching to the 47 essays of *The Oxford Handbook of Holocaust Studies*; his essays and arguments are absent from the state-of-the-art treatments of Donald Bloxham and Dan Stone; he figures nowhere in the mapping of the field by Jürgen Matthäus and the other contributors to Stone's 2004 anthology; nor for that matter is he mentioned by Yehuda Bauer.[126]

This surprising bifurcation, between this most searching of the attempts to unravel the skein of German complicity and those most insistent on the necessity of doing so, reflects certain difficulties with *Verstehen*, or with the kind of empathy from which most histories of the Jewish experience under Nazism tend to be written. Lüdtke's unsparing scrutiny of everything that helped to motivate people for doing the Third Reich's worst work – soldiers in the killing squads of a genocidal army, or skilled workers wielding authority over viciously exploited eastern forced laborers, to cite the two especially upsetting instances – confronts the willingness on the part of otherwise decent and upstanding individuals not just to "go along" and to "put up with" the regime's crimes, but even to make a virtue of doing so. Into the darkest corners of human motivation, Lüdtke shines a discomforting interpretive light whose grim results may be unlikely to inspire historians working on Jewish victimhood, who almost necessarily retain some redemptive or recuperative purpose. Despite all the talk of the "gray zone," with certain individual exceptions, there remains little willingness to examine comparably upsetting aspects of the agency of Jewish victims. Refusing to absolve ordinary actors of complicity proves easier in some cases than others, one might cautiously observe.[127]

That is where the crucial power differential – who was *inside* the *Volksgemeinschaft* and who was *not*, along with all the unrestrained physical violence, elaborate machineries of law, social sanctions, ideological work, moral coerciveness, and cultural othering needed to erect those boundaries – remains irreducibly key. Lüdtke pursues the implications unremittingly. He turns the binary of coercion and consent into a dialectic. With career-long consistency, on the one hand, he continues examining the processes and relations through which all forms of power (political rule and class dominance, social authority, policing and militarism, material and symbolic forms of state violence) become embedded, contested, and diffused during the nineteenth and twentieth centuries in ordinary social life.[128] In that way the violence of the Nazi drive for rule, the material and coercive exorbitance of Nazi power, is never allowed to drop from view. On the other hand, few historians have tried more persistently to get inside the question of consent – to understand not just how so many people became so open to finding positive reasons for accommodating the post-1933 exigencies, to the new rules for how lives would now have to be made, but also the anxiously extreme drivenness of the new regime's need to secure that approval, its restless desire to *extract* that consent. This was the dualism around which fascism sought to order itself – ruthless imposition of anti-democratic rule, equally compulsive thirst for popular endorsement.[129]

Notes

1 Recently biography is undergoing a notable resurgence, marked especially in Ian Kershaw's authoritative two volumes *Hitler 1889–1936: Hubris* and *Hitler 1936–1945: Nemesis*, New York: Norton, 1998 and 2000. These were preceded by U. Herbert's *Best: Biographische Studien über Radikalismus, Weltanschauung und Vernunft 1903–1989*, Bonn: Dietz, 1996. In the meantime we now have the following: P. Longerich, *Heinrich Himmler*, Oxford: Oxford University Press, 2012; T. Thacker, *Joseph Goebbels: Life and Death*, Houndmills: Palgrave Macmillan, 2009; R. Gerwarth, *Hitler's Hangman: The Life of Heydrich*, New Haven: Yale University Press, 2011; and C. Epstein, *Model Nazi: Arthur Greiser and the Occupation of Western Poland*, Oxford: Oxford University Press, 2010.

2 Best guides to the historiography are I. Kershaw, *The Nazi Dictatorship: Problems and Perspectives of Interpretation*, 4th ed., London: Arnold, 2000, and J. Caplan (ed.) *Nazi Germany*, Oxford: Oxford University Press, 2008.

3 See W. S. Allen, *The Nazi Seizure of Power: The Experience of a Single German Town, 1922–1945*, New York: F. Watts, 1984; orig. ed: Chicago: Quadrangle Books, 1965; J. Noakes, *The Nazi Party in Lower Saxony, 1921–1933*, Oxford: Oxford University Press, 1971; M. Broszat, E. Fröhlich, and F. Wiesemann (eds), *Bayern in der NS-Zeit*, 6 vols., Munich and Vienna: Oldenbourg, 1977–1983.

4 M. Kater, *The Nazi Party: A Social Profile of Members and Leaders, 1919–1945*, Cambridge: Harvard University Press, 1983; M. Jamin, *Zwischen den Klassen: Zur Sozialstruktur der SA-Führerschaft*, Wuppertal: Peter Hammer Verlag, 1984; R. Bessel, *Political Violence and the Rise of Nazism: The Storm Troopers in Eastern Germany 1925–1934* New Haven: Yale University Press, 1984; E. G. Reiche, *The Development of the SA in Nürnberg, 1922–1934*, Cambridge: Cambridge University Press, 1986; C. Fischer, *Stormtroopers: A Social, Economic, and Ideological Analysis 1929–35*, London: George Allen and Unwin, 1983; T. Childers, *The Nazi Voter: The Social Foundations of Fascism in Germany, 1919–1933*, Chapel Hill: University of North Carolina Press, 1983; R. F. Hamilton, *Who Voted for Hitler?* Princeton: Princeton University Press, 1982; J. Falter, *Hitlers Wähler*, Munich: C. H. Beck, 1991; and T. Childers (ed.) *The Formation of the Nazi Constituency 1919–1933*, London: Croom Helm, 1986.

5 See P. Fritzsche, *Rehearsals for Fascism: Populism and Political Mobilization in Weimar Germany*, New York: Oxford University Press, 1990; Fritzsche, *Germans into Nazis*, Cambridge: Harvard University Press, 1998; and Fritzsche, "The NSDAP 1919–1934: From Fringe Politics to the Seizure of Power," in Caplan (ed.) *Nazi Germany*, pp48–72. Another excellent synthesis can be found in R. J. Evans, *The Coming of the Third Reich*, London: Allen Lane, 2003, pp155–230.

6 H. Mommsen, *Beamtentum im Dritten Reich. Mit ausgewählten Quellen zur nationalsozialistischen Beamtenpolitik*, Stuttgart: Deutsche Verlags-Anstalt, 1966; M. Broszat, *Der Staat Hitlers*, Munich: Deutscher Taschenbuch Verlag, 1969. See also P. Hüttenberger, *Die Gauleiter*, Stuttgart: Deutsche Verlags-Anstalt, 1969; R. Bollmus, *Das Amt Rosenberg und seine Gegner. Studien zum Machtkampf im nationalsozialistischen Herrschaftssystem*, Stuttgart: Deutsche Verlags-Anstalt, 1970; E. N. Peterson, *The Limits of Hitler's Power*, Princeton: Princeton University Press, 1969.

7 Both Mommsen and Broszat were tendentiously caricatured by their opponents. See Broszat's classic article "Soziale Motivation und Führer-Bindung des Nationalsozialismus," *Vierteljahrshefte für Zeitgeschichte*, vol. 18, 1970, pp329–65, whose "structuralist" emphasis on institutional dynamics simultaneously upheld the ethical and historical decisiveness of human agency. For general guidance, see the judicious overview of J. Noakes, "Hitler and the Nazi State: Leadership, Hierarchy, and Power," in Caplan (ed.) *Nazi Germany*, pp73–98.

8 See P. Hüttenberger, "Nationalsozialistische Polykratie," *Geschichte und Gesellschaft*, vol. 2, 1976, pp417–42; H. Mommsen, "Hitler's Position in the Nazi System," in *From Weimar to Auschwitz: Essays in German History*, Oxford: Berg, 1991, pp163–88; J. Caplan, "Bureaucracy, Politics, and the National Socialist State," in P. D. Stachura (ed.) *The Shaping of the Nazi State*, London: Croom Helm, 1978, pp234–56. Coined originally by Carl Schmitt, "polycratic rule" was used by Karl D. Bracher, Wolfgang Sauer, and Gerhard Schulz in *Die nationalsozialistische Machtergreifung. Studien zur Errichtung des totalitären Herrschaftssystems in Deutschland 1933–34*, Cologne and Opladen: Westdeutscher Verlag, 1960, though paradoxically within a "totalitarianism" framework. See Kershaw, *Nazi Dictatorship*, p74, note 24.

9 The quoted phrases are taken from L. Dawidowicz, *The War against the Jews 1933–1945*, New York: Bantam Books, 1976, pp193–208. See the discussion in Kershaw, *Nazi Dictatorship*, pp94–102. The Windsor conference papers were published as G. Hirschfeld and L. Kettenacker (eds) *Der "Führerstaat": Mythos und Realität*, Stuttgart: Klett-Cotta, 1981.

10 See the following works by Mason: *Arbeiterklasse und Volksgemeinschaft: Dokumente und Materialien zur deutschen Arbeiterpolitik 1936–1939*, Opladen: Westdeutscher Verlag,

1975; *Social Policy in the Third Reich: The Working Class and the National Community*, Providence: Berg, 1993; and J. Caplan (ed.) *Nazism, Fascism, and the Working Class: Essays by Tim Mason*, Cambridge: Cambridge University Press, 1995.

11 T. Mason, "The Workers' Opposition in Nazi Germany," *History Workshop Journal*, vol. 11, 1981, p120.

12 The usual German word for "resistance" in the sense of the illegal underground is *Widerstand*, which after 1945 carried connotations of ethical commitment and organized preparation inseparably linked with the myth of the military and aristocratic 1944 July Plot. Explicitly distinguished from "resistance," Broszat's *Resistenz* took its meanings from medicine and physics, suggesting "immunity" or a countervailing ability to impede the flow of a current. It signified those elements of social life (actions, practices, structures, relations) "limiting the penetration of Nazism and blocking its total claim to power and control." This quotation is from Kershaw's exposition in *Nazi Dictatorship*, p194.

13 Ibid, p204. In Kershaw's exposition, resistance "embraced all forms of limited and partial rejection, whatever the motives, of specific aspects of Nazi rule. Instead of dealing in images of black and white, resistance was portrayed in shades of grey; as a part of the everyday reality of trying to adjust to, and cope with, life in a regime impinging on practically all aspects of daily existence, posing a total claim on society, but – as a direct consequence – meeting numerous blockages and restrictions in its attempt to make good this claim." Ibid, p193. Kershaw himself was part of the Bavaria Project. See I. Kershaw, *Popular Opinion and Political Dissent in the Third Reich 1933–1945*, Oxford: Oxford University Press, 1983, new edn 2002, and *The "Hitler Myth". Image and Reality in the Third Reich*, Oxford: Oxford University Press, 1987.

14 Kershaw, *Popular Opinion*, pp281, 373, 314.

15 See the following works by Peukert: *Die KPD im Widerstand. Verfolgung und Untergrundarbeit an Rhein und Ruhr 1933 bis 1945*, Wuppertal: Peter Hammer Verlag, 1980; *Ruhrarbeiter gegen den Faschismus. Dokumentation über den Widerstand im Ruhrgebiet 1933–1945*, Frankfurt am Main: Röderberg-Verlag, 1976; *Die Edelweisspiraten: Protestbewegungen jugendlicher Arbeiter im Dritten Reich*, Cologne: Bund-Verlag, 1980; *Inside Nazi Germany. Conformity and Opposition in Everyday Life*, New Haven: Yale University Press, 1987. By social histories of the working class under Nazism, Mason, Peukert, and others sought to reconstruct an argument about progressive working-class agency once organized political and trade union representation by a labor movement was wiped out.

16 R. Bridenthal, A. Grossman and M. Kaplan (eds) *When Biology Became Destiny: Women in Weimar and Nazi Germany*, New York: Monthly Review Press, 1984; G. Bock, *Zwangssterilisation in Nationalsozialismus: Studien zur Rassenpolitik und Frauenpolitik*, Opladen: Westdeutscher Verlag, 1986; C. Koonz, *Mothers in the Fatherland: Women, the Family, and Nazi Politics*, New York: St. Martin's Press, 1987; A. Grossmann, *Reforming Sex: The German Movement for Birth Control and Abortion Reform*, New York: Oxford University Press, 1995. For critical surveys, see A. von Saldern, "Victims or Perpetrators? Controversie about the Role of Women in the Nazi State," in D. Crew (ed.) *Nazism and German Society, 1933–1945*, London: Routledge, 1994, pp141–65; A. Grossmann, "Feminist Debates about Women and National Socialism," *Gender and History*, vol. 3, 1991, pp350–58. I take up this particular thread in detail in Chapter 4.

17 See, for example, A. Lüdtke, "What Happened to the 'Fiery Red Glow'? Workers' Experiences and German Fascism," in A. Lüdtke (ed.) *The History of Everyday Life: Reconstructing Historical Experiences and Ways of Life*, Princeton: Princeton University Press, 1995, pp198–251, and "The Appeal of Exterminating 'Others': German Workers and the Limits of Resistance," in M. Geyer and J. W. Boyer (eds) *Resistance against the Third Reich, 1933–1990*, Chicago: University of Chicago Press, 1994, pp53–74; L. Niethammer (ed.) *Lebensgeschichte und Sozialkultur im Ruhrgebiet: 1930 bis 1960*. vol. 1: *"Die Jahre weiss man nicht, wo man di heute hinsetzen soll": Faschismuserfahrungen im Ruhrgebiet*, Berlin: Dietz, 1983; A. von Saldern, *The Challenge of Modernity: German Social and Cultural Studies 1890–1960*, Ann Arbor: University of Michigan Press, 2002.

18 The literature is voluminous, pioneered by H.-W. Schmuhl, *Rassenhygiene, Nationalsozialismus, Euthanasia: Von der Verhütung zur Vernichtung "lebensunwerten Lebens", 1890–1945*, Göttingen: Vandenhoeck und Ruprecht, 1987; P. Weindling, *Health, Race and German Politics between National Unification and Nazism, 1870–1945*, Cambridge: Cambridge University Press, 1989; and R. N. Proctor, *Racial Hygiene: Medicine under the Nazis*, Cambridge: Harvard University Press, 1988. The best general survey, now already somewhat dated, is M. Burleigh and W. Wippermann, *The Racial State: Germany, 1933–1945*, Cambridge: Cambridge University Press, 1991. A key essay is D. J. K. Peukert, "The Genesis of the 'Final Solution' from the Spirit of Science," in T. Childers and J. Caplan (eds) *Reevaluating the Third Reich*, New York: Holmes and Meier, 1993, pp234–52. Though Mason's coinage of "biological politics" occurred at the end of the conference behind the Childers and Caplan volume, it is not in his written reflections. See T. Mason, "Whatever Happened to 'Fascism'?" *Radical History Review*, vol. 49, 1991, reprinted as an appendix to Childers and Caplan (eds) *Reevaluating*, pp253–62, and in Mason, *Nazism, Fascism, and the Working Class*, pp323–31.

19 The best introduction is via Kershaw, *Nazi Dictatorship*, "Hitler and the Holocaust," pp93–133. See also G. Eley, "Ordinary Germans, Nazism, and Judeocide," in Eley (ed.) *The "Goldhagen Effect". History, Memory, Nazism – Facing the German Past*, Ann Arbor: University of Michigan Press, 2000, pp1–32, and Chapter 6 in this volume.

20 For the ramifications of this shift in its West German setting, see G. Eley, *A Crooked Line: From Cultural History to the History of Society*, Ann Arbor: University of Michigan Press, 2005, pp61–114, treating Tim Mason in detail as an exemplary case, esp. pp102–13.

21 Proctor, *Racial Hygiene*, pp6–7.

22 Ibid.

23 M. Broszat, "Resistenz und Widerstand. Eine Zwischenbilanz des Forschungsprojekts 'Widerstand und Verfolgung in Bayern 1933–1945,'" in H. Graml and K.-D. Henke (eds) *Nach Hitler: Der schwierige Umgang mit unserer Geschichte*, Munich: Oldenbourg, 1987, pp75–6.

24 My reference here is to Peukert's hugely influential essay "The Genesis of the 'Final Solution' from the Spirit of Science."

25 See above all the works of U. Herbert: *Hitler's Foreign Workers: Enforced Foreign Labour in Germany under the Third Reich*, Cambridge: Cambridge University Press, 1998; orig. German edn. 1986; (ed.) *Europa und der "Reichseinnsatz," Ausländische Zivilarbeiter, Kriegsgefangene und KZ-Häftlinge in Deutschland 1938–1945*, Essen: Klartext, 1991; and "Labour and Extermination: Economic Interest and the Primacy of *Weltanschauung* in National Socialism," *Past and Present* 138, 1993, pp144–95.

26 M. Nolan, "Rationalization, Racism, and *Resistenz*: Recent Studies of Work and the Working Class in Nazi Germany," *International Labor and Working-Class History*, vol. 48, 1995, p132. Other studies of industrial "rationalization" emphasize continuities between the Third Reich and similar histories of the 1920s and 1950s, further displacing German workers as agents. Such research stresses their objectification and disempowerment rather than the scope for self-assertion that interested Mason, or the room for modest negotiation expressed by *Resistenz*. See especially T. Siegel, *Leistung und Lohn in der nationalsozialistischen "Ordnung der Arbeit,"* Opladen: Westdeutscher Verlag, 1989; R. Hachtmann, *Industriearbeit im "Dritten Reich": Untersuchungen zu den Lohn- und Arbeitsbedingungen in Deutschland 1933–1945*, Göttingen: Vandenhoeck und Ruprecht, 1989; T. Siegel and T. von Freyberg, *Industrielle Rationalisierung unter dem Nationalsozialismus*, Frankfurt am Main: Campus, 1991; D. Reese, E. Rosenhaft, C. Sachse, and T. Siegel (eds) *Rationale Beziehungen? Geschlechterverhältnisse im Rationalisierungsprozeß*, Frankfurt am Main: Suhrkamp, 1993.

27 See the very moving reflections of Tim Mason, who had personally recoiled from the intellectual and emotional toll of trying to work on the genocidal murderousness of the war years: Mason, "Epilogue," in *Social Policy in the Third Reich*, pp276–83.

28 Nolan, "Rationalization, Racism, and *Resistenz*," pp132–3.

29 A. Bullock, *Hitler. A Study in Tyranny*, revised edn, London: Hamlyn, 1973; J. C. Fest, *Hitler*, New York: Harcourt Brace, 1974.
30 Kershaw, *Hitler 1889–1936*, p591.
31 The first of these treatments, "Marks of a Genocidal Mentality" (*Hitler 1936–45*, pp127–53) deals with "Reich Crystal Night" (9–10 November 1938), which drastically radicalized the regime's anti-Semitic purposes. Subsequent treatments are in Chapters 6 ("Licensing Barbarism," pp231–79) and 10 ("Fulfilling the Prophecy," pp459–95).
32 Out of 445 pieces of legislation in 1941, only 72 laws, published Führer decrees, and ministerial decrees represented any semblance of inter-ministerial policy formation. The remaining 373 decrees were produced by individual ministries without wider consultation. Ibid, pp420–1.
33 Ibid, p577.
34 Ibid, pxxxvii. Kershaw recurs to similar formulations throughout the book, including his treatment of the final collapse, where "industry" is replaced by the SS: "The institutional pillars of the regime – the Wehrmacht, the Party, ministries of state, and the SS-controlled security apparatus – remained intact in the second half of 1944." Ibid, p705. This analytic also reflects the enduring influence of Franz Neumann's *Behemoth: The Structure and Practice of National Socialism, 1933–1944*, Chicago: Ivan R. Dee, 2009, originally published in 1944.
35 Ibid, p407.
36 Ibid, p420.
37 Kershaw, *Hitler 1889–1936*, Ch. 13: "Working Towards the Führer," pp527–91.
38 The quotations are taken from Kershaw's discussion in *Hitler 1936–1945*, pp148–53.
39 Ibid, p241.
40 Ibid, pp248–9.
41 Ibid, p249. See also Kershaw's discussion of the so-called T-4 program for the euthanasia (more accurately called "medicalized mass murder" than "mercy-killing") of the mentally ill and incurably sick, named after its headquarters in Tiergartenstrasse 4 in Berlin. Authorized formally by Hitler on 9 October 1939, 70,273 people were killed under the first phase of the euthanasia program, which became disguised after 24 August 1941 in response to certain public pressure. After the killing resumed on that basis, total deaths by 1945 exceeded 200,000. The victims were psychiatric patients, asylum inmates, depressives, sick concentration camp inmates, young children of the latter, and nonconformists of various kinds. *Aktion-T4* was direct ancestor to the "Final Solution," providing an administrative model, key personnel, and gas as the method of killing. See E. Klee, *"Euthanasia" im NS-Staat: Die Vernichtung "lebensunwerten Lebens,"* Frankfurt am Main: Fischer, 1983; Schmuhl, *Rassenhygiene*; G. Aly, "Medicine against the Useless," in Aly, Chroust, and Pross, *Cleansing the Fatherland*, pp22–98; M. Burleigh, *Death and Deliverance. "Euthanasia" in Germany, c. 1900–1945*, Cambridge: Cambridge University Press, 1994; H. Friedlander, *The Origins of Nazi Genocide: From Euthanasia to the Final Solution*, Chapel Hill: University of North Carolina Press, 1995; "Medicalized Mass Murder" is the title of Burleigh's chapter in *The Third Reich: A New History*, New York: Hill and Wang, 2000, pp382–404.
42 Kershaw, *Hitler 1936–45*, p324.
43 Ibid, p317.
44 Ibid, pp324–5.
45 C. R. Browning, *Nazi Policy, Jewish Workers, German Killers*, Cambridge: Cambridge University Press, 2000, p56.
46 Ibid, p30.
47 Kershaw, *Hitler 1936–1945*, p463.
48 These questions are taken up again in Chapter 6 of this volume.
49 Kershaw, *Hitler 1936–1945*, pp461–2.
50 Ibid, pp234–5. The importance of newly occupied Poland as a racialist laboratory emerges strongly from M. Wildt, *An Uncompromising Generation: The Nazi Leadership of*

the Reich Security Main Office, Madison: University of Wisconsin Press, 2009, pp217–41; also A. B. Rossino, *Hitler Strikes Poland: Blitzkrieg, Ideologie, and Atrocity*, Lawrence: University Press of Kansas, 2003; P. T. Rutherford, *Prelude to the Final Solution: The Nazi Program for Deporting Ethnic Poles, 1939–1941*, Lawrence: University Press of Kansas, 2007; Epstein, *Model Nazi*, pp124–230; G. Wolf, *Ideologie und Herrschaftsrationalität: Nationalsozialistische Germanisierungspolitik in Polen*, Hamburg: Hamburger Edition, 2012.

51 Here Kershaw follows an unpublished paper by Eberhard Jäckel in seeing Heydrich rather than Himmler as the main architect of the "Final Solution." See *Hitler 1936–45*, p933, note 68, and p495. The case for Himmler's primary authorship is made by R. Breitman, *The Architect of Genocide: Himmler and the Final Solution*, London: Bodley Head, 1991. For this question, the accounts of Longerich, *Heinrich Himmler*, pp385–512, and Gerwarth, *Hitler's Hangman*, pp141–72, are now essential.

52 See R. L. Koehl's classic study *RKFDV: German Resettlement and Population Policy 1939–1945. A History of the Reich Commission for the Strengthening of Germandom*, Cambridge: Harvard University Press, 1957; and G. Aly, *"Final Solution": Nazi Population Policy and the Murder of the European Jews*, London: Arnold, 1999.

53 Kershaw, *Hitler 1936–1945*, p316.

54 Ibid, pp388–89. See also O. Bartov, *The Eastern Front, 1941–45: German Troops and the Barbarization of Warfare*, London: Macmillan, 1985, and *Hitler's Army: Soldiers, Nazis, and War in the Third Reich*, New York: Oxford University Press, 1991; R.-D. Müller and G. R. Ueberschär, *Hitler's War in the East, 1941–1945: A Critical Assessment*, 3rd edn., New York: Berghahn Books, 2009; Aly, *"Final Solution"*; H. Heer and K. Naumann (eds) *Vernichtungskrieg. Verbrechen der Wehrmacht 1941 bis 1944*, Hamburg: HIS-Verlagsges, 1995; Hamburg Institute for Social Research (ed.) *The German Army and Genocide: Crimes against War Prisoners, Jews, and Other Civilians, 1939–1944*, New York: The New Press, 1999.

55 P. Ayçoberry, *The Social History of the Third Reich, 1933–1945*, New York: The New Press, 1999.

56 Ibid, p97.

57 However, it remains unclear whether this means "the invasion of politics *by violence*" or the "the invasion of politics *into society*."

58 Ibid, p245.

59 See note 34 above.

60 Ayçoberry, *Social History*, p170.

61 Ibid, p209.

62 M. Burleigh, *The Third Reich: A New History*, New York: Hill and Wang, 2000.

63 Ibid, p157.

64 Ibid, p323.

65 Ibid, p342.

66 Ibid, pp336–7.

67 The five chapters on the war years occupy 391 pages of the book, as against 244 pages for the four chapters dealing with 1933 to 1939. Prewar foreign affairs receive only a short nine-page subsection of Chapter 3 on the public values of the regime. The wartime chapters are also considerably longer, with, on average, 20 pages more than the pre-1939 ones.

68 Ibid, p595.

69 Ibid, p811.

70 Ibid, p480.

71 The concept of political religion *per se* goes back to writings of Erich Voegelin, in particular P. J. Opitz (ed.) *Die politischen Religionen* 2nd edn, Munich: Wilhelm Fink, 1993 (originally 1938), translated as part of M. Henningsen (ed.) *The Collected Works of Eric Voegelin, Volume Five: Modernity without Restraint: Political Religions; The New Science of Politics; and Science, Politics, and Gnosticism*, Columbia: University of Missouri Press,

1999. See also H. Maier (ed.) *Totalitarismus und politische Religionen: Konzepte des Diktaturvergleichs*, 2 vols, Paderborn: Schöningh, (1996–1997); M. Levy and J. Schoeps (eds) *Der Nationalsozialismus als politische Religion*, Bodenheim: Philo, 1997. The most painless introduction to Voegelin's works and career is via the *Eric Voegelin Study Page* website at http://home.salamander.com/~wmcclain/ev-conferences.html. The concept's recent genealogy runs through the Emilio Gentile and George Mosse. For Gentile, see *The Sacralization of Politics in Fascist Italy*, Cambridge: Harvard University Press, 1996; *Politics as Religion*, Princeton: Princeton University Press, 2006. For Mosse's more diffuse conception, see the following of his works: *The Nationalization of the Masses: Political Symbolism and Mass Movements in Germany from the Napoleonic Wars through the Third Reich*, New York: Meridian, 1977; *Masses and Man: Nationalist and Fascist Perceptions of Reality*, New York: Howard Fertig, 1980; *The Fascist Revolution: Toward a General Theory of Fascism*, New York: Howard Fertig, 1999. See also R. Griffin (ed.) *Fascism, Totalitarianism, and Political Religion*, London: Routledge, 2005.

72 This summary is based on Burleigh, *Third Reich*, pp1–9, 104–13, 252–67, 717, 812. See also P. Burrin, "Political Religion. The Relevance of a Concept," *History and Memory*, vol. 9, 1997, pp321–52; R. Griffin (ed.) *Fascism, Totalitarianism, and Political Religion*, London: Routledge, 2005, and especially R. Steigmann-Gall, "Nazism and the Revival of Political Religion Theory," pp82–102. Burleigh himself cofounded a new journal of *Totalitarian Movements and Political Religions*, published by Frank Cass since 2000.

73 The most important specific studies are C.-E. Bärsch, *Die politische Religion des Nationalsozialismus: Die religiöse Dimension des NS-Ideologie in den Schriften von Dietrich Eckart, Joseph Goebbels, Adolf Rosenberg und Adolf Hitler*, Munich: Wilhelm Fink Verlag, 1998; K. Schreiner, "'Wann kommt der Retter Deutschlands?' Formen und Functionen von politische Messianismus in der Weimarer Republik," *Saeculum*, vol. 49, 1998, pp107–60; K. Vondung, *Magie und Manipulation: Ideologischer Kult und politische Religion des Nationalsozialismus*, Göttingen: Vandenhoeck und Ruprecht, 1971; and R. Steigmann-Gall, *The Holy Reich: Nazi Conceptions of Christianity, 1919–1945*, Cambridge: Cambridge University Press. 2003.

74 This is the argument of W. Hardtwig, "Poltical Religion in Modern Germany: Reflections on Nationalism, Socialism, and National Socialism," *Bulletin of the German Historical Institute*, vol. 28, 2001, pp3–27. See also the comment by J. Caplan, "Politics, Religion, and Ideology: A Comment on Wolfgang Hardtwig," ibid, pp28–36.

75 Burleigh, *Third Reich*, p266.

76 Ibid, p255.

77 Ibid, p8.

78 Ibid, p255.

79 Among such critiques, see above all B. Hagtvet, "The Theory of Mass Society and the Collapse of the Weimar Republic: A Re-Examination," in S. U. Larsen, B. Hagtvet, and J. P. Myklebust (eds) *Who Were the Fascists: Social Roots of European Fascism*, Bergen: Universitetsforlaget, 1980, pp66–117; R. Koshar, *Social Life, Local Politics, and Nazism: Marburg, 1880–1935*, Chapel Hill: University of North Carolina Press, 1986, pp210–11.

80 A useful beginning was made by I. Kershaw and M. Lewin (eds) *Stalinism and Nazism: Dictatorships in Comparison*, Cambridge: Cambridge University Press, 1997, along with H. Rousso (ed.) *Stalinism and Nazism: History and Memory Compared*, Lincoln: University of Nebraska Press, 2004, which anthologized responses to a specifically French controversy. The essential starting point is now M. Geyer and S. Fitzpatrick (eds) *Beyond Totalitarianism: Stalinism and Nazism Compared*, Cambridge: Cambridge University Press, 2009.

81 See M. Burleigh, *Germany Turns Eastwards: A Study of Ostforschung in the Third Reich*, Cambridge: Cambridge University Press, 1988; Burleigh and Wippermann, *Racial State*; and Burleigh, *Death and Deliverance*.

82 See Burleigh, *Third Reich*, respectively, pp105, 204, 153, 187.

83 R. J. Evans, *The Coming of the Third Reich*, *The Third Reich in Power*, and *The Third Reich at War*, London: Allen Lane, 2003, 2004, and 2008.

84 These include the somewhat older works by N. Frei, *National Socialist Rule in Germany: The Führer State 1933–1945*, Oxford: Blackwell, 1993, German original 1987; and J. Dülffer, *Nazi Germany 1933–1945: Faith and Annihilation*, London: Arnold, 1996, German original 1992; as well as the following more recent ones: W. Benz, *A Concise History of the Third Reich*, Berkeley: University of California Press, 2006, German original 2003; J. W. Bendersky, *A Concise History of Nazi Germany*, 3rd edn, Lanham: Rowman and Littlefield, 2007; T. Kirk, *Nazi Germany*, Houndmills: Palgrave Macmillan, 2007; M. Kitchen, *The Third Reich: Charisma and Community*, Harlow: Pearson Longman, 2008. See also R. Stackelberg, *Hitler's Germany: Origins, Interpretations, Legacies*, London: Routledge, 1999; J. Hiden, *Republican and Fascist Germany: Themes and Variations in the History of Weimar and the Third Reich 1918–1945*, Harlow: Longman, 1996. The best critical historiographical guides remain I. Kershaw, *Nazi Dictatorship*, and Caplan (ed.) *Nazi Germany*.

85 The quoted phrases are taken from Evans's chapter headings in *The Third Reich in Power*. The full sequence of chapters in this second volume's unfolds as follows: "The Police State" (pp19–118); "The Mobilization of the Spirit" (pp119–218); "Converting the Soul" (pp219–320); "Prosperity and Plunder" (pp321–411); "Building the People's Community" (pp413–503); "Towards the Racial Utopia" (pp505–610); and "The Road to War" (pp610–712).

86 This is a notable strength of the overall work. The economic recovery of the 1930s is considered integrally with the process of "Aryanization" (expropriating the Jews), for example, stressing thereby a key element of the anti-Semitic wish. Likewise, the third volume on the wartime both foregrounds the genocide of the Jews as such (in the extremely powerful Chapter 3, "'The Final Solution'," pp217–318) and builds highly ramified treatments of all aspects of "the new racial order" into the primary architecture of the whole account. See, in contrast, H.-U. Wehler, *Deutsche Gesellschaftsgeschichte, vol. 4: Vom Beginn des Ersten Weltkrieges bis zur Gründung der beiden deutschen Staaten 1914–1949*, Munich: Beck, 2003, pp652–75, 881–902, 767–71, who gives the accumulated scholarship on bio-politics and racialization only the briefest of nods, while subsuming a 20-page section on the Judeocide into the differently accentuated treatment of World War II. A cursory four-page mention of forced foreign labor is assigned to a separately organized chapter on social structure.

87 Burleigh, *Third Reich*, p716.

88 A crucial tipping point came with M. Geyer and J. W. Boyer (eds) *Resistance Against the Third Reich 1933–1990*, Chicago: University of Chicago Press, 1994, deriving from a conference held in Chicago in March 1990.

89 C. R. Browning, *Ordinary Men. Reserve Police Battalion 101 and the Final Solution in Poland*, New York: Harper Perennial, 1992.

90 This growing skepticism about the grounds for nonconformity or *Resistenz* under Nazism was perhaps not disconnected from the surrounding political conjuncture of the 1990s, which unmoored left-wing historians from their previous assumptions, disabling their confidence in progressive working-class agency. With the old economies de-industrialized, trade unions and socialist parties in decline, and politics reduced to consumption, it became much harder to begin thinking about resistance.

91 E. A. Johnson, *Nazi Terror: The Gestapo, Jews, and Ordinary Germans*, New York: Basic Books, 1999, p15, also for the following quotation.

92 Key works include R. Gellately, *The Gestapo and German Society: Enforcing Racial Policy 1933–1945*, Oxford: Oxford University Press, 1992; K.-M. Mallmann and G. Paul, "Allwissend, allmächtig, allgegenwärtig?: Gestapo, Gesellschaft und Widerstand," *Zeitschrift für Geschichtswissenschaft*, vol. 41, 1993, pp984–99; Mallmann and Paul (eds) *Die Gestapo: Mythos und Realität*, Darmstadt: Primus Verlag, 1995; also R, Mann, *Protest und Kontrolle im Dritten Reich: Nationalsozialistische Herrschaft im Alltag einer rheinischen Grosstadt*, Frankfurt am Main: Campus Verlag, 1987. For denunciations, in particular, see R. Gellately, "Denunciations in Twentieth-Century Germany: Aspects of Self-

Policing in the Third Reich and the German Democratic Republic," *Journal of Modern History*, vol. 68, 1996, pp931–67; and G. Diewald-Kerkmann, *Politische Denunziation im NS-Regime oder die kleine Macht der "Volksgenossen,"* Bonn: Dietz, 1995.

93 R. Gellately, *Backing Hitler: Consent and Coercion in Nazi Germany*, Oxford: Oxford University Press, 2001, p3.

94 Ibid, pvii.

95 Johnson, *Nazi Terror*; also Johnson, *Urbanization and Crime: Germany 1871–1914*, Cambridge: Cambridge University Press, 1995. Subsequently, Johnson also published an oral history based on almost 200 interviews and over 3,000 written responses to a survey whose findings reinforced his argumentation in *Nazi Terror*. As the jacket of the later book puts it, "the research confirms that Hitler and National Socialism were so immensely popular among most Germans that intimidation and terror were rarely needed to enforce loyalty." See E. A. Johnson and K.-H. Reuband, *What We Knew: Terror, Mass Murder, and Everyday Life in Nazi Germany*, Cambridge: Basic Books, 2005.

96 Johnson, *Nazi Terror*, p286.

97 Ibid, pp373, 151.

98 Johnson provides a clear summary to this effect, ibid, p20: "the key to understanding the sometimes brutal, sometimes quasi-legalistic, but always effective Nazi terror lies in its selective character."

99 Ibid, pp19, 79.

100 G. Paul, "Ganz normale Akademiker: Eine Fallstudie zur regionalen staatspolizeilichen Funktionselite," in Paul and Mallmann (eds.) *Die Gestapo*, p250.

101 Johnson, *Nazi Terror*, pp8, 27.

102 Ibid, p8.

103 See Burleigh and Wippermann, *Racial State*, p170; also W. Ayaß, *"Asoziale" im Nationalsozialismus*, Stuttgart: Klett-Cotta, 1995, p24.

104 If "policing" is applied only to the Gestapo *per se*, then "asocials" and other criminalized populations disappear from consideration, even though profoundly "terrorized." Here, Burleigh and Wippermann's *Racial State* presents a more accurate and well-defined account of Nazi terror than either Johnson or Gellately. See Ayaß, *"Asoziale"*; L. Pine, *Nazi Family Policy, 1933–1945*, Oxford: Berg, 1997, pp117–46; R. Gellately and N. Stoltzfus (eds) *Social Outsiders in Nazi Germany*, Princeton: Princeton University Press, 2001; and the various volumes edited by Götz Aly et al. in the series *Beiträge zur nationalsozialistischen Gesundheits- und Sozialpolitik*, Berlin: Rotbuch, 1985.

105 Gellately, *Backing Hitler*, p258.

106 Ibid, p262.

107 See F. L. Carsten, *The German Workers and the Nazis*, Aldershot: Scolar Press, 1995, p157.

108 Gellately, *Backing Hitler*, p257.

109 For a case study of "Aryanization" of Jewish property, see F. Bajohr, *"Aryanization" in Hamburg: The Economic Exclusion of Jews and the Confiscation of their Property in Nazi Germany*, New York: Berghahn Books, 2002; Bajohr, *Parevnüs und Profiteure. Korruption in der NS-Zeit*, Frankfurt am Main: Fischer, 2001; Bajohr, "The Holocaust and Corruption," in G. D. Feldman and W. Seibel (eds) *Networks of Nazi Persecution: Bureaucracy, Business, and the Organization of the Holocaust*, New York: Berghahn Books, 2005, pp118–38; M. Dean, *Robbing the Jews: The Confiscation of Jewish Property in the Holocaust, 1933–1945*, Cambridge: Cambridge University Press, 2008; P. Hayes, "Plunder and Restitution," in P. Hayes and J.K. Roth (eds) *The Oxford Handbook of Holocaust Studies*, Oxford: Oxford University Press, 2010, pp540–59.

110 Gellately's chapter on this subject, "Concentration Camps in Public Spaces" (pp204–23), builds on the now incontrovertible evidence provided by the detailed studies of particular camps, localities, and businesses accumulating during the 1990s. See W. Benz and B. Distel (eds) *Der Ort des Terrors: Geschichte der nationalsozialistischen Konzentrationslager*, 6 vols, Munich: Beck, 2005–2007; U. Herbert, K. Orth, and C. Dieckmann (eds) *Die*

nationalsozialistischen Konzentrationslager: Entwicklung und Struktur, 2 vols, Göttingen: Wallstein, 1998; K. Orth, *Das System der nationalsozialistischen Konzentrationslager. Eine politische Organizationsanalyse*, Hamburg: Hamburger Edition, 1999. J. Caplan and N. Wachsmann (eds) *Concentration Camps in Germany: The New Histories*, London: Routledge, 2010, is now the best guide in English along with Caplan's "Introduction" to G. Herz, *The Women's Camp in Moringen: A Memoir of Imprisonment in Germany, 1936–1937*, New York: Berghahn Books, 2006, pp10–18, 38–45, contains an excellent summary.

111 In some places Gellately acknowledges this intimidatory function, only to elide it in his general conclusions, e.g., *Backing Hitler*, p201. See P. Longerich, *"Davon haben wir nichts gewusst!" Die Deutsche und die Judenverfolgung 1933–1945*, Munich: Siedler, 2006.

112 Werner Best (1903–1989) was a highly educated lawyer who rose through the ranks of the SS, helped to build the Gestapo, assisted Heydrich in the SS central administration until 1940, and became Reich Plenipotentiary over Denmark. Formed politically in the radical nationalist and anti-Semitic milieu of the *völkisch* Right, he made a post-Nazi career in the West German Free Democratic Party. See Herbert, *Best*, along with the other major new biographies mentioned in note 1 above.

113 Burleigh, *Third Reich*, p227.

114 D. Peukert, *Inside Nazi Germany*, p243.

115 Ibid, pp79–80.

116 A. Lüdtke, "Zur Einleitung," *Sozialwissenschaftliche Informationen für Unterricht und Studium (SOWI)*, vol. 6, 1977, p147.

117 R. Williams, *Marxism and Literature*, Oxford: Oxford University Press, 1977, p82. See also Eley, *Crooked Line*, pp19–24.

118 P. Steege, in A. S. Bergerson, E. Mailänder Koslov, G. Reuveni, P. Steege, and D. Sweeney, "Forum: Everyday Life in Nazi Germany," *German History*, 2009, vol. 27, no. 4, p562.

119 Especially Chapters 3 and 4. See also G. Eley, "Labor History, Social History, *Alltagsgeschichte*: Experience, Culture, and the Politics of the Everyday – A New Direction for German Social History?," *Journal of Modern History*, 1989, vol. 61, no. 2, pp297–343; also E. D. Weitz and G. Eley, "Romantisierung des Eigen-Sinns? Eine e-mail-Kontroverse aus Übersee," *Geschichtswerkstatt*, vol. 10, 1995, pp57–64.

120 Sweeney in Bergerson et al., "Forum: Everyday Life in Nazi Germany," pp575–6.

121 Mailänder Koslov, ibid, p563.

122 Sweeney, ibid, p579, also for the following quotation.

123 Browning, *Ordinary Men*. For excellent guidance to the still-burgeoning wealth of regional and local studies, see D. Pohl, *Verfolgung und Massenmord in der NS-Zeit 1933–1945*, Darmstadt: Wissenschaftliche Buchgesellschaft, 2003; U. Herbert (ed.) *National Socialist Extermination Policies: Contemporary German Perspectives and Controversies*, New York: Berghahn Books, 2000. For more extensive citations, see Chapter 6.

124 See the following essays by Alf Lüdtke: "'Formierung der Massen' oder: Mitmachen und Hinnehmen? 'Alltagsgeschichte' und Faschismusanalyse," in H. Gerstenberger and D. Schmidt (eds) *Normalität oder Normalisierung? Geschichtswerkstätten und Faschismusnalyse*, Münster: Westfälisches Dampfboot, 1987, pp15–34; "What Happened to the 'Fiery Red Glow'?" (orig. pub. 1989); "The Appeal of Exterminating 'Others'"; "Funktionseliten: Täter, Mit-Täter, Opfer? Zu den Bedingungen des deutschen Faschismus," and "'Ehre der Arbeit': Industriearbeiter und Macht der Symbole. Zur Reichweite symbolischer Orientierung im Nationalsozialismus," in Lüdtke, *Eigen-Sinn. Fabrikalltag, Arbeitererfahrungen und Politik vom Kaiserreich bis zu den Faschismus*, Hamburg: Ergebnisse, 1993, pp283–350; "War as Work: Aspects of Soldiering in Twentieth-Century Wars," Lüdtke and Bernd Weisbrod (eds) *No Man's Land of Violence: Extreme Wars in the 20th Century*, Göttingen: Wallstein Verlag, 2006, pp127–51. Omer Bartov's works register the perspectives of *Alltagsgeschichte*, as does the second volume of Saul Friedländer's *magnum opus*, and Christopher Browning's study of Starachowice, although

neither of the latter makes this explicit. See Bartov's earliest works, *Eastern Front* and *Hitler's Army*, but also *Germany's War and the Holocaust: Disputed Histories*, Ithaca: Cornell University Press, 2003, and *Erased: Vanishing Traces of Jewish Galicia in Present-Day Ukraine*, Princeton: Princeton University Press, 2007; S. Friedländer, *The Years of Extermination: Nazi Germany and the Jews 1939–1945*, New York: Harper Perennial, 2008; C. R. Browning, *Remembering Survival: Inside a Nazi Slave-Labor Camp*, New York: Norton, 2010. See also E. Mailänder Koslov's remarks in Bergerson et al., "Forum: Everyday Life in Nazi Germany," pp562, 563, 565, 568, 569, 571, 572–3, 576–7; also Mailänder Koslov, *Gewalt im Dienstalltag: Aufsheherinnen im Konzentrations- und Vernichtungslager Majdanek*, Hamburg: Hamburger Edition, 2009, and Mailänder Koslov, "'Going East': Colonial Experiences and Practices of Violence among Female and Male Majdanek Camp Guards (1941–1944)," *Journal of Genocide Research*, 2008, vol. 10, no. 4, pp563–82.

125 For excellent guides to research and writing on perpetrators, see D. Stone, "The Decision-Making Process in Context," in *Histories of the Holocaust*, Oxford: Oxford University Press, 2010, pp64–112, esp. pp95–111; D. Bloxham, *The Final Solution: A Genocide*, Oxford: Oxford University Press, 2009, pp261–99; Bloxham and T. Kushner, *The Holocaust: Critical Historical Approaches*, Manchester: Manchester University Press, 2005, pp61–175; M. Roseman, "Beyond Conviction? Perpetrators, Ideas, and Action in the Holocaust in Historiographical Perspective," in F. Biess, M. Roseman, and H. Schissler (eds) *Conflict, Catastrophe, and Continuity: Essays on Modern German History*, New York: Berghahn Books, 2007, pp83–103; G. Paul, "Von Psychopathen, Technokraten des Terrors und 'ganz gewöhnlichen' Deutschen: Die Täter der Shoah im Spiegel der Forschung," in G. Paul (ed.) *Die Täter der Shoa: Fanatische Nationalsozialisten oder ganz normale Deutsche?*, Göttingen: Wallstein, 2002, pp13–90; G. Paul and K.-M. Mallmann, *Karrieren der Gewalt. Nationsozialistische Täterbriographien*, Darmstadt: Wissenschaftliche Buchgesellschaft, 2004. J. Matthäus, "Historiography and the Perpetrators of the Holocaust," in D. Stone (ed.) *The Historiography of the Holocaust*, Houndmills: Palgrave Macmillan, 2004, pp197–215, usefully sets the scene for the most recent scholarship. Y. Bauer, *Rethinking the Holocaust*, New Haven: Yale University Press, 2001, mentions none of the new approaches.

126 These are the works cited in the preceding note 125. In Browning's *Remembering Survival*, whose interpretive approach maps so closely onto ground that Lüdtke's ideas have marked out, his influence goes entirely unremarked.

127 The longer exception, of course, concerns the scholarship on the *Judenräte*, which has long acknowledged the impossible complexities surrounding experience in the ghettos. See I. Trunk, *Judenrat: The Jewish Councils in Eastern Europe under Nazi Occupation*, New York: Macmillan, 1972; more recently, G. Corni, *Hitler's Ghettos: Voices from a Beleaguered Society 1939–1944*, London: Arnold, 2003. The trope of the "gray zone" is associated above all with P. Levi, "The Gray Zone," in *The Drowned and the Saved*, New York: Vintage, 1989, pp36–79. See especially J. Petropoulos and J. K. Roth (eds) *Gray Zones: Ambiguity and Compromise in the Holocaust and its Aftermath*, New York: Berghahn Books, 2005.

128 See A. Lüdtke, *Police and State in Prussia, 1815–1850*, Cambridge: Cambridge University Press, 1989; "The Role of State Violence in the Period of Transition to Industrial Capitalism: The Example of Prussia from 1815 to 1848," *Social History* 4, 1979, pp175–221.

129 Michael Wildt calls this the "self-empowerment" or "self-authorization" (*Selbstermächtigung*) of the *Volkgsemeinschaft*. See his *Volksgemeinschaft als Selbstermächtigung. Gewalt gegen Juden in der deutschen Provinz 1919 bis 1939*, Hamburg: Hamburger Edition, 2007.

3

THE RETURN OF IDEOLOGY

Everyday Life, the *Volksgemeinschaft*, and the Nazi Appeal

From society to culture: Reviewing the *Volksgemeinschaft*

Among the vast changes in Third Reich historiography since the 1980s, one decisive shift above all stands out. During the heyday of the great social history wave of the 1960s and 1970s, the most creative scholarly work was preoccupied with locating the "limits on Hitler's power," which it sought to define by carefully reconstructing whatever survived of a pre-existing or autonomous "society," however cramped and compromised those autonomies might be. Social historians focused most commonly on the working class, guided by the conviction that class relations – the processes of capitalist accumulation and exploitation that sustained class consciousness and all the associated actions and solidarities – retained their own primary logic independently of anything the Third Reich might do, in ways obstinately unaffected by either the Nazis' coercive violence or their ideological reach. Martin Broszat, Tim Mason, and Detlev Peukert all struggled in their differing ways to craft sophisticated approaches to the Third Reich's social history in this sense. But since that time, partly with the growth in popularity of more "culturalist" types of analysis, partly with the increasingly pervasive historiographical dominance of the Holocaust and the "racial state," the picture has entirely changed. Rather than looking for the places of relative non-involvement or resilience against German society's Nazification, historians now work mainly with a model of unbounded and generalized societal impact. Rather than seeing the limits and imperfections in Nazi domination, they assume its all-pervasiveness.

If social historians sought to uphold society's damaged but meaningful intactness, their successors see only the regime's depth of penetration, the radicalism of its totalizing reach, and the comprehensiveness of its claims, which allowed the populace no safe place for retreat. Historians now see a society shot completely through with Nazi influences and presuppositions. If not always fully Nazified in formal ideological terms, then in a structural sense German society became insidiously incorporated and redrawn. Of course, the Third Reich was violently closed *against* masses of people too. For whole categories of population the regime's totalizing claims were brutally negative and exclusionary, whether Jews and other racialized minorities, Communists, Social Democrats, and similar political enemies, or the ever-widening circles of the socially undesirable. But once included inside the boundaries of the *Volksgemeinschaft*, precisely because those boundaries were sanctioned by such deadly force, Germans could no longer feasibly keep themselves apart. At best, they accommodated to the regime and found ways of getting by.

When approaching German society between 1933 and 1945, historians tend these days to presume an unavoidable "gray zone" of agonizingly painful, ethically compromised, and necessarily imperfect everyday decision-making that even the most decent of "ordinary" Germans would now have to face. Making some kind of workable life under Nazism *had* to entail such "grayness" so long as the options of emigration or illegality – or identifying positively with the regime – were not to be embraced. Moreover, historians now gravitate more toward the war years than the 1930s; they are ever more likely to see the coming Holocaust and German–Jewish relations as the main determinative context; they treat race *qua* the "racial state" as the principal organizing term; and they stress the practical conformities exacted by the regime's everyday functioning as much as its spectacular manifestations, overt ideological interventions, and manifest political presence. Highly particularized micro-histories, biographies and memoirs, and "memory work" of all kinds form one familiar setting. With the exception of the major biographies, current research likewise de-emphasizes the more traditional political and institutional sites of analysis, turning instead to areas such as leisure and tourism, sexuality, cinema-going, music, the arts, fashion, consumption, and popular culture in all of its ways. In the process, a far more nuanced appreciation for the complexities of living under Nazism has certainly developed, whether for discrete social categories of the populace or for the various dimensions of people's lives. Those old moral truths offered by the binaries of "victims *versus* perpetrators" and "resistance *versus* collaboration" are no longer quite as easily invoked.[1]

One consequence of these developments is, in principle, to reinstate the value of ideological analysis, which for many years social history's dominance tended effectively to banish from the field. For all their admirable subtlety, for example, convinced materialists such as Broszat and Mason treated "social context" and "ideology" *dichotomously*, giving unambiguous explanatory precedence to the former over the latter. Yet, once the impact of Nazi ideology is measured less by the conscious adoption of Nazism's formal ideas than by the more insidious permeation of its values, in myriad conscious and unconscious ways, then the sharpness of that separation between "social context" and "ideology" begins to fall away. If we can once stop seeing ideology only as a discrete force acting *on* society – as a readily recognizable program or codified body of dominant values and beliefs – but rather appreciate its less visible framing functions as well, showing how Germans became persuaded into reading their world differently than before, then we may be in a better position to grasp the efficacies of Nazi impact upon everyday life. The idea of the racial state has in many respects done that kind of work over the past two decades, as historians tracked its penetration by means of social administration, healthcare, family policy, schooling, organized recreation, policing, and other areas of public policy. By examining the institutionally and professionally bounded worlds of Nazi policy-making to show how racial ideas were applied on the ground, pioneers such as Götz Aly, Henry Friedlander, and Michael Burleigh did a huge amount to show how the social order was meant to be re-made. At the same time, this work rarely saw *itself* as doing ideological analysis as such.

The idea of the *Volksgemeinschaft* is now being pursued in a similar way, offering valuable insight into how popular consent to Nazi rule could be secured. In setting the scene for such a discussion, for example, Detlef Schmiechen-Ackermann uses the example of the popular enthusiasm surrounding the festivities on Hitler's 48th birthday on 20 April 1937 in order to focus the interpretive dilemmas involved, especially in light of the deceptively transparent photographic record.[2] Did the "jubilant crowd with arms raised high in the Hitler salute" signify genuine joy, he asks, or was this a carefully staged propaganda shot? How far did the adulation for Hitler translate into knowing support for the policies of his regime? Which policies were supported, and which not? Who was absent from the crowd, and why? During the heyday of social history these questions had long received a straightforward answer: the idea of the "people's community" had been just a trick, a "fictitious concept" and a false promise, a projection of unity by the triumphal Nazis who wanted to close the books on Weimar's divisiveness and legitimize themselves into the future.[3] However relentlessly trumpeted by the regime's propaganda, social historians argued, the vaunted "state of harmony in German society ... had in reality never existed."[4] Against the claims of the *Volksgemeinschaft*, the pioneers of Third Reich historiography in the 1970s typically invoked the absence of significant change in the social structure, contrasting the Nazi rhetoric with the stark continuities of inequality beneath – most imposingly of all in Tim Mason's *Arbeiterklasse und Volksgemeinschaft*, but also in Ian Kershaw's early works and in the positions consistently advanced by Hans Mommsen.[5] The appeal of the *Volksgemeinschaft* may have been "a potent mobilizing agent," one such commentator now concedes. But "between the exaggerated pseudo egalitarian propaganda that claimed to have transcended class, denominational, and political division and the essential continuities in the class structure of Nazi Germany" there remained a huge gap.[6] "What are the reasons," Heinrich August Winkler asked rhetorically, "why we should actually take the Nazi slogans for anything real?"[7]

For some, that skepticism persists. At a benchmark conference at London's German Historical Institute in March 2010, called to take stock of current thinking ("German Society in the Nazi Era: *Volksgemeinschaft* between Ideological Projection and Social Practice"), Hans Mommsen, Ulrich Herbert, and Horst Möller each warned against using *Volksgemeinschaft* as an analytical term.[8] In his keynote address, Ian Kershaw issued a similar caution. Invoking the interpretive shift mentioned at the outset of this chapter – from the resistant "non-permeability" of German society against Nazi ideology (Broszat's *Resistenz*) to the all-pervasiveness of its penetration – Kershaw pointed to a troubling lack of differentiation in the picture of German society that the use of the concept easily encouraged: "By the claim to have integrated all Germans into the regime while excluding all who did not and could not belong, '*Volksgemeinschaft*' becomes virtually the synonym for a perpetrator society (*Tätergesellschaft*)."[9] In seeking to show the generalized pro-Nazi identification they claim to have found ("as though practically all Germans had become [Hitler's] accomplices"), Kershaw argued, historians are making themselves beholden to an essentially flawed concept. Of the three possible uses Kershaw distinguished, he dismissed the first – actual change under the Third Reich toward greater degrees of social and political equality – on empirical grounds. To the second, the "affective integration" enabled by "the mobilizing power of the vision of a better society," he gave greater credence, for despite all the propagandist crudity and excess, the *promise* of the *Volksgemeinschaft* imparted great dynamism to the Third Reich's popular appeal.[10] The third version of the idea he found the most fruitful – namely, the processes of "exclusion and inclusion as decisive features of National Socialist society, with patent implications for the regime's policies of racist discrimination, persecution, and extermination."[11]

In some of the new literature on *Volksgemeinschaft* Kershaw's worries about conceptual imprecision and overgeneralization seem definitely borne out. In two complementary books Thomas Kühne has taken the argument to its furthest extreme. The first of these, *Kameradschaft*, examined the mythologies and social practice of soldierly comradeship, first as a powerful construct of the interwar years founded on a particular appropriation of the front experience of 1914 to 1918, then as an experiential history of World War II. The second, more essayistic book, *Belonging and Genocide*, generalized these claims about the dynamics of group solidarity under warfare and military training to German society under the Third Reich as a whole.[12] But if the first of these studies grounds its analysis in a rather carefully delimited context of small-group military socialization, assembling a tightly conceived archive appropriate to its setting, then the second casts its findings recklessly across an entire society and its imputed culture. Here is Kühne's particular rendition of the Nazi *Volksgemeinschaft*:

> Perpetrators and bystanders energized social life and built collective identity through committing genocide. The desire for community, the experience of belonging, and the ethos of collectivity became the basis of mass murder. Perpetrating and supporting the Holocaust provided Germans with a particular sense of national belonging: *the German nation found itself by committing the Holocaust.*[13]

Here the argument has become entirely unmoored. In contrast with the treatment of soldierly bonding – of *Kameradschaft* as an elaborately founded discursive formation constructed around very particular histories of the years after 1914 – any specificity of agency and its effects, the social historian's righteous insistence on exactness of context and occurrence, has disappeared. Building an explanatory context for committal of atrocities on the Eastern Front will certainly require depth of perspective, through which the earlier twentieth-century genealogies can be examined. But Kühne argues inferentially throughout, reaching constantly from the compellingly explicated readings of selected literary and other written documentation upwards and outwards to the grand-scale abstraction of the nation. In the course of a single essay, he can travel from the normalcies of SS pleasure-seeking in the concentration camps, back to the trench masculinity of 1914 to 1918, returning through the *Freikorps* and the SA to the Border Police Station of Novy Sacz in 1939 to 1942, before ending with the individual reportage of a few *Wehrmacht* officers from 1942 to 1944 – all somehow figured into an overarching narrative of the whole nation.[14] Along the way he pauses to postulate a kind of universal masculinity, while effectively reinstating the conceptual primacy of a victim/perpetrator duality.[15] The *Volksgemeinschaft* here becomes merely a proxy for explanation: "The band was the *Wehrmacht*, the spearhead of the *Volksgemeinschaft*, the German nation."[16]

If earlier discussions of *Volksgemeinschaft* had preserved the antinomies of ideology and social context, making the one distinctly epiphenomenal to the other, then in Kühne's treatment the explanatory relations are reversed. German society has become subsumed entirely into an argument about "belonging" as a shared collective value of the nation – effectively a redeployed version of George Mosse's conception of "German ideology," reworked in the meantime via the culturalist languages of identity, violence, and masculinity establishing their ascendancy in the years since the later 1990s ("desire for community ... experience of belonging ... ethos of collectivity").[17] Relative to the kind of understanding enabled 25 years ago by Burleigh and Wippermann's bold intervention and all the associated discussion, this is a step back. By its detailed elaborations, *The Racial State* allowed us to begin breaking out of the earlier frame – which set ideology *apart* from social context – as it showed the regime's values being carried, concretely and practically, deep into the domain of the social – by means of law, administrative action, social mobilization, and the manifold intrusions of state and party into workplaces, neighborhoods, and families. The Nazis' project, as Burleigh and Wippermann saw it, involved "a global remodelling of society in accordance with racial criteria," and to understand such a design the analysis of the action of ideas *inside* the practical settings of social life became essential.[18]

Efficacy and everyday life: How did Nazism make its appeal?

In the ensuing approach, the *Volksgemeinschaft* was thus the very opposite of "mere" ideology in that older dismissive social historians' sense. Rather, its claims were themselves *precisely social.* They became institutionalized into social relations and material practices that brought real changes in the forms through which anyone living in Germany now had to acquire an understanding of the social world. This extended definition of ideology that I am using – as the ideas, beliefs, values, prejudices, assumptions through which people bring meaning into their material lives – becomes vital if the issue of generalized societal complicity is to be handled sensibly – that is, by escaping the essentializing pitfalls of an argument couching its claims in terms of all "Germans" or the imputed agency of the "German nation." As the social historians of the 1970s understood, any assignment of collective agency – whether conceived as guilt, responsibility, complicity, or shame – required situating in carefully specified contexts. *Societal* complicity was only graspable via a theorized aggregation of such modestly constructed and empirically grounded analytical claims. Otherwise the true difficulty of that idea – what it might *mean* to make an entire society "responsible," given the intractable complexities of the myriad circumstances involved and the heterogeneity of all the resulting responses – could never be honored. From Broszat and Mason through Kershaw and Peukert, continuing through Browning and the pioneers of the regional historiography of genocide on the ground, this struggle to establish the practical locatedness of experience inside the social relations, institutional settings, and structured material environments that organize the scope of individual and collective lives remains the social historian's distinguishing commitment.[19] Only then, once the shaping constraints and possibilities have been clarified, might the contingent dynamics of feasible decision-making – and their ethical valences – whether for individuals or for groups, be grasped.

Clearly, then, we need a workable balance of perspectives: *not only* current recognition of Nazism's more successful societal penetration and the resulting breadth of popular acceptance, *but also* a modified version of that older social historians' struggle to find where the limits may have been. In extreme accounts of the first kind, German society was completely permeated with Nazi practices and understandings of the world. Propagation of the *Volksgemeinschaft* – systematic, unceasing, morally coercive, but also emotionally satisfying and socially enjoyable – engendered a desire for belonging that might well become all-consuming in Kühne's sense. Extreme advocates of the second view, on the other hand, presented a picture of German society in which the relationship with the regime started to seem only ever about accommodation and pragmatics: indifferent to Nazi ideology as such, ordinary Germans embraced its values invariably on "other" grounds, ranging from diffuse and pre-existing patriotic loyalties and anti-Bolshevik fears of disorder to careerism and material gain, including the desire simply to be left alone. *Neither of these by themselves will do*. But likewise, we will grasp neither Nazism's successful appeal nor the readiness of large numbers of Germans to embrace it unless we take seriously what each approach is able to offer.

The quotidian circumstances of the making of livable lives – of friendships and romance, wage packets and careers, schooling and hobbies, of selves fashioned and families raised, of festivities enjoyed, pleasures consumed, jobs well done, fresh lands seen – not surprisingly focus many of the best efforts that Third Reich historians are making to this end. Taking seriously the Nazis' eagerness to enlist German workers' positive sympathies, even as the old labor movements were being ground into the dirt, affords one such opportunity – for example, by showing how the official slogans of the "Honor of Labor" (*Ehre der Arbeit*) and the "Excellence of

German Work" (*Deutsche Qualitätsarbeit*) could offer a different space of job satisfaction and psychic reward once older measures of solidarity, collective strength, and the dignity of labor were taken brutally away.[20]

Practical improvement of the workplace via the "Beauty of Labor" (*Schönheit der Arbeit*) initiated by Strength through Joy (*Kraft durch Freude*, or KdF), the leisure organization established by the German Labor Front (DAF) on 27 November 1933, formed one dimension.[21] Despite the actual hierarchies, top-down authority, and policing that held the vaunted "factory community" (*Betriebsgemeinschaft*) together, such changes were never merely window-dressing. "Brighter lamps or bigger windows, more spaciously laid out machinery, freshly introduced or expanded washing facilities and cloakrooms, sitting areas for breaks away from the machines" – all of these "promised a new quality of recognition and practical welfare," Alf Lüdtke argues.[22] This new rhetorical climate also encouraged "a change in self-perception." If "the diffuse talk of 'community' in the factories" allowed individual workers, especially those with particular training or skill, to find their own ways of making it through, then "the justice of hoping for the 'good life' could be experienced symbolically in an unexpectedly intense manner." However, to find ways of reclaiming the elements of one's working personality in the absence of any of the earlier collective supports – the forms of pleasure and self-assertiveness, all the aspects of selfhood vested around work, the *Eigen-Sinnigkeiten*, as Lüdtke calls them – was to find oneself becoming entrapped, unavoidably, in a profoundly compromising contradiction. At a level of individual experience, unfortunately, the very process of "perpetually putting up" with things (the realities of Nazi rule), while "taking advantage of the new chances" for making it through, often meant simultaneously "going along" with the state's injustices, Nazi violence, and "the fascist drive for war."[23]

By following the penetration of Nazi values into the practical settings of the industrial workplace, Lüdtke and others have shown how the antinomies of ideology and the social can be overcome. Reading the meanings of the impact of Nazi ideology and analyzing the content of Nazi social practices become less easily distinguishable as projects. If Mason's early work had powerfully delineated the new institutional and policy-making frameworks that enabled the demands of the *Volksgemeinschaft* to be driven deep into workplaces and working-class neighborhoods, his own social histories – whose archival grounding and controlled analytical richness remain unsurpassed – were always meant to qualify or relativize, even to discount, the efficacies of the ideological effect. In Mason's case social history spoke back *against* ideology.[24] But Peukert's landmark general account, *Inside Nazi Germany: Conformity, Opposition, and Racism in Everyday Life*, then marked out the space of interconnectedness – the junctures and inter-articulations, through which ideas and practices were mixed up together, forming Raymond Williams's "specific and indissoluble real processes" – where further studies of the working class under Nazism have been able to begin.[25]

The *stakes* of doing such work – conceptually, historiographically, ethically, politically – are not always made clear. If the goal is the building of a case for the moral indictment of a whole nation or society, which under specific circumstances and conjunctures may well acquire compelling urgency, then generalizing arguments such as those of *Belonging and Genocide* perhaps have a point.[26] Yet, beyond the justified purposes of polemics and the righteousness of the passions involved, the most helpful reading of German responsibility is surely the kind that uses the language of contextualism, locatedness, heterogeneity, and differentiation that I have been emphasizing above, along with the kind of evidence necessary to ground one's claims in as much interpretive specificity as possible. *That* commitment serves us best – not just for making sense of Nazism and its disturbing efficacies of appeal, but also for any other comparably challenging situation, whether historically or personally in our own contemporary and immediate worlds. As Lüdtke has argued, it was in the micro-political contexts of everydayness that the spread of Nazi ideology would ultimately be found having – or not having – its effect. But the indissoluble dilemmas of human action on the ground neither allow for easy black-and-white ethico-political appraisal nor absolve us from making such a judgment *per se*:

> Analyzing the terms of fascist rule in Germany remains in thrall to the victim-perpetrator model. Yet unencompassed by that frame are the hybrid circumstances of dependency and self-actualizing, especially the elements of coping and collusion. Capturing the latter requires foregrounding the reconstruction of social practice: namely, the *simultaneities* of rule, resistance, and keeping silently out of the way. For individuals that meant: to consent, to put up with, to go along – but also "to duck," to distance oneself, even once in a while to oppose, none of which brought either lasting or necessary contradictions. Putting up with things wore many faces 'on the inside.' But measured by the results and the perspectives of the victims, such multiplicity collapsed: whether hesitantly putting up with things or happily consenting, collusion resulted just the same. On that, German fascism's system of domination and exploitation rested right up to the end.[27]

Building the *Volksgemeinschaft*: Ideology on the ground

Though especially important historiographically, the workplace was only one of the sites at which the demands of the *Volksgemeinschaft* were leveled. The gender, sexual, and generational dynamics within family and marriage described another.[28] Yet a further context would be the local reception and effects of the ritualized mobilizations forming the Third Reich's plebiscitary public culture. What people really did at those official events, and what they took away from them, also allow us to judge the efficacy of Nazi ideology and its limits – that is, the varying ways in which the Nazi spectacle may actually have been experienced, whether via the Nuremberg rallies, the 1936 Olympiad, and Hitler's birthday, or through the many other official holidays and festivals, the parades and pageants prompted by particular events, or the countless locally staged celebrations.[29] The spectacle carried very different meanings for the direct participants as against the various categories of immediate spectators, the wider audience listening to the radio, or the broader publics at still further remove, not to speak of the service labor who enabled the event to be staged.[30]

It is not hard to see these big events of the Nazi ritual calendar – elaborately managed displays of mass loyalty and disciplined uniformity, mobilizing all the latest technologies of radio, cinematography, light, and sound, while marshaling their symbolics around the charismatic authority of the *Führer* – as juggernauts of indoctrination: concentrations of ideological power in the narrower sense, vehicles for the transmission of National Socialism's doctrinal message. Taking their cue from Walter Benjamin's aestheticization thesis ("the logical result of fascism is the introduction of aesthetics into political life"), however, such inquiries stop too often at the imposing orthodoxy of Nazism's self-representations alone, accepting "that Nazi culture was epitomized by the deindividuating, conformist, and unifying spectacles of Leni Riefenstahl's films and Albert Speer's monumental architecture."[31] In contrast, we need to push much further to explore how the impact of the mass spectacle – "ideology" in this doctrinal and dramatically staged sense – worked its way into the minds and habits of individual German subjects ("ideology" in the extended sense developed above). Once again, the precise efficacies of the Nazis' intended message will only come better into view if we pursue its effects into the mundane and localized settings of daily life, away from the alarums and excitements of the performance of the spectacle *per se*.

If we adopt this differently elaborated approach to ideology, the evidence of film promises particular illumination. Earlier historical work on German cinema classically reflected that older dichotomous separation, which saw the vast top-down machinery of Goebbels's Propaganda Ministry as acting concertedly *on* society in order to manipulate the masses into conformity – what Scott Spector calls "the founding structural model of a coherent propaganda program disseminated to the masses through the vehicle of the Nazi propaganda films and features."[32] In its treatment of filmic content, such work was reductionist, too, simplifying complex fields of meaning into a story of indoctrination, even while acknowledging the entertainment qualities of the vast bulk of the films actually being produced. Thus, to the first binary opposition of *ideology* and *social context* was added a second one between *ideological indoctrination* and *escapist diversion* that worked against any more complex understanding of how films produced meanings for the people who watched them. Yet precisely as entertainment, films not only filled people's everyday lives by distracting them; they also offered a range of representations that framed a private realm of wants and desires in ways that stitched these into the racialized vision of the *Volksgemeinschaft*. Popular and official culture could be made to work together. Encompassing far more than the regime's explicit propaganda operations, Nazism developed a more complex aesthetic program that matched the mass spectacle to the different appeals of consumer pleasure and visual enjoyment. In the "seemingly unpolitical spaces of private commodity consumption" and "American-style consumerism," Nazi cinema projected a promise of private satisfactions, "even as it co-opted these 'to arrest and rechannel' them."[33] It was in the cinema's space of enjoyment, no less than in the audience for the Nuremberg rally, that Germans were invited to see themselves as Nazi subjects.

Finally, it was in the idiom of an aspirational consumerism that the claims of the *Volksgemeinschaft* were also to be made. At the most basic of all levels, the regime's popular legitimacy clearly required an improvement in the standard of living: beyond the restoration of employment and the re-imposing of public order, putting food on the table was a highest priority. "I have the ambition to make the German people rich and Germany beautiful," Hitler told a journalist. "I want to see the living standard of the individual raised."[34] Yet, in the peacetime years before 1939, by most of the usual criteria, that ambition had not been realized. By the later 1930s, neither the achievement of full employment nor the chances of upward mobility had become sufficient in themselves to allow positive consensus to coalesce strongly enough behind the regime, while the accomplishments of the various campaigns to deliver consumer durables to the people remained modest in the extreme. On the one hand, with the partial exception of the "people's radio" (*Volksempfänger*), the much-vaunted drive to supply specially subsidized goods deemed "particularly useful to the body politic" manifestly failed. "People's products" (*Volksprodukte*), most notably the "people's car" (*Volkswagen*), but also household appliances such as refrigerators and vacuum cleaners, were never produced in quantities remotely capable of affecting popular attitudes in the ways imagined. Nor were the meager results of the massive "people's housing" programs imagined by the DAF.[35]

On the other hand, the priorities of the national economy as the Nazis defined them militated structurally *against* the boosting of consumption on anything like that scale. Contrary to the sensationalizing claims of Götz Aly's *Hitler's Beneficiaries*, it makes no sense to see the German people as being straightforwardly "bought off" by the redistributive successes and consumer plenty of an aggressively expanding racialized and imperialist economy. Quite aside from the coarse materialist reductionism moving such claims, the performance of the Nazi economy showed none of the results required by Aly's thesis of a "consensus dictatorship" (*Zustimmungsdiktatur*), with its causal equations between purported consumer satisfaction, expanding welfare provision, booty from "Aryanization" and wartime occupation, and majoritarian pro-Nazi enthusiasm.[36] To be sure, "the state's support of mass entertainment and its pro-family schemes allowed [selected consumer] industries to flourish," including radios, cinema, furniture, and telephones. But paradoxically, it was precisely the two primary drains on working-class household budgets – food and housing – that received no relief:

> Consumption suffered under the reality that Nazi economic policy was overstretched: providing jobs, building loyalty, safeguarding precious raw materials, and preparing for German hegemony in Europe took precedence over providing bountiful consumer opportunities.[37]

By 1938, at a time when the country was "suffering from a chronic shortage of affordable accommodation, new mortgage lending was banned, and civilian housing construction came to a virtual halt," the drive for rearmament was accounting for fully 20 percent of national income. "Viewed in macro-economic terms," Adam Tooze points out, "the Third Reich shifted a larger percentage of national resources into rearmament than any other capitalist regime in history."[38] That translated necessarily into a running squeeze on consumption. From 1935, butter and meat were effectively rationed in many cities, while government increasingly cajoled consumers with its campaigns for saving and self-monitoring in an economy of scarcity, such as the 1936 "Struggle against Waste" (*Kampf dem Verderb*).[39] In the thinking of the Nazi leadership – evident already in 1934, intensifying from 1936 to 1937 – guns *did* decisively trump butter: "Managed consumption in the service of war – rather than unfettered access to the joys of material goods – was the reality for most Germans in the Third Reich."[40]

But if consumption remained so constrained, then how else might the *Volksgemeinschaft* have become materially grounded? If the pace of rearmament was not to be slowed by pandering to the needs of individuals and households, whether by raising wages, investing in consumer goods, or easing imports, how else were living standards to be improved? Here the wider array of cultural and recreational programs operated by Strength through Joy played a crucial role. Aside from *Schönheit der Arbeit* already discussed, KdF also gave much of the impetus to the *Volksprodukte* conception, and in 1937 it was the DAF head Robert Ley who was given responsibility for bringing the *Volkswagen* project to fruition. Effectively filling the spaces of sociality, sports, hobbying, cultural improvement, and associational life from which the former labor movements had been evicted, KdF operated fitness and sports facilities, while broadening access to previously exclusive sports such as horseback riding, sailing, and tennis; it provided discounted tickets for concerts, theater, art exhibitions, and museums, while subsidizing cinemas and theaters directly; it also organized adult education classes. Most successfully of all, it mobilized major resources in order to maximize working-class access to paid vacations and affordable package holidays, not only subsidizing day outings, weekend excursions, ski trips, and ocean cruises, but also developing a large-scale infrastructure of hostels, resorts, special trains, and cruise ships. Equipped with a staff of some 140,000, it became an engine for the growth of tourism: by 1938 an aggregate of 54 million Germans had passed through its hands; in the last year of peace it handled 8.5 million tourists. By 1939 KdF was running 12 cruise ships of its own, including the specially built *Wilhelm Gustloff* and *Robert Ley*.[41]

How should we judge this particular efficacy? Conceived as one of five specially designed mega-resorts for the Baltic and North Sea coasts, the intended KdF showcase was a 20,000-bed holiday complex at Prora on the island of Rügen, whose construction began in May 1936, intended for completion by spring 1940. Long synonymous with the summer luxuries of the wealthy, Rügen was ideally suited for realizing the DAF's drive to show the claimed harmony of a united nation where workers now found an honored place – capitalizing on the defeat of

Marxism, laying the ghost of class conflict, dismantling the trappings of privilege, and enacting the vaunted egalitarianism of the *Volksgemeinschaft*, the idealized community of the race–nation–people. In its designers' conception, Prora was a monument to KdF's particular pursuit of that purpose, whose benefits were to seal the destruction of class-based politics achieved with the smashing of the Social Democrats and Communists in 1933.

In a sustained fantasy of "hyperpoliticized nation-building," Strength through Joy sought the end of Germany's regional, religious, and class divisions: "In the Nazi 'national community,' the social boundaries that internally divided Germany would dissolve, and tourism would serve as a vehicle for achieving that goal."[42] Prora's designs were to include "a mammoth entertainment center, cafes, cinemas, billiard rooms, bowling alleys, parking garages for the Volkswagens of vacationers, and a restaurant atop an eighty-five-meter-high structure that dwarfed the Berlin radio tower." Fitted with a wave-making machine, measuring 40 by 100 meters, an indoor heated pool enabled the resort to function outside of the summer season. For an all-inclusive cost of 20 marks, working-class families would get a week's stay in one of the identical rooms ("simple but modern"), each with an ocean view, enjoying "such creature comforts as hot and cold running water, central heating, closets, and some upholstered furniture."[43]

Like the "people's car," Prora was never actually brought into commission: it was preempted by the war, and like the Volkswagen plant and model city intended to service it, *KdF-Stadt*, with its planned family housing and generous amenities, the uncompleted complex was quickly refitted for military use.[44] But Prora's potency was in its *promise* of improvement, seemingly guaranteed in the resort's imposing comprehensiveness, which combined the collectivist sameness of Germans being together with the personal pleasures of relaxation. This vision of the future, of a purified Germany beyond the former class divisiveness, in which the body of the nation (*Volkskörper*), healthful and united, purged of its weaknesses and foreign elements, could be strengthened and renewed in the pursuit of wholesome enjoyments, was continuously reaffirmed not just in the barrage of the KdF's happy propaganda, but in the tangible actualities of the goods it delivered:

> Strength through Joy catered to consumer expectations as economic recovery ended unemployment and raised family incomes, recognizing that individual pleasure and autonomy mattered as much as the collective experience of cultural uplift and national renewal. While KdF directed its low-cost, non-commercial consumption toward collective ends, it simultaneously embedded visions of future prosperity in the dream worlds of the present, advertising material "luxuries" to appeal to its audience.[45]

Racial uplift in the drive for war: The *Lebensraum* of consumption

However, two things should always be remembered about this Nazi culture of consumption, which together enabled the *Volksgemeinschaft* to extract the tribute, its political surplus value, thereby suturing these local scenes of enjoyment to the freshly racialized project of the nation. First, KdF activities were never innocent of the Nazis' political purposes, but rather bespoke "the regime's politicization of all manner of cultural practices toward its foremost aim, the creation of an enlarged, racially purified 'national community' (*Volksgemeinschaft*)."[46] As Baranowski observes, "the focal point of the Rügen project, an enormous multipurpose hall … designed to hold all 20,000 vacationers at once," was meant to stage all manner of mass demonstrations and cultural events, including concerts, plays, exhibitions of art, parades, pageants, rallies, and political addresses, as well as diversions and popular entertainments. "Given its explicitly political purposes, the neoclassical design of the structure, which departed from the functional architectural style of the resort as a whole, conformed to Speer's plans for the proposed reconstruction of Berlin: imperial architecture for the emerging German empire." Here, the fascist spectacle was drawn down into the affective worlds of the everyday – in other words, prising its way into the scenes of enjoyment and relaxed subjectivity, where German subjects might be found least on their guard:

> The Rügen project thus embodied the imperial and militarized side of Strength through Joy's tourism, in which discipline and regimentation served as the organizing principles of working-class "leisure." Family vacations for workers were not to be occasions for intimacy and privacy, or so it seemed. Rather, the resort would become a venue for creating loyal Germans, who would eagerly abjure their class identities and follow their *Führer* without reservation.[47]

Second, *racial uplift* supplied the ulterior purpose of KdF tourism. Whether in southern Europe – Greece, Yugoslavia, Italy, Portugal (notably the island of Madeira, previously a British upper-class destination) – or in East Prussia and the other borderlands, trippers were specifically enjoined to value their standard of living and higher culture over those of the local populations. In the promotional discourse surrounding tourism in the East, no chance was missed to extol the civilizing achievements of the Germans in the Slavic lands of the Middle Ages, while German travelers were encouraged to look down on the destitution and disorder they encountered in cities such as Naples, Palermo, and Lisbon. This pedagogy of racial differences was a primary theme of the KdF's popular literature and advertisements, internal documentation, public addresses, and the many testimonies and travelogues solicited from travelers for the organization's magazines. Ley and the KdF leadership insisted on the value of observing racial differences at firsthand: "worker comrades would be convinced that National Socialism [had] created a matchless level of care unequalled anywhere else in the world for the working people of our *Volk* by observing the living conditions of other people."[48]

The imperfections remained clear enough: travelers often reported badly on religious, regional, gender, and class divisions among their fellows; working-class cruise participants resented the evident distinctions still separating the wealthier passengers, especially the party bigwigs; travelers reacted negatively against the official didacticism; commercial tourism also flourished as before.[49] But, on balance, KdF travel culture won its participants over: "KdF's package tours gave flesh and blood to the imagined racial community by reaching across class lines for their tourist consumers." Far from being a "beautiful illusion" or an elaborate deception, "its touristic spectacles encouraged its participants to see a cause-and-effect relationship between their own well-being and the Nazi regime's attempts to make Germans into the master race":

> KdF revealed the ugly distinctiveness of the National Socialist approach to raising the standard of living … Its tourism forecasted a German imperium while confirming the racism of its vacationers and the regime's own legitimacy … Although aesthetically pleasing workplaces and smiling tourists appear tangential to emergency decrees, concentration camps, and genocide, Strength through Joy exposed Nazism's fusion of pleasure and violence.[50]

There was the rub. For Hitler and the Nazi leaders, the dialectics of guns and butter always involved a wager on deferral. At the most fundamental level, based on a geopolitical judgment centering on the United States, Hitler believed that Germany's economic future hinged on the acquisition of empire. Absent that necessary basis, the failings of consumption in the 1930s, from the *Volksprodukte* to housing and general popular purchasing power, were explicable enough precisely because the arms drive demanded such precedence: "Whilst Germans were constrained to inhabit an inadequate *Lebensraum* hedged around by hostile powers, egged on in their antagonism towards Germany by the global Jewish conspiracy, it was no surprise that Germans could not afford cars."[51] Indeed, the promise of a higher standard of living entirely rested upon *Lebensraum*. Without it, in Hitler's words, "all social hopes" would be "utopian promises without the least real value."[52]

In these terms, Adam Tooze urges, "guns" and "butter" were hardly antithetical. On the one hand, strategically speaking, "guns were ultimately viewed as a means to obtaining more butter, quite literally through the conquest of Denmark, France, and the rich agricultural territories of Eastern Europe. In this sense, rearmament was an investment in future prosperity." On the other hand, the arms economy itself supplied "a particular form of collective mass-consumption." Analytically speaking, "there is no difference between the purchasing of tanks and military aircraft and expenditure on the construction of public buildings, arenas, or gigantic vacation resorts on the Baltic." Likewise, the start of conscription in 1935 "amounted to an enormous collective holiday for millions of young men, who were fed and clothed at public expense whilst not engaged in productive labor." The military in those terms not only joined a seamless unity with the Third Reich's other mass organizations ("young men … moved from the Hitler Youth via the *Wehrmacht* into the ranks of the DAF and KdF"), but also "formed the centerpiece for many of the ritualized mass events of the regime." Thus, "rearmament in the 1930s was as much a popular spectacle as it was a drain on the German standard of living, a form in other words of spectacular public consumption."[53]

These militarized and imperialist aspects of the Nazi vision of Germany's prosperous destiny were hardwired around a dogmatically racist and aggressively anti-Semitic set of beliefs as the only possible grounds for national belonging. When Hitler rhapsodized about the future abundance, the life of plenty that *Lebensraum* was meant to secure, "Germans" alone were the beneficiaries. If in the 1930s new patterns of consumer-oriented industrialization characterized all the capitalist economies as they emerged from the Depression, the Nazi version was distinctive in two ways: it deferred its promises of mass consumption in the interests of the arms drive; and it centered them around ideas of racial purity and supposedly healthy commercial practices.[54] But the Nazis' incessant invoking of racial health, moral wholesomeness, and national renewal, brilliantly captured by Geoffrey Cocks in his recent *The State of Health*, bespoke an ambivalence in their outlook too, one deeply embedded in early twentieth-century *völkisch* thought: mass consumption was also associated with overindulgence and "wasteful spending," cheapness and corruption, "unfair competition" and shady practices, degeneracy rather than well-being – in short, with the corrosive presence of the "Jewish spirit" whose worldly power the Nazis now identified with "America," a shorthand for the "crassness, racial diversity, and cultural hybridity [of] mass culture in the United States."[55]

In this political cosmology, Jonathan Wiesen aptly summarizes, *German* consumption would not be an "an end in itself."[56] "Rather, [it] was to serve a higher purpose, namely the enrichment of the *Volk* ... during its struggle for global and racial dominance. In this respect, goods and services had a national, even moral, purpose." The resulting inclusiveness of the *Volksgemeinschaft* was then armored by the expulsion of the Jew and other undesirables:

> Social, political, and racial undesirables were to be shut out of the future consumerist utopia. Jews served as the villainous counterpoint to the Nazi ideal, and the 'rules' of consumption were always premised on their economic and social ostracization. The 1 April 1933 boycott of Jewish shops, which the Propaganda Ministry planned despite little enthusiasm from the populace, was primarily about severing daily acts of consumption from Jewishness, now linked to moral and racial danger.[57]

Thus, German fascism struck a complicated balance between celebrating what Tooze calls "the collective consumption of the full fruits of industrial modernity" and acknowledging the continuing influence of long-established and un-assuaged suspicions among large constituencies of supporters, those "shopkeepers, farmers, and others who saw hyper-capitalism as a threat to their livelihoods." As Wiesen continues:

> This confluence created a core dilemma for the National Socialist regime. The Nazis condemned mass consumption as decadent, American, Jewish, and

> as a force that threatened to undermine the integrity of the German nation. But they also recognized, correctly, that consumer society still embodied the dreams of many Germans. The regime responded to this dilemma by crafting a uniquely National Socialist vision of a mass consumer society, based on racial purity and sanitized commercial practices.[58]

These last paragraphs have brought us back to the formal and centered understanding of ideology – namely, Hitler's own leading ideas; the racialized imaginary of the *Volksgemeinschaft*; the organizing principles of KdF; the geopolitics of prosperity and survival; the drive toward war; the renaming of the nation in the language of racial purity; the demonizing of the Jewish enemy. Having followed the Nazi appeal down into the micro-political settings of the workplace and the pleasure cruise, in other words, we need now to track in the opposite direction, back to where the formal ideas themselves were produced. This back and forth is crucial to how the question of ideology can be grasped.

On the one hand, Nazi ideas circulated through German society extremely systematically and authoritatively, with the full weight of the Propaganda Ministry and the other mass organizations behind them, in the absence of countervailing sources of opinion or the free exchange of argument, and backed by the sanctions of social exclusion, physical endangerment, and presumed violence. In those terms the *Volksgemeinschaft* was the most morally coercive category possible. At the same time, when such ideas circulate so profusely and unrestrainedly, they acquire powerful purchase on social experience. They become *real*. The Third Reich's governmental practice and system of policy, its rhetorics, its fully mobilized academic and scientific knowledge, its big political ideas, but also its use of actual or imagined events such as the November Revolution and the "stab-in-the-back" legend or the signature crises of the Weimar Republic, its appropriating of powerfully mythologized histories, its use of the mass spectacle and well-orchestrated campaigns, not to speak of deep legacies within the culture, persistent patterns of default thinking, and widely diffused dogmas of commonsense understanding – all of these actions constructed categories that Germans then needed to inhabit. Those categories interpellated them. Such interpellation was not automatic, not inevitable, not a process over which people could exercise no choice. But after 1933 – after Nazism's breach of civility – that process came with brute force. Nazi ideas – race, empire, struggle, necessity of war, the Jewish enemy, above all the *Volksgemeinschaft* – created places where, in practice, with varying degrees of self-awareness, Germans had little choice but to dwell. As I have argued, that describes something more than an ideology somehow external or auxiliary to a materiality structured around something else (like class or a social interest) in that older 1970s social historian's sense. Rather, it describes a real social topography: forms of everydayness, actually existing patterns of organized social life, an entire architecture of common belonging, ways of regulating personal and public space, institutional machineries, practices of governmentality. Nazi ideas acquired their strength and resilience – notably in the forms of consent that persisted, remarkably, for the duration of the war – because they took hold in an actually existing world of practices and thought.

On the other hand, though, we *do* need to examine the Nazi regime's motivating ideas as such – that is, the strategic thinking that shaped the inventory of primary commitments listed above, set them into motion, and formed them into the dominant categories of understanding available to people after 1933. Those categories gave Germans the materials of their possible relations to the social and political world of the Third Reich. They structured what it became feasible for Germans to think and what they could not. If, in studying the formation of "new fascist subjectivities," we need to take seriously "the interpellative capacities of Nazi ideology," then it is to the core ideas that we should next turn.[59]

Nazi ideology at the core

Of course, we have very extensive older intellectual histories, many of them more broadly contextualized as histories of conservative, right-wing, or *völkisch* thought more generally, as well as studies of the formation of Hitler's own views and those of other Nazis. These lines of inquiry have continued, as have studies in particular areas, such as the arts and the churches, along with numerous biographies or critical commentaries of writers, painters, philosophers, and other prominent intellectuals. But with notable exceptions, these literatures stop short of engaging with the question of ideology in the particular way I am suggesting here – as a body of thought produced in the core institutions of the Nazi state, whose coherence transferred into policies and machineries of practice with the kinds of efficacy discussed at length above.[60] Highly elaborate and informative scholarship has recently accumulated around the institutionally and professionally bounded arenas of Nazi policy-making and the practical contexts of implementation, moreover, including a growing literature on the various academic disciplines.[61] But this work seldom ventures an explicitly theorized argument about ideology as such. Yet another body of work, as we have seen, reduces the impact of Nazi ideology to rather simplified models of social conformity and acquiescence. In the logic of even the most sophisticated social historical inquiry, moreover, the emphasis on "social context" can obscure the Nazis' success in shifting social values from below. In an especially influential instance, Hans Mommsen privileged the "political and bureaucratic mechanisms that permitted the idea of mass extermination to be realized" by setting these dichotomously *over* and *against* "ideological factors," which he dismissed as merely "the effects of antisemitic propaganda and the authoritarian element in traditional German political culture." In so doing, he downplayed the insidiousness of Nazism's discursive power.[62]

In the meantime, pioneers such as Götz Aly, Henry Friedlander, and Michael Burleigh have gone furthest with regard to the racial state's policy-making arenas by treating these institutional locations as the extended ideological contexts where Nazi practices were developed. Simply by the remarkable densities of their empirical–analytical accounts, these works allow the coherence of the motivating commitments and more elaborate networks of ideas to be reconstructed.[63] They are joined by the local and regional historians of the wartime implementation of Nazi racial and genocidal policies in occupied Eastern Europe, such as Dieter Pohl, Thomas Sandkühler, Walter Manoschek, Christian Gerlach, Christoph Dieckmann, and Andrej Angrick.[64] In both bodies of work, though, it was still the goal-oriented and interest-based outlook of the relevant Nazi cadres that tended to draw the most attention – the planes of equivalence and contiguity linking the ethos and practice of the SS and other core Nazi institutions to the necessary and predictable rhythms of business-as-usual in a complex modern economy and administrative state, including what seem to be the "normal" dynamics of career-building, professionalism, expertise, social advancement, and knowledge-production among particular cohorts of doctors, lawyers, statisticians, economists, and other civil servants.[65]

It is consequently to the new scholarship concerned specifically with the various categories of the leadership and cadres of the SS that we should look for the most important insights. Beyond the key biographies – Peter Longerich's of Heinrich Himmler, Robert Gerwarth's of Reinhard Heydrich, Ulrich Herbert's of Werner Best, David Cesarani's of Adolf Eichmann – a wider array of work now brings us to a quite new level of understanding, including Michael Thad Allen's intensive analysis of the managers and engineers in the SS Business Administration Main Office (*Wirtshaftsverwaltungshauptamt*, WVHA), Isabel Heinemann's study of the SS Racial-Hygienic and Population-Biological Research Center (*Rasse- und Siedlungshauptamt*, RHF), Karin Orth's collective biography of senior concentration camp administrators, and Hans Safrian's study of the officials originating in Adolf Eichmann's Central Office for Jewish Emigration in Vienna (*Zentralstelle für jüdische Auswanderung*), along with the essential regional studies already mentioned above.[66] Herbert's now-classic biography of the archetypal SS insider Best showed these possibilities early on, locating the evolving coherence and unnerving extent of Nazi ambitions in a combination of upwardly mobile professional drive, project-oriented administrative expertise, and a well worked-out philosophy of race, all framed in the longer-standing language of early twentieth-century radical nationalism and its mythologies, given free reign by the untrammeled capacities of the prerogative state.[67]

Amidst this new work, Michael Wildt's imposing account of the high leadership at the center of the SS state-institutional complex in the Reich Security Main Office (*Reichssicherheitshauptamt*, RSHA) contributed the essential piece.[68] Originating in the project on World View and Dictatorship (*Weltanschauung und Diktatur*) sponsored by Herbert during his directorship of the *Hamburg Forschungsstelle für die Geschichte des Nationalsozialismus* in 1992 to 1995 (where Orth and Dieckmann were also fellow collaborators), Wildt authoritatively analyzed the RSHA's leadership, organizational structure, and range of activities while carefully dissecting its centrality to the implementation of the Nazi state's racial grand design. Most obviously, his book belongs with the steadily accumulating sociologies and collective biographies of particular Nazi leadership sectors, including the studies by Allen,

Heinemann, Orth, Safrian, and others mentioned above; with the studies of the professions and expertise going back to the scholarship on racial hygiene, medicine, and eugenics which began appearing in the 1980s; and above all with the pioneering researches of Götz Aly and his collaborators.[69] Among this vital literature, Wildt's book now goes furthest in bringing ideology as such – in its coherent, centered, programmatic form – back to salience. Even more, it shows how an appreciation of ideology's importance can be fully combined not only with the best kind of social history, but with broad-gauged cultural analysis and an institutional approach to the study of politics, too.

Wildt divides his book into four parts, moving from ideology as such (entitled "Generation"), through institutional analysis to the war, with a substantial epilogue on what happened to RSHA personnel after 1945.[70] By far the longest of these sections is the third, in which he lays out the RSHA's wartime role in managing the escalating drive to remake the Eastern European social order along racialist lines. He does so in three stages, beginning with the aftermath of the Polish campaign, which created the needed laboratory for mass murder and deportation, continuing through the planning delirium and genocidal fury of 1940 to 1941, and ending with the atrocious descent from systematizing into chaos during 1942 to 1945. As he guides us through the dynamics of policy-making and executive action so exhaustively, making the passage of the RSHA administrators into the practice of killing seem so apparently seamless – from the corridors of power to the *Einsatzkommandos*, from the drawing-board to the killing fields – the central narrative of the "Final Solution" becomes compellingly clear. As we acquire ever more scholarly research of this kind, moreover, certain older fixations of the field, such as the earlier fighting among "intentionalists" and "structuralists" or the controversies over the exact timing of the specific decision for genocide, start to seem stunningly unimportant. Wildt manages to cut a path through those tired debates without discarding the valuable substance on either side. Thus, he foregrounds the instigating agency of Nazi ideology, but locates this in the particular dynamism of the RSHA as a distinctive Nazi "institution of a new type," itself linked to a specific generational formation defined by activism and the "unboundedness" or "heedlessness" marked in his book's title. Neither the decisiveness of Hitler's own outlook nor the wider, more heterogeneous formations of ideas and attitudes in the Nazi movement are diminished in the slightest as a result.

By the richness of his archival learning, as well as the careful density of his empirical analysis and the confidence of his historiographical reach, Wildt manages to pull together everything we have been learning about the atrocious extent of SS ambitions for transforming Europe's social landscape, while simultaneously grounding this argument in the particular institutional setting that evolved for policy-making between 1936 and the opening months of the war. He might have done more to connect the RSHA to other sectors of policy-making and executive action under the Third Reich, whose polycratic unreliability necessarily qualified and often disrupted what Himmler's ambitious young *Weltanschuungskrieger* ("warriors with a cause") wanted to achieve.[71] During the inception years of 1936 to

1939, both Göring and Goebbels remained forces to be reckoned with as Himmler began assembling his agenda, while during the wartime both the complexities of running the war economy and the continuing jurisdictional powers of the Nazi *Party* impeded the progress of the intended SS aggrandizement, not to speak of the incipient nightmare of trying to sustain popular morale.[72] There was a chance here to re-energize discussions of the Nazi state, which since the 1970s have remained somewhat stuck theoretically around still-valuable formulations of Franz Neumann and Ernst Fraenkel, along with various deployments of a Weberian argument about charisma.[73] At the same time, the strength and clarity of Wildt's analysis certainly benefit from the consistency of focus on the core of the RSHA *per se*. There are perhaps four major elements to his accomplishment, each corresponding to one of the main sections of the book.

First, Wildt makes one of the strongest and most convincing cases yet for tracing the Third Reich's distinctive dynamism to a particular constellation of generational experiences arising out of World War I. Using a sample of 221 among the 400 senior administrators of the 3,000-strong RSHA, he delivers a fascinating portrait of the SS inner leadership cohort, who worked at the very core of the racial state's wartime policy-making machinery. By emphasizing this group's high levels of academic qualification, upward mobility, and career-oriented professionalism, the resulting sociology confirms an emergent historiographical consensus, while adding a more pointed argument about the energizing ideological commitments involved. On the one hand, Wildt decisively lays to rest the residual if persistent image of the uprooted, displaced, marginal, or *déclassé* Nazi activist. Indeed, far from providing a refuge for the rejected, the Third Reich's policy-making arenas drew many of the most successful. Relative to the newly prevailing political values after 1933, the SS central leadership recruited the best and brightest of the aspiring generation. A career at the top of the SS made it possible to realize the sociocultural desideratum of a successful bourgeois identity. "If we examine the social background of RSHA leaders," Wildt argues, "we find that in general they were social climbers." He continues:

> The picture here is clear. The leadership corps of the RSHA recruited young men from the lower middle class, in particular the sons of merchants and mid-level civil servants, as well as those from the lower class who were often the first in their family to earn a college degree and who then embarked on a professional career, subsequently advancing to the RSHA and thus into leadership positions in the National Socialist state … [I]t appears that it was especially the younger age groups – those born after 1900 – who rose from the lower middle class to the RSHA. In any case, it is clear that these men did not constitute a degraded academic subproletariat but, rather, were active social climbers who had already sought to attain a higher social status than their own fathers even before joining the Gestapo and the SD.[74]

At the same time, the ambitions of this generational grouping were moved not just by the achievement-oriented careerism of its professional aspirations – in some generic and depoliticized story of upward mobility – but also by a highly specific political outlook, one shaped by the cultural and existential meanings of World War I and its consequences. If the SS inner core differed from the older stereotype of the brutish and uncultured Nazi hoodlum, nor were they the mere bureaucrats and pen-pushers so familiar from another tradition of analysis, the one descending from Hannah Arendt's *Eichmann in Jerusalem* or the seminal work of Raul Hilberg. Wildt exemplifies that second view by the supposed figure of the "technician of death, who maintained and optimized his part in the enormous machinery of annihilation, with no concern for the murderous meaning of the overall enterprise, to say nothing of developing any moral scruples."[75] Yet, so far from being the *Schreibtischtäter* ("desk-perpetrator") of Arendt's or Hilberg's imagination, he argues, the RSHAers were driven by a definite belief system, a zealously professed anti-democratic philosophy hardwired around a biologically conceived anti-Semitism. They prided themselves on their anti-conservative radicalism, their unpitying rigor, their cold and steely objectivity, their willing readiness for action. Their hard-headed progressivist understanding of Germany's future was dogmatically based in a biological or genetic theory of the movements of history. Racially defined peoples were the source of history's agency. The *Volkskörper* needed to be ruthlessly fortified against the degenerative effects of internal weakness, whether these derived from the demographic catastrophe of World War I, from the corruption of the genetic pool, or from the spread of criminal and asocial behavior. External dangers, above all coming from the power and influence of the Jews, were no less dire.

Wildt grounds this argument in the salient characteristics of the so-called "war youth generation" (*Kriegsjugendgeneration*), by which he means those born between 1902 and 1912 who were themselves too young to have served in the war, as distinct from the predecessor generation born during the 1890s who shared directly in the "front experience" so famously idealized by Ernst Jünger.[76] As Wildt shows, 77 percent of the RSHA leadership belonged to those who had missed the opportunity to experience the battlefield and its camaraderie, yet who were old enough to have coveted its meanings. They appropriated the martial disciplines of hardness, ruthlessness, and action, while repudiating the bombast of the discredited Wilhelmine generations and eschewing the naïve sentimentalism of the young "front generation" itself. Of course, they lived through the extreme revolutionary turbulence of the immediate postwar years too, invariably passing through the *Freikorps* and other radical nationalist formations, where they acquired virulent loathing for Communists and Jews. Crucially, they also entered the universities, emerging with higher degrees and a radicalized sense of their own political mission. Committed substantively to a racialized and biologically founded *völkisch* vision of a new Germany, they evinced a cold and objective ethic of action: "The criteria for leadership, according to this position, were belief, will, drive, and *success*, not the morality and humanity of a leader's goals. In the eyes of these twenty-year-old college students, truth was realized in the deed. They did not believe in analytical, skeptical doubt directed at all validity claims but instead in devotion and enthusiasm."[77] Wildt is excellent at tracking his future RSHAers through the multiform *völkisch* milieu of the pre-Nazi radical Right, using a series of succinctly drawn biographical portraits to make these trajectories admirably concrete. His efforts here will be especially appreciated by specialists on the Weimar and Wilhelmine periods, who continue to grapple with the vexed difficulties of establishing the precise continuities in which the Third Reich's political history needs to be grounded.

At the same time, Wildt refuses to find in these biographies any easy uniformity or to inscribe them with some straightforward proto-Nazi inevitability. His excellent recurring portraits of individuals, which are worked skillfully into the analysis, are particularly telling in this respect. The young radical nationalists of this "uncompromising" or "unconditional" generation may have professed a common activist, anti-bourgeois ethic of masculinity which celebrated charismatic leadership and the cult of the deed, but as students and aspiring professionals they also moved through a variety of particular political groupings and allegiances on the extreme Right before the decisive political breach of 1933 delivered them into a durable ideological home. This is the second major thesis that Wildt develops. The Nazi seizure of power opened the way. It allowed the meanings and implications of the outlook of the *Kriegsjugendgeneration* to coalesce. It created the institutional environment where their ambitions could be harnessed. Recruited into the central leadership of the SS as the *Sicherheitsdienst* (SD) transmuted into the new state's primary policy-making engine, these youthful ideologues were encouraged to think of themselves as the coming executive élite. Drawing astutely on Carl Schmitt's writings of the time, Wildt sees them as the ruthless shock troops of a pure politics unconstrained by anything short of the *Führer*'s will. The uncoupling of politics from the normalized routines of the constitutional state "expanded the possibilities for creating new political institutions in the National Socialist state for the *Volksgemeinschaft* that were capable of distinguishing between friend and enemy in 'battle,' in an 'emergency,' and in 'war'." The exponents of such a politics had license for every possible radicalization:

> The SD and Gestapo were ideal institutions for this conception of politics as an act of shaping or forming and as the field of the decisive deed. They were, on the one hand, organized as centers of executive power and centralized intelligence agencies for the investigation of political, ideological, and 'racial' enemies; on the other hand, neither was subject to any form of traditional administrative rules.[78]

In Reinhard Heydrich's conception, this became the ideal of a "fighting administration" (*kämpfende Verwaltung*), which envisaged the SS as a "shock troop for the party in all matters of domestic territorial security and the securing of National Socialist ideas."[79] During 1935 to 1938, a steady stream of policy documents concerning the fate of the Jews issued from the desks of Heydrich's thrusting young team, steadily sharpening and expanding the terms of racial policy, while Heinrich Himmler's elevation to supreme chief of the German Police on 17 June 1936 gave this activity a clear institutional impetus.[80] In this regard, Wildt decisively questions the older desire of Broszat and Mommsen to find the key to the regime's radicalization in the dynamics of its polycratic disorder because, on the contrary, the shared ideological commitments of Heydrich's administrative vanguard gave their efforts coherence, intensity, and direction. If Himmler dreamed of using the SS to create a new ruling élite, what he called "an upper class that has been selected repeatedly over centuries, a new nobility continually supplemented with the best sons and daughters of our *Volk*," then Heydrich sought to anchor the pursuit of this "racist biopolitical utopia" in an unprecedented concentration of executive authority, procedurally untethered from any of the usual constitutional or bureaucratic restraints.[81] During 1938 to 1939, Werner Best and Walter Schellenberg advocated differing models of administrative reorganization to achieve this goal, and the merging of the SD with the Gestapo and Criminal Police into the RSHA on 27 September 1939 was the eventual outcome.

That this "institution of a new type" was formally established at the very moment of the inception of the war was certainly no accident. As Wildt points out, the RSHA "was an institution of movement" whose élan of activism and ruthlessness embodied Nazism's core self-understanding.[82] Although the racialized planning and the associated administrative coalescence had been proceeding since 1936, accordingly, it was the outbreak of war that gave Nazi designs their headway. Indeed, for the new RSHA the Polish campaign functioned as the founding act of violence. It was through the massacres and deportations of the anti-Polish terror during the autumn of 1939, which were at their most horrendously unrestrained against the Jews, that Nazi intentions acquired their requisite institutional form.[83] This was true of the new administrative arrangements created for the occupied territories, of the expeditious handling of local tensions between the army and the SS, and, above all, of the latter's emerging primacy. As Wildt shows in the third of the major theses I want to highlight, the war was essential not only to realizing the planning blueprints of resettlement and deportation, exploitation and enslavement, mass killing and eventually genocide, but also to enacting the vaunted cult of the deed. The RSHA arose "from the practice of racist mass murder."[84] It became a crucible for the unity of theory and practice.

It is this fungibility of roles – of the ease of passage of leading RSHA functionaries back and forth between paper pushing and mass murder, between the drafting of policy documents and the actuality of killing on the ground – that arises most shockingly from Wildt's account. This highly educated élite of ideologically driven administrators proved completely adept at moving from the one context into the other. They were not at all removed from or protected against the practical meanings of their desk-bound administrative measures, let alone immunized against them in the manner Arendt's trope of the "banality of evil" had implied. At one level, Wildt's account of the war years covers what by now has become extremely well-trodden ground, while appropriately re-centering the narrative actively around the RSHA. But if the successive phases of "Persecution, Expulsion, Extermination" and their regional specificities have become only too horrifically familiar, Wildt's emphasis on the self-justifying grandiosity of the RSHA élite's driving motivations – what amounted to a ghastly ethic of genocide – forms his distinctive contribution.[85] Some earlier studies have developed such an analysis around individuals – Herbert's biography of Best is the outstanding case; but Wildt comes closer than almost anyone to grounding such particularized understandings in a collective portrait of an entire category of crucial perpetrators, which pays attention to their sociology, their cultural formation, and their explicit political values, while connecting the complex fusion of these characteristics to a dynamic story of institutional development.

Finally, Wildt adds a fascinating chapter to the now burgeoning scholarship on the distressing ease of the post-1945 normalization in the West German Federal Republic, which allowed so many convinced and willing adherents of the Third Reich to become re-assimilated into an officially de-Nazified society ("Back in Civil Society").[86] While describing the immediate transition to post-Nazism, including the Nuremberg trials and subsequent desultory efforts at prosecution, the heart of this fourth part of the book is formed by further exemplary biographies. The more spectacular of these included the former adjutant to the Kripo head Artur Nebe, Karl Schulz, who emerged unscathed from British de-Nazification proceedings to re-establish his police career in Schleswig-Holstein, rising to become head of the *Landeskriminalamt* in Social Democratically (SPD) governed Bremen in September 1952; and the literary scholar Hans Rößner, who joined the SD in 1934 as a 23-year-old, worked under Otto Ohlendorf in the SD-Inland, and rebuilt a successful career after 1945 in publishing, culminating at the top of the Piper Verlag, where he became Hannah Arendt's editor![87]

Of course, careers such as these under the changed postwar circumstances of an officially liberal polity presupposed intricate and sustained machineries of concealment and obfuscation. But the more disquieting implications of Wildt's account concern the degree of openness and collective self-deception that accompanied these trajectories, allowing the resumption of professional lives to be accomplished in such apparently good conscience. Here he adds an especially atrocious chapter to an already well-established and elaborately drawn picture of the manifold ways in which continuities stretched unproblematically from the core areas of the Third Reich's racial state into the most respectable territories of West German professional and public life. The civil service, medicine, the law, business, the academic professoriat, and the other professions – all remained thickly inhabited by those who had built successful careers under fascism, when the practice of killing had never been far from the respectable performance of professional life. To Herbert's surgical exposure of Werner Best's particular trajectory through the Federal Republic's founding institutional landscape, Wildt adds the generalized account of the high SS leadership's more or less unhampered collective survival.[88]

Wildt's book does not satisfy in all respects. For example, it isolates the RSHA unnecessarily from other parts of the Nazi state – whether we consider other key areas of the SS, such as the *Ordnungspolizei* and especially the WVHA studied so revealingly by Michael Thad Allen, or the complex apparatus of the Nazi state more generally. Having plotted the passages of his RSHAers so carefully through the radical right-wing affiliations of the Weimar years, moreover, he somewhat separates them from these surrounding histories once they arrive in the precincts of the SD during the 1930s. At the same time, no single book can hope to accomplish everything, least of all one that in its German original already contained almost 1,000 pages. *An Uncompromising Generation* is an extremely imposing achievement. It confirms above all that the importance of Nazi ideology is centrally back on the table – *not* as the old-style expository history of ideas, but as the careful and grounded critical analysis of all the forms of Nazi praxis. After three decades in which forms of social, institutional, and cultural history tended to push ideological analysis more to the margins, it becomes increasingly clear that any future understanding will require looking at the ideas, cultural outlooks, mental energy, and ethico-philosophical motivations of those who felt able to identify their futures with the Third Reich and willingly made their careers there, too.

Notes

1 Emblematic would now be P. Fritzsche, *Life and Death in the Third Reich* which draws these insights brilliantly together.

2 See D. Schmiechen-Ackermann, "'Volksgemeinschaft': Mythos der NS-Propaganda, wirkungsmächtige Verheißung oder soziale Realität im 'Dritten Reich'? – Einführung," in Schmiechen-Ackermann (ed.) *"Volksgemeinschaft": Mythos der NS-Propaganda, wirkungsmächtige Verheißung oder soziale Realität im "Dritten Reich"?*, Paderborn: Ferdinand Schöningh, 2012, pp13–18. This volume resulted from a major conference in Hanover on 2 to 3 October 2009, forming the first in an intended series under the title *Nationalsozialistische "Volksgemeinschaft". Studien zu Konstruktion, gesellschaftlicher Wirkungsmacht und Erinnerung*, sponsored by the Lower Saxon Universities of Göttingen, Hanover, Oldenburg, and Osnabrück.

3 Characteristically, this was Martin Broszat's position, as quoted by W. J. Mommsen, "Einleitung," in G. Hirschfeld and L. Kettenacker (eds) *Der "Führerstaat,"* 1981, p18: "the unity of the *Volksgemeinschaft*, which was so strongly stressed in the propaganda ... fell apart ... in an increasing chaos of specific powers."

4 Quoted phrases come from Norbert Frei's critical rendition of this earlier orthodoxy in his succinct "People's Community and War: Hitler's Popular Support," in H. Mommsen (ed.) *The Third Reich between Vision and Reality: New Perspectives on German History 1918–1945*, Oxford: Berg, 2001, p59.

5 See Mason (ed.) *Arbeiterklasse und Volksgemeinschaft*, whose introduction was published separately (1977) and later translated as *Social Policy in the Third Reich*. Also Kershaw, *Popular Opinion* and *The "Hitler Myth"*; H. Mommsen, "Nationalsozialismus also vorgetäuschte Modernisierung," in W. H. Pehle (ed.) *Der historische Ort des Nationalsozialismus*, Frankfirt am Main: Fischer, 1990, pp13–46; B. Weisbrod, "Der Schein der Modernität: Zur Historisierung der 'Volksgemeinschaft'," in K. Rudolph and C. Wickert (eds) *Geschichte als Möglichkeit. Über die Chancen von Demokratie*, Essen: Klartext, 1995, pp224–42; H. A. Winkler, "Vom Mythos der Volksgemeinschaft," *Archiv für Sozialgeschichte* 17, 1977, pp484–90.

6 D. Welch, "Nazi Propaganda and the *Volksgemeinschaft*: Constructing a People's Community," *Journal of Contemporary History*, 2004, vol. 39, no. 2, p213, note 1.

7 Winkler, "Vom Mythos," p485.

8 See the conference report by J. Steuwer, *German Historical Institute London Bulletin*, 2010, vol. XXXII, no. 2, pp120–8.

9 I. Kershaw, "'*Volksgemeinschaft*': Potenzial und Grenzen eines neuen Forschungskonzepts," *Vierteljahrshefte für Zeitgeschichte*, 2011, vol. 59, no. 1, p2.

10 Ibid, pp3, 7.
11 Ibid, p3.
12 T. Kühne, *Kameradschaft: Die Soldaten des nationalsozialistischen Krieges und das 20. Jahrhundert*, Göttingen: Vandenhoeck und Ruprecht, 2006, and *Belonging and Genocide: Hitler's Community, 1918–1945*, New Haven: Yale University Press, 2010.
13 Kühne, *Belonging and Genocide*, p1. My italics.
14 Kühne, "The Pleasure of Terror: Belonging through Genocide," in P. E. Swett, C. Ross, and F. d'Almeida (eds) *Pleasure and Power in Nazi Germany*, Houndmills: Palgrave Macmillan, 2011, pp234–55.
15 "Leagues of men forming themselves into communities of the illicit and the criminal were not peculiar to the military or to Germany in the Nazi period. As historical, sociological, psychological, and anthropological research in other military organizations and in certain gangs and rites of initiation show, such social mechanisms are widespread perhaps all over the world and throughout history." Ibid, p246.
16 Ibid, p249. This critique should not detract from the importance of Kühne's delineated analysis of the gender order constructed around soldierly masculinities in the years 1914 to 1945, which retains its interest and acuity. See T. Kühne, "Comradeship: Gender Confusion and Gender Order in the German Military, 1918–1945," in K. Hagemann and S. Schüler-Springorum (eds) *Home/Front: The Military, War, and Gender in Twentieth-Century Germany*, Oxford: Berg, 2002, pp233–54; "Male Bonding and Shame Culture: Hitler's Soldiers and the Moral Basis of Genocidal Warfare," in O. Jensen and C.-C. W. Szejnmann (eds) *Ordinary People as Mass Murderers: Perpetrators in Comparative Perspective*, Houndmills: Palgrave Macmillan, 2008, pp55–77.
17 While based avowedly in the twentieth century, *Belonging and Genocide* has some affinities with T. Rohkrämer, *A Single Communal Faith? The German Right from Conservatism to National Socialism*, New York: Berghahn Books, 2007, discussed in Chapter 1. An important lineage also runs through the writings of G. L. Mosse, beginning with *The Crisis of German Ideology. Intellectual Origins of the Third Reich*, London: Weidenfeld and Nicolson, 1966. See especially *Nationalism and Sexuality. Middle-Class Morality and Sexual Norms in Modern Europe*, Madison: University of Wisconsin Press, 1985; *Fallen Soldiers: Reshaping the Memory of the World Wars*, New York: Oxford University Press, 1990; and *The Image of Man: The Creation of Modern Masculinity*, New York: Oxford University Press, 1996.
18 M. Burleigh and W. Wippermann, *The Racial State: Germany, 1933–1945*, Cambridge: Cambridge University Press, 1991, p304. Also ibid, p306: "The main object of social policy remained the creation of a hierarchical racial new order." The final part of this book, with chapters on "Youth," "Women," and "Men," is titled "The Formation of the '*Volksgemeinschaft*'," even if the term is translated as "National Community," ibid, pp199–303.
19 Kühne himself gestures toward such complexity, stressing the need to "distinguish different types of initiative, enthusiasm, compliance, complicity, shared knowledge, qualms, and choices." *Belonging and Genocide*, p3.
20 See the citations to Lüdtke's essays in note 124 of Chapter 2.
21 See especially S. Baranowski, *Strength through Joy: Consumerism and Mass Tourism in the Third Reich*, Cambridge: Cambridge University Press, 2004, pp75–117; the classic study is A. Rabinbach, "The Aesthetics of Production in the Third Reich," in G. L. Mosse (ed.) *International Fascism: New Thoughts and New Approaches*, London and Beverly Hills: Sage Publications, 1979, pp189–222.
22 A. Lüdtke, "'Ehre der Arbeit'," p333.
23 Ibid, p335.
24 Thus, in Mason, *Social Policy*, the chapter on "Social Policy and Social Ideology, 1934–1936" (pp151–78) is preceded by those on "The Condition of the Working Class in Germany, 1933–1936" (pp109–50) and "The Transformation of Class Relations" (pp88–108). The back and forth between these two levels is always insightfully conducted, but the

priority remains clear. Likewise, his brilliant reading of the inception of the 1934 Law on the Organization of National Labor emphasizes the economic logics of rationalization and imposition of industrial peace over Nazi understanding of "an ideological solution." See Mason, "The Origins of the Law on the Organization of National Labor of 20 January 1934. An Investigation into the Relationship between 'Archaic' and 'Modern' Elements in Recent German History," in J. Caplan (ed.) *Nazism, Fascism, and the Working Class*, esp. pp81, 102–3. A similar analytical precedence organizes "Women in Germany, 1925–1940. Family, Welfare, and Work," ibid, pp131–211, though again always with subtlety and complex precision.

25 Peukert, *Inside Nazi Germany*, first published as *Volksgenossen und Gemeinschaftsfremde – Anpassung, Ausmerze und Aufbegehren unter dem Nationalsozialismus*, Cologne: Bund-Verlag, 1982; R. Williams, *Marxism and Literature*, Oxford: Oxford University Press, 1977, p82. The two major studies of working-class formation during the 1930s have been R. Hachtmann, *Industriearbeit im "Dritten Reich"* and M. Schneider, *Unterm Hakenkreuz. Arbeiter und Arbeiterbewegung 1933 bis 1939*, Bonn: Dietz, 1999. Strikingly, neither Burleigh, *Third Reich*, nor Evans, *Third Reich in Power*, treats workers separately. Caplan's edited volume *Nazi Germany* contains no entry on workers or class formation.

26 This was the ground from which the postwar Nuremberg prosecutions and later proceedings such as the trial of Adolf Eichmann (1961) and the Frankfurt Auschwitz Trial (1963–1965). By the time of the *Historikerstreit* of 1985–1986, such ethico-political terrain was still being passionately contested, while the reception of Daniel Goldhagen's *Hitler's Willing Executioners: Ordinary Germans and the Holocaust*, New York: Knopf, 1996, marked a key watershed. For the trials *per se*, see especially D. Bloxham, *Genocide on Trial: War Crimes Trials and the Formation of Holocaust History and Memory*, Oxford: Oxford University Press, 2003; R. E. Wittmann, *Beyond Justice: The Auschwitz Trial*, Cambridge: Cambridge University Press, 2005; D. O. Pendas, *The Frankfurt Auschwitz Trial, 1963–1965: Genocide, History, and the Limits of the Law*, Cambridge: Cambridge University Press, 2006; H. Earl, *The Nuremberg SS-Einsatzgruppen Trial, 1945–1958: Atrocity, Law, and History*, Cambridge: Cambridge University Press, 2009. For the context of public controversy in the 1980s and 1990s: C. S. Maier, *The Unmasterable Past: History, Holocaust, and German National Identity*, Cambridge: Harvard University Press, 1988; and G. Eley (ed.) *"Goldhagen Effect."*

27 A. Lüdtke, "Die Praxis von Herrschaft: Zur Analyse von Hinnehmen und Mitmachen im deutschen Faschismus," in Berlekamp and Röhr (eds) *Terror, Herrschaft und Alltag, Probleme einer Sozialgeschichte des deutschen Faschismus*, Münster: Westfälisches Dampfboot, 1995, p240.

28 This will be taken up further in Chapter 4. An excellent overarching treatment is M. Mouton, *From Nurturing the Nation to Purifying the Volk: Weimar and Nazi Family Policy, 1918–1945*, Cambridge: Cambridge University Press, 2007; also N. R. Reagin, *Sweeping the German Nation: Domesticity and National Identity in Germany, 1870–1945*, Cambridge: Cambridge University Press, 2007, pp110–43. In comparison, L. Pine, *Nazi Family Policy 1933–1945*, Oxford: Berg, 1997, observes the older separation between "Nazi family ideology" and the social contexts of policy implementation. See especially the work of G. Czarnowski, "'The Value of Marriage for the *Volksgemeinschaft*': Policies towards Women and Marriage under National Socialism," in R. Bessel (ed.) *Fascist Italy and Nazi Germany: Comparisons and Contrasts*, Cambridge: Cambridge University Press, 1996, pp94–112; "Hereditary and Racial Welfare (*Erb- und Rassenpflege*): The Politics of Sexuality and Reproduction in Nazi Germany," *Social Politics: International Studies in Gender, State, and Society*, 1997, vol. 4, no. 1, pp114–35; *Das kontrollierte Paar: Ehe- und Sexualpolitik im Nationalsozialismus*, Weinheim: Deutscher Studien Verlag, 1991. For an illuminating case study, see P. Szobar, "Telling Sexual Stories in the Nazi Courts of Law: Race Defilement in Germany, 1933 to 1945," in D. Herzog (ed.) *Sexuality and German Fascism*, New York: Berghahn Books, 2005, pp131–63.

29 For a discussion of the Third Reich's festive calendar, see P. Reichel, *Der schöne Schein des Dritten Reiches. Faszination und Gewalt des Faschismus*, Munich: Carl Hanser Verlag, 1992, pp208–31.

30 For these complexities on the example of the Nuremberg Party Rallies, see M. Urban, "Die inszenierte Utopie. Zur Konstruktion von Gemeinschaft auf den Reichsparteitagen des NSDAP," in Schmiechen-Ackermann (ed.) *"Volksgemeinschaft,"* pp135–57, and the same author's exhaustive book-length study, *Die Konsensusfabrik. Funktion und Wahrnehmung der NS-Reichsparteitage, 1933–1941*, Göttingen: V&r Unipress, 2007.

31 S. Spector, "Was the Third Reich Movie-Made? Interdisciplinarity and the Reframing of 'Ideology'," *American Historical Review*, 2001, vol. 106, no. 2, 482–3, citing the argument from L. Koepnick, "Fascist Aesthetics Revisited," *modernism/modernity*, vol. 6, 1999, 51–73. See W. Benjamin, "The Work of Art in the Age of Mechanical Reproduction," in H. Arendt (ed.) *Illuminations*, London: Collins/Fontana, 1973, p243.

32 Spector, "Was the Third Reich Movie-Made?," p464.

33 Here I am quoting Spector's rendition of Koepnick's argument: Koepnick, "Fascist Aesthetics," pp52–54; Spector, "Was the Third Reich Movie-Made?," p483.

34 W. König, "Das Scheitern einer nationalsozialistischen Konsumgesellschaft," *Zeitschrift für Unternehmensgeschichte*, vol. 48, 2003, pp152–3.

35 S. J. Wiesen, "National Socialism and Consumption," in F. Trentmann (ed.) *The Oxford Handbook of the History of Consumption*, Oxford: Oxford University Press, 2012, p45. For an authoritative study, see W. König, *Volkswagen, Volksempfänger, Volksgemeinschaft: "Volksprodukte" im Dritten Reich. Vom Scheitern einer nationalsozialistischen Konsumgesellschaft*, Paderborn: Schöningh, 2004. By 1941 almost 75 percent of German households had radio receivers, up from only 25 percent in 1933, but these were not exceptional figures internationally: Denmark and Sweden recorded still higher figures, while Norway and France showed faster growth with lower investment. See also A. Tooze, "The Economic History of the Nazi Regime," in Caplan (ed.) *Nazi Germany*, p183. The most dramatic failure was the *Volkswagen*: though 340,000 customer orders were placed during 1938 to 1945, no single car was produced in the purpose-built plant, which after September 1939 was converted for military production.

36 See G. Aly, *Hitler's Beneficiaries: Plunder, Racial War, and the Nazi Welfare State*, New York: Metropolitan, 2007. See J. A. Tooze, "Einfach verkalkuliert," *die Tageszeitung*, 12 March 2005, with subsequent exchange between Aly and Tooze, ibid, 15–16 March 2005; M. Vogt et al., "Essays zu Götz Alys *Hitlers Volksstaat*," *Neue Politische Literatur*, 2005, vol. 50, no. 2, pp185–217; R. J. Evans, "Parasites of Plunder?," *The Nation*, 8 January 2007; C. R. Browning and R. Overy, "Review Forum," *Journal of Genocide Research*, 2007, vol. 9, no. 2, pp303–10.

37 Wiesen, "National Socialism and Consumption," p438.

38 A. Tooze, *The Wages of Destruction: The Making and Breaking of the Nazi Economy*, New York: Viking, 2006, pp163, 192–3; Tooze, "Economic History," p180.

39 See König, *Volkswagen, Volksempfänger, Volksgemeinschaft*, pp137–50; Reagin, *Sweeping the German Nation*, pp144–80.

40 Wiesen, "National Socialism and Consumption," p438. Tooze, *Wages*, pp162–5, importantly complicates the formula of "guns or butter."

41 S. Baranowski, "Strength through Joy: Tourism and National Integration in the Third Reich," in S. Baranowski and E. Furlough (eds), *Being Elsewhere: Tourism, Consumer Culture, and Identity in Modern Europe and North America*, Ann Arbor: University of Michigan Press, 2001, p216; and for full detail, Baranowski, *Strength through Joy*, pp118–61. See also K. Semmens, *Seeing Hitler's Germany: Tourism in the Third Reich*, Houndmills: Palgrave Macmillan, 2005; R. Koshar, "Savage Tourism" in *German Travel Cultures*, Oxford: Berg, 2000, pp115–59.

42 Baranowski, "Strength through Joy," pp225, 213.

43 Ibid, p218. For greater detail: Baranowski, *Strength through Joy*, pp155–61; H. Spode, "Ein Seebad für Zwanzigtausend Volksgenossen: Zur Grammatik und Geschichte des

Fordistischen Urlaubs," in P. J. Brenner (ed.) *Reisekultur in Deutschland: Von der Weimarer Republik zum "Dritten Reich,"* Tübingen: Max Niemeyer Verlag, 1997, pp7–47; J. Rostock and F. Zadniček, *Paradiesruinen: Das KdF-Seebad der Zwanigtausend auf Rügen*, Berlin: Ch. Links Verlag, 1995.

44 For the *Volkswagen* planned city (today Wolfsburg), see H. Mommsen and M. Grieger, *Das Volkswagenwerk und seine Arbeiter*, Düsseldorf: Econ, 1997, pp250–82.

45 Baranowski, *Strength through Joy*, p6.

46 Baranowski, "Strength through Joy," p213.

47 Baranowski, *Strength through Joy*, p159. For Spode, "Ein Seebad für Zwanzigtausend Volksgenossen," this was a "Fordist" model of mass tourism, whereas Baranowski sees the attentiveness to individuated enjoyments too. Baranowski, *Strength through Joy*, p161.

48 Ibid, 142. Baranowski provides an excellent distillation of KdF publications from this point of view, ibid, pp142–54.

49 See Semmens, *Seeing Hitler's Germany*, pp72–97, and for the tense relations between commercial tourism and KdF, pp98–128.

50 Baranowski, *Strength through Joy*, pp177, 10. The "beautiful illusion" reference is to Reichel, *Der schöne Schein des "Dritten Reiches."*

51 Tooze, *Wages of Destruction*, p162.

52 G. Weinberg (ed.) *Hitlers Zweites Buch: Ein Dokument aus dem Jahr 1928*, Stuttgart: Deutsche Verlags-Anstalt, 1961, p144, cited by Tooze, *Wages of Destruction*, p162. See Tooze, pxxiv: "by one last great land grab in the East [Germany] would create the self-sufficient basis both for domestic affluence and the platform necessary to prevail in the coming superpower competition with the United States."

53 Ibid, pp163–4.

54 Here I am following Wiesen's helpful formulation, "National Socialism and Consumption," p447.

55 Ibid, 435. See G. C. Cocks, *The State of Health: Illness in Nazi Germany*, Oxford: Oxford University Press, 2012.

56 Wiesen, "National Socialism and Consumption," p435, quoting the Nazi economist B. Kiesewetter, "Kartell, Marktordnung, Recht und Verbrauch," *Die deutsche Volkswirtschaft*, 2 June 1936, vol. 6, no. 17, pp536–8.

57 Wiesen, "National Socialism and Consumption," p436. See here F. Bajohr and M. Wildt, "Einleitung," in Bajohr and Wildt (eds) *Volksgemeinsschaft: Neue Forschungen zur Gesellschaft des Nationalsozialismus*, Frankfurt am Main: Fischer, 2009, pp7–23.

58 Tooze, *Wages of Destruction*, p164; Wiesen, "National Socialism and Consumption," p449. See also S. J. Wiesen, *Creating the Nazi Marketplace: Commerce and Consumption in the Third Reich*, Cambridge: Cambridge University Press, 2011.

59 D. Sweeney in A. S. Bergerson, E. Mailänder Koslov, G. Reuveni, P. Steege, and D. Sweeney, "Forum: Everyday Life in Nazi Germany," *German History*, 2009, vol. 27, no. 4, p579. For the full quotation, see my discussion in the concluding part of Chapter 2 at note 122.

60 Exceptions need to be made for such works as E. Jäckel's short classic, *Hitler's Weltanschauung: A Blueprint for Power*, Middletown, C. T.: Weslyan University Press, 1972, or R. Bollmus, *Das Amt Rosenberg*. Early pioneers include A. Barkai, *Nazi Economics: Ideology, Theory, and Policy*, New Haven: Yale University Press, 1990; W. D. Smith, *The Ideological Origins of Nazi Imperialism*, New York: Oxford University Press, 1986; Proctor, *Racial Hygiene*; R. Griffin, *The Nature of Fascism*, London: Routledge, 1991. Among current literature: O. Plöckinger, *Geschichte eines Buches: Adolf Hitlers Mein Kampf, 1922–1945*, Munich: Oldenbourg, 2006; N. Gregor, *How To Read Hitler*, London: Granta Books, 2005; T. W. Ryback, *Hitler's Private Library: The Books That Shaped His Life*, New York: Knopf, 2009; R. Weikart, *From Darwin to Hitler: Evolutionary Ethics, Eugenics, and Racism in Germany*, Houndmills: Palgrave Macmillan, 2004; C. Koonz, *The Nazi Conscience* Cambridge: Harvard University Press, 2004. Evans, *The*

Third Reich in Power, now provides the best overall guide, especially pp220–320. See also R. J. Evans, "The Emergence of Nazi Ideology," in Caplan (ed.) *Nazi Germany*, pp26–47.

61 For work on the natural sciences, see M. Renneberg and M. Walker (eds) *Science, Technology, and National Socialism*, Cambridge: Cambridge University Press, 1994; M. Szöllösi-Janze (ed.) *Science in the Third Reich*, Oxford: Berg, 2001; S. Heim, C. Sachse, and M. Walker (eds) *The Kaiser Wilhelm Society under National Socialism*, Cambridge: Cambridge University Press, 2009. For the historical profession: W. Oberkrome, *Volksgeschichte. Methodiche Innovation und völkische Ideologisierung in der deutschen Geschichtswissenschaft 1918–1945*, Göttingen: Vandenhoeck und Ruprecht, 1993; K. Schönwälder, *Historiker und Politik. Geschichtswissenschaft im Nationalsozialismus*, Frankfurt am Main: Campus, 1996, and "The Fascination of Power: Historical Scholarship in Nazi Germany," *Historical Workshop Journal*, vol. 42, 1996, pp19–40; W. Schulze and O. G. Oexle (eds) *Deutsche Historiker im Nationalsozialismus*, Frankfurt am Main: Fischer, 1999. See also M. Burleigh, *Germany Turns Eastwards*; I. Haar and M. Fahlbusch (eds) *German Scholars and Ethnic Cleansing, 1919–1945*, New York: Berghahn Books, 2005.

62 H. Mommsen, "The Realizable of the Unthinkable: The 'Final Solution of the Jewish Question' in the Third Reich," in Mommsen, *From Weimar to Auschwitz*, Princeton: Princeton University Press, 1991, p252.

63 See Burleigh and Wippermann, *Racial State*; G. Aly, *"Final Solution"*; H. Friedlander, *The Origins of Nazi Genocide*; Burleigh, *Death and Deliverance*.

64 See, in particular, P. Longerich, *Holocaust: The Nazi Persecution and Murder of the Jews*, Oxford: Oxford University Press, 2010, and *The Unwritten Order: Hitler's Role in the Final Solution*, Stroud: Tempus, 2001; D. Pohl, *Nationalsozialistische Judenverfolgung in Ostgalizien 1941–1944: Die Organisierung und Durchführung eines staatlichen Massenverbrechens*, Munich: Oldenbourg, 1996; T. Sandkühler, *"Endlösung" in Galizien: Der Judenmord in Ostpolen und die Rettungsinitiativen von Berthold Beitz, 1941–1944*, Bonn: Dietz, 1996; W. Manoschek, *"Serbien ist Judenfrei." Militärbesatzungspolitik und Judenvernichtung in Serbien 1941/2*, Munich: Oldenbourg, 1993; C. Gerlach, *Kalkulierte Morde. Die deutsche Wirtschafts- und Vernichtungspolitik in Weißrussland 1941 bis 1944*, Hamburg: Hamburger Edition, 1999; C. Dieckmann, *Deutsche Besatzungspolitik in Litauen 1941–1944*, Göttingen: Wallstein, 2011; A. Angrick, *The "Final Solution" in Riga: Exploitation and Annihilation, 1941–1944*, New York: Berghahn Books, 2009. For a general guide to the new regional research, see U. Herbert (ed.) *National Socialist Extermination Policies: Contemporary German Perspectives and Controversies*, New York: Berghahn Books, 2000; and, more recently, W. Gruner and J. Osterloh (eds) *Das "Großdeutsche Reich" und die Juden: Nationalsozialistische Verfolgung in den "angegliederten" Gebieten*, Frankfurt am Main: Campus, 2010.

65 For a valuable entrée to the burgeoning historiography of the professions and expertise, see L. Raphael, "Ordnungsdenken und die Organisation totalitärer Herrschaft: Weltanschauungseliten und Humanwissenschaftler im NS-Regime," *Geschichte und Gesellschaft*, vol. 27, 2001, pp5–40. Two key pioneering accounts were G. Aly and S. Heim, *Architects of Annihilation: Auschwitz and the Logic of Destruction*, Princeton: Princeton University Press, 2002; orig. German edn. 1991; and Burleigh, *Germany Turns Eastwards*.

66 See Longerich, *Heinrich Himmler*; Gerwarth, *Hitler's Hangman*; Herbert, *Best*; D. Cesarani, *Becoming Eichmann: Rethinking the Life, Crimes, and Trial of a "Desk Murderer,"* Cambridge: Da Capo Press, 2004; M. T. Allen, *The Business of Genocide: The SS, Slave Labor, and the Concentration Camps*, Chapel Hill: University of North Carolina Press, 2002; I. Heinemann, *"Rasse, Siedlung, deutsches Blut": Das Rasse- und Siedlungshauptamt der SS und die rassenpolitische Neuordnung Europas*, Göttingen: Wallstein, 2003; K. Orth, *Die Konzentrationslager-SS. Sozialstrukturelle Analysen und biographische Studien*, Göttingen: Wallstein, 2000; H. Safrian, *Eichmann's Men*, Cambridge: Cambridge University Press, 2010. See also J. Banach, *Heydrichs Elite: Das Führerkorps der Sicherheitspolizei und des SD,*

1936–1945, Paderborn: Ferdinand Schöningh, 1998; Y. Lozowick, *Hitler's Bureaucrats: The Nazi Security Police and the Banality of Evil*, New York: Continuum, 2002. Among older works, R. L. Koehl, *The Black Corps: The Structure and Power Struggles of the Nazi SS*, Madison: University of Wisconsin Press, 1983, remains valuable, while H. F. Ziegler, *Nazi Germany's New Aristocracy: The SS Leadership, 1925–1939*, Princeton: Princeton University Press, 1989, no longer seems adequate.

67 Herbert, *Best*. See also L. Hachmeister, *Der Gegnerforscher: Die Karriere des SS-Führers Franz Alfred Six*, Munich: Beck, 1998. Among the older literature, P. G. Black, *Ernst Kaltenbrunner. Ideological Soldier of the Third Reich*, Princeton: Princeton University Press, 1984, remains important.

68 M. Wildt, *An Uncompromising Generation: The Nazi Leadership of the Reich Security Main Office*, Madison: University of Wisconsin Press, 2009, orig. pub. as *Generation des Unbedingten: Das Führungskorps des Reichssicherheitshauptamtes*, Hamburg: Hamburger Edition, 2003.

69 See Proctor, *Racial Hygiene*, and Weindling, *Health, Race, and German Politics between National Unification and Nazism*, pp489–564, along with Friedlander, *Origins of Nazi Genocide*, and Burleigh, *Death and Deliverance*. Excellent conspectuses may be found in Evans, *Third Reich in Power*, pp506–33; M. Burleigh, *The Third Reich*, pp345–404; T. Kirk, *Nazi Germany*, Houndmills: Palgrave Macmillan, 2007, pp150–72. For Götz Aly and his collaborators, see Aly and Heim, *Architects of Annihilation*; Aly, *"Final Solution"*; Aly, P. Chroust, and C. Pross, *Cleansing the Fatherland: Nazi Medicine and Racial Hygiene*, Baltimore: Johns Hopkins University Press, 1994; M. Burleigh, "A 'Political Economy of the Final Solution'? Reflections on Modernity, Historians, and the Holocaust," in *Ethics and Extermination: Reflections on Nazi Genocide*, Cambridge: Cambridge University Press, 1997, pp169–82. See also I. Haar and M. Fahlbusch (eds) *German Scholars and Ethnic Cleansing, 1919–1945*, New York: Berghahn Books, 2005.

70 See Wildt, *Uncompromising Generation*, pp21–121, 125–214, 217–357, and 361–424, respectively. In the German edition the first part is titled *Weltanschauung*, whose inflection of meaning in this context is more toward "vision of the world" than to "ideology."

71 Here I am following Mark Roseman's formulation in "Beyond Conviction?," pp84, 92.

72 The starting point for considering these questions is now Tooze, *Wages of Destruction*.

73 See Neumann, *Behemoth*; E. Fraenkel, *The Dual State: A Contribution to the Theory of Dictatorship*, New York: Oxford University Press, 1941. "Charismatic rule" is treated most elaborately, if schematically, in Wehler, *Deutsche Gesellschaftsgeschichte, vol. 4: Vom Beginn des Ersten Weltkrieges bis zur Gründung der beiden deutschen Staaten 1914–1949*, Munich: Beck, 2003, pp551–63, 623–35, 675–9, 866–72, 884–7, 933–7, and L. Herbst, *Hitlers Charisma: Die Erfindung eines deutschen Messias*, Frankfurt am Main: Fischer, 2010. More successful is I. Kershaw, *The End: The Defiance and Destruction of Hitler's Germany, 1944–1945*, New York: The Penguin Press, 2011, which embeds the explication in its detailed analytical narrative. For Kershaw's definition, see ibid, pp13–14; also Kershaw, *Hitler: A Profile in Power*, London: Longman, 1991, pp10–14. For critical surveys, see van Laak, "Adolf Hitler," in F. Möller (ed.) *Charismatische Führer der deutschen Nation*, Munich: Oldenbourg, 2004, pp149–70; E. Horn, "Work on Charisma: Writing Hitler's Biography," *New German Critique*, 2011, vol. 38, no. 3, pp95–114. For the earlier state discussion, see the writings of Jane Caplan: *Government Without Administration: State and Civil Service in Weimar and Nazi Germany*, Oxford: Oxford University Press, 1988; "Bureaucracy, Politics, and the National Socialist State;" "Theories of Fascism: Nicos Poulatzas as Historian," *History Workshop Journal*, vol. 3, 1977, pp83–100; "'The Imaginary Universality of Particular Interests': The 'Tradition' of the Civil Service in German History," *Social History*, 1979, vol. 4, no. 2, pp299–317; also M. Geyer, "The State in National Socialist Germany," in C. Bright and S. Harding (eds) *Statemaking and Social Movements: Essays in History and Social Theory*, Ann Arbor: University of Michigan Press, 1984, pp193–232.

74 Wildt, *An Uncompromising Generation*, pp38, 39–40.
75 Ibid, p7.
76 This argument goes back to Peukert, *Die Weimarer Republik. Krisenjahre der Klassischen Moderne*, Frankfirt am Main: Suhrkamp, 1987, pp25–31; also J. Reulecke, "Im Schatten der Meißnerformel: Lebenslauf und Geschichte der Jahrhundertgeneration," in W. Mogge and J. Reulecke (ed.) *Hoher Meißner 1913. Der Erste Freidutesche Jugendtag in Dokumenten, Deutungen und Bildern*, Cologne: Verlag Wissenschaft und Politik, 1988, pp11–32. The idea of a "war youth generation" was initially popularized by G. Gründel in *Die Sendung der jungen Generation*, Munich: Beck, 1932, pp31–42. See A. Donson, *Youth in the Fatherless Land: War Pedagogy, Nationalism, and Authority in Germany, 1914–1918*, Cambridge: Harvard University Press, 2010, p249, note 15.
77 Wildt, *An Uncompromsing Generation*, p71.
78 Ibid, p121.
79 Ibid.
80 See Wildt's earlier edition of these memoranda, M. Wildt (ed.) *Die Judenpolitik des SD 1935 bis 1938: Eine Dokumentation*, Munich: Oldenbourg, 1995.
81 The statement is taken from a speech delivered by Himmler to the SS leadership in Tölz on 18 February 1937. See Wildt, *An Uncompromisig Generation*, p110.
82 Ibid, p210. Wildt's treatment of the clashing rationales developed by Werner Best and Walter Schellenberg for the putative RSHA during 1938 to 1939, drawing on Fraenkel's theory of the "dual state" (the coexistence of the "normative" and the "prerogative"), is an excellent starting-point for theorizing the state under fascism. See ibid, pp125–64, 210–14. His discussion of the initial "structure and staff" in the newly established RSHA may be found ibid, pp165–210.
83 See now the crucial work of Wildt's student G. Wolf, *Ideologie und Herrschaftsrationalität: Nationalsozialistische Germanisierungspolitik in Polen*, Hamburg: Hamburger Edition, 2012; Rutherford, *Prelude to the Final Solution*; Epstein, *Model Nazi*, pp124–230.
84 This phrase forms the title of Wildt's concluding section (*Uncompromising Generation*, pp240–41) in his chapter on "Poland, 1939: The Experience of Racist Mass Murder," pp217–41. In the German original the section is considerably longer: *Generation des Unbedingten*, pp480-85. The leader of Einsatz gruppe I, Bruno Steckenbach advanced to become Chef des RSHA-Amtes I Personal in June 1940, having served during 1933 to 1938 as chief of Gestapo in Hamburg. His emblematic career forms one of Wildt's excellent recurring biographical illustrations.
85 "*Verfolgung, Vertreibung, Vernichtung 1940/41*" is the title of the relevant chapter in the German edition (*Generation des Unbedingten*, pp486–606), which is differently organized than the English translation.
86 "Postwar: Back in Civil Society," is the title of Wildt's relevant chapter, *An Uncompromising Generation*, pp361–403.
87 Ibid, pp389–93 and 393–403, respectively.
88 In addition to Herbert, *Best*, pp403–521, see N. Frei, *Adenauer's Germany and the Nazi Past: The Politics of Amnesty and Integration*, New York: Columbia University Press, 2002.

4

MISSIONARIES OF THE *VOLKSGEMEINSCHAFT*

Ordinary Women, Nazification, and the Social

Putting women into the history of Nazism

This book has spent much of its time worrying about questions of consent and responsibility. What were the bases of support for the Nazi regime? How did the Nazis make and secure their popular appeal? How should we think about their various categories and sources of support, and what sustained that popularity for so long, indeed right up to the very end of the war? Certain aspects of these questions have been answered confidently in great detail for a very long time, with compelling analytical care and unimpeachable archival backing, in a scholarly historiography extending now across five decades. We know an enormous amount about the seizure of power, the process through which the Nazis established their regime and enforced its hold. By this stage, we need hardly know more about the detailed sociologies of their direct strength – about who voted for them and who joined the various arms of the movement, from the NSDAP (Nazi Party) itself and the SA (*Sturmabteilung*: Stormtroopers or Storm Divisions), through the SS, to the Hitler Youth (*Hitler Jugend*, HJ), League of German Maidens (*Bund Deutscher Mädel*, BDM), the National Socialist Womanhood (*NS-Frauenscahft*, NSF), and the other auxiliary organizations. We also know how that strength was distributed regionally across different economies and types of community, along with its rhythms over time. We can claim similar knowledge of the wider reserves of support in society at large, especially among the full range of the professions, across the various sectors of the economy, and among the titled nobility.

But what were the patterns of endorsement, complicity, and identification, and who was left on the other side of those boundaries? What did those relations concretely mean? Who was a culprit and who a victim? Who an accomplice and who a bystander? What were the different registers of coercion, conformity, complicity, and consent? Are these even sensible categories any more, given all that we continue to learn about the constraints and complexities of agency and action? Might not a different spectrum of terms be more useful in the end – like "making it through," "putting up with things," "swallowing one's tongue," "going along," "staying out of the way," and so forth. Whatever our preferred language, though, how should we judge the ethics and the pragmatics of living one's life under Nazism? If nothing directly drew the regime's attentions – absent any record of enmity or vulnerability, whether from opposition and dissent, from being classified as "asocial" or "unfit," or from being a Jew or some other "enemy of the race" – how far could you preserve some integrity? The ordinary elements of daily living – schooling, employment, neighborliness, healthcare, charity, religion, sport, all the forms of sociability, not to speak of the obligatory contacts with the state, from taxation and welfare to military service and enrollment in the HJ or BDM – made it impossible to separate completely from society. So what were the consequences – existentially, ethically, psychologically, intellectually, politically – for selfhood and subjectivity? Given all those inescapable points of connection, how should we think about the condition of trying not to be involved?

The search for an approach adequate to these questions – to the demands of analyzing society's complicity in the violence of Nazi rule – continues to preoccupy Third Reich historians. Women's history has faced this in an especially acute form, amid debates that echoed the impact of early feminist historiography in other places. One early instance surrounded a 1976 essay by Annemarie Tröger, who sought to lay the myth that women bore the blame for Hitler's accession, having supposedly voted for him in disproportionately high numbers amid a kind of "masochistic hysteria."[1] In fact, as a series of careful analyses proceeded to show, while in 1928 to 1932 large numbers of women were clearly voting for them, the Nazis were not notably interested in appealing to women until very late in the day. For most of Weimar, women were voting disproportionately for the Catholic Center and the two conventional right-wing parties, the German National-People's Party (DNVP) and German People's Party (DVP), instead. The DVP counted on women for about 52 to 55 percent of its votes, the DNVP for 56 to 60 percent; and together they drew about a third of the female electorate by 1924. In comparison, like the Social Democrats (SPD) and Communists (KPD), the Nazis found it harder to win women's support. Indeed, after the first rush of women's suffrage in 1919 – that year some 80 percent of freshly enfranchised women went to the polls, helping to elect the broad democratic majority of the National Assembly – female turnout dwindled toward 60 percent in many cities by 1928, while the right-wing parties underwent "a gradual 'feminization' … especially at the provincial level."[2] Female piety also played its part, for women continued giving their votes in greater numbers than men to both the Catholic Center and the heavily Protestant DNVP, even as the latter's electorate began deserting to the NSDAP after 1928.[3]

For the Nazis, women as such were simply not an evident priority. It was only during 1932 that they began relaxing an aggressively masculinist stance by developing a form of positive appeal, though strictly on the basis of the most reactionary of separate-sphere maternalisms. "Equal rights for women," in Hitler's view, "means they receive the respect they deserve in the sphere nature intended for them."[4] What public statements the Nazis addressed toward women emphasized only their place in the home as wives and mothers, removed from politics, public responsibility, the professions, and ideally the paid workplace. "In January 1933," Tim Mason aptly remarked, "the new regime thus had some leeway to make up in gaining the confidence of German women."[5]

The debate about the Nazis' women voters, in some respects brought to closure by the turn of the 1990s, displays much of the same schematism on the subject of ideology discussed earlier in this book.[6] Thus, on the one hand, Helen Boak concludes, rightly, that "it can no longer be denied that women's votes did, indeed, play a substantial part in bringing Hitler to power."[7] Given both the greater numbers of women in the overall electorate and the enormous surge in Nazi popular votes during 1930 to 1932, in fact, this had to be true.[8] But in settling that empirical question, on the other hand, Boak immediately takes back its significance, playing down the meaningful agency or consequences involved for women in deciding to switch their allegiances from one party to another, as though the violent extremism of the Nazis, which by 1932 had become so patently clear, was just a banal variation on an already familiar theme. Women "turned to the NSDAP" because of its "growing prominence and respectability," its "dynamism," its youthfulness, "its growing strength, the disintegration of the liberal and local conservative parties, and the general disillusionment and dissatisfaction with what the Republic had brought or failed to bring" – indeed, for any reason *other than* the Nazis' own distinctive profile or ideas.[9]

Yet, against the backcloth of what was actually happening in 1932 – the pervasive violence and confrontationalism, the febrile, frenetic quality of public life, the sense of everything falling apart – this denial of specific significance to the act of giving one's vote to the Nazis, as if Hitler was tantamount to Hugenberg, seems perverse. The fullest consequences of putting the Nazis into power were not known, of course. As Matthew Stibbe says, "a vote for the Nazi Party (especially in the circumstances of depression-hit Germany)" may not have been "necessarily the same thing as a vote for fascist-style dictatorship or one-party rule."[10] But the general entailments were still perfectly apparent by the middle of 1932. After 30 January 1933, moreover, those new cohorts of Nazi voters, women and men, then declared themselves perfectly happy with the terms of the order that was now being reimposed.[11]

In other words, in reading the significance of Nazi attitudes toward women it is scarcely enough to observe the absence of references to women in the party program, the vagueness of the generalities in the rhetoric of Nazi newspapers, leaflets, and electioneering, or the particular contradictions on policy matters from one Nazi speech to another. Nor is it convincing to flatten Nazi views on "women's role in society" into the similar "views held by the DVP, DNVP, Center Party, and BVP."[12] Citing that convergence, Boak downgrades Nazi anti-feminism to a mere "element of Nazi propaganda" in the sense discussed in Chapter 3, so that, for example, the attack on married women's employment becomes attributed "more to opportunism, with the party realizing the feelings this issue generated among the general public, than to party ideology."[13]

But if in no party's case did its stance on women "play a decisive part in voter choice," that hardly renders perceptions of gender meaningless for politics. Nazi rhetoric dripped with gendered references to the *Volkskörper* and the health of the nation, to family and youth, to war, struggle, and manhood, to sacrifice and renewal, with all of the associated imagery, and that was a discourse where women were certainly inscribed, in however mediated and coded a fashion. Moreover, how exactly the primary dynamics of the political crisis of the early 1930s were to work themselves out – those of "family, welfare, and work," to use Tim Mason's triplet – had implications for women so palpable for the Nazis as to require little explicit address or targeted appeal: restoring the health of the family was *essentially* about women, after all. The Nazis' opponents certainly grasped this: as Julia Sneeringer has shown, during 1932 the other parties "put the spotlight" so brightly "on what a Nazi victory would mean for women's rights" that this issue was returned to the agenda for the first time since 1919, thereby constraining the Nazis themselves to respond.[14]

Though the stakes for Boak in making her argument remain obscure, it seems clear that after 1928 neither the Center nor the DNVP, "the parties of the Weimar Republic which benefited most from female suffrage," laid much emphasis on "gender-specific propaganda." Rather, they "emphasized women's role within the family and Christian values."[15] Thus, the public priorities most pertinent for women were deemed to reside with all those practices of governance concerned with stabilizing Germany's moral-political order – pre-eminently via the family and households, but also through religion and schooling, private hygiene and public health, wholesome recreation and sober entertainment, responsible consumption, and all the other elements of orderly living.

In the Nazi case, those commitments were not only ratcheted upwards to a stridency whose radicalism marked a quantum jump, but were also organized more explicitly and consistently via the language of race. In Mason's words: "The purity of the blood, the numerical power, the vigor of the race were ideological goals of such high priority that all women's activities other than breeding were relegated in party rhetoric to secondary importance."[16] In short: across this full spectrum of issues centrally affecting "women's role in society," the Nazis surely *did* have an aggressively expounded program that was definitely "coherent" and "cohesive."[17] Indeed, in "its attitudes and policies towards women, National Socialism was the most repressive and reactionary of all modern political movements." In these terms, Mason's strong thesis still stands: "anti-feminism was not a minor or opportunistic component of National Socialism, but a central part of it, and a part the importance of which in the years 1929–33 has probably been underrated."[18]

Women's agency and the gendering of political capacities

During the course of the 1980s, women's history moved to the center ground of German historical discussion in North America in very exciting ways, in large part via the scholarship and collective impact of the German Women's History Study Group based in New York. Strongly oriented toward the Weimar and Nazi years, that group's influence moved forward through two major conferences, the first at the University of Pennsylvania in April 1984 ("Public Spheres and Private Spaces: Politics and Society in Weimar Germany"), the second at Rutgers University in April 1986 ("The Meaning of Gender in German History"), while strongly shaping the discussion in a third at Penn in April 1988 ("Reevaluating the Third Reich").[19] Women's history was also getting under way concurrently inside West Germany, with a notable growth of discussion in the early 1980s whose Third Reich benchmark was certainly Gisela Bock's powerful study of forced sterilization appearing in 1986.[20] In the English language, these early discussions were framed between pioneering interventions by Renate Bridenthal and Claudia Koonz and Tim Mason in the mid 1970s and the appearance of the anthology *When Biology Became Destiny* in 1984. That latter volume not only convened the best new work specifically on women, but also helped to decisively shift the agenda for the historiography of Nazism overall. As an emblematic text it belongs with Detlev Peukert's *Inside Nazi Germany* and Michael Burleigh and Wolfgang Wippermann's *Racial State* in that regard.[21]

With the advent of this new work, women's historians quickly confronted the issues posed at the head of this chapter. Thus, while much of the earliest work had foregrounded the Third Reich's overwhelming misogyny, presenting women straightforwardly as the victims of the Nazis' family, reproductive, and racialized social policies, the first synthetic general account to appear, Claudia Koonz's *Mothers in the Fatherland*, emphasized instead the forms of female involvement and collusion. The central, disconcerting feature that Koonz discerned grew from the material conditioning, political compulsions, and motivating ideologies shaping women's idealistic but subordinated complicity in the Nazi project. Here the Nazis' own outlook and policies provided the more familiar part of the story, both in the rationalized ferocity of their misogyny and in the simultaneous celebration of a sentimentalized domesticity – a story in which a nurturing maternalism would succor the harshness of the public struggle, first against the enemies within, and then for the greater glories of the revivified race-people. Koonz added her own distinctive insight by exploring the resonance of the idea of *Lebensraum* for the idealized construction of a specifically women's space. Some of the more organizational matters, involving the specifically female aspects of the *Gleichschaltung* (the post-1933 process of coordination/articulation of the existing public sphere into a unitary framework of Nazi institutions), were better known, and there Koonz pulled together a range of detail from the newly emerging research, notably the contributions of Jill Stephenson.[22]

The more original – and troubling – features of the argument concerned the bases of Nazism's positive appeal. At first, women figured insignificantly in the Nazis' own movement culture, contributing by 1933 less than 6 percent to the NSDAP membership, or less than 1 percent of the entire female population.[23] As Boak acknowledged: "Alone of the political parties the NSDAP refused to allow women to hold positions of leadership or to represent it at any level."[24] But from the surge of Nazi electoral popularity it was also apparent that existing women's organizations had come to provide a deep reservoir of sympathy and potentially active identification. The more conservative women's groups, such as the Housewives' and Countrywomens' Associations whose growth during Weimar developed supports for women's independent capacities in the narrowly separatist sense, proved a particularly fertile recruiting ground.[25] As Koonz argued, the Nazis' appeal to such groups reflected a basic convergence of values around motherhood, the family, and domesticity. Given the massive anxieties on which the Nazis played in the early 1930s, including the widespread and over-determined hostility to the image of the "New Woman," the notion of a morally privileged woman's sphere also offered powerful leverage for Nazi ideology, much as the "motherhood-eugenics" discourse left another sector of opinion vulnerable to the appeal of the Nazis' racialism.[26] Very quickly after 30 January 1933, in fact, reflecting the broad congruence of thinking among politically active right-wing women, the women's organizations of the DNVP and DVP, along with most of the League of German Women's Organizations (*Bund Deutscher Frauenvereine*, BDF), had no difficulty in swinging over to the new regime. In the patriotic concentration accomplished by the Nazis during the first half of 1933, right-wing women took their enthusiastic place. As Agnes von Zahn-Harnack, BDF president, emphasized in the negotiations with the NSF, "the new Germany will undoubtedly have especial understanding for a whole series of tasks which the [BDF] believes to be urgent; in the first place a 'biological policy' which supports the German family through economic and eugenic measures."[27]

Later, a more systematic conception of feminine virtue then became worked into a central feature of the Nazi social order as a necessary compensation for the unrelenting public brutalities of the regime, becoming all the more indispensable once the wartime violence of military service and genocidal killing intensified the demands on patriotic masculinity. By performing the emotional work the system needed in order to function, partly inside the family, partly through professions such as teaching, social work, and nursing, but also via Nazism's public enforcement of its rigid regime of femininity, Koonz argued, German women became positioned as its "accomplices." It was in this sense that women became key participants in what the Nazis were intending to pursue. They became drawn ineluctably into the practical everydayness of the Third Reich's system of rule. This was how they colluded. With whatever degree of consciousness or intention, women necessarily participated in Nazi practice – by providing "the image of humane values that lent the healthy gloss of motherhood to the 'Aryan' world of the chosen," and by offering "a doll's house of ersatz goodness," as "a haven from public horror for the men who arrested, deported, tortured, and killed those they defined as the enemies of the *Volk*."[28] Such complicity was especially marked in the female sector of public service employment. Even if such women – nurses, kindergarten helpers, social workers, teachers, clerical workers in any number of institutional settings – withheld their active endorsement, morally compromised forms of non-involvement could only ever result, amounting to passive but knowing acquiescence (turning a blind eye and looking the other way), given the racial state's daily actualities. As for the privacy of domestic life, "family" had in any case ceased to be available as a refuge in any "innocent" or protected sense. To a disquieting degree, under the Third Reich, the boundaries between "public" and "private" were effectively dissolved.[29]

Koonz's book drew a scathingly hostile response from Gisela Bock, with a resulting controversy whose terms owed as much to extraneous differences – the contrasting dynamics of contemporary West German and US feminisms as they emerged from the 1970s, with their sharply differing lexicons for the politics of motherhood, for example, or the unresolved generational angst of German women historians born to mothers who had lived under the Nazis – as to the immediate historiographical ground *per se*.[30] Against Koonz's thesis of an aggressively pronatalist Third Reich, whose promotion of motherhood not only cemented the social order but also created a structure of professional and practical opportunity that successfully coopted many women into its goals, Bock's own work had "insisted that the true 'novelty' of Nazi policy had been its extreme *anti-natalism*," one that potentially victimized all women by threatening their (biological and social) maternal identity."[31] In a path-breaking analysis of the roughly 400,000 forcible sterilizations under the Third Reich, Bock explicated the purposes and effects of that policy as paradigmatic for the operation of the racial state, showing how the categories of race and gender worked intimately – and lethally – together in marking women as primary targets of the regime's race-defined population politics. That mutually constitutive interconnectedness of race and gender, the particular ways in which the forced sterilization policy sutured those categories and their wider meanings together, with effects that extinguished a woman's procreative and feminine relation to motherhood rather than securing it, does indeed complicate the persuasiveness of the Koonz argument. The machinery of the racial state and its operations – including many of the policies directly targeting women as mothers – were organized by ruthlessly administered assumptions of social value that could deny women the ability to bear and raise children as easily as promote it. For those deemed "unfit" or "inferior," Bock reminded us, "National Socialism pursued a policy not of family welfare, but of family destruction."[32] Furthermore, there was nothing *specifically* Nazi about the system of benefits directed through the family, for this was comparable with the welfarism introduced concurrently elsewhere. The *real* specificity, again, was in the viciousness of the Nazis' anti-natalism.[33]

Yet, Bock also produced simplifications of her own. If half of those who were forcibly sterilized were actually *men*, that is surely a problem. While women were nine-tenths of those dying from the procedure and may have suffered worse (physically, emotionally, socially) from the consequences of childlessness, or at least suffered differently, then it remains unclear what this might then enable us to say. Universalizing the experience of sterilized women as Bock does, making a very particular minority stand in for the whole category, seems tendentially essentialist: "In making this argument Bock structurally locates all women as victims because they were all disciplined and oppressed by the threat of forced abortion and sterilization if they did not live up to the proper standards of social and physical fitness."[34] Moreover, the starkness of the binary – "anti-natalism" versus "pro-natalism" as the main truth of Nazi attitudes – is itself unhelpful. The very desire for a single primary or superordinate system of meaning seems misplaced, notably at odds with the new emphasis on the "gray zone" already under way even as Bock published her book. The most important intervening specialists, Gabriele Czarnowski and Atina Grossmann, each show the complicated *concurrencies* of anti-natalist and pro-natalist politics after 1933, most notably with respect to abortion. As Grossmann says, Nazi policies might either uphold the necessity of motherhood or require termination, depending on the requirements of the health of the *Volk*: "The most salient feature of Nazi abortion policy therefore was its clear selectivity." She continues:

> Voluntary abortions desired by women themselves and not state-sanctioned for reasons of the health of the *Volk*, were severely repressed – up to and including the death penalty for those performing the abortions (including doctors but usually midwives). Abortions on racially, physically, and mentally valuable women were to be stamped out. Abortions on the racially undesirable and "unfit" were coercively performed according to decisions made by the same medical commissions that determined sterilizations, and generally not severely punished if performed illegally.[35]

Once we shift focus from population politics *per se* to the broader societal contexts stressed by Koonz, Bock's skepticism about the salience of pro-natalist ideas becomes hard to credit.[36] Jill Stephenson and others provide ample evidence of the efficacy of the regime in enlisting the social energies of young and older women, whether for the ritualized celebrations of Mother's Day and other actions sponsored by the People's Welfare Organization (*Nationalsozialistische Volkswohlfahrt*, NSV), the introduction of the Mother Cross in 1939, the child-raising classes provided by the Reich Mothers' Service (*Reichsmütterdienst*, RMD), courses in household management offered by the Women's Bureau (*Frauenwerk*), or use of the mothers' advice centers.[37] At a level of small-scale social leadership, women were certainly not absent from the landscape of practical participation in the *Volksgemeinschaft*:

> Over one million of the approximately 3,300,000 women in the *Frauenschaft* and *Frauenwerk* in 1939 held some official position. In the *Frauenschaft* they were responsible for the ideological and political development of members, collected membership dues, distributed propaganda and headed the organization's weekly evening meetings. In the *Frauenwek* they concentrated on their clientele's domestic and mothering skills, helped set up training centers for mothers, and, in the tradition of bourgeois women's associations, ran welfare schemes.[38]

Yet, these were precisely the settings where we would certainly expect to find heavily maternalist pressure toward embracing the normativities of marriage and family, providing Koonz, indeed, with most of her sources for the Nazism-as-motherhood thesis.[39] Especially given the evidence for the continuing entry of women into the waged labor force, accordingly, "can we assume this exhausts the National Socialist conception of the woman?"[40] By probing brilliantly inside the appeal to girls and young women of another of the Nazi mass organizations, the League of German Maidens, Dagmar Reese extends the argument about female agency into a further complicated direction. The realm and activities of the BDM gave girls chances to be independently among themselves, to develop generational *esprit*, to build self-esteem, and to acquire and practice leadership. The BDM precisely *did not* preach the conventional virtues of domesticity and female compliance. Rather, it gave girls ways to push pleasurably *against* the confines of family. In loosening those restrictions, the BDM showed young women a form of independence just as they were being opened toward the messages of party and state.[41]

While Bock and Koonz each address vital parts of the Third Reich's relationship to women, neither of their respective frameworks sufficiently captures the fullness of the latter. The complexities in how the regime actually functioned in the widest arenas of female activity seriously upset the binary terms of the Bock-Koonz dispute. If they make Bock's extrapolations from the very particular case of the forcible sterilization policy seem too schematically abstract, then they also exceed Koonz's particular construction of separate spheres. But now, at two decades distance, it has become much easier to think beyond the limits those dichotomies allow. As Michelle Mouton observes, it was much rather the capacity of the Nazis to disorganize and remake the overall bases of the socio-political order in Germany, within an extremely wide repertoire of racially driven and ruthlessly applied policies and precepts, that requires our primary attention – their readiness "to alter dramatically the relationship between motherhood and the state" as a field of extraordinarily intrusive bio-political intervention far wider than either a pro-natalist or anti-natalist framework alone might suggest.[42]

The place from which Koonz began – what I called "the material conditioning, political compulsions, and motivating ideologies shaping women's idealistic but subordinated complicity in the Nazi project" – provides much scope for fruitful thought. My earlier chapters gave extensive attention to each of the latter two aspects – political compulsions and motivating ideologies – and in what follows I now turn to the material conditioning – the structural circumstances that shaped women's socio-political options during the Nazi years. Those conditions both confined the possibilities for conscious agency, particularly under the coercive weight of Nazism's anti-democratic political rule, and significantly eclipsed the otherwise decisive political ruptures of 1933 and 1945. I will then end by returning to the motivating ideologies as such, looking directly at a category of women whose activism fed directly into building the *Volksgemeinschaft*.

Women, work and welfare

The relationship of women to work under Nazism forms one of the classic instances of the older approach to ideology. Tim Mason brilliantly laid this out 40 years ago in terms that were revelatory for the time.[43] On the one hand, the Nazis made no bones about their intentions: women had no place in the industrial labor force, least of all those who were married ("double earners"), belonging instead strictly in their families; once women were back in the home and men in their jobs, health could return to the nation.[44] Yet, on the other hand, the growth in women's paid employment continued much as before, especially once the arms drive intensified from 1936. By 1938 numbers of women in all branches of industry had grown to 1.85 million from 1.21 million in 1933, affecting the heavy-industrial and manufacturing core no less than the more predictable sectors of textiles, clothing, and food: iron, steel, and machine tools saw women's presence grow from 13 to 19 percent, electrical engineering from 12 to 29 percent of the workforce. Where else could women be found working? Aside from all the unpaid work they supplied in households, shops, farms, and other family businesses, and their statistically unseen labors in the informal cash economy of neighborhoods (as child minders, laundresses, seamstresses, and so forth), they appeared above all in the expanding service sector – as shop assistants, clerks, stenographers and typists, secretaries, telephonists, waitresses, canteen-workers, teachers, nurses. Overall, between June 1933 and May 1939, the total numbers of all women working for a wage rose from 11.5 to 13.8 million, among whom married women increased from 4.5 to 6.4 million.[45]

For historians of Nazism, beginning with Tim Mason and Dörte Winkler, the real story behind these numbers concerned the gap that opened between the Nazis' ideas and their realization, between *ideology* and *social history*, once the policies hit against the realities of society and economy, some of which came from the normal functioning of a capitalist economy and its social relations (e.g., the operation of labor markets or the maximizing of household incomes), others from the effects of what the Nazis themselves were doing. The resulting problems were then hugely exacerbated by a state-party institutional structure whose polycratic disorder characteristically hampered its ability to sort out the conflicts. For one thing, Nazi family policies – or, at least, those aimed at strengthening the ties of women to domestic motherhood – clashed consistently with the realities of women's economic behavior and the material needs of their households, for in practice women *had* to remain gainfully active, whether for wages in industry and services, in the family economies of farming, shop keeping, and artisanal trades, or in the commercial networks of city life, irrespective of what Nazi ideologues might insist they should be doing.[46] The needs of the arms drive, which themselves clashed with a motherhood-centered family program in a variety of complicated ways, then also faced the intractable qualities of labor markets – that is, the types of jobs that women were actually willing to seek. Any one instance of these over-determined conflicts would then pit different interests against one another (ministries, policy-making agencies, bodies of expertise, party and governmental entities, the array of interests in the economy), whether at the highest levels in Berlin or all the way down the system to the ground. Invariably, given the interconnectedness of the issues involved, the conflicts and confusions ran *through* individuals and entities rather than cleanly between and among them.

In Mason's pioneering account Nazi dilemmas were irreducible. With admirable care and clarity, he presented them by juxtaposing the actualities of women's employment in the 1930s ("Women's Place") with the constellation of Nazi policies in relation to family, motherhood, and population ("Procreation"), before showing how the two conjoined in an impasse of crisis proportions on the eve of the war ("Women, the Labor Market, and the State in the Later 1930s").[47] Just as the economic recovery began generating needs for women workers in consumer industries and services, the demand for industrial labor under the Four-Year Plan also trumped arguments for keeping women out of the labor force: the bans on the paid employment of the wives of Marriage Loan recipients were incrementally rescinded in 1936 to 1937, while a variety of incentives were devised tempting women, single and married, into seeking paid employment. Labor scarcity effectively bared the contradictions in how the Nazis thought they were treating German women. Here is Mason's summary:

> In the late 1930s the question of women's work came to pose one of the most intractable and embarrassing sets of problems which the Nazi regime faced in internal affairs. The immediate cause of these difficulties was immediate and obvious – women's employment was essential to the rearmament program and the war effort – but their resolution called for measures which were diametrically opposed to the direction of all earlier Nazi policies. Attempts to mobilize women for war production also came up against many of the irreducible facts about the nature of women's work in the capitalist system of that epoch, and they threatened to destroy a large part of the regime's basis of popular support. The regime found itself impaled upon a set of contradictory imperatives.[48]

Here again, then, social history is called upon to show the hollowness of Nazi ambitions and the limited efficacy of Nazi ideology. In effect, Nazi designs for motherhood are deemed to have been countermanded by the superordinate logics of the economy – the entailments of the Four-Year Plan, the exigencies of labor recruitment during the arms drive, and the varying needs of industry, sector by sector, for labor power. Still more, Nazi policies had to contend with the actual behavior of women, whose statistical regularities are shown to have had powerful countervailing effects. For Matthew Stibbe, this was about "image" versus "reality"; for Mason, "the paternalist anti-feminist ideology" colliding with "the realities of social change."[49] None of the above arguments are false as such. But as far as ideology goes, surely, the contradictions were precisely the point. The degree of *programmatic coherence* of the Nazi prescriptions (or otherwise) was only one level of meaning. The clashing perspectives and priorities outlined above was another – the *incoherent* and *contradictory* character of Nazi aspirations when taken as a whole. Yet a third level, the most complex and important for our purposes, was the *moment of the clash* itself, the point at which Nazi policies encountered the recalcitrance of the social, the autonomous patterning of social forces and trends, the obstinate idiosyncrasies of the human materials they were seeking to mold. For this, above all, is what ideology actually *does*: it handles the contradictions; it works with differences and difficulties in order to manage them, sometimes successfully but as often not.

Thus, the real import should be found not in the confusions of Nazi policy when faced with the "contradictory imperatives" Mason described, or the twisting and turning on the part of this or that Nazi ideologue. The really interesting questions about Nazi ideology, rather, concern the complex ways in which those contradictions were negotiated out on the ground. The typical manifestation of a labor policy running into problems at the grassroots, which a social historian might traditionally expect to find, after all, would be opposition or dissent, or at least a disruption of some kind, like a protest or a riot or a strike. That such resistance failed to occur very much under Nazism, and that popular compliance lasted instead through the dying days of the regime, was not a sign of Nazi ideology's failure or ineffectuality, but of its opposite – namely, *precisely its ability to go on doing its work*.[50] While ideology stays schematically separated from "society" or counterposed against it – against the realities of the labor market or the actual behavior of women – we are unlikely to grasp the extensiveness of its full force. Whereas the ideas themselves were important, Nazi ideology was as much to be found embedded and embodied in social practices and social relations as it was inside people's heads: in what they did as well as what they thought, in their relationships and their actions, and in the structured circumstances – small scale, material, quotidian – where they did them. As Alf Lüdtke showed us, once we follow ideology into the micro-historical contexts of the workplace or the neighborhood in that way – and for our current purposes into the family, the welfare office, the NSF meeting, the BDM troupe, and the Strength through Joy (*Kraft durch Freude*, KdF) trip, but also the farmhouse, the typing pool, the department store, and the assembly line – we become better equipped to see how its persuasiveness, or compulsions, took hold.[51]

Dagmar Reese's study is still a rare effort fully to do this, distinguishing the complexities of motivation – from the overtly political through the pressures of socialization to simple social climbing, but also a kind of rebelliousness against the family – that drew girls into joining the BDM, while nonetheless stressing the power of the organization's underlying system of values, its grammar of belonging. Nazism's societal norms and expectations became textured into everything the BDM *did* as well as into the formal rhetoric of its public influence so that the extraction of loyalty from its members resulted in a culture of obedience and conformity that appeared "to be passively tolerated" while being, in fact, "actively maintained."[52] That so little work has yet been done to pursue this kind of insight into the domains of specifically women's work remains extremely striking. It certainly reflects the more general recession of labor history and social-historical interest in the working class during the past several decades, a neglect further reinforced by the general migration of interest toward the war years, where the overwhelming bulk of the new scholarship, including those studies seeking an everyday-life or micro-historical perspective, concentrates on the various categories of foreign and coerced laborers, rather than the German-ethnic "core" of the working class *per se*.[53] At this stage we know far more about the everydayness of the camps and the killing fields than the workplace relations in industry.

In seeking to bring everyday experience and state-political action into closer reciprocal alignment, we can find some vital help by going back in time slightly to treatments of World War I.[54] Proceeding from the complex interrelations linking the character of wartime labor markets, the distribution of shortages, the pressures of family survival strategies, and the impact of state intervention, for example, Ute Daniel sought to show how the "thoughts and behavior of anonymous, unorganized masses of people" could help shape "the development of political structures" by exploring "how far and under what circumstances everyday ways of thinking [could] develop political force." Conversely, "working-class women's life-world relations, whether they concerned wage work or housework, women's familial situation or their political consciousness and activity, cannot be analyzed without considering the state's labor-market and rationing policy, demographic structural data, hypotheses about patterns of collective behavior, and so forth."[55] The key is to be able to move back and forth between these different levels or regions of analysis – from the structure of the wartime labor markets to the policy-making processes of government and army, from the administrative and social-policy consequences of labor mobilization to the demographics of family life, from issues of sexuality and the raising of children to the question of rationing and strategies of subsistence – for it is only then that popular attitudes toward the war can properly be grasped. By studying the complex transmissions and mediations among each of these areas, especially the experiential and the structural, we might bring the limits and possibilities of working women's agency better into view.

Nazi dilemmas in organizing the industrial labor markets of the late 1930s were not only anticipated by this earlier experience but directly influenced by its legacies. Thus, the highly visible infusion of women into previously male jobs in the metalworking and chemicals sectors so crucial to the war effort after 1914 was only accomplished by drawing women who were already employed in services and elsewhere in industry, so that the main effect of the war was rather a syphoning of female labor from some sectors to others. The real *growth* in women's employment actually occurred not in the factories but inside the household in the form of homework. Either way, the war mainly confirmed a pre-established trend toward increased women's employment, which was well under way before 1914. It was also resumed after 1918, while the recruitment of women into metalworking was equally suddenly reversed, so that in the longer haul the war had produced more of a temporary distortion. At the same time, the real novum was a highly intrusive turn to intervention on the part of the civilian and military arms of the state in relation to labor, which created a range of new capacities and expectations, with associated implications across a much wider spectrum of social policies. At the core of this process was the crucial Patriotic Auxiliary Service Law of December 1916. It was the fallout surrounding this centerpiece of the drive for "total" mobilization that suggests an especially interesting set of continuities with the predicament faced later by the Nazis.[56]

Two years into the war, it had become clear to the military high command, given the army's escalating needs for manpower at the front, that the key to mobilizing labor effectively for the war effort was now the recruitment of women. After the corporative opening toward the SPD-aligned Free Trade Unions, the furthest-reaching aspects of the official discussion of the new law concerned the resulting tortuous back-and-forth around the implications of bringing women *en masse* into the workforce. As later under Nazism, major anxieties attended the presumed disturbances for normal family life that such an increase in women's employment was expected to bring. As one key statement of the military Supreme Command (OHL) put it: "After the war, we will need the woman as spouse and mother." "For the development of our people *after* the war," it continued, "healthy social conditions, i.e. in the first place the protection of the family, are necessary."[57] Thus, the prospect of women's mobilization brought trepidation from the start. Several months later, in March 1917, a representative for the Imperial Office of the Interior found "something disturbing about this entire development." Seeing "women in armaments factories, driving coaches, and cleaning the streets" destabilized the norms of sexual difference. As the same government spokesman put it, "through the employment of women in male occupations, the entire female organism and the entire female sensibility are being pushed down other paths." Consequently, it was not just in the interest of male workers but for the "good of the people" (*im Interesse unseres Volkswohls*) that this be a strictly temporary state of affairs.[58]

To manage the feared disruptions, women's employment was surrounded with a new apparatus of welfare, coordinated through a Women's Department and Women's Labor Office attached to the new War Office created in November 1916. Nurseries were established; women munitions workers were given readier access to food; social workers were used to assist working women with their family obligations, notably via the new figure of the factory nurse or "company housewife," whose brief extended across both workplace and home. This new machinery of social policy was explicitly double-edged. On the one hand, it was the necessary substitution for female conscription. Once the option of full-scale compulsory mobilization was rejected, that is, women's recruitment into industry had to presume this kind of systematic social support. As Marie-Elisabeth Lüders, the future liberal parliamentarian and first head of the Women's Department, put it:

> The conditions under which women live and work are by Nature indissolubly linked, and this means that … any attempt to recruit women by force in an emergency stands no chance of success … Introducing compulsory

> recruitment is bound to fail because of the physiological, psychological, and sociological limitations of female life, and whoever tries to enforce demands which are impossible by their very nature can only be repaid by defeat.

Laden with ideology, this statement nonetheless captured the practical constraints of women's increasingly complex and arduous family burdens. As Daniel remarks, "Lüders believed that ways and means had to be found that took these limitations of women's lives into account – and that this would lead directly to a social policy tailored specifically to the needs of women and families."[59]

On the other hand, though, such social policy had a necessary *disciplinary* purpose. It was meant to manage and neutralize as far as possible the disruptive effects of women's mobilization on the "healthy" social relations the family was responsible for organizing. The degree to which wartime conditions were tearing apart the social fabric cannot be exaggerated. By 1916 two-thirds of adult males aged 18 to 45 were under uniform and away from home; varying by region, "30 to 65 percent of fathers, teachers, policemen, judges, and youth workers were conscripted"; and "close to half of the civilians living in Germany were under 18."[60] With fathers absent, authority visibly depopulated, schools closed, mothers at work, and young daughters running households, official fears for the family were hardly baseless. Increasingly obsessed with sexuality, criminality, and the control of youth, public policy became sucked into this vacuum in order to compensate for the suspension of "normal" family circumstances for the duration of the war:

> … it was exactly this decline in the reproductive functions of the family caused by the war, in other words the separation of many families, the decline in the birth and marriage rates and the increase in the number of women who no longer lived with a husband or other family members … that moved those aspects of human coexistence previously situated in the context of the family into the arena of public interest, where they were then defined as symptoms of a crisis affecting the entire society.[61]

This moral crisis in the family's normalizing functions incited the state toward an expanding inventory of regulative concerns, whose urgency long outlasted the war years. Transmuted beneath Weimar's liberalized public sphere and permissive cultural climate, they persisted throughout the 1920s, then to acquire virulent form under the Third Reich. In the immediate terms of 1916 to 1917, these were specifically keyed to the wartime, but *mutatis mutandis* they defined a vital space of governmentality for the longer term: interruption of sexual relations within marriage and its consequences for fertility and family formation; prostitution at home and at the front; sexually transmitted disease; control of the independent sexuality of women; the general discourse of sexual danger flourishing so luxuriantly during the war.[62]

The flip side of this recession of reproductive functions was an equally powerful growth in the family's economic importance for the production and consumption of goods. This was a practical response to the growing pressure of shortages, the inadequacies and particular operation of the rationing system, and the effective collapse of the money economy by the winter of 1915 to 1916. It meant partly a resurgence of productive activity within the family itself, and partly an illegal consumer economy of informal barter arrangements, pilfering, and theft, and the massive turn to "hamstering" (hoarding and foraging expeditions to the countryside).[63] Immensely time consuming, these essential subsistence strategies became a powerful disincentive for women to enter industrial employment, as did the task of tracking the official distribution of goods through the rationing system. The exigencies of family survival militated consistently against the state's drive to draw women into industry. Other factors worked similarly, including the system of welfare relief instituted early in the war for so-called *Kriegerfrauen*, or "warrior wives," which might substitute for waged income, particularly when the latter involved such a loss of time. In the end, the state was compelled to acquiesce in these impediments – its tacit acceptance that working-class survival required an illegal subsistence economy largely organized by women, the countervailing effects of the welfare system for conscripts' families, and its own ideological ambivalence about mobilizing women for the war effort in the first place.[64]

This struggle for economic survival was crucial to the radicalization that eventually produced the political collapse of 1918. The state's inability to guarantee adequate supplies of food and other necessities, and its forced toleration of a system of illegal popular procurement, disastrously undermined its ability to sustain the necessary patriotic consensus (the "civic truce," or *Burgfrieden*). Even as official rhetoric continued stressing the primacy of patriotic solidarity and an implicitly egalitarian notion of sacrifice, participation, and community (*Volksgemeinschaft*), the political urgency of the food shortages opened a space, willy-nilly, where a new oppositional discourse of citizenship and sovereignty could coalesce, braced by the practical logics of negotiation and empowerment which official languages of patriotic unity had encouraged. A cumulative withdrawal of consent occurred through the everyday encounters with ineffectual authority, which in turn shifted the entire perception of the war. Such experiences were converted into oppositional sentiments via informal systems of communication which gradually amounted to a kind of alternative public sphere based in the constant crowds and queues entailed by the war – in the food lines, in railway stations, by notice boards, on foraging expeditions, and so on – together with the masses of letters that passed between women and their men at the front. Rumors and jokes proved as vital as slogans and political agitation in generating oppositional capacities. In this sense, the informal context of the everyday became the decisive terrain of popular disaffection. The focusing of the resulting conflicts around the category of the citizen-consumer inadvertently conferred a political identity and eventually a political voice on women.

Any fuller discussion of this politics of Imperial collapse in 1917 to 1918 would outgrow my present purposes, but the work of Davis, Daniel, and others makes a major contribution to our understanding of how the German Revolution was able to occur. If the state's ability to function ideologically and administratively had been fatally compromised long before the events of autumn 1918, then the response of working-class women to the war's deprivations had a key part in that process. This story vitally complements the more familiar narrative of industrial militancy, shop-floor disaffection, and working-class radicalization in industry. For women, moreover, the German Revolution registered a genuine moment of emancipation – certainly juridically, in terms of political enfranchisement and the associated constitutional freedoms under the law. The complicated dynamics of the years 1917–1918 to 1923–1924 led to outcomes with decisive bearing on the gendered dimensions of the rise of Nazism discussed earlier in this chapter. In Kathleen Canning's words, "The catastrophic conditions on the German home front and the deepening divide between militarized state and civic public opened spaces for citizenship claims that would have been unthinkable before the war." The promise of women's political equality in 1918 to 1919 was integral to the founding of the democracy that German fascism became so brutally intent on destroying. For Canning, these years "marked the period of citizenship's greatest resonance and promise, at least for the period of German history from 1848 to 1933. It might be said that citizenship became a new object of desire, a social identity Germans *wanted* or aspired to fulfill."[65] In all of these ways the relationship of everyday life to the forming of women's political identities and their relationship to political action at the level of the polity and the state has proven incredibly illuminating.

How is all of this relevant to the immediate subject under discussion, the history of women under the Third Reich? It matters because, whether under the accelerating circumstances of duress in the economy during 1936 to 1939, or in the years of wartime mobilization of the 1940s, a comparable dynamic of change, involving collective disaffection, delegitimizing of public authority, and the tottering of the state simply *did not happen*. In other words, if the analysis of everyday life during World War I can provide such illuminating access to the oppositional agency of women, why did the same process not recur, in whatever particular forms, during World War II?

At a level of compelling general explanation, we know what much of the answer will comprise. The quality, effectiveness, and scale of Nazi coercion, combined with the indelible demonstration-effects of its violence, reaching from 1933 to 1934 through 1938 to the war years themselves, dwarfed anything the Imperial state was remotely able to muster. The full and elaborate extensiveness of the machinery of the racial state, which far exceeded the penetrative reach of Wilhelmine welfarism, added further to that coercive capability. Likewise, from 1943 the effects of the bombing war imposed conditions of everydayness profoundly different from those accompanying the shortages after 1915 to 1916. My discussion in earlier chapters has also emphasized the specific forms of collective patriotism engendered so effectively by the *Volksgemeinschaft*, whose morally coercive intrusions into the local settings of ordinary life left no space for dissenting conceptions of citizenship of the kind identified by Belinda Davis and Kathleen Canning during the course of World War I. We know, from the empirical record of the wartime, no less than from the accumulated historiography, that nothing began to materialize that looked even marginally comparable to the popular democratic capacities that coalesced so impressively during 1917 to 1918.

So we would not expect the 1940s to replicate the patterns and dynamics of identity formation Davis reconstructed from the everydayness of women's experience in World War I Berlin. But research of equivalent richness and imagination should certainly give us far better access to the processes that allowed German women to go on giving the regime their positive acquiescence and even their keenness of support – that allowed them to go on behaving as Nazi subjects. Of course, as Mason long ago pointed out, the Nazis were themselves obsessed with this precedent of the previous war and the analogy with 1918 to 1919 and devoted great efforts to ensuring that things would not again fall so badly apart, which in this context meant paying primary attention to the questions of food supply and distribution on which the legitimacy of the Imperial state so disastrously foundered.[66] That attentiveness to the basics of popular consumption, a recurring concern about how far the population might be pushed before its readiness for sacrifice started to fray, remained a default reflex for the Nazi leadership during the 1930s and into the early years of the war, although once the military tide started to run against them from 1942 to 1943 the whole context of the calculus changed.[67]

But the fear of working-class disaffection, of a repetition of the debacle of morale in 1918 and the November Revolution, was not the only legacy descending from World War I. As intimated above, the entailments of the Auxiliary Labor Law of December 1916 had also produced remarkably ambitious plans for the centralized regulation of a nationally conceived labor market along with a quite new machinery of social policy provision. Under the Weimar Republic, the newly expanded welfare state then acquired an institutional architecture that was far denser than anything before, interconnected in multiple ways with the economy, for which the omnipresent discourse of "social rationalization" promised the visionary glue. Each of those arenas of the 1920s, the innovations of the welfare state and the rationalization drive, had the most far-reaching of implications for women.[68] It was this very extensiveness of the innovations, and their particular adaptations under the Third Reich, that played a big part in disorganizing the capacities available for pushing back against the regime after 1933.

Social policy, the family, and the rationalizing of private life

How should we think about Nazism's relationship to that continuously burgeoning twentieth-century context of social policy, welfare legislation, and social governmentality we call the welfare state? Everything encompassed by the theory and practice of the "racial state" supplies an unpleasant answer to this question, probably the most important one: forcible sterilization, abortion, and other aspects of reproductive health; marriage laws and other policies for the family; treatment of "asocials" and the "socially unfit"; treatment of the physically and mentally disabled; euthanasia; public health, eugenics, and "racial hygiene." Thus, the entire complex of policies devoted to securing the health of the national body (*Volkskörper*) formed the organizing core of the characteristically Nazi form of the welfare state. But around it there radiated other bodies of social legislation and governmental practice corresponding to the areas more commonly associated with welfare states elsewhere – employment (and joblessness), housing (and homelessness), poverty and poor relief, nutrition, and so forth. One older strand of historiography picks up on these areas and considers Nazi social policies for their relation to structural continuities, both earlier and subsequent, often inside an argument about longer-term modernization processes in an industrial society.[69] With this important distinction in mind – between the more generic conception of the welfare state and the Third Reich's extremely specific racialized version – I will look closely at a particular case.

If we go back to earlier moments of social policy, the gendered quality of the discourse already rises clearly from the terms of debate. Thus, while the late nineteenth-century apparatus of poor relief, charity, and social insurance may not have been formally organized around strategies of sexual difference, the discursive repertoire (including ideas of Christian responsibility, capitalist rationality, political calculation, social discipline, and national efficiency) was predicated upon gendered assumptions, particularly regarding the social importance of the family. This was true of national and local state provision, charitable work, and company-provided welfare, all of which reflected definite assumptions about what constituted orderly domestic living arrangements. From the 1890s, moreover, with the changing bases of women's work (waged and unwaged, domestic and industrial, blue and white collar), the growth of urban living and associated housing problems, the rising industrial and electoral strength of labor, and the manifold concerns of German national efficiency, the discourse of social reform became charged with new meanings, not least through the involvement of new forms of professional expertise in social policy and the complex pressure of the emergent women's movement. When we add other issues, such as child and maternal welfare, public health, policies for the control of youth, and the general regulation of morality and sexuality, all of which became increasingly central for the social-policy complex, we have a major domain of political intervention where the state and other agencies were intensively engaged. World War I brought a further concentration of activity in those directions.

The intimate connections between work and home are what concern me here – the continuous tendency of dominant social-policy discourse to collapse women's identities back into the family and its household organization of reproductive functions, even allowing for the wide variation of welfare strategies across different times and places. In the German case, the particular dynamism of pre-1914 industry, along with the exceptionally high levels of concentration in key sectors (especially heavy industry and the new electro-chemical complex), enabled unusually elaborate systems of company-based social provision compared with, say, Britain and France, which in turn allowed the preservation of certain company-based autonomies against the encroachment of government social policies. The early launching of such initiatives – involving everything from company housing, company welfare, and company stores to the organizing of company-based unions – also allows the exploring of continuities from the *Kaiserreich* to the Federal Republic across the various political caesuras of 1918, 1933, and 1945. Not least because of its liberal political affiliations during its foundation years before 1914, the major Berlin-based electro-technical concern, Siemens, provides a very good basis for exploring the intersections of racial, social, and labor policies affecting women in the specific context of the industrial firm.

A series of contrasts help to constitute the value of the Siemens example. The first is between the Wilhelmine and Weimar periods, setting the authoritarian paternalism of company welfare politics familiar before 1914, which aspired to general surveillance over the lives of the workforce by means of company unions, company stores, and the general management of social life, against the more finely tuned strategies of a firm such as Siemens after World War I. But this was also the difference between the heavy industries of the Saar and the Ruhr, which had to create industrial settlements virtually out of an empty landscape, and the electro-technical industry of Berlin, where the big-city environment created very different conditions of labor recruitment and retention, along with a much different logic of housing and other social provision.[70] Whereas coal, iron, and steel were among the pioneers of Germany's industrial transformation, thirdly, electrical engineering was the classic bearer of the so-called second industrialization in which the benefits of science, sophisticated mechanization, marketing strategies, and a more finely specialized division of labor formed the main engine of accumulation. This new industrial configuration sustained an elaborate and highly creative discourse of organizational innovation focused on maximizing the efficiencies the new technical advances allowed, and it was here that the characteristic Weimar discourse of "rationalization" became inscribed.

Rationalization in this context meant modernization of the labor process and its technology for the purposes of fine tuning worker productivity, a language of improvement centered on the idea of a production "flow." For this purpose, the "human factor" was a major complication, and a key element in the associated labor policies became the management of worker attitudes and behavior to avoid interruptions and inefficiencies in the production process. As one Siemens director put it in 1941: "Industrial technology is realized in industrial plants. An industrial plant may in turn be regarded as the place where two flows merge: a flow of people and a flow of goods … If an industrial enterprise is to thrive, these two flows must never be interrupted."[71] This wholly instrumentalized conception of workers' relationship to production translated into an elaborate machinery of testing, evaluation, and supervision for regulating workers' performance: physical and psychological aptitude testing of individual workers (from IQ to vision, dexterity, reflexes, health, and highly specific factors such as hand moisture); timekeeping studies; measurement of behavior against the technical requirements of machinery, workshop, and plant; careful attention to plant hygiene and workers' health; meticulous cost-accounting; and the grounding of managerial strategy in the collection of statistics. The resulting "science of work" then allowed the authority structures, promotion tracks, and especially the wages system and bonus schemes, as well as the technical organization of the work, to be managed to maximum efficiency. Much less calculable, of course, was what happened off the job, and it is here that we need to move from work to the wider social policy domain.[72]

Here the Siemens strategy became highly specific in ways that projected a paradigmatic "modernity," in Carola Sachse's account. By contrast with the heavy industrial paternalism of the period before 1914, where capital aspired to regulate the private sphere and the social life of its workers through a system of direct control, Siemens developed a mixed model of public and company-based social provision. In a sense, the ideological resistance to basic social democratic ideas – namely, trade unionism and the beginnings of a welfare state – was becoming less important for the company after 1918 than the "depoliticized" and consensual acceptance of efficiency (*Leistung*) as the primary goal of managerial politics: so long as public agencies, including even the trade unions and Social Democratic leisure organizations, were promoting values conducive to a culture of productivity among the working class (sobriety, orderly family living, healthy lifestyles, the desire to get on in the world, and self-motivated discipline), the question of controlling one's labor force politically was becoming far less crucial. There were indications of this before 1914. Thus, although Siemens actually pioneered company unionism before 1914, in a confrontation with the SPD union in 1905 that successfully broke the latter's strength in the firm, this was aimed specifically at containing strikes, and management appeared to feel no compulsion to contest the SPD's influence more generally – for example, in the areas of recreation and sports. Thus, the company was able to abandon its own "yellow" organization (company union) very easily in 1918, once the corporative Central Working Agreement (*Zentralarbeitsgemeinschaft*) between the unions and big employers seemed to guarantee the stable industrial relations that Siemens above all required.

In effect, Siemens pursued a "social-policy dual strategy," a division of labor with the state, in which public provision of general welfare allowed a clearer definition of the realistic extent of company-provided benefits. This was perhaps clearest in the ruthlessly individualizing personnel policy which rejected notions of the family wage based on the male worker's marital status and number of children in favor of strictly applied criteria of "scientifically" measured individual efficiency and productivity. It was the state's business to provide support for the citizenry at large within the limits of its political and fiscal capacities; the company's priority was to focus on its own workers, sorting them out into labor units of higher and lower value according to the best available scientific techniques. Moreover, the relentless productivism of Siemens's internal social policy was also calculated to identify a very specific group of employees as the real beneficiaries of company largesse – namely, "skilled workers employed in machine assembly and work preparation, plant engineers and other specialists," who in effect constituted the stable core of particularly valuable workers whom the company wanted to bind to itself for the longer term.[73] Sachse uses housing as a telling example to this effect because (again by contrast with the company housing of the Ruhr before 1914) only small numbers of company apartments were actually built (only 2,900 for the 85,000 employees who worked in Berlin-Siemensstadt by 1939, or enough for only 3.4 percent of the total workforce), and these were offered at non-subsidized market rents; in practice, they were reserved for important employees "to live in the vicinity of the plant and be on constant call to deal with disruptions of the 'production flow' as they arose."[74]

One of the key characteristics of these particularly valued employees was that they were all *men*. There was certainly no feminization of the Siemens workforce. During the 1920s and 1930s, the overall gender distribution remained remarkably constant – some 47 percent male blue-collar, 23 percent female blue-collar, 25 percent male and 5 percent female white-collar – and it was only in exceptional times, during the two World Wars and the depth of the Depression, that the proportions changed, with numbers of women increasing in wartime, male white-collars growing at the expense of blue-collar men in the Depression.[75] Moreover, in the "selection of human material," women were consistently treated as marginal. They were essentially excluded from the rewards system by specifically female wage categories at the bottom of the scale; and this practice was pioneered in the salary designations for the newly important female white-collar labor that outlasted the end of World War I. In practice, women's access to the rewards of the industrial *Leistungsgesellschaft* ("efficiency society") came only through marriage, "mediated by the successful career of the husband."[76] Indeed, the non-working wives, mothers, and daughters of male Siemens employees could expect far more such rewards than "their working sisters who had no husband, father or son in the company."[77]

Through this hierarchy, women employees were effectively erased as a visible and independent agency in the company culture. This was very striking in the case of factory social work, which had emerged in World War I as a distinctive field of women's activity, for while this figured heavily in Siemens's general managerial strategy, the factory nurses became formally subordinated to the male heads of the new Social Policy Department in the reorganization of the early 1920s. The latter certainly had a key part in company policy and was the main vehicle of its influence on the mass of the workforce, as opposed to the privileged core of employees serviced by the wages policy and benefit schemes. But the presence of women as the functionaries of this new social work activity had little effect on the prevailing norms of women's subordination. Moreover, the productivist logic of factory social policy stopped the latter short of maternity policies and any measures for the protection of pregnant workers and mothers. Thus, quite aside from the systematic downgrading of women employees, factory social policy lacked all enabling effects for women even in the conservative sense of the validation of motherhood and domesticity. Such an approach was simply not functional for the efficiency-related goals of the company, and while the housewife performed valuable reproductive labor, this was strictly ancillary to the main productivist ideology then organizing the company culture.

Having said this, the "rationalization of private life" was a key motif of company thinking. Company spokesmen, including Carl Friedrich von Siemens himself, had publicly expounded the belief since 1917 "that the efficiency of labor inside the factory and the living arrangements outside the factory are closely connected together," and careful attention was paid to keeping them in productive alignment.[78] Siemens used "all kinds of measures to secure definite forms of family life among its employees, promoting some types of social behavior, and opposing others." The aim was "to 'rationalize' the family as the workshop in which labor power was produced." "Factory family policy was the means for institutionally combining the familial production and factory consumption of labor power under the reign of modern management."[79] Great effort was spent on promoting "healthy" attitudes to the physical and psychic needs of work. Health education and rational recreation were to produce a developed sense of "self-responsibility" via an ideological apparatus of factory nurses and company doctors, counseling and home visits, recreational opportunities, the company newspaper, the library, lectures, and classes. Once again, core material provision, whether in company housing, access to the rest homes, or the main use of cultural and sporting facilities, tended to be reserved for the favored core of (male) officials, engineers, and skilled workers. But the propaganda effect was much wider. The factory should provide a "model of hygienic living for after the work is done." This was the larger challenge for management:

> The individual's organization of non-work time into sleeping, eating, and travel to and from work, together with nutrition, clothing, and housing arrangements, were all taken to be relevant factors for the politics of production, even though their extra-factory location made them harder for the company to influence.[80]

The priorities of Siemens's rationalizing strategy were brought sharply into focus during the Nazi time, when parts of the party-state, specifically the German Labor Front (DAF) as opposed to the Ministry of Labor and agencies more attuned to the autonomous needs of capital, developed an aggressively aggrandizing strategy for uniting state and company social policy on the racialist basis of the *Volksgemeinschaft*. Sachse provides an excellent analysis of the resulting tensions. On the one hand, the whole ideology and apparatus of testing and "selection" entailed by the "science of work" was quite compatible with the goals and practice of Nazi racial politics, and in some ways the respective values were fully continuous with one another. The stress on physical and psychic health, the measurement of skills and innate aptitudes, the assessment of working-life expectancy and the capacity for efficiency, the encouragement of desires for advancement – all of these implied notions of human and social value that aligned very well with the Nazi pursuit of "joy in work," as did the stress on domestic hygiene and the reproductive importance of orderly family life. To this extent, Sachse's treatment of the discursive relations among work, family, housing, and home makes an important case for seeing Nazism's continuity with the "normal" logics of pre-Nazi life.[81]

The convergence was also apparent during the war when Siemens began participating in the system of forced foreign labor, including the slave labor of the concentration camps, whose deployment was in many ways an extreme version of the technocratic instrumentalizing of labor power that the company's productivism had been applying since the 1920s. Relative to their extra-factory living circumstances, coerced workers were sometimes the beneficiaries of the factory's internal regime of hygienic order. From the company's point of view, the use of slave labor had some dysfunctional consequences for the ideal of continuous production flow, not least because of minimal training times and standards of health and nutrition the company recognized for workers to reach their optimal productivity. However, proceeding on the basis of the expendability of some categories of labor power was a logical development of the company's established practices, and Siemens's behavior during the war is another example of industry's remarkably consistent facility in accommodating Nazism. At the very least, the Siemens tradition was consistent with much of wartime experience and in itself gave no principled basis for opposing the forced labor system. As Sachse laconically remarks:

> At the very bottom of the factory ... hierarchy were the male and female workers from the concentration camps. Under the conditions of National Socialism, once their health was so badly destroyed by the hardships in the plant and all the other chicaneries that they could no longer manage the demands of the work, they were delivered up to the extermination apparatus of the SS. How strongly the firm of Siemens opposed this situation cannot be reconstructed from the available documents.[82]

On the other hand, the social-policy program of the DAF did create serious tensions. Aspiring to general competence for social-policy matters in industry, the DAF began a campaign in 1933 to secure this influence by appointing social workers in the factories themselves, recruited from the internal workforce and directly responsible to itself. Not surprisingly, major companies like Siemens resisted such a move: it threatened to disturb an existing system of company-internal social policy, replacing professionally trained social workers responsible to management with women from the shop floor appointed, paid, and instructed by the DAF. Even more, it intruded a set of inappropriate ideological goals that were external to the efficiency-oriented content of the existing productivism that the rationalization drives of the 1920s had put into place. This was especially true of the central theme of DAF propaganda in this respect – namely, the importance of women to the racially constructed ideal of the *Volksgemeinschaft* in their primary identity as mothers, for the resulting stress on "racial hygiene" worked directly counter to the Siemens tradition of social policy, which had addressed the family as the modular unit for the renewal of labor power rather than as the object of population policies in the maternalist sense.

This conflict, which was regulated in an agreement of December 1935 between industry and the DAF, but which resurfaced in a variety of ways during the life of the Third Reich, allows Sachse to typologize what were in effect two variants of social rationalization: the productivist model exemplified by Siemens, and the broader population-oriented social policy, which in the DAF case was also linked to the Nazis' overall racialist project. In the first case, we have the two-child nuclear family centered on the housewife. Functionally speaking, its purpose was the renewal of the husband's labor power, and company social policy was to shape its internal regime to this end, focusing on the identity of company and family interests vested in the husband's career. In the second case was the large and racially pure family with at least four children:

> In this family it was not the modern housewife, but the 'racially conscious mother,' who owed allegiance to the state and the *Volksgemeinschaft*, rather than to her husband. The Labor Front, together with other Nazi institutions, carried out a policy of simultaneously biologizing the family and politicizing the relationships between its members. The tendency of such a policy was to disintegrate the family as a social unit by atomizing the family and ranking each of its members in the German "community of efficiency and performance" (*Leistungsgemeinschaft*) according to race and mastership. They were recruited as individuals into age and sex specific mass organizations and were sworn into the *Volksgemeinschaft* and so were made into objects of state politics.[83]

To some extent, the outcome of this conflict followed practical lines. The DAF strategy, which targeted women *in* the workplace, was realized best in small and medium-sized firms with a mainly female labor force, producing a total of some 3,000 workplace-recruited social workers by 1943. In the bigger companies, in contrast, where numbers of women workers (as in mining and other parts of heavy industry) were often very low, management could resist the DAF with greater success: as the social work efforts would be forced outside the factory gates, a company such as Siemens could claim that its provision was already very good, and the claims of the DAF to competence could be more effectively fought.

In all of these ways the case of Siemens seems excellently suited for a post-Foucauldian analysis. In its several variants, factory-based social work clearly offered a site for the deployment of norms and values increasingly postulated for the family across a spectrum of the new human sciences by different schools of psychologists, in particular. Families were being "policed" in the sense intended by Jacques Donzelot – that is, precisely *not* via the coercive imposition of conformity using the threat of penalties or reprisals (unless, of course, the women concerned should transgress some other part of the Third Reich's penal code).[84] Rather, the normality envisaged by the new expertise would be secured by producing mothers who themselves would actively desire hygienic homes, well-ordered households, and healthy, efficiently nourished children. In the Siemens conception, the familial ideal could succeed only "to the extent that it managed to solicit the active engagement of individuals in the promotion of their own bodily efficiency."[85] The

Siemens experts sought to implant in their family subjects a set of expectations about the character of a successful domestic sphere, images that were likewise always keyed to perceptions of reward. Such families were encouraged "to govern their intimate relations and socialize their children according to social norms," but their means of doing so involved self-monitoring and self-activation based on cultivating "their own hopes and fears." Women should become the technicians of their own familial competence: "Parental conduct, motherhood, and child rearing can thus be regulated through family autonomy, through wishes and aspirations, and through the activation of individual guilt, personal anxiety, and private disappointment."[86]

Yet, in the actual day-to-dayness of their working and family lives, the Siemens women, whether workers themselves or workers' wives, encountered far more than the Siemens managers, social workers, industrial psychologists, testers, and psychotechnicians alone. They also dealt with neighbors, friends, workmates, other family members, and the often relentless attentions of the various agencies of the Nazi state, including those of the organization with its own interest in molding the working environment – namely, the DAF. Ordinary life is never without its various forms of rockiness even under the most stable and harmonious of political conditions, after all, whether these come from social problems, marital or parental crises, neighborhood tensions, or the sheer arduousness of balancing work and home. Beneath the added hardships, massive uncertainties, palpable violence, and spectacular politics of the years from 1930, even allowing for the partial hiatus of 1936 to 1938, this was even more likely to be true, especially given the relentlessly hortatory pressures coming from the Nazi regime. For some of the time these different parts of life may have worked harmoniously together. But what if they did not? How would a young woman living in Berlin-Siemensstadt with relatives in the SPD or KPD, with deep religious convictions, with a desire for education, with professional aspirations, or simply with a yen for the ideals of sexual freedom and feminine independence associated with the New Woman cope with the resulting tensions, whether *en route* to full adulthood or after the presumptive arrival in marriage?[87]

The point here is not to imply some hitherto unacknowledged or underappreciated space of "resistance," although we might certainly anticipate finding traces of Broszat's *Resistenz* or Mason's "opposition," no less than the complex patterns of socialization Reese reported from the BDM. Given the general balance sheets of complicity and acquiescence, the predominant story was clearly one of accommodation, however discomforting, tortuous, unfinished, and even jagged the details may have been. Yet, exactly in such details will the important illuminations be found. Faced with Nazism's attested success – its ability, beyond the brute facts of coercion and violence, to go on renewing its support – we need to know as much as possible about how, amid the practice of ordinary living, the work of continuing to produce Nazi subjects could be accomplished. How, under such circumstances, did women negotiate or handle the relays between the various parts of their lives? In Sachse's telling, women were caught in a permanently incomplete process of mediation, oscillating back and forth between familial values and the demands of work (including its demands on reproduction), in a process that asked them "to bridge the unbridgeable … and, by 'swinging' between the spheres, to internalize real contradictions subjectively, and day by day to discover 'new resolutions'."[88] However extensively or efficaciously it may have been practically realized, the Siemens model of the mobility-oriented nuclear family projected a discursive space of enormous continuing resonance and power: "comprising a skilled worker risen to plant engineer, a hygiene-conscious wife, a boy in whose education a maximum of money and effort was invested, and a decently educated daughter who worked in the office until marriage, with well-groomed, discreetly fashionable appearance."[89] The micro-historical settings of the workplace, as Alf Lüdtke has shown, offer opportunities for close readings of workers' attitudes and behavior that revealed fascism's ability to turn the best impulses and satisfactions to its purpose. Next to the "honor of labor" (*Ehre der Arbeit*), the "honor of family" should now have its turn.

Women activists and the making of Nazi subjects

What about those women who were avowedly Nazi in their convictions and loyalties, the Nazi women activists themselves? This is in itself a capacious and variegated category. It comprises most obviously those women who took leadership roles in the various organizations, from the NSF and BDM, through the Women's Bureau, the Reich Mothers' Service, and League of Schoolgirls (*Nationalsozialistischer Schülerrinnenbund*), to the numbers of women who took paid or voluntary positions in the Third Reich's charitable and welfare agencies and those considerable numbers who worked in jobs and professions actively promoting a Nazi outlook. Thus, Dagmar Reese suggests a fourfold working typology for the leadership group of the BDM in these regards, with the first category comprising the politically conscious adherents or activists as such. The second contingent comprised those girls who were primarily concerned with maintaining some aspect of their social standing; the third were the rebels reacting against family and home; and the fourth were the opportunists and straightforward social climbers. The positive attractions of joining were usually real enough, but in each case the proximate reasons were as much to do with personal or private motives of one kind or another. But as Reese also goes on to argue, the greatest efficacy may have come from the cumulative and habituated dailiness of everything that becoming a loyally active member entailed. That was most likely to be true where the young women were being enlisted in idealistic service for the *Volksgemeinschaft*.[90]

The complexities emerge in compelling detail from the circumstances of the young German women recruited during the war into lower-grade and ground-level professionalized service work in the Nazi-occupied East. Here the social history of Nazi expansionism into the eastern borderlands may be used to examine the forms and meanings of female participation in Nazi policies with particular concreteness.[91] The women concerned were activists: teachers in elementary schools and kindergartens, school assistants, "settlement advisers," and functionaries in Nazi auxiliary organizations like the BDM, as well as students posted to the East in their summer vacations.[92] Most were in their 20s when they volunteered or were sent off to occupied Poland, although the Nazi officials might often be somewhat older, such as two of the cases cited by Elizabeth Harvey, one a university-educated press officer for the NSF and the other a full-time BDM leader, each of whom were in their 30s. Among the youngest were the 19- and 20-year-old trainee-teachers assigned to village schools in the Polish general-government or the new Reich provinces of the Warthegau and Danzig-West Prussia. While considerably far from the Eastern Front until the last year of the war, these young women had ample chance to experience the building of the Nazi New Order in all its ruthless brutality, particularly in the Zamosc area to the southeast of Distrikt Lublin, where the SS leader Odilo Globocnik unleashed a notably vicious program of Germanization. While responsible directly for the schooling, welfare, and advising of the ethnic German settlers, female activists necessarily joined in the dispossession and continuing persecution of the indigenous Polish population, who, of course, included a high proportion of Jews.[93]

To become fully intelligible these young women's experience and expectations require the layered context of earlier designs for "Germanizing" the so-called eastern borderlands as they cascaded downwards from the later nineteenth century and World War I. Thus, Harvey shows first how patriotic women found a place in the radical-nationalist public sphere of the Weimar Republic by committing themselves to the "womanly" tasks of child welfare, pedagogy, and charitable work; then how the Nazis appropriated "women's borderland activism" after 1933; and finally how women became recruited for actual deployment in the East after 1939. At one level, the settlement programs in occupied Poland provided young women in the feminized lower-status professions of teaching, childcare, and social work with some limited but significant outlets for occupational advancement. But at another level, this promise of bettering their lives was profoundly infected by the terms of the Nazis' racial-political project. Recruitment to the East endowed these young women with a distinctive place in the nation. It offered a rhetorically prestigious future as the missionaries of a culturally superior "Germanness," in this case aimed not at civilizing a conquered and exploited native people out of its ascribed savagery and backwardness, but at molding an ethnic German population into its new destiny as the master race. Composed both from the established German-speaking residents of prewar Poland and from the new colonists transplanted from elsewhere in Eastern Europe, including Bessarabia, Galicia, Bukovina, Dobrujda, Volhynia, and the Baltic, and precariously instated in these vulnerable outposts of the *Volksgemeinschaft*, the ethnic Germans now needed to be carefully fortified in their imputed sense of "greater German" belonging.

As Harvey says, the women recruited for this purpose approached the East as either a strange and "uncanny space" or a reclaimed "German homeland."[94] They were deployed mainly as "settlement advisers," in schooling, and in early childcare.[95] Their subjectivities were shaped by mixtures of naïve career-mindedness, ingrained racism, hapless idealism, and practical complicity in Nazi crimes. As the first study of eastward expansionism centrally focused on women's involvement, Harvey's account brings into sharp particular focus the question of German responses to the racialized maltreatment of the regime's many categories of enemies, in this case posed all the more starkly by the extremes of the maltreatment meted out to the non-German inhabitants of occupied Poland. Those day-to-day actualities of the German presence incorporated all the most vicious practices of a conquering and colonizing power: the systematic and peremptory violating of rights; the endemic seizures of property, land, and goods; assaults on indigenous cultural practices and institutions; callous and self-righteous disregard not only for the accumulated conventions of civility, but even for the most elementary human decencies; the forced dispossession and deportation of local populations; and, of course, the everyday machinery of physical violence, killing, and mass murder associated with the Nazi New Order in the East. The German women enlisted into this effort on the ground, however naïve or consciously "non-political" their self-descriptions or later protestations, simply could not have failed to be complicit. Though not directly involved in the fighting on the Eastern Front (or in the killing operations of Christopher Browning's "ordinary men"), these female auxiliaries of Germanization did their bit for the appalling accomplishments of racialized exploitation, imperialist expansion, and genocidal killing just as surely as the enlisted men of the army. In that sense, Harvey's book forms an essential companion study to the growing volume of scholarship on the "crimes of the *Wehrmacht*."[96]

At the same time, there was much that might still sustain misgivings. The ambivalence emerged clearly from the diary kept by "Frieda Hagen," the 29-year-old director of the school for village advisers opened by the NSF in the General Government in December 1943. Located in Zamosc County, at the storm center of Globocnik's resettlement drive (which altogether displaced over 100,000 Poles from 300 villages), this school implemented its charge amid hostile territory subject to inadequate resources, bureaucratic arbitrariness and indifference, and widening partisan attacks. Even as "the military situation was turning her rural refuge into an outpost under siege," Hagen continued sustaining "her belief in Germany and the German cause while becoming increasingly outraged by the occupation regime and its Party and SS representatives." Regardless of this practical disillusionment, her idealism in the cause *per se* remained: Nazi officialdom was at fault, betraying the settlers' trust and driving the Poles into resistance. The SS undermined all the other good work: "There were decent Germans who strove to create a viable relationship with the colonized population, but the regime, embodied above all in the SS, vandalized and destroyed the basis of such relationships, starving and oppressing the Poles and driving them … to attack German villagers."[97] But actual fellow feeling for the Poles, let alone for the Jews, was never allowed to be posed.

This self-deceiving dialectic of idealism and unease set the common pattern for how these young women responded to what they encountered in the Nazi East. The same also held good for how they processed those experiences after the war, tracked by Harvey through the substantial memoir literature as well as by means of her 16 elaborate interviews.[98] In that respect, Harvey's subjects were a very specific contingent among the more than 12 million German-speakers who later fled or were expelled from Eastern Europe in the wake of the end of the war and its aftermath. Those numbers undoubtedly included masses of the so-called *Volksdeutsche* (ethnic Germans) from the Baltic states, eastern Poland, the Balkans, and the Soviet Union, numbering over half a million, whom the Third Reich had resettled in occupied Poland during 1939 to 1941; and the women auxiliaries of the Nazi occupying administration also joined the legions of officials, professionals, civilian employees, and camp followers who either fled the Red Army's advance or were eventually repatriated.[99] As such, they had much in common with the French, British, Dutch, and Belgian officials, commercial employees, and settlers who were repatriated from Africa, South Asia, and Southeast Asia during the decolonizations of the 1950s.

Indeed, Nazi eastward expansion may be linked more generally to comparative studies of colonialism. It implies no diminishment of the peculiar enormity of the genocidal war against the Jews and other peoples to show the important planes of equivalence linking the Nazi New Order in the East with the colonizing practices of European powers elsewhere in the world, not least – for our present purposes – because of the cultural centrality ascribed to women in the so-called "civilizing mission." For the effort at implanting a "German culture" in the occupied East entailed not only the population policies of uprooting and mass murder, resettlement and dispossession, together with the usual machinery of language policies, schooling, and the celebration of an invented German customary culture. This "Germanization" drive also embraced a wider social program of housewifery, domestic hygiene, and orderly family life, for which the generations of girls and young women socialized during the 1930s provided the necessary cadres of teachers, social workers, instructors in domestic science and mothercraft, volunteers, and role models needed in order to socialize the local ethnic-German populace into the ideals required by the *Volksgemeinschaft*.

As Ann Stoler and others have made clear in the contexts of overseas Western European colonialism, the exclusionary boundaries so essential to the securities and stabilities of European colonial rule rested on elaborately administered codes of racial superiority, for which the Nazis' eastern imperium offers an accelerated, overheated, short-lived, and exceptionally brutal illustration. For the purposes of constructing and maintaining the necessary systems of distinction, those codes always made domesticity and the intimacies of private life essential: that is, matters of marriage, courtship, and cohabitation; sexuality and intimate relations, especially prostitution; child-raising and education; the role of native servants; in general, the orderly management of households. When the boundaries were transgressed via *métissage* or miscegenation, the mixing of race, the resulting affront "challenged middle-class family order and racial frontiers, norms of childrearing and conjugal patriarchy, and made it increasingly difficult to distinguish between true nationals and their sullied pseudo-compatriots."[100] For sustaining the *moral integrity* of colonial rule in this sense, women became crucial. It was by means of their decorum, their personalities, and their bodies that the boundaries could be marked. But women were not only policed by the norms and expectations of colonial rule. They were also the active agents of its reproduction. *That* was the dualism the young women recruited into the Nazi occupying administration inhabited only too well.

Finally, these youthful missionaries of the *Volksgemeinschaft* return us to the questions where this chapter began. I have tried throughout the preceding discussion to hold in fruitful tension two complementary understandings of ideology – one focusing on Nazism's big ideas, the driving motivations of Hitler and other key figures, and the movement's programmatic goals; the other looking for the practical and material ground – in social relations, institutional settings, cultural practices, concrete events – where such ideas became translated into action, where their meanings had to be negotiated, their contradictions managed, and their efficacies secured. In assessing the character of Nazism's popular appeal – its "interpellative capacities," in Dennis Sweeney's formulation – I have also weighed the material conditioning and structural circumstances that both shaped the strength of the appeal and disposed the potential constituencies toward various kinds of opposition, acquiescence, indifference, or support. In that respect, the welfare complex of social policies focused on workplace and family, whether managed by the state or by the exceptional resources of a large private company such as Siemens, revealed a great deal about women's political agency quite beyond Gisela Bock's somewhat monofocal stress on anti-natalism as the regime's primary way of relating to women.[101] In their varying ways both Carola Sachse and Elizabeth Harvey show how the primacy of motherhood stressed by Claudia Koonz might become translated into a social program of activist engagement *in* society, in the interest of social governmentality and its political pedagogies, rather than *only* fortifying the family's protective functions as the proverbial "haven in a heartless world."[102] Dagmar Reese's pioneering account of what drew girls into becoming activists in the BDM also goes beyond the dichotomous framework of the Bock–Koonz polemic (anti-natalism *versus* pro-natalism, family destruction *versus* family welfare) by suggesting registers of female independence beyond a straightforward familialism altogether.

Work of this kind on women under Nazism can help our understanding of the big question running through this book – namely, the nature of the shifting and permeable boundary between the dyed-in-the-wool Nazis themselves (Hitler, Himmler, Goebbels, and the other national leaders, the wider networks of the highest leadership, the party ideologues and the "old fighters," and all those in the movement who were socialized consciously into its commitments and ideas) and that broader reservoir of sympathies available to be activated in society at large. For in pursuing its goals, whether during the 1930s or during the wartime, the regime *had* to presume such broader reserves of potential support. From the onslaught against opponents in the earliest days of violent and confrontational consolidation in 1933 to 1934, through the demonizing of the Jews and other enemies of the *Volk*, to the war-driven patriotism of the later 1930s, the Nazis wagered on their ability to draw upon exactly that breadth. They relied on a variety of encouraging dispositives: the positive affinities of entire political constituencies elsewhere on the right, especially those parts of the 1933 electorate still with the DNVP; the unformed idealism of younger generations; the straightforward pragmatics of the desire for a successful and secure life; last but not least, the elements in the outlook even of opponents that might be turned in their favor – sundry patriotisms, yearnings for the good life, prejudices against the Jews, fantasies of the nation, desires for the wholeness of a conflict-free social world. Essential to the Nazis' success in realizing their purposes, this kind of popular concurrence mattered as much as – probably *more* than – any focused adherence to the particularities of the doctrinal message *per se*. As I hope to have made clear, treating one as "ideology" and not the other makes no sense. It was in the *process* of producing the concurrence that ideology did its most important work.

That does not cancel or displace the questions of accommodation and complicity, but it does complicate presumptions of the transparency of women's "agency" and its ethical valence. On the one hand, Harvey shows "how and why ideas about home, family, and domestic culture came to be a crucial component of the drive to create the Nazi 'New Order' in the East," illuminating a great deal "about women and constructions of 'Germanness' as well as the place of female activism in the Nazi state and its imperialism."[103] On the other hand, though, she shows the messy combinations of idealism and pragmatics so often moving individuals on the ground – taking orders and fitting in; suspending ethical judgments under repressive duress; enjoying the challenge and adventure of the frontier; embracing the rhetorics of patriotic service and sacrifice; losing oneself in the pleasures of solidarity in the *Volksgemeinschaft*. This was the process of producing Nazi subjects. What German women thought they were doing in the East was certainly laid down for them in fundamentally prescriptive ways by the Nazi state. But the details of *how exactly* they delivered their collusion can tell us much about how fascist subjectivities could be made.

Notes

1 A. Grossmann, "Feminist Debates about Women and National Socialism, *Gender and History*, 1991, vol. 3, no. 3, p353. See A. Tröger, 'Die Dolchstoßlegende der Linken' 'Frauen haben Hitler an die Macht gebracht'," in Gruppe Berliner Dozentinnen (eds) *Frau und Wissenschaft. Beiträge zur Berliner Sommeruniversität für Frauen Juli 1976*, Berlin: Courage Verlag, 1976, pp324–55.

2 M. Stibbe, *Women in the Third Reich*, London: Arnold, 2003, p15.

3 For women in the DNVP and DVP, see R. Scheck, *Mothers of the Nation: Right-Wing Women in Weimar Germany*, Oxford: Berg, 2004, and K. Heinsohn, *Konservative Parteien in Deutschland 1912 bis 1933. Demokratisierung und Partizipation in geschlechterhistorischer Perspektive*, Düsseldorf: Droste Verlag, 2010. More generally: E. Schöck-Quinteros and C. Streubel (eds) *"Ihrem Volk verantwortlich." Frauen der politischen Rechten (1890–1933)*, Berlin: Trafo Verlag, 2007; C. Streubel, *Radikale Nationalistinnen. Agitation und Programmatik rechter Frauen in der Weimarer Republik*, Frankfurt am Main: Campus Verlag, 2006.

4 Ibid, p2. Compare this statement from an article about the main Nazi women's organization formed in 1923, the German Women's Order (*Deutscher Frauenorden*, DFO), in

Nationsozialistische Monatshefte, 1930, vol. 1, no. 1, p43, cited by C. Koonz, *Mothers in the Fatherland: Women, the Family, and Nazi Politics*, New York: St. Martin's Press, 1987, p54: "The National Socialist movement is an emphatically male phenomenon as far as the political struggle is concerned. Women in parliament are a depressing sign of liberalism. They insult feminine values by imitating men. We believe that every *genuine* woman will, in her innermost being, pay homage to the masculine principle of National Socialism. Only then will she become a total woman!" Or this one by Emma Witte, a leading DFOer, in 1924, quoted by Stibbe, *Women*, p19: "The coming racial state must be masculine – or it will not be at all!"

5 T. Mason, "Women in Germany, 1925–1940: Family, Welfare, and Work," in Caplan (ed.) *Nazism, Fascism, and the Working Class*, p156. See now K. Schmersahl, "Die Demokratie ist weiblich. Zur Geschlechterpolitik der NSDAP am Beispiel nationalsozialistischer Karikaturen in der Weimarer Republik," in G. Boukrif, C. Bruns, K. Heinsohn, C. Lenz, K. Schmersahl, and K. Weller (eds) *Geschlechtergeschichte des Politischen. Entwürfe von Geschlecht und Gemeinschaft im 19. Und 20. Jahrhundert*, Münster: Lit Verlag, 2002, pp141–74.

6 In addition to the works cited in what follows, see also R. J. Evans, "German Women and the Triumph of Hitler," *Journal of Modern History*, 1976, vol. 48, no. 1, pp123–75, revised in Evans, *Comrades and Sisters*, Brighton: Weatsheaf, 1987, pp157–95; Childers, *The Nazi Voter*, pp260, 264; Stibbe, *Women*, pp25–9, provides a helpful summary.

7 H. L. Boak, "'Our Last Hope': Women's Votes for Hitler," *German Studies Review*, 1989, vol. XII, no. 2, p304.

8 In 1925, there were 21,025,998 women aged 20 and over, as against 18,769,662 men. Thus even as female turnout dropped behind that of the men, the actual numbers of women voting might still often exceed those of men. Ibid, p291.

9 Ibid, p303.

10 Stibbe, *Women*, p28.

11 See here K. Heinsohn, "'Volksgemeinschaft' als gedachte Ordnung. Zur Geschlechterpolitik der Deutschnationalen Volkspartei," in Boukrif et al (eds) *Geschlechtergeschichte des Politischen*, pp83–106.

12 Boak, "'Our Last Hope'," p302. The Bavarian People's Party (*Bayerische Volkspartei*, BVP) was the separately constituted, predominantly agrarian, heavily clerical party that functioned effectively as the Bavarian wing of the center.

13 Ibid, also for the following phrase.

14 J. Sneeringer, *Winning Women's Votes: Propaganda and Politics in Weimar Germany*, Chapel Hill: University of North Carolina Press, 2002, p231.

15 H. Boak, "Mobilizing Women for Hitler: The Female Nazi Voter," in A. McElligott and T. Kirk (eds) *Working towards the Führer: Essays in Honor of Sir Ian Kershaw*, Manchester: Manchester University Press, 2003, p82. But see now Heinsohn, "'Volksgemeinschaft' als gedachte Ordnung."

16 Mason, "Women in Germany," p151.

17 See Boak, "'Our Last Hope'," p302: "The Nazis did not seem to have a coherent or cohesive program with regard to women's role in society."

18 Mason, "Women in Germany," pp132, 154. Disagreement with this last statement seems to have motivated Boak's own article; see Boak, "'Our Last Hope'," p302. Mason's cautious and succinct explanation remains an excellent starting point. See "Women in Germany," pp149–56.

19 Interestingly, neither of the first two events produced a published volume, an omission hardly imaginable now. The third conference resulted in T. Childers and J. Caplan (eds) *Reevaluating the Third Reich*, New York: Holmes & Meier, 1993. For an interdisciplinary conference on "Women, Fascism, and Everyday Life" at the Ohio State University in April 1983, see J. Caplan's report in *History Workshop Journal* 17, 1984, pp197–8.

20 See G. Bock, *Zwangssterilisation im Nationalsozialismus*; also Frauengruppe Faschismusforschung (ed.) *Mutterkreuz und Arbeitsbuch. Zur Geschichte der Frauen in der*

Weimarer Republik und im Nationalsozialismus, Frankfurt am Main: Fischer, 1981; M. Schmidt and G. Dietz (eds) *Frauen unterm Hakenkreuz*, Berlin: Elefanten, 1983; R. Wiggershaus, *Frauen unterm Nationalsozialismus*, Wuppertal: Hammer, 1984. Two earlier pioneers were J. Stephenson, *Women in Nazi Society*, New York: Barnes and Noble, 1975, and *The Nazi Organization of Women*, London: Croom Helm, 1981; and D. Winkler, *Frauenarbeit im "Dritten Reich,"* Hamburg: Hoffmann und Campe Verlag, 1977. See also U. Frevert, *Women in German History: From Bourgeois Emancipation to Sexual Liberation*, New York: Berg, 1989; orig. German 1986, pp205–52.

21 See R. Bridenthal, A. Grossmann, and M. Kaplan (eds) *When Biology Became Destiny*; Peukert, *Inside Nazi Germany*; Burleigh and Wippermann, *The Racial State*; R. Bridenthal and C. Koonz, "Beyond *Kinder, Küche, Kirche*: Weimar Women in Politics and Work," in B. A. Carroll (ed.) *Liberating Women's History*, Chicago: University of Chicago Press, 1976, pp301–29, revised in *When Biology Became Destiny*, pp33–65; Mason's "Women in Germany" appeared first in *History Workshop Journal*, vol. 1, 1976, pp74–113, and vol. 2, 1976, pp5–32. For the general historiographical shift, see the discussion in Chapter 2.

22 Stephenson, *Women in Nazi Society*, and *Nazi Organizatiion of Women*; also C. Koonz, "The Competition for Women's *Lebensraum*, 1928–1934," in Bridenthal, Grossmann, and Koonz (eds) *When Biology Became Destiny*, pp199–236.

23 J. Falter, *Hitlers Wähler*, Munich: Beck, 1991, p143.

24 Boak, "Mobilizing Women," p73.

25 See R. Bridenthal, "Organized Rural Women and the Conservative Mobilization of the Countryside in the Weimar Republic," in L. E. Jones and J. Retallack (eds) *Between Reaction, Reform, and Resistance: Studies in the History of German Conservatism from 1789 to 1945*, Providence: Berghahn, 1993, pp375–405, and Bridenthal, "Professional Housewives: Stepsisters of the Women's Movement," in Bridenthal, Grossmann, and Kaplan (eds) *When Biology Became Destiny*, pp153–73.

26 See A. Grossmann, *Reforming Sex*, especially ppvii–viii.

27 R. J. Evans, *The Feminist Movement in Germany 1894–1933*, London and Beverly Hills: Sage Publications, 1976, p258. For women in the DNVP and DVP, see Scheck, *Mothers of the Nation*, here pp4–5, 163; Heinsohn, *Konservative Parteien*; Schöck-Quinteros and Streubel (eds) *"Ihrem Volk verantwortlich"*; Streubel, *Radikale Nationalistinnen.*

28 Koonz, *Mothers in the Fatherland*, pp419–20.

29 See this statement by DAF head Robert Ley, quoted by Frevert, *Women*, p243: "We start when a child is three years old. As soon as he even starts to think, he's given a little flag to wave. Then comes school, the Hitler Youth, military service. But when all that is over, we don't let go of anyone. The Labor Front takes hold of them again, and keeps hold until they go to the grave, whether they like it or not."

30 See G. Bock, "Die Frauen und der Nationalsozialismus: Bemerkungen zu einem Buch von Claudia Koonz" *Geschichte und Gesellschaft*, vol. 15, 1989, pp563–79, also published in *Bulletin of the German Historical Institute, London*, 1989, vol. XI, no. 1, pp16–24. For response by Koonz, *Geschichte und Gesellschaft* 18, 1992, pp394–9, and Bock's rejoinder, "Ein Historikerinnenstreit?," ibid, pp400–4. For the elements of generational complaint, whose terms could be extremely raw, see especially L. Gravenhorst and C. Tatschmurat (eds) *Töchter-Fragen. NS-Frauengeschichte*, Freiburg: Kore, 1990. For critical commentary, see Grossmann, "Feminist Debates," to which Bock's "Ein Historikerinnenstreit?" also directly responded; von Saldern, "Victims or Perpetrators?;" D. Reese and C. Sachse, "Frauenforschung und Nationalsozialismus – eine Bilanz," in Gravenhorst and Tatschmurat (eds) *Töchter-Fragen*, pp73–106; B. Kundrus, "Frauen und Nationalsozialismus," *Archiv für Sozialgeschichte*, vol. 36, 1996, pp481–99; U. Weckel, K. Heinsohn, and B. Vogel, "Einleitung," in Heinsohn, Vogel, and Weckel (eds) *Zwischen Karriere und Verfolgung. Handlungsräume von Frauen in nationalsozialistischen Deutschland*, Frankfurt am Main: Campus Verlag, 1997, pp7–23.

31 Grossmann, "Feminist Debates," p351 (my italics).

32 G. Bock, "Antinatalism, Maternity, and Paternity in National Socialist Racism," in Crew (ed.) *Nazism and German Society*, p129.
33 Bock insists that family welfare privileged fathers rather than mothers too. See ibid.
34 Grossmann, "Feminist Debates," p352.
35 Grossmann, *Reforming Sex*, p153; also G. Czarnowski, *Das kontrollierte Paar.* In this light Bock's claim that the June 1935 amendment to the 1933 Sterilization Law sanctioning medically and eugenically indicated abortions had made abortion legal for the first time ("Abortion was now no longer prohibited") seems highly tendentious. See Bock, *Zwangssterilisation*, p99.
36 See this statement in Bock, "Anti-Natalism," p112: "the view of National Socialist gender policies as essentially consisting of 'pro-natalism and a cult of motherhood' is largely a myth." While consistent with Bock's binary framework, the use of "essentially" in this sentence is presumably meant to hedge, leaving space open for pro-natalist politics in subsidiary or less important ways.
37 By March 1939, 1.7 million women had attended 100,000 RMD courses provided across Germany; by 1938, 1.8 million had been taking the Women's Bureau courses; 25,000 advice centers had been established serving 10 million women. Frevert, *Women*, pp231–34, provides a good summary; also Stephenson, *Nazi Organization*, pp165–6, and *Women in Nazi Society*, pp45–6; S. Dammer, "Kinder, Küche, Kriegsarbeit: Die Schulung der Frauen durch die NS-Frauenschaft," in Frauengruppe Faschismusforschung (ed.), *Mutterkreuz und Arbeitsbuch*, pp215–45.
38 Frevert, *Women*, p242.
39 In illustrating the prevalence of the separate-spheres ideology, Koonz relied largely on the statements of the officials of Nazi, Protestant, and Catholic women's organizations, rather than outlook of ordinary "non-political" mothers and housewives.
40 D. Reese, *Growing up Female in Nazi Germany*, Ann Arbor: University of Michigan Press, 2006, p42.
41 Ibid, especially pp1–10, 247–51, and the following essays: D. Reese, "Emanzipation oder Vergesellschaftung: Mädchen im 'Bund Deutscher Mädel'," in H.-U. Otto and H. Sünker (eds) *Politische Formierung und soziale Erziehung im Nationalsozialismus*, Frankfurt am Main: Suhrkamp, 1991, pp203–25; Reese, "Verstrickung und Verantwortung. Weibliche Jugendliche in der Führung des Bundes Deutscher Mädel," in Heinsohn, Vogel, and Weckel (eds) *Zwischen Karriere und Verfolgung*, pp206–22; Reese, "The BDM-Generation: A Female Generation in Transition from Dictatorship to Democracy," in M. Roseman (ed.) *Generations in Conflict: Youth Revolt and Generation Formation in Germany, 1770–1968*, Cambridge: Cambridge University Press, 1995, pp227–46; also D. Reese (ed.) *Die BDM-Generation. Weibliche Jugendliche in Deutschland und Österreich im Nationalsozialismus*, Berlin: Verlag für Berlin-Brandenburg, 2007. More generally now, see especially S. Steinbacher (ed.) *Volksgenossinnen. Frauen in der NS-Volksgemeinschaft*, Göttingen: Wallstein Verlag, 2007.
42 M. Mouton, *From Nurturing the Nation*, p108.
43 See Mason, "Women in Germany."
44 "National Socialism aims to allow the German woman the opportunity to fulfill the calling that nature has given to her, namely to be a wife and mother! She has no desire to work in the factory and no desire to enter parliament. A comfortable home, a loving husband, and a multitude of happy children are much more to her taste. National Socialism will ensure that the men get jobs again so that they can establish and feed a family and so that they can rescue women from the current need to work [outside the home]." *Das ABC des Nationalsozialismus*, published in 1933, cited by Stibbe, *Women*, p84.
45 See Winkler, *Frauenarbeit*, p198. Stibbe provides an excellent analytical summary in *Women*, pp85–91. There were still key distinctions. If in 1939 "over 90 percent of all single women were in some kind of employment," then "two-thirds of married women of working age remained outside the workforce, indicating a relative (but by

no means absolute) failure to mobilize female labor in the run-up to war." The 1939 census also embraced the expanded territories of the Greater German Reich (Saarland, Austria, Sudetenland, Bohemia-Moravia), thereby somewhat inflating the contrast with 1933. Ibid, p89.

46 The population politics exemplified in Bock's study of forcible sterilization implied an additional but very different range of complications, treating the populace less for its potential sources of labor power than for its degrees of "racial" health. During the wartime, when the Nazi imperium enabled the comprehensive racializing of labor markets, these goals of the racial state very directly intersected with the efforts at mobilizing labor, further complicating and disrupting the latter. The indispensable guide is now the brilliant analysis of A. Tooze in Chapter 16, "Labor, Food, and Genocide," of his *The Wages of Destruction: The Making and Breaking of the Nazi Economy*, New York: Viking, 2007, pp513–51, which supersedes all other general accounts.

47 These three sections may be consulted in Mason, "Women in Germany," in J. Caplan (ed.) *Nazism, Fascism and the Working Class,* pp156–62, 162–78, and 178–207, respectively.

48 Ibid, p178.

49 Stibbe, *Women*, p84; Mason, "Women in Germany," p160. Mason continues: "If the question is first taken as a whole, it is evident that the Conservative, Catholic, and Nazi attack on the *regular* employment of women in general (whether married or single) was most vociferous at a time (1929–33) when women were anyway leaving the labor market in very large numbers and at a rapid pace for elementary social and economic reasons. On this broad front the anti-feminist reaction was rushing with an impressive display of virile energy through a wide-open door. Exactly the opposite was the case, however, on the narrower front that concerned *married*, economically active women, and in particular married wage-earners. Here the anti-feminist reaction found itself in head-on collision with a long-term process of social and economic change, which was drawing ever more married women into trade and industry; here paternalists, eugenist zealots, and misogynists flailed about themselves with an irrational and noisy mendacity, which was powerless to disrupt the nexus of the joint interests of employers and married women workers. The irreducible facts were that more and more married women workers were working, partly because more and more women of working age were getting married."

50 I am fully aware here of the forms and scale of dissent of various kinds that did actually happen during the war years, although disentangling the precise meanings contained in each of the available categories remains notoriously difficult. See the figures quoted in Chapter 2 for the first six months of 1943: 982 convictions for treason, with 948 executions; 8,850 Germans charged with left-wing activity, 8,727 with "resistance," and 11,075 with "opposition"; 10,773 arrested for fraternizing with prisoners of war and foreign slave laborers. See Carsten, *German Workers*, p157. By 1943, in other words, popular compliance was breaking down in all sorts of ways. My purpose is to stress the degree to which the consequences remained contained.

51 See the following essays by Alf Lüdtke: "'Formierung der Massen'"; "What Happened to the 'Fiery Red Glow'?"; "The Appeal of Exterminating 'Others'"; "Funktionseliten: Täter, Mit-Täter, Opfer?"; "'Ehre der Arbeit'"; "War as Work."

52 Reese, "Verstrickung und Verantwortung," p219. We now have the further evidence assembled in Steinbacher (ed.) *Volksgenossinnen.*

53 Neither of the major general histories, Hachtmann, *Industriearbeit im "Dritten Reich,"* and Schneider, *Unterm Hakenkreuz*, treat women workers remotely adequately. Company-based studies rarely approach the labor process and the socio-cultural dynamics of the shop floor in ways suggested by Lüdtke's work. See, for instance, B. Bellon, *Mercedes in Peace and War: German Automobile Workers, 1903–1945*, New York: Columbia University Press, 1990; N. Gregor, *Daimler-Benz in the Third Reich*, New Haven: Yale University Press, 1998; and H. Mommsen and M. Grieger, *Das*

Volkswagenwerk und sein Arbeiter im Dritten Reich, Düsseldorf: Econ, 1996, each in their respective ways really excellent. See Chapter 3, note 25.

54 See, above all, U. Daniel, *The War Within: German Working-Class Women in the First World War*, Oxford: Berg, 1997, orig. German. 1989; B. J. Davis, *Home Fires Burning: Food, Politics, and Everyday Life in World War I Berlin*, Chapel Hill: University of North Carolina Press, 2000; E. Domansky, "Militarization and Reproduction in World War I Germany," in G. Eley (ed.) *Society, Culture, and the State in Germany, 1890–1930*, Ann Arbor: University of Michigan Press, 1996, pp427–64; M. Geyer, *Verkehrte Welt. Revolution, Inflation und Moderne: München 1914–1924*, Göttingen: Vandenhoeck und Ruprecht, 1998; K. Canning, "Claiming Citizenship: Suffrage and Subjectivity in Germany after the First World War," in Canning, *Gender History in Practice: Historical Perspectives on Bodies, Class, and Citizenship*, Ithaca: Cornell University Press, 2006, pp212–37; S. Dobson, *Authority and Upheaval in Leipzig, 1910–1920: The Story of a Relationship*, New York: Columbia University Press, 2001; A. Donson, *Youth in the Fatherless Land: War Pedagogy, Nationalism, and Authority in Germany, 1914–1918*, Cambridge: Harvard University Press, 2010, pp137–53.

55 Daniel, *War Within*, p8.

56 The classic study is that of G. D. Feldman, *Army, Industry, and Labor in Germany, 1914–1918*, Providence: Berg, 1992; orig. edn, Princeton: Princeton University Press, 1966, esp. pp149–348, along with J. Kocka, *Facing Total War: German Society 1914–1918*, Leamington Spa: Berg, 1984, originally published as *Klassengesellschaft im Krieg. Deutsche Sozialgeschichte 1914–1918*, Göttingen: Vandenhoeck und Ruprecht, 1978. However, by placing women's labor and its social-policy entailments at the center, Daniel's *War Within* now supplants all earlier accounts.

57 Daniel, *War Within*, p69.

58 Ibid, p101.

59 Ibid, p76. I have slightly adjusted the Lüders translation.

60 Donson, *Youth in the Fatherless Land*, pp10–13.

61 Daniel, *War Within*, p138.

62 By taking a longer view of the first half of the twentieth century, a variety of recent works allow these questions to be engaged in the way suggested here. See A. F. Timm, *The Politics of Fertility in Twentieth-Century Berlin*, Cambridge: Cambridge University Press, 2010; V. Harris, *Selling Sex in the Reich: Prostitutes in German Society, 1914–1945*, Oxford: Oxford University Press, 2010; Mouton, *From Nurturing the Nation to Purifying the Volk*; N. R. Reagin, *Sweeping the German Nation: Domesticity and National Identity in Germany, 1870–1945*, Cambridge: Cambridge University Press, 2007; D. Herzog (ed.) *Sexuality and German Fascism*, New York: Berghahn Books, 2005; E. D. Heineman, *What Difference Does a Husband Make? Women and Marital Status in Nazi and Postwar Germany*, Berkeley: University of California Press, 1999; Grossmann, *Reforming Sex*; C. Usborne, *Cultures of Abortion in Weimar Germany*, New York: Berghahn Books, 2007, and *The Politics of the Body in Weimar Germany: Women's Reproductive Rights and Duties*, Ann Arbor: University of Michigan Press, 1992.

63 In the English edition of Daniel's book, *hamster* is translated rather oddly as "squirrel" and the practice of hoarding as "squirreling." Of course, either could be metaphorically appropriate. On the other hand, the hamster is arguably more efficient, storing food in its capacious cheeks, whereas the squirrel (*Eichhörnchen*) leaves random deposits of nuts that it commonly fails to retrieve. See Daniel, *War Within*, pp197 and 228 (note 220).

64 These paragraphs are based on Davis, *Home Fires Burning*, which meticulously charts the shifting dynamics among food, politics, and everyday life in wartime Berlin, making a brilliant case for the decisive effects of women's activism in destabilizing the legitimacy of government.

65 Canning, "Claiming Citizenship," p117.

66 See especially T. W. Mason, "The Legacy of 1918 for National Socialism," in *Social Policy in the Third Reich*, pp19–40. See also Tooze, *Wages of Destruction*, pp1–33, 513–51.

67 For Mason's reflections on what remained valid in his arguments about the severity of the Nazi dilemmas on the eve of war, including a detailed engagement with the scholarly research and debates as of the later 1980s, see his 90-page "Epilogue" in *Social Policy in the Third Reich*, pp275–369. For our intervening knowledge, see Tooze, *Wages of Destruction*, esp. pp135–65, 285–325.

68 Not accidentally, the German Women's History Study Group moved during the later 1980s quite strongly toward thematics of "modernity, gender, rationalization, and the welfare state." See A. Grossmann, "Gender and Rationalization: Questions about the German/American Comparison," *Social Politics: International Studies in Gender, State, and Society*, 1997, vol. 4, no. 1, p16. See especially Reese, Rosenhaft, Sachse, and Siegel (eds) *Rationale Beziehungen?*; T. Siegel, "It's Only Rational: An Essay on the Logic of Social Rationalization," *International Journal of Political Economy*, 1994–1995, vol. 24, no. 4, pp35–70; M. Nolan, *Visions of Modernity: American Business and the Modernization of Germany*, New York: Oxford University Press, 1994; H. Homburg, *Industriearbeit und Rationalisierung. Das Beispiel des Siemens-Konzerns Berlin 1900–1939*, Berlin: Haude and Spner, 1991; C. Sachse, *Siemens, der Nationalsozialismus und die moderne Familie*, Hamburg: Rasch und Röhring, 1990; A. Rabinbach, *The Human Motor: Energy, Fatigue, and the Origins of Modernity*, Berkeley: University of California Press, 1992, pp238–88.

69 See, in particular, L. Preller, *Sozialpolitik in der Weimarer Republik*, Düsselddorf: Droste, 1978, orig. edn. 1949; M.-L. Recker, *Nationalsozialistische Sozialpolitik im Zweiten Weltkrieg*, Munich: Oldenbourg, 1985; M. Prinz and R. Zitelmann (eds) *Nationalsozialismus und Modernisierung*, Darmstadt: Wissenschaftliche Buchgesellschaft, 1991; M. Prinz, "Wohlfahrtsstaat, Modernisierung und Nationalsozialismus. Thesen zu ihrem Verhältnis," in H.-U. Otto and H. Sünker (eds) *Soziale Arbeit und Faschismus*, Frankfurt am Main: Suhrkamp, 1989, pp47–62; K. Teppe, "Zur Sozialpolitik des Dritten Reiches am Beispiel der Sozialversicherung," *Archiv für Sozialgeschichte*, vol. 17, 1977, pp195–250; T. Harlander and G. Fehl (eds) *Hitlers soziale Wohnungsbau 1940–1945: Wohnungspolitik, Baugestaltung und Siedlungsplanung*, Hamburg: Hans Christians Verlag, 1991; G. Schulz (ed.) *Wohnungspolitik im Sozialstaat. Deutsche und europäische Lösungen 1918–1960*, Düsseldorf: Droste, 1993. Mason's discussion in *Social Policy in the Third Reich*, esp. Chapter 5 ("Social Policy and Social Ideology, 1934–1936") and Chapter 6 ("Social Policy, Rearmament and War, September 1936 to December 1939"), observes this more classical understanding.

70 For a brilliant dissection of the character of heavy industrial paternalism before 1914, with a highly original argument about the "racialization of industrial work" and its relationship to a post-1918 future of fascism, see D. Sweeney, *Work, Race, and the Emergence of Radical Right Corporatism in Imperial Germany*, Ann Arbor: University of Michigan Press, 2009. My own arguments may be found in G. Eley, "Capitalism and the Wilhelmine State: Industrial Growth and Political Backwardness, 1890–1918," in Eley, *From Unification to Nazism: Reinterpreting the German Past*, London: Allen and Unwin, 1986, pp42–58.

71 C. Sachse, "Rationalizing Private Life. German Factory Family Policy: Siemens in Berlin, 1918–1945," in C. Sachse, I. Lenz, and T. Siegel, *Personnel Management as Gender Policy*, Diskussionspapier, 10–90, Hamburg: Hamburger Institut fur Sozialforschung, 1990, p11.

72 Here I am following the detailed argument in Sachse, *Siemens, der Nationalsozialismus und die moderne Familie*.

73 Sachse, "Rationalizing Private Life," p16.

74 Sachse, *Siemens, der Nationalsozialismus und die moderne Familie*, p246.

75 Ibid, p106.

76 Ibid, p247.

77 Ibid, p22.

78 Ibid, p246.

79 Ibid, p21.

80 Ibid, p250.
81 These complicated but definite planes of equivalence, including countless practical intersections and collaborations, are confirmed by the findings of new research on the history of the natural and social sciences under Nazism. See, above all, S. Heim, C. Sachse, and M. Walker (eds) *The Kaiser Wilhelm Society*. For earlier stages of this research, see the two valuable anthologies: Szöllösi-Janze (ed.) *Science in the Third Reich*; Renneberg and Walker (eds) *Science, Technology, and National Socialism*. The earlier of those volumes still emphasized weapons-related technology, as against racial and population related research, biology and botany, industrial chemistry, and so forth. Some of the 1994 contributors gave credence to the autonomies and even "passive opposition" of the sciences, a standpoint adopted by K. Makrakis in *Surviving the Swastika: Scientific Research in Nazi Germany*, New York: Oxford University Press, 1993, esp. pp202–4. Also pioneering was G. Aly and K. H. Roth, *Die restlose Erfassung. Volkszählen, Identifizieren, Aussondern im Nationalsozialismus*, Berlin: Rotbuch Verlag, 1984, translated as *The Nazi Census: Identification and Control in the Third Reich*, Philadelphia: Temple University Press, 2004. See, in particular, G. Aly and S. Heim, *Architects of Annihilation*; Aly, Chroust, and Pross, *Cleansing the Fatherland*; Aly, *"Final Solution"*. For the most important critique of Aly and Roth, *Nazi Census*, see J. A. Tooze, *Statistics and the German State: The Making of Modern Economic Knowledge*, Cambridge: Cambridge University Press, 2001, esp. pp36–9, 285–97.
82 Sachse, *Siemens, der Nationalsozialismus und die moderne Familie*, p197.
83 Sachse, "Rationalizing Private Life," p19.
84 The reference here is to J. Donzelot, *The Policing of Families*, New York: Pantheon Books, 1979. See also the work of N. S. Rose, whose theoretical interest far exceeds its primarily British focus: *Governing the Soul: The Shaping of the Private Self*, London: Routledge, 1989; *The Psychological Complex: Psychology, Politics, and Society in England, 1869–1939*, London: Routledge, 1985; "Governing the Social," in N. Gane, *The Future of Social Theory*, London: Continuum, 2004, pp167–85; and also M. Dean, *Governmentality: Power and Rule in Modern Society*, London: Sage, 1999.
85 Rose, *Governing the Soul*, p130.
86 Ibid.
87 This is precisely where Dagmar Reese's work becomes so excitingly suggestive. See especially *Growing up Female in Nazi Germany*, but also the other works listed in note 41 above.
88 Sachse, *Siemens, der Nationalsozialismus und die moderne Familie*, p17.
89 Ibid, p256.
90 See Reese, "Verstrickung und Verantwortung," pp90–5. For the broader context of women's patriotic identification under the Third Reich, see Steinbacher (ed.) *Volksgenossinnen*.
91 Here I am relying on E. Harvey, *Women and the Nazi East: Agents and Witnesses of Germanization*, New Haven: Yale University Press, 2003, also the following: " 'Die deutsche Frau im Osten': 'Rasse,' Geschlecht und öffentlicher Raum im bestzten Polen 1940–44," *Archiv für Sozialgeschichte*, vol. 38, 1998, pp191–214; "Pilgrimages to the 'Bleeding Frontier': Gender and Rituals of Nationalist Protest in Germany, 1919–1939," *Women's History Review*, vol. 9, 2000, pp201–28; "'We forgot all Jews and Poles': German Women and the 'Ethnic Struggle' in Nazi-Occupied Poland," *Contemporary European History*, 2001, vol. 10, no. 3, pp447–61; "Remembering and Repressing: German Women's Recollections of the 'Ethnic Struggle' in Occupied Poland during the Second World War," in Hagemann and Schüler-Springorum (eds) *Home/Front*, pp275–96.
92 At the center of Harvey's account are 16 direct informants with whom she conducted intensive interviews.
93 For fruitful comparison, see E. Vlossak, *Marianne or Germania? Nationalizing Women in Alsace 1870–1946*, Oxford: Oxford University Press, 2010.

94 The phrases come from the title of Chapter 5, "'Uncanny Space' or 'German Homeland'," Harvey, *Women and the Nazi East*, pp119–46.

95 See Chapter 6, "Motherliness and Mastery: Making Model Germans in the Annexed Territories," ibid, pp147–90; Chapter 7, "Moulding the Next Generation: Village Schoolteachers in the 'Reichsgau Wartheland'," ibid, pp191–231; Chapter 8, "Child-care and Colonization: Kindergartens on the Frontiers of the Nazi Empire," ibid, pp232–60. Chapter 9, "Building on the Volcano," ibid, pp261–82, adds a compelling case study of the area around Zamosc, based on the diary of the woman who was made responsible for training village advisers there.

96 See Browning, *Ordinary Men*; O. Bartov, A. Grossmann, and M. Nolan (eds) *Crimes of War: Guilt and Denial in the Twentieth Century*, New York: The New Press, 2002; H. Heer and K. Naumann, *War of Extermination: The German Military in World War II, 1941–1944*, New York: Berghahn Books, 2000.

97 *Women and the Nazi East*, pp262, 273.

98 Here she adds another valuable piece to the now enormous literature dealing with the vagaries of German postwar memory, providing excellent insight into the particular repressor mechanisms available to women. See R. G. Moeller, *War Stories: The Search for a Usable Past in the Federal Republic of Germany*, Berkeley: University of California Press, 2001; B. Niven (ed) *Germans as Victims: Remembering the Past in Contemporary Germany*, Houndmills: Palgrave Macmillan, 2006.

99 These categories of newly migrated German nationals (as opposed to the long-term German-speaking pre-1939 residents of the various countries) are not usually broken out of the general statistics provided for the expellees in the available accounts. See Moeller, *War Stories*, p201, note 7, for the necessary citations, plus the following: R. Schulze, "Forced Migration of German Populations During and After the Second World War: History and Memory," in J. Reinisch and E. White (eds) *The Disentanglement of Populations: Migration, Expulsion, and Displacement in Post-War Europe, 1944–1949*, Houndmills: Palgrave Macmillan, 2011, pp51–70; P. Ahonen, *After the Expulsion: West Germany and Eastern Europe 1945–1990*, Oxford: Oxford University Press, 2003, pp15–24; V. Lumans, *Himmler's Auxiliaries: The Volksdeutsche Mittelstelle and the German National Minorities of Europe, 1933–1945*, Chapel Hill: University of North Carolina Press, 1993.

100 A. L. Stoler, "Sexual Affronts and Racial Frontiers: European Identities and the Cultural Politics of Exclusion in Colonial Southeast Asia," in G. Eley and R. G. Suny (eds) *Becoming National: A Reader*, New York: Oxford University Press, 1996, p312. See also Stoler, *Race and the Education of Desire: Foucault's History of Sexuality and the Colonial Order of Things*, Durham: Duke University Press, 1995; Stoler, *Carnal Knowledge and Imperial Power: Race and the Intimate in Colonial Rule*, Berkeley: University of California Press, 2002; P. Levine, *Prostitution, Race, and Politics: Policing Venereal Disease in the British Empire*, London: Routledge, 2003; A. Burton, *Dwelling in the Archive: Women Writing, House, Home, and History in Late Colonial India*, Oxford: Oxford University Press, 2003.

101 In the meantime, Bock also modified her views. Contrast her earlier disposal of Koonz with the more recent "Ordinary Women in Nazi Germany: Perpetrators, Victims, Followers, and Bystanders," in D. Ofer and L. J. Weitzman (eds) *Women in the Holocaust*, New Haven: Yale University Press, 1998, pp85–100.

102 The reference here is to C. Lasch, *Haven in a Heartless World*, New York: Basic Books, 1977, which Koonz evokes in her statement quoted at note 28 above. See Koonz, *Mothers in the Fatherland*, p419.

103 Harvey, *Women and the Nazi East*, pp1–2.

5

EMPIRE, IDEOLOGY, AND THE EAST

Thoughts on Nazism's Spatial Imaginary

Space, Nazism, and historiography

Perhaps the strongest consensus among historians of the Third Reich at large still presumes the inherence of expansionism at Nazism's essential core: war and the drive for an imperialist "new order" were inscribed in the regime's future from its start. Of late, the specifically spatial aspects of that drive, with its binary ambitions both to recast the social order "at home" and to remap the ethno-cultural geographies and territorial sovereignties of Europe as a whole, have also been receiving marked attention.[1] Of course, in the throes of such an imperialism, the very meanings and possibilities of "home" – its cultural coordinates, its political geographies, its existential borders and their entailments – would be thrown inevitably into flux. That was occurring with the earliest steps in the creation of the "Greater German Reich" even before the war itself had begun, a remapping of Germanness initiated still earlier via the Nazis' relentless propaganda of word and image. The geopolitical enormity of what the Nazis had in mind, the extent of the reordering of the European space this putative "Germany" would require, became incrementally clearer with each of Hitler's peacetime triumphs, whose impact enabled Germans to begin placing themselves on a very different mental map: the return of the Saarland via plebiscite in January 1936; remilitarizing of the Rhineland in March; *Anschluß* with Austria (March 1938); the taking of Sudetenland (September 1938), Bohemia-Moravia (March 1939), and Memel (also March); plus the signing of the Anti-Comintern Pact with Japan (November 1936) and Italy (November 1937).

That impact was intensely accelerated by the war as German armies swept over the rest of the continent. If this was a re-territorializing of Europe under the sign of Germany's imperial rule, with drastic reassignments of sovereignty and citizenship, then the physical geography of German space was also being literally re-visualized, as millions of Germans began encountering these far-flung lands at first hand – as soldiers, administrators, settlers, experts, planners, professionals, civilian workers, carpetbaggers, profiteers. This radical indeterminacy of the German home was produced, too, in the movements and alterity of populations inside Germany itself. Around half a million *Volksdeutsche* were brought back to Germany (*heim ins Reich*) from the Baltic, Galicia, Bessarabia and Bukovina, elsewhere in the Balkans, and parts of the Soviet Union, with the intention of resettling them on expropriated Polish farmland in the newly annexed territories. Still more alien were the millions of foreign laborers drafted into German industry during the course of the war, including 8.4 million civilian workers, 4.6 million prisoners of war, and the many thousands of concentration camp inmates.[2]

This shifting of Germany's borders, and the scrambling of how they could be understood, may be set in a much longer context. Far more than other polities shaped by the European constitution-making of the 1860s, Germany's continuity as a national state has been repeatedly interrupted. Its official borders have been frequently and significantly redrawn; within the claims to nationhood, the gaps between territorial integrity and cultural formation have been variable and extreme; its constitutional forms have run the gamut from centralism to federalism, dictatorship to democracy, monarchy to republic. "Germany" has been an abstract, mobile, contingent, and highly contested term. It has only ever approximated to the vaunted unity of land, language, law, institutions, high-cultural traditions, and customary heritage that nationalist discourse – and the usages of commonsense – would like to presume. Within one and a half centuries, with special and continuous intensity during the "thirty years' war" of 1914 to 1945, after all, *six major ruptures* have occurred: in 1864 to 1871, in 1914 to 1918, in 1918 to 1923, in 1936 to 1945, in 1945 to 1949, and finally in 1989 to 1990.[3] With each succeeding territorial-cum-constitutional rearrangement, the languages of nationhood either cleared a space for democratic experiment or else closed it down. Whatever the outcomes of the immediate political contests, "Germany" was only ever defined within complex and uncertain fields of relations linking nationhood, cultural belonging, and the state.

With these reference points in mind, I will explore some of the uses of a spatial perspective in studying Nazism. What do we gain, theoretically and methodologically, by subjecting Nazism to the analytics of "space"? What is the value added by adopting this particular approach? What does it allow us to think that was not as easy to think before? As with any language of widening cross-disciplinary currency, *space* and *spatiality* can be invoked all too easily without sufficiently considering the possible valences.

Thus, one way of approaching the salience of space for historiographies of Nazism could be straightforwardly empirical-analytical. The longstanding influence of regional and local studies since the 1960s forms an obvious example, whether applied to the distinctiveness of particular localities, both institutionally understood and in terms of community organization, or to spatially defined case studies of movement and regime, dealing either with the rise of Nazism before 1933 or with the reach of the power of the Third Reich and its impediments. In the English-language historiography, each of the pioneering studies of the Nazi Party's (NSDAP's) rise to power produced during the earliest phase of scholarly historiography had been regional or local studies, just as the earliest attempts to explore the "limits of Hitler's power" took the same kind of approach too.[4] If we fast forward to the present, then we find a similar prioritizing of region and locality – of *place* – as the best ground from which to approach Nazi empire and the Holocaust by referring policy formation, genocidal practice, and the decision-making behind the "Final Solution" to the situational dynamics of variable regional and local histories.[5]

A second path to grasping the spatial dimensions or dynamics of Nazism is certainly via its own explicit languages. Not only the rhetorics of *Lebensraum*, *Großraum*, *Raumwirtschaft*, *Raumplanung*, and so forth come into question here, but also the entire discourse of planning, population politics, clearances, deportations, transfers, reclamation, resettlement, and repopulation that became so crucial to the Nazi imperium after 1939, whether in the latter's imaginings or in its means of practical realization. Yet, here we can already see the opening of a somewhat wider space (sic) between the institutional and social-historical materialities of Nazi policy and practice, on the one hand, and the greater amorphousness of Nazi outlook and ideology, on the other, where extremely complicated fields of imagining, projection, representation, contestation, and general indeterminacy developed through which the actions of the regime had to be negotiated.

Here the element of the *spatial* starts to describe not so much a firm social-historical and materialist ground of geographies, economies, and social structures, but rather a metaphorical realm of projections, ideology, cultural claims, mythologizing, narrative aggrandizement, and geopolitical fantasy. "Space" in that sense was defined not only by the physical boundaries marking out a territory and the restored sovereignties taken away by Versailles, but also by the imagined future of Nazi empire-making – historically licensed expectations of conquest, colonial desire in all of its explicit and unconscious modalities, the technocratic drivenness of a kind of social engineering, and all of those ambitions now treated as part of Nazism's utopian wish. These questions may be followed into the most obvious part of the Nazis' spatial imaginary – namely, the ideology of *Lebensraum* (living space), which has some claims to having been the master concept through which Hitler himself and other leading Nazis understood what they were doing.

Respatializing German history: The nation as an empire

As already mentioned, the very largest scale of the Nazi spatial order – the continent-wide *Großraum* housing the new German empire imposed across Europe during 1938 to 1942 – has been drawing much interest, most notably in the major syntheses of Mark Mazower and Shelley Baranowski, but also via the remarkable efflorescence of wider scholarly attention to German colonialism under the *Kaiserreich* and its aftermaths, through which discussions of continuity between Bismarck and

Hitler have taken on a new lease of life. Pertinent, too, is the growth of comparative genocide studies, for which the German record of colonial killing in Southwest Africa and East Africa, no less than the exterminatory violence of World War II, has become increasingly emblematic.[6] In this regard the spatial coordinates of the Nazis' expansionist thinking could draw on a diversity of precedents. These ranged from the shame and bitterness of Versailles to the "stab in the back" legend encrusting the military debacle of 1918 and the panoramic delirium of conquering the East during 1915 to 1918, back through the prewar discourse of *Mitteleuropa* (Central Europe), the much longer memory of the *Drang nach Osten* (drive to the East), and the pervasive post-1880s social Darwinian consensus about the necessary rivalries of the great world empires. Each of these contexts composed a complex fund of antecedents and prefigurative experience, whose possible relevance became unevenly sifted and partially appropriated in the various planning and policy-making networks of the 1930s and 1940s. Flagging these precedents does not require an oversimplified model of causal or explanatory continuity, whether biographically, ideologically, or in some other way. As Birthe Kundrus has argued, the links between Nazi expansionism and those earlier moments may be concretized more cautiously around specific "chains of influence, transfers, and situational parallels" by seeing earlier colonial histories as a future reservoir of possible models and policies, ideas and attitudes, dreams and fantasies, usable practices, modalities of planning, and available blueprints, as well as a variety of paths *not* to be followed.[7] Nazi expansionism also had its own terrible specificities that may never be straightforwardly subsumed inside any such larger-scale temporal framework. But the fruitfulness of situating the Nazi imperium inside those deeper and longer-term histories, both in the abstract and for the purposes of comparison, has surely become non-controversial.

In light of current thinking about the dynamics of later nineteenth-century globalization and the multidirectional interconnectedness between "the national" and "the global," historians have been arguing recently for a *respatializing* of German history by following the tracks of that history (or the "boundaries of Germanness") out onto a transnational stage.[8] Thus, even during the very inception of Germany's unification in 1866 to 1871, the possible materials for German nationhood were *always-already* distributed across far wider-than-national worlds, whether in the global circuits of migrancy and commerce, in the complex European geographies of language, residence, and cultural self-identification, or in the sheer unformed amorphousness of the relations between German-speaking populations and the given territorial sovereignties. By the later nineteenth century, nationhood in Europe more generally was, in any case, fast becoming "imperialized" within a set of transnational logics, bound into a set of economic, geopolitical, and cultural exigencies that simply dictated energetic participation on a world stage. To secure its popular legitimacy, whether in the new nations of Germany and Italy or the older ones of Britain and France, government had to be capable of preserving national interests amidst the intensities of international competition, as well as sustaining the power of national culture overseas, and creating a system of practical and emotional ties strong enough for keeping the allegiances of those migrants who were leaving the homelands in their prodigiously disquieting numbers. In other words, even as the German nation was first being created, national horizons were being fashioned that were expansive and far-flung rather than being confined just to contiguous German-speaking Europe itself – ones that encompassed German interests, influences, and populations in the world at large rather than simply the European heartlands of German nationality. In a cognate sense, they also looked *past* the core territories of 1871 toward the dispersed topography of German settlement further to the east, in Poland, Bohemia, elsewhere in the Habsburg Empire, the Balkans and the Ottoman Empire, and parts of Tsarist Russia.[9]

This importance of empire was experienced both in the abstract and extremely concretely. As political advocacy, it was aggressively reiterated around a breadth of ideological consensus after the 1880s that Germany's future prosperity and survival would necessarily presuppose some basis of successful competition against the rival world empires of Britain, Russia, and the United States. Such "empire talk" forged connections across the presumptively interlinked priorities of distinct domains in the life of the nation. First came the sphere of foreign policy and international conflict *per se*, defined by the arms drive and a diplomacy of aggressive interventions once *Weltpolitik* was proclaimed in the later 1890s. Just beyond was the burgeoning discourse of national efficiency in the economy. Harnessed to projections of future economic growth, this encompassed everything deemed necessary to secure Germany's competitiveness in the world market, including the aggressive deployment of tariffs, bilateral trading treaties, and state-aided export offensives.[10] Then came the entire domain of social welfare, likewise conceived under the sign of national efficiency. While any particular social policy only ever emerged from complicated interactions among economic, socio-political, ethico-religious, institutional, and short-term political motivations, sometimes strategically conceived and woven together, but as often discretely undertaken out of expediency, most major initiatives were at some level consciously framed in the cause of social cohesion and political stability.[11] From the mid-1890s these discussions, too, increasingly occurred under the sign of empire.

Between the 1880s and 1914 the drumbeat of world-political advocacy developed symbiotically across each of these domains. But the resulting urgencies were also experienced by the German people in myriad practical ways, whether in the circulation of images and ideas in the public worlds of the press, literature, and the arts or in the wider everydayness of popular culture. The latter, in particular, was becoming an environment saturated with representations of the exotic in the colonial overseas. German publics were being invited to register the necessity of empire at every turn: via museums and archaeology; travel, tourism, and exploration; commodification, marketing, and consumption; aviation, steamships, and other technologies of travel; medicine and eugenics; ethnology and racial classification; exhibitions, zoos, and commercial entertainments; formal and informal pedagogies of multiple kinds; and the new visual paraphernalia of posters, postcards, collectors' picture cards in packets of consumer goods, commercialized bric-a-brac, caricatures and newspaper illustrations, as well as the new visual languages of film, photography, and advertising.[12]

One of the biggest shifts registered by National Socialism's distinctive ambitions of empire, along with the differing salience of "race," the primacy of anti-Semitism, and the alacrity of the turn to genocidal violence enabled by the experience of World War I, was the decisive withdrawal from these older priorities of a globalized *Weltpolitik*. Of course, the latter had always been tethered to a conception of continental dominance too. Even during its hegemony, extending between the colonial enthusiasm of the early 1880s and the watershed of 1910 to 1911, "world-political" thought was hardwired around a grand project of continental integration under German dominance usually styled as *Mitteleuropa*, which from the turn of the new century became increasingly imbricated with the emergent ideology of *Lebensraum*. The longer-standing emigrationist anxieties about population loss now conjoined with new political worries about the birth rate, the social question, and racial vitality, so that the belief in the national struggle for existence, keyed to the dialectics of prosperity and survival, became harnessed to a continental vision of landward expansion to the East. It was in the widening gap between radical nationalist expectations and the negligible returns on the government's *Weltpolitik* after 1896 to 1897 that the space for a disillusioned politics of "national opposition" began to grow. As hopes of overseas gains became deferred, projections of a "greater Germany" fastened increasingly onto the idea of *Mitteleuropa*, with evident implications for the vexed question of the future of the Habsburg Empire. Radical nationalists now staked the prospects for overseas expansionism on the prior attainment of the project of a *völkische Großraumordnung*, or the remaking of the Central European spatial order along ethno-racial lines. In so doing they aggressively advocated the arms race, militarization, and the embrace of the necessity of war.[13]

Wilhelmine radical nationalism: Three legacies

I spend so much time on these earlier contexts because they delivered the "space of experience" where the Third Reich's "horizons of expectation" were formed.[14] This indebtedness of Nazi thinking to the spatial imagination of late Wilhelmine radical nationalism was threefold. The *first* such element, substantive and programmatic, was the ruthlessly elaborated and engineered vision of a continental eastward imperium *per se*. The discursive architecture of the Pan-German outlook, in particular, had been constructed around the keywords of "nation," "people," and "race" in ways that made social Darwinian assumptions of struggle and survival into an operative ideological matrix. As Peter Walkenhorst has argued, this saw the breakthrough into a new kind of bio-political thinking that focused obsessively on "the three bodies of the nation" (individual, socio-political, bio-reproductive), while helping to shape the nationalization of citizenship in the new law of 1913 and suturing into place a new unity of the *Staatsvolk* and the *Volksgemeinschaft*.[15] Already before 1914, in tracts such as Heinrich Claß's pseudonymously published

Wenn ich der Kaiser wär and other writings, but especially during the war aims discussions of World War I, the Pan-Germans displayed an *avant-garde* readiness for extreme bio-political interventions, whose terms chillingly prefigured the direction of National Socialist policies. These had embraced not only the mass deportation (*Evakuierung*) and ethnic cleansing (*völkische Flurbereinigung*) of non-German peoples in the interests of future imperial expansion, but also the expulsion of foreign Jews and the reduction to second-class citizenship of those who had been born in Germany. For domestic policy, elaborate schemes of social engineering envisaged the planned eugenic improvement of the population stock (*planmässige Züchtungspolitik*) so that "those who were inferior" (the "mentally ill, imbeciles, epileptics, alcoholics, criminals, also the seriously tubercular") might be eliminated.[16]

The *second* legacy came from the final stage of World War I in the extraordinary panorama of imperialist opportunity opened for Germany in the East by the Russian military collapse and the Treaty of Brest-Litovsk. If the ambitions of the *Oberost*, the military command on the Eastern Front established under Erich Ludendorff in the autumn of 1915, had been expansive enough, projecting "a total mobilization and comprehensive economic exploitation of land and people" in Germany's favor, a complete reordering of the East under German rule, then March 1918 brought still more extravagant and unanticipated vistas of aggrandizement.[17] From Poland and the Baltic, German ambitions now transferred to Ukraine: "The possibility, which leaped to the fore in the spring of 1918, of winning the entire, expansive eastern sphere [*Ostraum*] with its supposedly inexhaustible supplies of raw materials as a 'German hinterland'," radicalized the German leaders into thinking that the former Russian Empire could now be "broken apart."[18] The aim was "getting out of Ukraine what there is to be gotten," binding it over the longer term into the greater German economy.[19] That meant appropriating grain surpluses, Germanizing the iron and manganese industries, administering the railways and Black Sea ports, indeed controlling the entire Ukrainian infrastructure. There were parallel schemes for the Baltic, or the *Baltikum* as the unified military command there became named in the summer of 1918. This would be the basis for exploiting what was left of Russia and opening the way to the Middle East. The long-term significance can hardly be overstated. When war ended in the west, German troops were still holding a line from Finland to the Caucasus: "Hitler's long-range aim, fixed in the 1920s, of erecting a German Eastern Imperium on the ruins of the Soviet Union was not simply a vision emanating from an abstract wish. In the *Ostraum* established in 1918, this goal had a concrete point of departure. The German Eastern Imperium had already been – if only for a short time – a reality."[20]

These continuities between the *Oberost* vision and the later "drive to the East" of the Nazis were crucial. The rapidly emerging nationalist mythology of the undefeated army betrayed by the duplicity of treasonous politicians and a revolutionary uprising at home (the infamous "stab in the back" legend) was fueled by perceptions of the Eastern war's glorious success, a missionary vision further reinforced by the fear of Bolshevism. After the war, these perceptions hardened into a new language of "*Volk und Raum*" or "race and space," in which the meanings of "*Land*" or "country" became emptied out of valid or allowable human associations. Freed from the inconvenience of acknowledging any actually existing histories, the language of *Raum* offered instead the neutral and abstract framing for a racialized ideology of German expansionism that professed indifference to the peoples already living in the region.[21]

Acquiring "scientific" weight and legitimacy during the 1920s from the academic fields of geopolitics and *Ostforschung* ("East-research"), this program reflected a ruthlessly modernizing and self-interested drive to reconquer the region. Devoid of coherent histories, dynamic cultures, or viable claims to statehood, German expansionists insisted, the East was merely a disorganized and empty expanse of primeval landscapes, primitive economies, inchoate ethnicities, and insanitary settlements. Mired in dirt, superstition, and backwardness, with no credible claim to independence, the East could only deliver the *Lebensraum* or "living space" needed by its dynamic and racially superior neighbor to the west. The German invaders had experienced that East as an empty, under-populated, and under-cultivated land – a place of sheer "*Unkultur*," as the head of the military administration in Lithuania-Bialystok, Theodor von Heppe, had called it.[22] In Courland, German soldiers found a land that seemed verminous, plague ridden, and devoid of healthful inhabitants.[23] It was a land that could be cleared, resettled, and exploited for the good of Germany's superior economy and general civilization. As Victor Klemperer, who during World War I worked in the press section for *Oberost*, reflected: "Here, without question, we are the bringers of *Kultur*!"[24]

The exceptional brutality of the civil warfare raging across the former Tsarist lands during 1918 to 1919 also had its long-term effects. Amidst those disorders the marauding of the *Freikorps* was especially notorious, wreaking appalling havoc in the politics and social life of the new Baltic states between January and December 1919. Those exploits, too, an extraordinary story of semi-official military subcontracting, patriotic bravado, political entrepreneurship, and straightforward brigandage, powerfully stamped German nationalist perceptions of the East.[25] At one level, the *Freikorps* adventurers aspired to a brutalized, undisciplined, and microcosmic caricature of the abortive imperium of the *Oberost*, which darkly prefigured the systematized lawlessness of the Nazi invasion of Soviet territory two decades later. The Baltic rampage compensated not only for the shame of the lost war, whose wounds were gouged into rage by the news of the Versailles Treaty on 28 June 1919, but also for the sense of degeneracy at home, where the Left presided over the hated Republic. In the characteristic rhetoric of one leading *Freikorps* militant and future Nazi: "while in the homeland bullets whipped through the cities, while confused comrades carried the red flag of a utopian *Internationale* through the streets, a secret murmuring went through the gray front of the genuine warriors: *Off to the Baltikum!*"[26] Amidst the growing wantonness of the violence against the Latvian and Lithuanian peoples, the volunteers easily conjured mystical associations of heroes past, from the Teutonic Knights to the figure of the *Landsknecht*, the freebooter mercenary of the Thirty Years' War, and thence to the leaders of the War of Liberation against Napoleon. *Freikorps* militants armored themselves in fantasy scenarios of national rebirth: "Soldiers in the *Baltikum* sang a marching song, whose first verse began, 'We are the last Germans, who stayed opposite the enemy'," the revered rightwing author and terrorist Ernst von Salomon remembered. His next sentence captured the apocalyptic hankering: "Now we felt ourselves to be the last Germans, period."[27]

Not only did the idea of a stolen victory in the East become widely diffused in Germany, but for many nationalists that East also functioned as the place of special destiny. It became the natural direction for Germany's future expansion, a region containing only "people with little cultural development" who took what German beneficence provided while grasping ungratefully for an independence that could never be sustained.[28] The East was also the source from which destructive and demoralizing contagion was believed to flow. This was perceived literally, as refugees, evacuees, displaced populations, demobilized soldiers, and migrants of all sorts crowded across Eastern Europe's still indeterminate borders after 1918, many of them made homeless or stateless by the drastic remapping of the region's political geography. This hooked into older fears of epidemics and contagious disease, whose immediate reference point was Germany's now dismantled wartime system of public health regulations and disease control in the occupied borderlands, based in quarantine, disinfection, delousing, and epidemiological surveillance: "German bacteriologists characterized Russia as 'a land of hunger and famine,' and as drenched in disease," constantly prey to "epidemics of typhus, cholera, typhoid, and malaria." Such overheated anxieties climaxed in the terrible Russian famine of 1921 to 1922, when the spectacle of mass starvation further sharpened these racialized perceptions of the East. By the time Germany's borders had successfully stabilized after the flux at the end of the war, the government had proceeded to rebuild what its Health Office called "an epidemic protection wall" of medical inspection facilities, or an epidemiological "iron curtain."[29] The dangers of infection were now firmly associated in the minds of German nationalists with any uncontrolled influx of racially inferior peoples, among whom eastern Jews (*Ostjuden*) were increasingly singled out. Of course, the elision to anti-Bolshevism was then easily made. The fear of Bolshevik infection became an integral part of the imagery of a threat from the East.[30]

This history was the crucible for National Socialism's vision of the East, the basic architecture of its spatial imagination. When Adolf Hitler trumpeted eastward expansion as Germany's destiny in the immediate aftermath of the *Kaiserreich*'s demise, he bespoke all of the above.[31] Thus, the *third* legacy of late Wilhelmine radical nationalism was more diffusely ideological, the generalized and protean "German myth of the East," as opposed to the more programmatic bio-political projections associated with the Pan-Germans. As Robert Nelson aptly observes, during World War I "the Rubicon was crossed when it came to what was possible to 'think' about the East," encouraging radical nationalists toward three primary commitments: "the pioneer engagement with the frontier, and the concomitant notion of 'emptiness'; the slow but sure evolution from cultural chauvinism to biological racism … and finally the notion of the colonial laboratory, the idea that massive projects of social engineering could take place with little restraint in the non-metropole space."[32]

But the resulting ideological array should not be reduced too straightforwardly to a tightly structured and misleading coherence. The conjoining of "race" to "space" in the Nazi outlook issued in a very wide diversity of particular systems, projects, and beliefs, which themselves derived from broader repertoires of knowledge, science, and ideology in the larger world of early twentieth-century radical nationalist discourse. For example, Wendy Lower's pioneering work makes very clear not only the focused specificity of those self-consciously and overtly colonizing initiatives launched by the SS in occupied Poland, the Baltic, and Ukraine, but also the far messier actualities that materialized on the ground: if the former envisaged Germanization as a ruthlessly consistent application of rigidly formal precepts based on "racial science" and its classifications, then the latter revealed a far more compromised history of improvised measures and enforced pragmatics.[33] Moreover, whether on the scale of the vast expanses of the occupied East as a whole or in the many ground-level negotiations required by the Nazi state's polycratic disorders, the hard core of the SS contended with other perspectives and understandings, including differently founded *völkisch* outlooks and older models of Germanization, which in consistency and primary orientation might be no less racist than their own. In his treatment of the maneuvering between Albert Forster and Heinrich Himmler over the use of the *Deutsche Volksliste*, for example, in one of the most important studies of Nazi racial policies in the occupied East, Gerhard Wolf shows exactly this complexity at work, producing "a stand-off not between pragmatists and ideologues but between *völkisch* and racial ethnocrats."[34]

Historiography and the return of ideology

With the extraordinarily important return of ideology to the historiographical center ground of the Third Reich, a key tension needs to be marked. On the one hand, we now have a large scholarly corpus analyzing the ethos and practice of the Nazi state's core institutions. As traced in the preceding chapters, the strongest impetus behind the new work came from a convergence of interest in the ideas organizing the operations of the racial state. However repugnant and outlandish, those ideas required meticulous reconstruction if the efficacies of their appeal were to become at all intelligible, particularly where they resonated more widely among Germans of the time, articulated successfully with other bodies of thought, and worked with the grain of developments displaying evident societal force. As I have argued, that scholarship has come to concentrate above all around the SS, whether at the center in the work of Ulrich Herbert, Michael Wildt, Michael Thad Allen, and the rest, or in the wealth of studies now scrutinizing SS practice on the ground. This work has compellingly reinstated the importance of analyzing Nazi ideology by extending the history of ideas toward the institutional, professional, and policy-related settings where Nazi ideas were translated into active materialities and types of practice.

In foregrounding the technocracy, project-oriented enthusiasms, and managerialism of the racial state, such studies have helped us to see how easily careers, ordinary ambitions, and optimistic professional futures came to be imagined within the framing of the new normal the Third Reich had now established. Very recently, some work has begun carrying this argument about ideology onto the wider societal stage by exploring how the moral boundaries of national belonging, civic obligation, social responsibility, and human intercourse could be coercively remade under the aegis of the *Volksgemeinschaft*. This again broadens the concept of ideology by following the impact of ideas *into* society and seeing how they became converted into *practices*. By hammering so relentlessly on the rules of inclusion and exclusion, the propagandists, advocates, and functionaries of the *Volksgemeinschaft* redefined Germans' access to possible forms of personhood. Rather than the "moral calculus" of liberalism that "turns on the concept of universal human rights," Claudia Koonz has argued, "the Third Reich extolled the well-being of the ethnic German community as the benchmark for moral reasoning." Using the concepts of "ethnic fundamentalism" and "the Nazi conscience," she makes the case for a "comprehensive ethical revolution … that prepared Germans to tolerate racial crime well before the advent of genocidal murder battalions and extermination camps."[35] In all of these ways, recent work recovers the centered coherence, perverse epistemology, and concerted power that allowed the Nazi outlook to enlist so many people so persuasively.[36]

On the other hand, though, precisely this *centeredness* may easily be overstated or misconstrued. In the preceding chapters I have emphasized at some length the complexities of the distance that separated the shaping of ideas "at the top" (in the Nazi bureaucracy, in the Propaganda Ministry, in Hitler's head) from the meanings they may have carried as they encountered the various categories of ordinary Germans "on the ground." My purpose in doing so is to dismantle the opposition of "ideology" *versus* "social context" used so often in the past to frame that distinction. Thus, rather than being defined just by its point of conception, the work of ideology should be taken to include the highly material and practical aspects of the manner of its entry into the local and the everyday, where its meanings were necessarily shifted and modified in the course of the ensuing impact and negotiation. But the accumulated scholarship on the population politics and planning scenarios of the higher SS also runs a danger of suggesting too great a degree of coherence at the top, imputing an over-unified political conception to the officialdom of the Reich Security Main Office (*Reichssicherheitshauptamt*, RSHA), quite aside from their differences with other parts of the Third Reich's state–party institutional complex, particularly after the invasion of the Soviet Union in June 1941. The planning that preceded the latter during 1940 to 1941 was reasonably successfully integrated, but thereafter things quickly fell apart. Weighing the significance of the RSHA's programmatic intentions within this wider political field becomes extremely difficult amidst the jurisdictional confusions, duplications, and personal rivalries that now routinely broke out across the RSHA, Hermann Göring's Office of the Four-Year Plan and its constellation of ministerial interests, Alfred Rosenberg's Ministry for the Occupied Eastern Territories, Martin Bormann's Party Chancellery, the Reich Chancellery under Hans-Heinrich Lammers, and, of course, the army and private industry. However coherent the intentions formulated inside the planning offices of the RSHA, they could never lastingly trump that endemic disorder.[37]

Once we turn to Nazi empire more directly, the importance of these points becomes very apparent. They should alert us to the instabilities in how the projection of "race" into "space" might actually have occurred. Building from his own primary focus on the "engineering of waterways" and the metaphorical as well as the literal meanings of "drainage," for example, David Blackbourn has brilliantly described one such context in the "conquest of nature" and its relation to the "mystique of the frontier." His book both captures the euphoria of the eastward gaze and accepts the multiplicity of projects that followed. The planning delirium of the eastward expansion, the *Ostrausch* ("intoxication of the East"), brought into play projects and ideas whose terms and reach necessarily exceeded any strictly managed program, quite apart from the complexities of implementation they actually encountered on the spot:

> There were proposals to extend the Autobahn system east, schemes for rural electrification, and proposals to conjure up towns where they ought to be (in line with central place theory), not where they – with scandalous haphazardness – actually were. The occupiers harnessed soil experts, botanists, plant geneticists, population specialists, aerial photographers, meteorologists, and (not least) regional and landscape planners.[38]

But once that machinery of planning and speculation was up and running, whether under the aegis of *Generalplan Ost* or in the many other university units, policy agencies, and research institutes now involved, the outcomes were not always as reliable as some depictions of the voraciously aggrandizing jurisdictional expansion of the SS might encourage us to expect. Even at the core of the newly annexed territories of occupied Poland, designated in Himmler's thinking as the primary setting for a racially engineered New Order based on expropriation, resettlement, and exploitation, Germanization proceeded only by means of unanticipated, protracted, and unresolved conflicts of perspective and administrative action. So, far from establishing the central coordinating machinery for straightforwardly implementing such plans, the creation of the Reich Commission for the Strengthening of Germandom (*Reichskommissariat für die Festigung deutschen Volkstums*, RKF) under Himmler on 7 October 1939 initiated only the earliest stages in a long haul of negotiation in Berlin, through which Göring's office, the Finance and Transportation Ministries, the Gauleiters concerned, and Hans Frank as the head of the Polish general-government were at first effectively able to apply the brakes. Still more to the point, Himmler's RSHAers proved unable to assert uncontested competence for the process of Germanization once the planning did get more seriously under way from May 1940, facing severe jurisdictional opposition from the Interior Ministry and the Gauleiters. Most significantly of all, Himmler's efforts at enforcing strictly *racial* criteria for defining which parts of the Polish populace might be selected for positive integration proved incapable of displacing the rival perspectives of the civil administration, whose advocates tended to emphasize a *völkisch* model of Germanization instead, one based on malleable social and cultural criteria and far more continuous with the earlier Germanization drives before 1914.[39] Here, in other words, in the very crucible of the RSHA's earliest forays into large-scale, race-based population politics, neither "Nazi ideology" nor the "racial state" could be found functioning homogeneously.[40]

Gerhard Wolf's account of the labyrinthine maneuvering over Germanization policies in occupied Poland becomes exemplary in this regard, showing vividly how policy disagreements and diversities of practice could easily run through the interiors of the SS racial agencies and the RKF, too. This is further confirmed if we widen our perspective to the colonization plans more generally. Though certainly extensive in their geographies and spatial reach, the territories slated for actual settlement under the New Order were actually rather specific as well as poorly conceived and chaotically experimental – the directly annexed parts of Poland (Danzig-West Prussia, Upper Silesia, Warthegau), plus the Baltic states, and the Hegewald, Halbstadt, and Nikopol colonies in the Zhytomyr, Dnepropetrovsk, and Nikoleav regions of Ukraine. Moreover, occupied *Western* Europe revealed a quite different history of spatial contestation, for which neither settlement plans (apart from Alsace-Lorraine) nor successful SS designs ever became as salient. While carrying the RSHA brief in Paris, for example, Werner Best had to concede defeat in his bid to replace a Western Europe of nation-states with an expressly racialized political geography, succumbing to the superordinate preferences of the military and diplomats.[41] If himself an archetype of the SS ideologue, moreover, Best also behaved with notable flexibility during his subsequent time in Denmark.[42]

Thus, the spatial imaginary structuring Nazi conceptions and practices of empire was borne by a series of complexly cascading histories, whose ideological meanings accumulated efficacy as they emerged from World War I and its violent revolutionary aftermaths. Many of those meanings have not been treated in detail here – for example, the North American referents for Blackbourn's "mystique of the frontier," which were never very far from the minds of Hitler ("The Volga must be our Mississippi"), Himmler (under German settlement, the barren and empty lands of the East "could become a paradise, a European California"), and other leading Nazis.[43] As a more heterogeneous discursive formation, the grandiose spatial trope of "the East" had enlisted many radical nationalists during the first three decades of the century whose generative influence then diverged from Nazi thinking in the 1930s, including Friedrich Ratzel, Karl Haushofer, Max Sering, Theodor Reismann-Grone, and Heinrich Claß, among other telling examples.[44]

But at this general level the fantasies of a verdant, fecund, and luxuriant future ("Out of the eastern territories, we must make a Garden of Eden") remained operative across such differences while drawing on a deep past.[45] In contrast with the Jewish "tyranny" and the "culture-negating and culture-destroying forces of Bolshevism," argued the head of the police training programs in Kiev in 1942, the pioneering German colonists and merchants of earlier centuries had brought "fertile fields, blooming cities, outstanding buildings, and artistic [and] scholarly works of the highest value."[46] It was there, in the land of metaphor and fantasy, that the common fund found its strongest expression. Here is Reinhard Heydrich giving his maiden address as Reich Protector of Bohemia-Moravia:

> These are spaces that one should in reality deal with like the dyking of new land on the coast, by building a protective wall of peasant protection (*Wehrbauern*) well to the east in order to seal this land off once and for all against the storm floods of Asia, then subdividing it with transverse walls so that we gradually reclaim this earth for ourselves, then far away on the margin of the true Germany, which was colonized with German blood, we slowly lay down one German wall after another so that, working towards the East, German people of German blood can carry out German settlement.[47]

To be rendered intelligible, such flights of fancy have to be referred to larger-than-Nazi histories. In fact, we need *both* the illuminating new work on the brutally managed project-driven coherence of the race-based ideological drives of the SS *and* continuing studies of the wider radical nationalist outlook where many of the potentials for that more programmatic set of commitments were housed and embedded. That remains an abiding challenge for anyone seeking to understand the dynamism of the Third Reich. The complexities here are multiform because the wider heterogeneity of imperialist thinking was not arranged neatly on either side of a Nazism *versus* wider-than-Nazism divide. That particular older-established dichotomy certainly retains important meaning – namely, between the National Socialist "true believers" and the far broader cultures of complicity and accommodation needed to ensure both the regime's capacity for implementing its policies and the full extent of its wider support. But those boundaries were themselves also both shifting and permeable, so that great care is needed in order to show how the complexities of any particular project and its implementation actually played themselves out.

Furthermore, those differences over the relative salience of "German culture" or "German blood" in defining the practical coordinates for concretely building the Nazi imperium in the various sectors of the "East" ran *through* the Nazi ranks, rather than outside them, and in many respects reached far inside the "hard core" of the SS itself, too – differences over who was to be allowed onto the *Volksliste* (German Ethnic Registry) and its equivalents and who was not, for example, and for that matter over how the extraordinarily diffuse concept of *Lebensraum* was to be endowed with some practicable contents and coherence.[48] Any easy distinction between SS "ideologists" ruthlessly and consistently wedded to their race-based projects and other Nazis (such as Arthur Greiser in Epstein's portrayal or Albert

Forster in Wolf's) whose relationship to *völkisch* and other strands of earlier radical nationalist thought supposedly made them into "pragmatists" and therefore somehow "less Nazi" is really not helpful. The dialectics of "pragmatics" and "ideology" could be found operating in each part of the Nazi policy-making machinery, just as the varying ideological repertoire of "race" could be constitutive for the latter in a wide variety of differing ways. "Nazi ideology" was not something owned by the SS, whose coherence and authenticity somehow diminished the further away from the notional core that it moved. Moreover, this is precisely where the ideological heterogeneity emphasized so strongly above – those "complexly cascading histories" of engagement with the East that accumulated as a consequence of World War I, together with all of the deeper histories we would also want to add – becomes so important.[49]

In other words, in breaking down the complexities of Nazi rule and how it worked, we need to study *not just* the processes that secured the necessary conformities and accommodations in society at large, but also the contingencies of how agency was produced inside the Nazi apparatuses themselves. The first of those purposes has undoubtedly predominated during the past two decades. As in most other areas of Nazi policy-making, especially during the war years, the short-term effectiveness of the atrocious occupation regime of the East presumed a vast reservoir of conformity quite beyond any necessary enthusiasm for either the specifics of the ideological message or the programmatic violence *per se* – including a willingness to stay in line and accept orders, a readiness to sink one's individuality in the coercive ideological community of the *Volksgemeinschaft*, a suspension of ethical agency under conditions of reliably heedless repression, and the usual appeals of adventure and sacrifice during wartime's heightened patriotic service. The regionally and locally grounded scholarship on the Judeocide and other aspects of the occupied East has moved our understanding on this score decisively forward, whether in relation to the *Wehrmacht*, to the role of the police auxiliary formations, to the presence of German civilian personnel, or to the elaborate machineries of professional expertise – that is, all those who were enlisted into the practical mechanics of the various versions of the Germanization drive.[50] But the same kind of analysis now needs to be applied to the interior histories of the Third Reich's state apparatuses too.

In its explicit foregrounding of spatial politics, Thomas Lekan's reading of Nazi treatments of landscape can be helpful here. In considering Nazism's apparently contrary impulses – its enthusiasm for technology's empowering consequences, yet its mystical venerating of the past of the *Volk* – Lekan rightly queries the influential formula of "reactionary modernism" that has often allowed them to be far too glibly reconciled. For if variously anticipated during preceding decades, the Nazis' specific reimagining of the national past in elaborately racialized ways was less some "reactionary" throwback than itself an outlook forged specifically in the 1930s, where Lekan uncovers sites of complexity that far exceed what the paradoxically hinged binary of "reactionary modernism" can be expected to contain.[51] Thus, the *Autobahn* planners "were hardly nostalgic about the traditional countryside," but instead "wielded ecological discourse to legitimate a transformation … of cultural landscapes" that sought effectively to reinvent them in "a more 'natural' state." Similarly, "Spatial planning and ecological restoration were also integral to the regime's racist and imperialist goals; measures designed to protect German Soil cannot be divorced from the regime's desire to restore Aryan Blood."[52] Indeed, the Nazi "synthesis of environmental planning and racial hygiene [created] a new sense of time and space that went far beyond nineteenth-century dichotomies of progress and tradition." Here Lekan describes the Nazis' especially driven relationship to ideas of the past and the future, which found its violent expression in the exorbitantly demanding spatial imaginary of race, empire, and colonization:

> In place of what Walter Benjamin deemed modernity's "homogeneous, empty time," the Nazis used organic metaphors of *Ewigkeit*, or eternity, to recapture what Benjamin termed 'Messianic' time, a simultaneity of past and future in an instantaneous present. The Nazis grounded their belief in racial character on supposedly objective laws of the natural world; Germans past, present, and future were thus eternally connected by blood. Though Germany's primordial landscape was gone forever, ecological restoration and spatial planning held out the promise that the natural balance in the contemporary cultural landscape could be restored. By preventing landscape deterioration through careful planning and restoration, the German nation would endure forever; both *Volk* and *Landschaft*, Blood and Soil, would renew themselves in a never-ending cycle of birth, growth, death, and rebirth. As the poet Karl Broeger remarked: "Nothing can take away our love and faith in our land. We are sent to preserve and shape it. Should we die, it is the duty of our heirs to preserve and shape it. Germany will not die." Blood and soil interacted symbiotically to create a closed organic circle that would replace the relentless linearity of nineteenth-century progress. By returning to their primordial *Lebensraum*, the *Volk* would perpetuate the thousand-year Reich and live, perhaps, forever.[53]

Space, place, and the imaginary

This is where cultural geography, as the particular disciplinary context where "space" is an organizing concept, can provide a great deal of help. If one vital feature of the intellectual history of historiography during the last 40 years has been a continuous worrying of materialist types of analysis, then the cultural geographer's version of this conundrum concerns the relationship between "space" and "place." Thus, if older notations of regionalism, area, and location – traditional geography in those senses – implied a set of place-based materialities, then more recently, ever since the late 1980s, cultural geographers have proposed a culturalist or representational conception of "landscape" instead in order to capture the social and subjective meanings through which a particular envisioning of place becomes constructed and imagined. "Space" then becomes the broader philosophical ground for thinking about human spatial experience, while place can denote the material realization or concretizing of the human wroughtness of space. More dynamically put, the dual processes of discursive space-making and phenomenological emplacement become the particular meaningful material practices that articulate, institutionalize, and attempt to fix human experience.[54]

One of the main effects of this really decisive theoretical, or perhaps epistemological, move has been to render as problematic an older model of the relationship between time and space, in which time functioned as the superordinate category, while place signified stasis or a kind of permanence, the solid and perduring ground of unchangeability, in ways akin to Fernand Braudel's geographical time, the deep structures of the environment and their *longue durée*. Against those older habits of thought, the more recent rethinking of space overturns that presumed authority of time. From functioning as the mere "container" of historical experience, space reemerges as its constitutive medium. We now have in its stead a mobile, processual field of time and space in which neither of those terms any longer exercises primacy, but rather become enfolded together in a much more dynamic conception of the flows and forms of a society's collective life. While hardly part of the "cultural turn" in human geography *per se*, standing rather for extremely classical materialist commitments, thinkers such as Henri Lefebvre and David Harvey have also played their part, as has Raymond Williams, by seeking the ground upon which *society* and *space* could be re-theorized. Each posed the question of how social analysis might become spatialized.[55] The old question of what is space gives way to a new one – namely, how is it that particular human practices, experiences, and imaginings both create and deploy distinctive constructions of space? Thinking about space in such a way helps ground and illumine certain other terms now commonly used by historians as a matter of course, like maps, mapping, and landscapes. Each of these conceptual devices originates metaphorically as a means not only of helping to explain how representations and imaginings can occur, but also re-describing how such processes become naturalized into fixed and centered narratives such that place begins to appear settled and obvious.[56]

In the German field, studies of *Heimat* have been the classic instance of the gains of taking on board these complexities of space and spatialization.[57] In this regard the cultural geographer's understanding of space becomes extremely helpful in handling questions of center and periphery, or center and margins. There are many particular ways of deploying, and beginning to deconstruct, that familiar binary framework. We might, for instance, approach the margins most obviously via questions of ethno-cultural and ethno-religious minorities, or by foregrounding treatments of gender and region. Our contemporary language of *margins*, *frontiers*, *borderlands*, *liminality*, *hidden histories*, and so forth also contains a wider menu of approaches in that kind of way, so we also need to explore more metaphorical and allegorical uses of the language in question – that is, the representational and ideational meanings of the margin as well as the more practical and material ones. Any discussion of margins should also encourage us to consider how the centeredness of German history in the Nazi time might then be rethought. In other words, we should not stay in the margin without returning to the center in order to try to understand what difference this may have made.[58]

Finally, the idea of the "imaginary" as developed from the thought of Cornelius Castoriadis also becomes extremely helpful – namely, as the cognitive ground of thought, beliefs, and assumptions from which human agency may materialize, or the mental landscape where homes can be imagined and purposeful explorations occur, what Dirk Moses calls "the symbolic, generative matrix within which people imagine their social world and constitute themselves as political subjects."[59] The "political imaginary" suggests the contexts of thought, some of them willfully intended but others only partially understood, even entirely unreflected, that set people into motion. It is what allows them to become political actors; it enables political agency. It describes the cumulative and congealed givenness of "the background assumptions about reality that makes daily praxis possible." More than any specific set of ideas, it is what makes the forming and framing of ideas possible in the first place. Charles Taylor puts this extremely well in saying that the imaginary is a pre-theoretical sense of the commonalties and disjunctions of social life, one "carried in images, stories and legends" that allow people to "imagine their social existence, how they fit together with others, how things go on between them and their fellows, the expectations that are normally met, and the deeper normative notions and images that underlie these expectations."[60] In Moses's words, the imaginary "underlies and enables the repertoire of actions available for any particular society."

Yet, the imaginary can never be permanently naturalized into a stable and entirely predictable source of legitimacy, rendered reliably authoritative or impermeable against change. It has to be renewed and reproduced; it has to be confirmed. Sometimes that happens "naturally" and unconsciously, as "a matter of course." At others it requires active and deliberate labor, whether by individuals in order to situate themselves more comfortably within a set of familiar or changed relations, or by organized agencies of some kind such as a government, a church, or a party. That process of renewal may succeed to varying degrees or it may come apart. Its terms may shift as a result of contestation, whether subtle and insidious or via large-scale upheaval and transformations. "Deeper than the immediate 'background' understanding needed to interpret social life, the imaginary is also temporally constituted," constituted through and by time, because in order to work effectively "social interpretation necessarily entails a narrative of the collective becoming of the primary social group, for instance the nation, standing internationally in history." For this, "a culture's sense of moral order" also becomes crucial.[61]

This seems to me to be one way of handling the problems of ideology. National Socialism aspired to remake Germany's social imaginary in the terms that I have just laid out. As the following chapter will continue to explore, the extraordinary scale of that ambition remains unintelligible without a grasp of Nazism's catastrophic sensibility, both as a view of the past and as an anticipation of the future. That is where the analytics of space become vital – in the form, that is, of the language of *Raum*, *Lebensraum*, *Großraum*, *Raumplanung* and the complicated ways in which those contexts shaped and were shaped by the drive for a new German imperial imaginary in terms of the embrace of a particular conception of Europe and its Nazified New Order.

Notes

1 Here I cite only three major synthetic works: M. Mazower, *Hitler's Empire: How the Nazis Ruled Europe*, New York: Penguin Press, 2008; S. Baranowski, *Nazi Empire: German Colonialism and Imperialism from Bismarck to Hitler*, Cambridge: Cambridge University Press, 2011; Tooze, *The Wages of Destruction*.

2 The impact of these numbers of foreigners upon Germany's wartime visual landscape – in a visual environment massively denuded of adult German men younger than 40 and not in uniform, populated increasingly by women, teenagers, and old men – has not been fully explored. At a time when Germany's external borders were being pushed brutally *outwards*, with obsessive attention to the bases of separation between Germans and the subject peoples, a vast army of the latter were brought forcibly into the very heartland of Germany itself. To take just one example, the Rheinmetall-Borsig anti-aircraft factory in Laurahütte (Silesia) employed only 650 German nationals alongside 850 forced laborers and 900 inmates supplied by Auschwitz. See R. J. Evans, *The Third Reich at War*, New York: Penguin Press, 2009, pp367–8. The fundamental works on forced labor are now M. Spoerer, *Zwangsarbeit unter dem Hakenkreuz: Ausländische Zivilarbeiter, Kriegsgefangene und Häftlinge im Dritten Reich im bestezten Europa 1939–1945*, Stuttgart: Deutsche Velags-Anstalt, 2001, along with U. Herbert, *Hitler's Foreign Workers* and Herbert (ed.) *Europa und der "Reichseinsatz."* For a masterful synthetic analysis see Tooze, *Wages of Destruction*, pp513–51; and for a succinct summary account, Evans, *Third Reich at War*, pp347–72.

3 I define these ruptures by simultaneous occurrence of territorial revision (loss or addition of new lands to the state) and upheavals in state forms and political arrangements. In contrast with their frequency in German history, there was only a single clear instance of such a rupture in France – that of 1940 to 1946 – because the other major political and constitutional crises, with the possible exception of 1870 to 1871, lacked territorial changes on anything like the German scale.

4 See Allen, *The Nazi Seizure of Power*; Noakes, *The Nazi Party in Lower Saxony*; Peterson, *The Limits of Hitler's Power*.

5 This is the underlying conceptual and methodological working basis for the works cited in note 64 to Chapter 3.

6 Mazower, *Hitler's Empire*; Baranowski, *Nazi Empire*. For scholarship on German colonialism and its legacies: V. Langbehn and M. Salama (eds) *German Colonialism: Race, the Holocaust, and Postwar Germany*, New York: Columbia University Press, 2011; M. Perraudin and J. Zimmerer (eds) *German Colonialism and National Identity*, London: Routledge, 2011; A. D. Moses and D. Stone (eds), *Colonialism and Genocide*, London: Routledge, 2007, especially J. Zimmerer, "The Birth of the *Ostland* out of the Spirit of Colonialism: A Postcolonial Perspective on the Nazi policy of Conquest and Extermination," pp101–23; G. Eley and B. D. Naranch (eds) *German Colonialism in a Global Age, 1884–1945*, Durham: Duke University Press, forthcoming 2014. See also the forum involving J. Baberowski, M. Dabag, C. Grlach, B. Kundrus, and E. D. Weitz, "Debatte: NS-Forschung und Genozidforschung," *Zeithistorische Forschungen/Studies in Contemporary History, Online Ausgabe*, 2008, vol. 5, no. 3, http://www.zeithistorische-forschungen.de/16126041-Debatte-3-2008.

7 B. Kundrus, "Kontinuitäten, Parallelen, Rezeptionen. Überlegungen zur 'Kolonisierung' des Nationalsozialismus," *WerkstattGeschichte* vol. 43, 2006, pp45–62, here p60. See also D. van Laak, *Imperiale Infrastruktur. Deutsche Planungen für eine Erschließung Afrikas 1880 bis 1960*, Paderborn: Ferdinand Schöningh, 2004.

8 The latter phrase is taken from the subtitle of K. O'Donnell, R. Bridenthal, and N. Reagin (eds) *The Heimat Abroad: The Boundaries of Germanness*, Ann Arbor: University of Michigan Press, 2005. See especially the following: S. Conrad, *Globalisation and the Nation in Imperial Germany*, Cambridge: Cambridge University Press, 2010; A. Zimmerman, *Anthropology and Antihumanism in Imperial Germany*, Chicago: University of Chicago Press, 2001, and *Alabama in Africa: Booker T. Washington, the German Empire, and the Globalization of the New South*, Princeton: Princeton University Press, 2010; H. G. Penny and M. Bunzl (eds) *Worldly Provincialism: German Anthropology in the Age of Empire*, Ann Arbor: University of Michigan Press, 2003. For recent commentaries, see especially J. Jenkins, "Locating Germany," *German History*, 2011, vol. 29, no. 1, pp108–26; B. Naranch, J. Jenkins, K. Manjapra, H.-E. Kim, Y.-S. Hong, and C. R. Unger, "Asia, Germany and the Transnational Turn," *German History*, 2010, vol. 28, no. 4, pp515–36.

9 In thinking through this specifically transnational perspective, I have learned a great deal from Bradley D. Naranch and his writings, above all his forthcoming *Blood and Empire: Global Expansion and the Making of Modern Germany*.

10 H.-U. Wehler, *Bismarck und der Imperialismus*, Cologne: Kiepenheuer und Witsch, 1969, pp112–42, 423–53; W. Spohn, *Weltmarktkonkurrenz und Industrialisierung Deutschlands 1870–1914*, Berlin: Olle und Wolter, 1977; C. Torp, *Die Herausforderung der Globalisierung: Wirtschaft und Politik in Deutschland 1860–1914*, Göttingen: Vandenhoeck und Ruprecht, 2005; Conrad, *Globalisation and the Nation*, pp27–76.

11 See here G. Eley, "Social Imperialism in Germany: Reformist Synthesis or Reactionary Sleight of Hand?" in Eley, *From Unification to Nazism: Reinterpreting the German Past*, London: George Allen and Unwin, 1986, pp154–67.

12 See above all D. Ciarlo, *Advertising Empire, Consuming Race: Colonialism and Visual Culture, 1887–1914*, Cambridge: Harvard University Press, 2010; E. Ames, *Carl Hagenbeck's Empire of Entertainments*, Seattle: University of Washington Press, 2008; S. Wolter, *Die Vermarktung des Fremden*, Frankfurt am Main: Campus, 2005; J. Zeller, *Bilderschule der Herrenmenschen: Koloniale Reklamesammelbilder*, Berlin: Ch. Links, 2008; V.M. Langbehn (ed.) *German Colonialism, Visual Culture, and Modern Memory*, London: Routledge, 2010.

13 This is necessarily a highly compressed rendition of a complicated set of histories before 1914. The indispensable starting point remains F. Fischer, *War of Illusions: German Policies from 1911 to 1914*, along with his *Germany's War Aims in the First World War*, each London: Chatto and Windus, 1969 and 1967. For current research and argument, see M. Hewitson, *Germany and the Causes of the First World War*, Oxford: Berg, 2004; and for a fine conspectus, Baranowski, *Nazi Empire*, pp9–66. For greater detail, see G. Eley, "Empire by Land or Sea? Germany's Imperial Imaginary, 1840–1945," in Eley and Naranch (eds) *German Colonialism*. The continuing reach of the earlier discourse is brilliantly examined in J. Hell, "Katechon: Carl Schmitt's Imperial Theology and the Ruins of the Future," *The Germanic Review*, vol. 84, no. 4, 2009, pp283–356, and the same author's forthcoming *Ruins: From the Roman Empire to the Third Reich*.

14 The reference here is to R. Koselleck, "'Space of Experience' and 'Horizon of Expectation': Two Historical Categories," in Koselleck (ed.) *Futures Past: On the Semantics of Historical Time*, Cambridge: MIT Press, 1985, pp255–76.

15 P. Walkenhorst, *Nation–Volk–Rasse: Radikaler Nationalismus im Deutschen Kaiserreich 1890–1914*, Göttingen: Vandenhoeck und Ruprecht, 2007, pp128–49. For the "three bodies of the nation," see U. Planert's brilliant "Der dreifacher Körper des Volkes: Sexualität, Biopolitik und die Wissenschaften vom Leben," *Geschichte und Gesellschaft*, vol. 26, 2000, 539–76.

16 Ibid, p115. See D. Frymann (H. Claß), *Wenn ich der Kaiser wär: Politische Wahrheiten und Notwendigkieiten*, Leipzig: Dietrich, 1912.

17 V. G. Liulevicius, *War Land on the Eastern Front: Culture, National Identity, and German Occupation in World War I*, Cambridge: Cambridge University Press, 2000, pp54–5.

18 A. Hillgruber, *Germany and the Two World Wars*, Cambridge: Harvard University Press, 1981, pp45–6.

19 Karl Hellferich, leading banker and politician, successively Secretary of the Treasury (1915–1916) and the Interior (1916–1917), quoted by J. G. Williamson, *Karl Helfferich 1872–1924: Economist, Financier, Politician*, Princeton: Princeton University Press, 1971, p267.

20 Hillgruber, *Germany and the Two World Wars*, p47. See also G. Eley, "Remapping the Nation: War, Revolutionary Upheaval, and State Formation in Easter Europe, 1914–1923," in P. J. Potichnyj and H. Aster (eds) *Ukrainian–Jewish Relations in Historical Perspective*, Edmonton: Canadian Institute of Ukrainian Studies, 1988, pp205–46.

21 See this remark recorded in his diary in April 1941 by Hermann Voss, an anatomist newly appointed to a chair in the Medical Faculty at the new Reich University of Posen, the intended flagship of German education in the occupied territories: "I quite like the city of Posen; if one could only get rid of the Poles, it would be very pleasant here." See G. Aly, "The Posen Diaries of the Anatomist Hermann Voss," in Aly, Chrost, and Pross, *Cleansing the Fatherland*, p122. I have slightly amended the translation.

22 Liulevicius, *War Land*, p29. At 27 people per square kilometer, *Oberost*'s population density was only half that of neighboring East Prussia, a quarter of that for Germany as a whole. The war itself decimated the demographic landscape, removing a third of *Oberost*'s prewar population either as casualties or refugees, or some 1.3 out of 4.2 million people, varying from an extraordinary 54.4 percent in Courland to 26.6 percent in Lithuania. Not only ruined in numbers, the remaining inhabitants were also disproportionately female, juvenile, or old-aged.

23 "It was a horrifying sight, these villages, deserted, half-burned out and haunted by hungry crows, in which only on occasion, out of a stark, barricaded house with blind, covered windows, from a disgusting door crack would lean out a sad figure, wasted down to bones, which in terrible greeting would vomit on the doorstep and then immediately crawl back into the darkness of these unhealthy, forbidden houses." See B. von der Marwitz, *Stirb und Werde. Aus Briefen und Kriegstageesbuchblättern des Leutnants Bernhard von der Marwitz*, Breslau: Wilh. Gottl. Korn, 1931, quoted by Liulevicius, *War Land*, p42.

24 V. Klemperer, *Curriculum Vitae. Erinnerungen, 1881–1918*, Berlin: Aufbau Verlag, 1996, p467, quoted by Liulevicius, *War Land*, p46.

25 The *Freikorps* were originally raised in Germany under the authority of SPD Defense Minister Gustav Noske in early January 1919 to assist in suppressing the radical Left. They were then deployed for sundry other purposes, including the shielding of troops during evacuation from the East and the protection of Germans in border conflicts, while effectively becoming feral, most notoriously in the Baltic. Officially recalled to Germany in July 1919, the Baltic units mutinied into a 14,000-strong German legion. Parasitic on the land, they kept up a ferociously predatory presence in the region, clutching fantasies of a German military redoubt, until finally expelled from Lithuania in December 1919. See R. G. L. Waite, *Vanguard of Nazism: The Free Corps Movement in Postwar Germany 1918–1923*, Cambridge: Harvard University Press, 1952, pp94–139; Liulevicius, *War Land*, pp227–46. See also K. Theweleit's still unrivaled, if disorderly and speculative, treatment of the resulting discourse of violent, xenophobic, and misogynist masculinity in *Male Fantasies, Vol. 1: Women, Floods, Bodies, History*, and *Vol. 2: Psychoanalyzing the White Terror*, Minneapolis: University of Minnesota Press, 1987, 1989.

26 F. W. Heinz, "Der deutsche Vorstoß in das Balitkum," in C. Hötzel (ed) *Deutscher Austand: Die Revolution des Nachkrieges*, Stuttgart: Kohlhammer, 1934, p47, quoted by Liulevicius, *War Land*, p233.

27 E. von Salomon, *Die Geächteten*, Berlin: Rowohlt, 1930, p111, quoted by Liulevicius, *War Land*, p237. Salomon (1902–1972) was involved in planning Walther Rathenau's assassination in June 1922, though not in the act itself. Sentenced to five years

in prison, he gained later renown with autobiographical fictions about his youthful wartime experiences and service in the *Freikorps*. Keeping his distance from Nazism, he re-emerged after 1945 as a pacifist.

28 W. von Gayl, quoted by Liulevicius, *War Land*, p249. An anti-Polish activist and Prussian civil servant before 1914, specializing in internal colonization and close to the Pan-Germans, Gayl became head of the Political Section of the *Oberost* administration in 1916 to 1918.

29 P. J. Weindling, *Epidemics and Genocide in Eastern Europe, 1890–1945*, Oxford: Oxford University Press, 2000, pp153, 176, 152.

30 All of these dimensions of Germans' relation to the East are brilliantly engaged in A. H. Sammartino, *The Impossible Border: Germany and the East, 1914–1922*, Ithaca: Cornell University Press, 2010.

31 "We National Socialists consciously draw a line beneath the foreign policy of our prewar period. We take up where we broke off six hundred years ago. We stop the endless German movement to the south and west, and turn our gaze to the east. At long last we break off the colonial and commercial policy of the prewar period and shift to the soil policy of the future." See A. Hitler, *Mein Kampf*, Boston: Houghton Mifflin, 1971, p656, cited by W. Lower, "Hitler's 'Garden of Eden' in Ukraine: Nazi Colonialism, *Volksdeutsche*, and the Holocaust, 1941–1944," in J. Petrupoulos and J. K. Roth (eds) *Gray Zones*, pp185–204, here p189.

32 R. L. Nelson, "Introduction: Colonialism in Europe? The Case against Salt Water," in Nelson (ed.) *Germans, Poland, and Colonial Expansion to the East: 1850 Through the Present*, New York: Palgrave Macmillan, 2009, pp1–9, here p4. See also G. Thum (ed.) *Traumland Osten: Deutsche Bilder vom östlichen Europa im 20. Jahrhundert*, Göttingen: Vandenheock und Ruprecht, 2006; V.G. Liulevicius, *The German Myth of the East: 1800 to the Present*, Oxford: Oxford University Press, 2009.

33 W. Lower, *Nazi Empire-Building and the Holocaust in Ukraine*, Chapel Hill: University of North Carolina Press, 2005; D. Farber and W. Lower, "Colonialism and Genocide in Nazi-Occupied Poland and Ukraine," in A. D. Moses (ed.) *Empire, Colony, Genocide: Conquest, Occupation, and Subaltern Resistance in World History*, New York: Berghahn Books, 2008, pp372–400; Lower, "Hitler's 'Garden of Eden' in Ukraine."

34 See G. Wolf, *Ideologie und Herrschaftsrationalität* and esp. Wolf, "Suitable Germans – Enforced Assimilation Policies in German Occupied North Western Poland, 1939–1945," in C.-C. W. Szejnmann and M. Umbach (eds) *Heimat, Region and Empire. Spatial Identities under National Socialism*, Houndmills: Palgrave Macmillan, forthcoming, from which the quotation is taken.

35 Koonz, *The Nazi Conscience*, pp2–3, 16.

36 Such an approach to Nazi ideas reaches a kind of apogee in the grandiose fictionalized rendition of SS thinking in J. Littell's controversial novel, *The Kindly Ones*, New York: HarperCollins, 2009, which uses an invented SS narrator, Max Aue, in order to stage a series of elaborately detailed explications of Nazi thought during the time of genocide. For a searching discussion of Littell's novel, see D. LaCapra, "Historical and Literary Approaches to the 'Final Solution': Saul Friedländer and Jonathan Littell," *History and Theory*, vol. 50, 2011, pp71–97; also "Toward a Critique of Violence," in LaCapra, *History and its Limits: Human, Animal, Violence*, Ithaca: Cornell University Press, 2009, pp90–122.

37 For the specifics of the planning process during the 12 months before the invasion of 22 June 1941, see A. J. Kay, *Exploitation, Resettlement, Mass Murder: Political and Economic Planning for German Occupation Policy in the Soviet Union, 1940–1941*, New York: Berghahn Books, 2006. The indispensable guide to the overall predicament of German occupation administration, its competing exigencies, and insurmountable problems is Tooze, *Wages of Destruction*, pp429–589. For excellent summary accounts, see Chapter 8: "Designing a 'War of Annihilation'," in I. Kershaw, *Hitler. 1936–45: Nemesis*, pp339–89; Mazower, *Hitler's Empire*, pp179–256.

38 D. Blackbourn, "The Conquest of Nature and the Mystique of the Eastern Frontier in Nazi Germany," in Nelson (ed.) *Germans, Poland, and Colonial Expansion to the East*, pp141–70, here p147; also Blackbourn, *The Conquest of Nature: Water, Landscape, and the Making of Modern Germany*, New York: W. W. Norton, 2006, Chapter 5: "Race and Reclamation: National Socialism in Germany and Europe," pp251–309.

39 Here see above all G. Wolf's new study, *Ideologie und Herrschaftsrationalität*, esp. pp191–342. For the RKF, Koehl, *RKFDV*, remains an excellent starting point. See also Longerich, *Heinrich Himmler*, Oxford: Oxford University Press, 2012, Chapter 16, "A New Racial Order," pp437–68; Epstein, *Model Nazi*, pp124–230; Rutherford, *Prelude to the Final Solution*; Rossino, *Hitler Strikes Poland*; M. G. Esch, *"Gesunde Verhältnisse": Deutsche und polnische Bevölkerungspolitik in Ostmitteleuropa 1939–1950*, Marburg: Verlag Herder-Institut, 1998. For cognate events in the Czech–German borderlands: T. Zahra, *Kidnapped Souls: National Indifference and the Battle for Children in the Bohemian Lands, 1900–1948*, Ithaca: Cornell University Press, 2008, pp169–251.

40 However, Wolf himself constructs perhaps too sharp an opposition between "racial" and *völkisch* thinking. The SS race experts *per se* had certainly hardened their own understanding, but the distinction remained otherwise more permeable. As *völkisch* thought coalesced among late Wilhelmine radical nationalists during the early 1900s it acquired an expressly racialist outlook. That the rivalries between Himmler and the Gauleiters came to center on the racial/*völkisch* opposition was keyed situationally to the technical requirements and operation of the *Volksliste*. In other contexts of debate, the modes of thought might not have been so sharply in tension let alone mutually exclusive. See especially Walkenhorst, *Nation–Volk–Rasse*, pp80–165.

41 His ambition to merge The Netherlands, Flanders, and French territory north of the Loire River into the Reich, transform Wallonia and Brittany into protectorates, merge Northern Ireland with the Irish Republic, create a decentralized British federation, and declare independence for the Basques, Catalonians, and Galicians from Spain foundered on the resistance of the military and the foreign office, [who] preferred the existing national states, albeit under German domination. See S. Baranowski, "Against 'Human Diversity as Such': *Lebensraum* and Genocide in the Third Reich," in Langbehn and Salama (eds) *German Colonialism*, pp51–71, here p61; also Baranowski, *Nazi Empire*, pp290–1; Herbert, *Best*, pp295–8.

42 For the Danish episode, see Herbert, *Best*, pp323–400; Evans, *Third Reich at War*, pp389–92.

43 See Blackbourn, "Conquest of Nature," pp152, 158; and in full detail, *Conquest of Nature*, pp293–309; also C. P. Kakel, *The American West and the Nazi East: A Comparative and Interpretive Perspective*, Houndmills: Palgrave Macmillan, 2011.

44 The diversity of radical nationalist projections of eastward expansion may be approached via the following: Smith, *Ideological Origins*; Burleigh, *Germany Turns Eastwards*; Haar and Fahlbusch (eds) *German Scholars and Ethnic Cleansing*; M. Bassin, "Race contra Space: The Conflict between German *Geopolitik* and National Socialism," *Political Geography Quarterly*, 1987, vol. 6, no. 2, pp115–34, and "Imperialism and the Nation State in Friedrich Ratzel's Political Geography," *Progress in Human Geography*, vol. 11, 1987, pp473–95; H. Heske, "Karl Haushofer: His Role in German Geopolitics and in Nazi Politics," *Political Geography Quarterly*, 1987, vol. 6, no. 2, pp135–44; D. T. Murphy, *The Heroic Earth: Geopolitical Thought in Weimar Germany, 1918–1933*, Kent, O. H.: Kent State University Press, 1997; R. L. Nelson, "The *Archive for Inner Colonization*, the German East, and World War I," in Nelson (ed.) *Germans, Poland, and Colonial Expansion to the East*, pp65–93; I. Stoehr, "Von Max Sering zu Konrad Meyer – ein 'machter greifender' Generationswechsel in der Agrar- und Siedlungswissenschaft," in S. Heim (ed.) *Autarkie und Ostexpansion. Pflanzenzucht und Agrarforschung im Nationalsozialismus*, Göttingen: Wallstein, 2002, pp57–90; G. Stoakes, *Hitler and the Quest for World Domination: Nazi Ideology and Foreign Policy in the 1920s*, Leamington Spa: Berg Publishers, 1986; S. Frech, *Wegbereiter Hitlers? Theodor Reismann-Grone. Ein völkischer*

Nationalist (1863–1949), Paderborn: Ferdinand Schöningh, 2009, pp318–412; J. Leicht, *Heinrich Claß 1868–1953. Die politische Biographie eines Alldeutschen*, Paderborn: Ferdinand Schöningh, 2011.

45 The statement was made by Hitler in a meeting on 16 July 1941 to discuss the political plan of action for occupied Soviet land. He continued: "they [the eastern territories] are vital to us … [overseas] colonies play an entirely subordinate role." See Lower, "Hitler's 'Garden of Eden' in Ukraine," p200.

46 Ibid, p195.

47 Blackbourn, *Conquest of Nature*, p273.

48 Conflicts over the qualifying criteria for getting onto the *Volksliste* (racial-biological versus a demonstrated record of social and cultural identification) were at the heart of the rivalry between Himmler and the two Gauleiters most affected, Arthur Greiser (Warthegau) and Albert Forster (Danzig–West Prussia). See the account in Epstein, *Model Nazi*, pp208–30, and for full detail Wolf, *Ideologie und Herrschaftsrationalität*, pp376–488.

49 In developing this argument I am grateful to Gerhard Wolf for a number of clarifying conversations.

50 See here Elizabeth Harvey's excellent *Women and the Nazi East*. As she shows, the effort at implanting a "German culture" in the occupied East entailed not only the population policies of uprooting and mass murder, resettlement and dispossession, together with the usual machinery of language policies, schooling, and the celebration of an invented customary culture. But Germanization also embraced a wider program of housewifery, domestic hygiene, and orderly family life, for which the generations of girls and young women socialized during the 1930s provided the necessary cadres of teachers, social workers, instructors in domestic science and mothercraft, volunteers, and role models.

51 The reference is to J. Herf, *Reactionary Modernism: Technology, Culture, and Politics in Weimar and the Third Reich*, Cambridge: Cambridge University Press, 1984.

52 T. M. Kehan, *Imagining the Nation in Nature: Landscape Preservation and German Identity, 1885–1945*, Cambridge: Harvard University Press, 2004, p250.

53 Ibid, p251.

54 For reflections on contemporary historiography in the sense suggested by this paragraph, see G. Eley, *Crooked Line*.

55 See H. Lefebvre, *The Production of Space*, Oxford: Blackwell, 1991, and *State, Space, World: Selected Essays*, Minneapolis: University of Minnesota Press, 2009; D. Harvey, *The Urban Experience*, Baltimore: Johns Hopkins University Press, 1989; Harvey, *Justice, Nature and the Geography of Difference*, Oxford; Wiley–Blackwell, 1997, pp207–328; Harvey, "Reinventing Geography," *New Left Review*, Second Series 4, 2000, pp75–97; and R. Williams, *The Country and the City*, New York: Oxford University Press, 1975.

56 For guidance in the intellectual landscape of cultural geography, I am hugely indebted to Jessica Dubow. See, in particular, D. Cosgrove, *Social Formation and Symbolic Landscape*, Madison: University of Wisconsin, 1998, 1st edn, 1984; and Cosgrove, "Towards a Radical Cultural Geography," *Antipode*: 1983, vol. 15, no. 1, pp1–11, followed by Cosgrove and S. Daniels (eds) *The Iconography of Landscape: Essays on the Symbolic Representation, Design, and Use of Past Environments*, Cambridge: Cambridge University Press, 1989. See also D. Gregory, *Geographical Imagination*, New York: HarperCollins, 1991; Cosgrove (ed.) *Mappings*, London: Reaktion, 1999; T. Cresswell, *Place: A Short Introduction*, Oxford: Wiley–Blackwell, 2004.

57 Discussion was pioneered by C. Applegate, *A Nation of Provincials: The German Idea of Heimat*, Berkeley: University of California Press, 1990, reinforced by A. Confino, *The Nation as a Local Metaphor: Württemberg, Imperial Germany, and National Memory, 1871–1918*, Chapel Hill: University of North Carolina Press, 1997; also J. Jenkins, *Provincial Modernity: Local Culture and Liberal Politics in Fin de Siècle Hamburg*, Ithaca: Cornell University Press, 2002. For important reflections: C. Applegate, "A Europe of Regions: Reflections on

the Historiography of Subnational Places in Modern Times," *American Historical Review*, 1999, vol. 104, no. 4, pp1157–82.

58 For further reflections, see G. Eley, "How and Where is German History Centered?," in N. Gregor, N. Roemer, and M. Roseman (eds) *German History from the Margins*, Bloomington: Indiana University Press, 2006, pp268–86.

59 A. D. Moses, "Redemptive Antisemitism and the Imperialist Imaginary," in C. Wiese and P. Betts (eds) *Years of Persecution, Years of Extermination: Saul Friedländer and the Future of Holocaust Studies*, London: Continuum, 2010, pp233–54, here p237, also for the following. See C. Castoriadis, *The Imaginary Institution of Society*, Cambridge: Polity, 1987; and for essential background, M. van der Linden, "*Socialisme ou Barbarie*: A French Revolutionary Group (1949–1965). In memory of Cornelius Castoriadis, 11 March 1922–26 December 1997," *Left History*, vol. 5, no. 1, 1997, pp7–37.

60 C. Taylor, "Modern Social Imaginaries," *Public Culture*, vol. 14, no. 1, 2002, pp91–124, here p106; also Taylor, "What is a 'Social Imaginary?'," in Taylor (ed.) *Modern Social Imaginaries*, Durham: Duke University Press, 2004, pp23–30.

61 Moses, "Redemptive Antisemitism," p237. My own thinking about the "imaginary" is indebted to long-running conversations with my late friend Keith Nield, and more recently with Dirk Moses. See also G. Eley, "Imperial Imaginary, Colonial Effect: Writing the Colony and the Metropole Together," in C. Hall and K. McClelland (eds) *Race, Nation and Empire: Making Histories, 1750 to the Present*, Manchester: Manchester University Press, 2010, pp217–36.

6

PUTTING THE HOLOCAUST INTO HISTORY

Genocide, Imperial Hubris, and the Racial State

Histories sacred and profane

"A sacrifice wholly consumed by fire; a whole burnt offering … A complete sacrifice or offering … A sacrifice on a large scale … Complete consumption by fire, or that which is so consumed; complete destruction, esp. of a large number of persons: a great slaughter or massacre." Such is the *OED*'s definition of the word "holocaust."[1] As always, the etymology discloses a finer pattern of meaning. As Paul Mendes-Flohr and Jehuda Reinharz point out in their compilation *The Jew in the Modern World*, the term begins in theology. It "derives from the Septuagint, the Jewish translation of the Hebrew Scripture into Greek from the third century BC, in which *holokaustos* ('totally burnt') is the Greek rendering of the Hebrew *olah*, the burnt sacrificial offering dedicated *exclusively* to God."[2] By the nineteenth century the term has passed into wider secular usage, denoting simply any example of vast devastation, particularly by fire. It became a term of no particular political or cultural charge.

How did present usage develop? It existed in the 1950s, but with no capital "H," and without the proprietorial charge. Filip Friedman, who pioneered the earliest historiography of the Jews in occupied Poland, used it, but only as a descriptive equivalent with several others, preferring instead the expression "the Jewish Catastrophe."[3] At that stage "holocaust" more commonly attached to the nightmare of nuclear war. The shift came after the controversy surrounding Hannah Arendt's *Eichmann in Jerusalem* in 1963, which began an intense public interrogation of Jewish conduct during the Nazi persecution.[4] A chillingly apt term coined during the war itself – "genocide" – now gave way to an expression more patently partisan.[5] In the meantime, the Jewish cultural presence evinced a self-confidence, an institutional weight, and a recognition that permitted both the Jewish and the universal importance of the genocide to be more assertively claimed. This was not unconnected to the novel existence of a territorial Jewish state, which played increasingly complicated parts in how German historians came to approach this history. In the wake of the 1967 Six Day War, an awareness of Israel's relationship to its origins helped to instate the genocide in public consciousness, across the Western European and English-speaking worlds, for Jews and non-Jews alike, in quite new ways.

In the process genocide became "The Holocaust," and the drive for a Nazi New Order became "the War against the Jews." Insistence on the event's uniquely Jewish character inescapably ensued. Lucy Dawidowicz described the "Holocaust" as "another link in the historic chain of Jewish suffering," for "once again in their history the Jews are victims, sacrifices."[6] Rhetorically, this had the ring of terrible, disquieting truth. But the sacral tone easily followed. Here is philosopher Emil Fackenheim in 1970 at a conference in Jerusalem: "A Jew knows about memory and uniqueness. He knows that the unique crime of the Nazi Holocaust must never be forgotten – and, above all, that the rescuing for memory of even a single innocent tear is a *holy task*."[7] Writings from that time embraced the mythical dimensions, from Elie Wiesel's best-selling fiction to George Steiner's *In Bluebeard's Castle* and Richard Rubenstein's *The Cunning of History*.[8] This easily passed into exclusivity, claiming empathic privilege and even Jewish ownership. Seven years later, at another conference, Fackenheim attacked those who questioned the Holocaust's uniqueness for "insulting" and "betraying" the dead. As Yehuda Bauer, then emerging as a key Israeli voice, put it: "if what happened to the Jews was unique, then it took place outside of history, and it becomes a mysterious event, an upside-down miracle, so to speak, an event of religious significance in the sense that it is not man-made as that term is normally understood."[9]

By the late 1960s "Holocaust" was appearing regularly in titles of essays and books, equipped with both capital letter and definite article. By the time of the *Encyclopaedia Judaica* volume in 1972, it was firmly established.[10] Concurrently, Jerusalem and Tel Aviv finally became key centers of research rather than, say, Warsaw, Paris, and New York. One notable watershed was a 1968 Yad Vashem conference, whose proceedings appeared in English as *Jewish Resistance during the Holocaust*.[11] Not only did the Jews begin re-emerging as historical subjects, whose reactions to Nazi persecution showed all the grayness of accommodation and resistance many earlier accounts had effaced; but the proceedings also marked the transition from testimony to scholarship. Filip Friedman and others had always observed the historian's evidentiary and disciplinary protocols. But it was only now, during the 1970s, that the historiography began coming more fully of age.

The mid 1980s already saw an ever-growing mountain of literature. Holocaust drew generous endowments across the United States, seeding an elaborate infrastructure for research and discussion. "Holocaust Studies" entered the curriculum in North American schools and colleges. It became endlessly discussed in books, TV shows, dramas, fictions, and films. By the 1980s enrolments at the University of Michigan for History 386 on "The Holocaust" far outran any of the Modern European surveys; in Ann Arbor's largest bookstore, Jewish history claimed more space than German, French, Italian, Spanish, Russian, and Eastern European history combined. Memoirs, anthologies, coffee-table books, novels, and textbooks ran ever more thickly from the presses. In November 1978 Jimmy Carter had named his President's Commission on the Holocaust under Elie Wiesel. A year later, it recommended a National Holocaust Memorial/Museum, an Educational Foundation, and a Committee on Conscience to monitor outbreaks of genocide in the world.[12]

For the place of the Holocaust in German history, this quickening of public interest becomes the indispensable background. Much critical intellectual history now tracks the shifts in public consciousness since the late 1940s, country by country, including Peter Novick's *The Holocaust in American Life*; Tony Kushner's *The Holocaust and the Liberal Imagination* on Britain; Tom Segev's *The Seventh Million* on Israel; and so forth.[13] We might draw an arc from the showing of the NBC television drama *Holocaust* in April 1978 to the release of Stephen Spielberg's *Schindler's List* in 1993, which then launched an especially intense media cycle of public memorializing, one intimately interlinked with the commemorative activity descending from the 40th anniversary of World War II in 1985. These same patterns of public interest became massively ramped up in West Germany around the showing of *Holocaust* in 1979.[14]

From the late 1960s, public memory work around the meanings of German responsibility for Nazism has been insistently tied into debates about the health of German democracy. In principle, this syndrome differed little from equivalent memorializing elsewhere, likewise linked to the working through of complex political legacies, collective identifications, and generational tensions descending from the war. Similar stories certainly surround other national historiographies. Convergent fields of controversy elsewhere in Europe mobilize the concurrent concerns of scholars and wider publics, sometimes focusing on the fate of the Jews, in the usual talk of perpetrators, bystanders, and victims, sometimes raising broader questions of resistance and collaboration. Continuing debates in Italian public life regarding legacies of fascism and anti-fascism, coming to terms with the "Vichy syndrome" in France, reconfiguring the war's legacies in Britain in a process extending now across three decades, and so on – in each case, country by country, the war's longer-term meanings are being opened up and interrogated.[15]

Bringing the Holocaust back home

That German historians now see the "war against the Jews" as Nazism's defining feature is quite new. It was only slowly that history of the Holocaust left its very particularized niche, whose links to German historians' acknowledged priorities remained quite thin. Until the 1990s it was virtually entirely sidelined by German historians. In most German histories it made only negligible appearances. Gordon Craig's Oxford History, *Germany 1866–1945*, published in 1978, supposedly the most authoritative general account of its time, gave the "Final Solution" barely three pages in its larger treatment of "Hitler's War, 1939–1945."[16] The worlds of

German historians working on Nazism and Jewish historians working on Holocaust were minimally interlinked. During the 1980s, that profoundly changed. *Now*, all aspects of Nazi policy and practice toward the Jews, along with every dimension of the "racial state," form overwhelmingly *the* primary concern of the field. Concurrently the bulk of new research has shifted markedly *away* from the dictatorship's founding years and *toward* the war years themselves.

From the mid 1960s to the early 1980s the main dividing lines among historians of Nazism on the "Final Solution" involved radically contrasting views of agency and causation. Whereas debates focused on Nazi aggression more generally, treatment of the Jews was a topic clearly nested therein. Should responsibility for genocide be drawn tightly around Hitler and the Nazis themselves, or should it be expanded to German society at large?[17] For so-called "intentionalists," such as Klaus Hildebrand and Andreas Hillgruber or Lucy Dawidowicz and Gerald Fleming, the answer was completely straightforward: the Final Solution came from the fundamental beliefs and direct authorship of Hitler as clearly laid out in *Mein Kampf* from the earliest years of the movement, unfolding with the force of a "blueprint" or "grand design."[18] Exterminating the Jews came from the uniqueness of Nazi racialism and Hitler's personal ideology, so that any actual decisions became the logical culmination of "the distinctive murderous will of the Nazi leadership."

On the other side were "structuralists" such as Hans Mommsen and Martin Broszat, who certainly accepted Hitler's underlying authority and the impetus of Nazi ideology, but saw anti-Semitism more complexly related to the movement's makeup, treating the "Final Solution" as the unevenly evolving consequence of the opportunities and disorder created by the military victories of 1940 to 1941. They saw Hitler as a "weak dictator," whose personal impact upon governing mattered far less than the "cumulative radicalization" of Nazi practice. If the murderousness of Nazi intentions was clear enough, the turning to genocide *per se* was new and produced situationally out of the war years during 1939 to 1941. Thus, historians should focus on the circumstances leading earlier combinations of policies to be jettisoned, including surreally unworkable schemes of mass deportation, projections of slow death by concentrating populations with no means of livelihood, and mass killings behind the military lines of the Eastern Front's "war of annihilation."[19] It was only the exhaustion of these earlier plans, compounded by the fresh millions of Jewish population in occupied Polish and Soviet lands, that brought Nazi planners to the killing of the entire Jewish people.

This structuralist case decisively widened German responsibility because it linked Nazi policies to the necessary collusion of all manner of civil servants, managers, businessmen, and professionals. Simply to become feasible, genocide presumed this widespread practical complicity of large sections of German society. That complicity was just as vital for the shaping of the "Final Solution" as the continuities in Hitler's ideological hatred of the Jews since *Mein Kampf*. Whereas "intentionalists" personalized the explanation of the "Final Solution" around Hitler's ideological outlook and dictatorial will, couching responsibility in terms of Nazi ideological fanaticism, "structuralists" moved attention away from Hitler himself toward a much broader-based conception of German responsibility, stressing instead the social and institutional structures engendering the regime's radical drive. Structuralist approaches tied the anti-democratic, terroristic, racialist, and anti-Semitic aspects of Nazism to a *generalized notion of German societal complicity*. By focusing on the broader social, political, and cultural dispositions in German society, they insisted, we could understand far better how "ordinary Germans" learned how to kill. We could understand how "normal" German society could become deformed into accepting the regime's racialist and anti-Semitic goals.[20]

That concept of normality corresponds roughly to the idea of the "banality of evil," as it emerged from the controversies surrounding Hannah Arendt's *Eichmann in Jerusalem*.[21] It helps us to think about the ways in which Nazi dynamism presumed *not only* an animating will among the leaders, *but also* the compliance and collusion of "non-Nazis" at all levels of German society after 1933, especially among the respectable layers in business, the professions, the armed services, and the civil apparatuses of the state. Without such larger reservoirs of acceptance, the functioning of the Third Reich's "racial state" was simply not thinkable. There were also key affinities here with the work of the great pioneer Raul Hilberg, whose classic account, *The Destruction of the European Jews*, had appeared in 1961, but only properly entered currency in this later time.[22] Like the structuralists, Hilberg took an avowedly administrative approach to all aspects of the Holocaust, eschewing either complex analysis of perpetrator motivations and ideas or detailed social histories of the killing process on the ground, while purposefully disregarding the testimony and experiential history of Jewish victims themselves.[23]

Each of these pioneering figures – Arendt, Mommsen/Broszat, Hilberg – remained contentiously disliked by wide circles inside the immediate field. But in combination they decisively shaped the broader intellectual climate in which younger generations of German historians, those embarking on dissertations in the late 1960s and 1970s, were now able to think. The image of the perpetrator as an emotionless bureaucrat, a "desk-murderer" (*Schreibtischtäter*) or "cog in the wheel," whose willingness to follow orders and adapt to the system fundamentally allowed it to function, now became paradigmatic for how the new historiography of the Holocaust could unfold. As *German* historians started bringing the subject for the first time centrally into the study of Nazism *per se*, *this* was the ground from which their understanding had grown. By the late 1980s, as argued in earlier chapters, a new historiography began resituating Nazi anti-Semitism inside much larger formations of the *racial state*. That, in turn, meant understanding the Holocaust in relation to more general patterns of *modernity*, whose pressures toward order-making and rule-following, planning and standardization, social exclusion and fear of difference, procedural rationality and social governmentality were deemed to have acquired, in early twentieth-century Germany, exceptional force.[24]

One direct effect of the intentionalist–structuralist controversy was a determination on the part of scholars working on the central decision-making machinery of the Nazi state to produce the most careful and authoritative account feasible of how the decision for the "Final Solution" actually occurred, leaving in the process no archival stone unturned. Much of that resolve was spurred by the claims of sundry "Holocaust deniers," including the widely published private scholar David Irving, that Hitler was uninvolved in either the central planning of the Judeocide or the details of implementation.[25] Absent any single written directive documenting Hitler's authorship in that excessively literal sense (the proverbial "smoking gun"), historians such as Christopher Browning and Ian Kershaw undertook a long and painstaking evidentiary odyssey to establish, via compellingly detailed empirical analysis, what the archival record could nonetheless allow us to say. As a result, and over the longer term since the late 1980s, the old conflict between intentionalists and structuralists practically died away.

As the mechanics and chronology of the decision-making process in 1939 to 1942 became exhaustively reconstructed, especially in light of newly accessible former Soviet and Eastern European archives, that older polarized framework seemed less and less helpful. Instead, we have broad agreement on the importance of both elements – a cumulative radicalization of anti-Jewish policies toward a decision for genocide, whose rationale had always presumed Hitler and the Nazis' fundamental ideological commitment. Historians still differ on when exactly the crucial line was crossed, whether as early as July to September 1941 or during the first half of December. But all share a "moderate structuralist" consensus. Indeed, we now possess three definitive general accounts reflecting this standpoint: Christopher Browning's 615-page *Origins of the Final Solution* (2004); Saul Friedländer's 870-page second volume, *The Years of Extermination* (2007); and Peter Longerich's 645-page magnum opus *Holocaust* (2010).[26]

On this basis a number of confident generalizations can follow. While there was patently a desire to settle the "Jewish question" once and for all, in callous and complete disregard of Jewish lives and livelihoods, with the willing embrace of mass killings and all possible ruthlessness, there was no originary blueprint of the kind eventually ratified at Wannsee in January 1942. The drive to destroy the Jewish historical and future presence in a German-dominated Europe arises incontrovertibly from the entirety of the documentary record between autumn 1939 and summer 1941, whether from Hitler's own public and private statements, from the planning agencies of the SS, from the wider governmental discussions, or from what the SS and civilian authorities actually *did* – practically, concretely, situationally, systematically – on occupied Polish ground. But the Final Solution *per se* resulted in the event from the Nazis' repeated inability to realize their earliest plans for resettlement and expulsion of racially defined populations, among whom the Jews were most brutally at risk. In the 18 months after the occupation of Poland in fall 1939, *resettlement*, *mass expulsion*, and *ghettoization* were each implemented in roughly overlapping sequence, with huge disorder and resulting problems, including mass starvation, appalling hardships, generalized brutality, and indiscriminate killing.[27]

By spring 1941, these plans were a clear practical failure. The anti-Soviet war then offered a double solution: Jews in the freshly occupied territories would be killed on the spot; ultimate victory would allow Jews previously concentrated in occupied Poland to be deported further to the very far east, where they would be left to die.[28] It was thus the war of annihilation begun on 22 June 1941 and the mass killings perpetrated by the *Einsatzgruppen* that fully escalated these intentions into genocide. The extension of systematic murder to women and children as well as to Jewish men occurred, region by region, between the end of July and early September 1941, after which there was no going back. The invasion of the Soviet Union blasted open the pathway leading from wanton but still localized mass murder to the pan-European project of systematized genocide decidedly in place by early 1942.[29]

Whether before or after June 1941, though, there was enormous room for local initiative. Situated decisions played a key part in driving radicalization forward, notably during the key months of July to December 1941. Each of the specialists on the central decision-making process – above all, Christopher Browning, Peter Longerich, Ian Kershaw, Michael Wildt, as well as the best synthesizers, such as Mark Roseman and Dan Stone – stresses the crucial back and forth between murderous practice in the field and the authorizing importance of a central political will. Partly responding to the calamitous disorder created by the regime's wartime population policies, partly taking initiatives consistent with the ruthlessness required by the latter, partly adhering to the anti-Semitic and security-related injunctions emanating from Berlin, now increasingly focused on the need for more systematic mass killings as the logistical nightmares resulting from the deportations and concentration of unwanted populations continued to grow, key regional satraps began escalating toward full-scale genocide. Roseman rightly stresses the process of crossing "a psychological threshold" and the breaking of taboos, so that possibilities unleashed by the *Einsatzkommandos* on Soviet territory could be taken up further to the west: "The acceptability of killing was spreading out from the Soviet Union, an invitation to key Nazis all over Europe."[30] The escalation of the mass murders of Soviet Jews between July and the end of September, itself showing the same dialectic of local initiative and central direction, had these powerful transfer effects.[31] They opened the way for genocide elsewhere in occupied Eastern Europe, too: "What began as a Soviet experiment was thus disseminated and modified piecemeal, by improvisation and example, over the period from September to November 1941."[32]

As key accelerators of genocide, four regional cases are now recognized from October 1941, recording both a common logic of radicalization and the same reciprocal causality of decisions at the center and events on the ground. The first involved a complex negotiation over the logistical entailments of the recklessly implemented deportation and settlement policies: these were creating growing calamities of overcrowding, provisioning, and public health in the Warthegau as a principal transit territory for resettling *Volksdeutsche*, dispossessed Poles, and Jews being deported to the East. For agreeing to resume deportations to the already overcrowded ghetto in Lodz, the Gauleiter Arthur Greiser was authorized by Himmler to proceed with the killing of 100,000 Jews, an early instance of which was the murder of some 3,000 in the southern district of Konin. Concurrently, a decision was taken to build a gassing facility at Chelmno. As Roseman comments: "While authorization for the killings came from the top, the initiative had come from the locality, and the goal was the solution of a regional 'problem' rather than the implementation of a more comprehensive program."[33]

Second, realizing to their dismay that the Jews concentrated in General-Government Poland could not, after all, be deported to the East, the authorities there "began to think about a 'final solution' to the 'Jewish Question' on [their] own territory," leading on 14–21 October to a series of high-level consultations in the district capitals of Warsaw, Lublin, Radom, and Lvov.[34] Newly equipped with direct authorization from Himmler, the Lublin SS chief Odilo Globocnik agreed with the Governor Hans Frank that his district henceforth should be cleared of Jews. The upshot was the establishment of the extermination camp at Belzec, where the first gassings occurred at the end of the first week in December.

Next, on 6 October, a huge killing operation was launched in eastern Galicia, with some 2,000 men, women, and children murdered in Nadvorna and further massacres continuing through the following weeks, including 10,000 to 12,000 deaths on 12 October alone. Soviet-occupied until the invasion of 22 June, East Galicia already saw mass executions in the latter's wake, making the continuity with events on Soviet territory especially direct. Here "the shootings seem to have been a regional initiative designed in the short term to thin out the population so that 'manageable' ghettos could be created."[35] As in the first two instances, proposals were apparently mooted for a gassing facility in the vicinity of Lvov.[36]

Finally, in occupied Serbia the newly arriving military commander Franz Böhme began a policy of reprisals against the local population, intensifying during early October into a generalized killing of incarcerated Jews: some 2,000 on 9–13 October, another 9,000 over the next two weeks, 8,000 at the start of November; by the following May all 7,500 Jewish women and children had also been killed, a gassing truck being dispatched from Berlin for the purpose.[37]

These four instances added up to a murderously convergent pattern. Yet, the formal decision to exterminate the Jews of all Europe remained something more than the sum of their parts, a future conclusion still waiting to be written. The situational logic and compulsion of events had become exceptionally powerful, enlisting not only the ideological warriors of the SS, but also the Nazi civilian authorities such as Greiser in the Warthegau who ceded nothing in ruthlessness as a *génocidaire*, and – as the Serbian example makes plain – the military too.[38] Roseman describes "a fatal two-pronged development" here: "The hard-line radicals in Himmler's almost autonomous police empire in Poland undertook increasingly violent measures, while the civilian administration imposed exclusionary and persecutory measures on the Jewish population that made killing seem the only option."[39] As Longerich points out, moreover, "An important feature common to all four regions (Warthegau, Lublin, Galicia, Serbia) is the use of gas to murder people. This method of murder fitted into a high-level policy that can also be demonstrated to have operated in winter 1941–42 in Auschwitz (Zyklon B) and in the occupied Soviet areas (gas vans)."[40] These initiatives could also draw on the euthanasia program initiated inside Germany during summer 1939, whose actions received official endorsement in October as Operation T-4. Whether in technology or personnel, this proved a key precedent: while the T-4 killings started with injections and poison, gassing was already in use by January 1940, initiating a continuity of genocidal practice that reached directly to the systematic murdering of the Jews.[41]

What all of this suggests is "that the transition from murderously neglectful and brutal occupation policies to genocidal measures occurred initially without a comprehensive set of commands from the top."[42] At the same time, each ratcheting forward of the genocidal logic *presumed* authorization from the very highest level, sometimes with physical presence, as in Himmler's touring of the occupied Soviet territory during July to October. At the source were Hitler's own express intentions. Only the latter's procedural detail remains unsettled: "whether we should conceive of such authorization as a single instruction, as a series of orders, or as the general empowerment of one of his subordinates (Himmler, for example), and whether the initiative for the policy came from him in the first instance or from someone else."[43] On the one hand, there was still no concerted and codified pan-European decision for genocide as such: "in the autumn of 1941 no overall plan for the murder of the European Jews had been set in motion step by step." But, on the other hand, region by region, from the Eastern Front to the four locations just discussed, events were cumulatively acquiring deadly force: "subordinate organizations – albeit within the context of a centrally controlled policy – were largely developing their own initiatives."[44]

Excepting a few outliers, we now have broad concurrence on a chronology.[45] Between the middle of September and early December 1941, the Nazi higher leadership reached the decision to systematically murder all the Jews of Europe. The infamous Wannsee Conference was convened on 20 January 1942 to pull all the needed preparations together. Importantly, Heydrich and his fellow participants were still assuming that the full-throttle prioritizing of the purpose would wait until *after* the victory over Bolshevism: so "Only in spring and early summer 1942 was it gradually realized that the 'final solution' was to be implemented during the course of the war itself."[46] Given everything we have learned, as well as what we probably can never know (absent any single written directive), it seems immaterial whether to place the watershed earlier in autumn 1941 amid the euphoria of the early anti-Soviet advance (Browning) or stress rather the incremental continuity of annihilatory intent through a series of escalations during 1939 to 1942 (Longerich, Kershaw). While the empirical quest to be as specific as possible about the timing of the crucial decisions was absolutely essential, one might say, as it vitally fueled the engine of clarification, it was ultimately self-canceling, too, as certain disagreements will always remain irreducible.[47] Since the ebbing of the anger of intentionalists and structuralists, moreover, the *stakes* are no longer the same. Ulterior investments in the virtues of one interpretation over another seem not to be driving the disagreements.[48] Ethico-political and philosophical purposes have not ceased to matter but, on the contrary, patently move the main participants.[49] Saul Friedländer, nothing if not ethically invested in the object of study, ventures only: "The decision was taken sometime during the last three months of 1941."[50]

"Working towards the *Führer*"

The new scholarship has also confirmed and deepened what we know about the Nazi state. It further vindicates the value of Ian Kershaw's widely adopted formula of "working towards the *Führer*." Taken originally from an unexceptional speech by a Nazi official in 1934 ("it is the duty of everybody to try to work towards the *Führer* along the lines he would wish"), this sought to capture the particular dynamics in Hitler's version of charismatic rule: "I saw the radical dynamic of the regime rooted in Hitler's embodiment of a utopian vision of national redemption through racial purification within Germany as the platform for imperial conquest through racial extirpation."[51] Hitler's relative indifference to the daily business of governing left a space where aspiring supporters, powerful subordinates, regional satraps, ambitious specialists, and other members of the leadership could maneuver for advantage, while observing the rules of loyalty and actively pursuing the Leader's redemptive vision for Germany. Once the war had begun, this mechanism operated to deadly effect. Taking their cue from the Leader's authorizing statements, the lieutenants acted. Absent a paper trail leading back to Hitler's own desk, his centrality may be reconstructed inferentially from the very density of the actions, exchanges, and commentaries among subordinates, from Himmler and the others at the center to the Greisers and Globocniks in the field. The meticulous detail of the local studies now allows us to work *back* from the *effects* of decisions to reconstruct the central originating impulse of the decisions themselves. Peter Longerich's short book shows brilliantly how this can be done.[52]

Consistent with the Mommsen-Broszat idea of "cumulative radicalization," Kershaw's formula illumines the distinctive exercise of power inside the Nazi state. It shows how the drives to realize Hitler's perceived intentions could gather momentum. It animates Longerich's account of the inception of the "Final Solution" and most of the other major efforts to specify Hitler's role in decision-making. It obviates the need for a documented *Führerbefehl*. Finally, it showed how Hitler personally ratcheted forward the radicalism being aimed against the Jews. Citing his Reichstag "prophecy" of 30 January 1939, which declared the next war the occasion for the Jews' final destruction, Kershaw describes a process of repeated rhetorical incitement, which worked pointedly inside a shared discursive community:

> As the "Final Solution" was being ushered in, Hitler used this "prophecy" on several telling occasions to signal the need for radical action by his underlings. They, in turn, understood the "prophecy" to indicate the "wish of the *Führer*" without any need for explicit orders. The "prophecy" had an additional function: to spread to the general public an awareness, while avoiding detailed or explicit information, that the destruction of the Jews was

> inexorably taking place. In this way, the "prophecy" became a key metaphor for the "Final Solution" and, functionally, served to indicate how in this crucial area the presumed "wish of the *Führer*" activated the most terrible of the regime's crimes.[53]

Equally clearly, the Nazi governing system was a "polycratic" one that rested upon a proliferation of agencies, institutional initiatives, and administrative functions, created sometimes deliberately but as often capriciously, with unclear and frequently clashing jurisdictions that typically pitted existing state bureaucracies and a variety of Party offices (themselves rivalrously subdivided) against each other. "Whether one looks at the civil service or the Order Police," Dan Stone observes, "one sees a state and a regime with a polycratic character, that is to say, a multiplicity of agencies competing for control of policy and vying with each other for the ear of the *Führer* … ."[54] Though seen too easily as a deliberate strategy of divide and rule through which factional in-fighting neutralized potential opposition, polycracy was certainly essential to the practice of charisma behind personal rule and the *Führerprinzip* (leadership principle). As the example of the *Deutsche Volksliste* (German Ethnic Register) in the annexed Polish territories showed only too well, factionalism and inefficiencies could frequently ensue, whether in such particularized conflicts or in far larger-scale difficulties of managing the national labor supply and other aspects of the war economy.[55] Yet, in many ways the Wannsee Conference demonstrated the contrary, bringing together six separate ministries (a seventh was unable to attend), two agencies for the occupied East (a third person was otherwise engaged), and an array of agencies of the SS. This was a striking case of inter-agency coordination.[56]

By the same characteristic, Wannsee also showed the sheer depth of the institutional preparation and collaboration that imagining and planning the Judeocide required. Some early research focused on the logistics of transportation and railway timetables, broadening attention away from the camp system and the SS themselves to capture the widening constituencies of involvement.[57] In discussing October 1941, Longerich points to exactly this degree of carefully negotiated coordination: "the execution of these complex operations involved a whole series of organizations outside the SS and the police, such as the *Reichstatthalter* in the Warthegau, the civil administration of the General-Government, the Foreign Ministry, the *Wehrmacht*, and the Chancellery of the *Führer*."[58] The invaluable growth of regional and local studies, including studies of particular ghettos and particular camps, allows this insight to solidify. These show, beyond any doubt, that the killing process necessitated the practical involvement of ordinary people at many different levels. To organize genocide required mobilizing the largest-scale human and administrative resources of a society. Perpetrators included not just the killers of the SS, but also the civil servants who planned the logistics; the managers who supervised all along the chain of implementation; the businessmen who supplied the goods that kept the process working (and exploited the resources it delivered); the academics who furnished the knowledge; the clerks who staffed the offices; and the railway men who drove the trains.[59] The perpetrators included *not only* the brutal and sadistic killers on the ground, *but also* the many categories of helpers behind the scenes.

Widening the contexts

If the most basic of structuralist commitments – the need to theorize and empirically locate a groundable idea of societal complicity – is well established, it has not precluded the probing of individual motivations and responsibility. As local studies remind us again, graphically and compellingly, emphasis on administrative logics should *not* blind us to the horrors of the actual violence genocide required. Yet, a tension may certainly be marked here. Especially under the sign of "the banality of evil," the "Final Solution" appears for some commentators as the worst manifestation of the dehumanizing potentials of modern bureaucracy and technological reason, with its apotheosis in the anonymous death factory of Auschwitz or the faceless bureaucrat safe behind his desk. In much structuralist work, a certain distancing from the graphic immediacy of the atrocities did tend to occur, making the material more assimilable to the "objective" and emotionally neutral conventions of academic history.[60]

In contrast with this foregrounding of bureaucratic process and its languages of presentation, local studies bring us closer to the horrendous suffering, physical pain, and sadistic excess. They show us that the killing was *not* an impersonal process, but happened via countless face-to-face acts, committed by real individuals and supervised by decision-makers who lived in the epicenter of the carnage itself. While Daniel Goldhagen's *Hitler's Willing Executioners* was sometimes credited with naming this ground, the growth of an extensive locally based historiography was well under way when that book appeared. Unlike Goldhagen, these works held on to the enduring structuralist insights, building analysis of how Nazi government worked explicitly into their accounts.[61] The key, surely, is to keep both perspectives together – *not just* the graphic detailing of atrocities in the vivid awfulness of everyday life in the Jewish work camps of Lublin (to cite one of Goldhagen's cases), *but also* the systematic accounting of the administrative deployment of forced labor on a German-wide scale. As Ulrich Herbert, Wolf Gruner, and others have each shown, it is perfectly feasible to combine both registers of analysis inside a common narrative and conceptual frame.[62]

On this point Hans Mommsen and Manfred Grieger's massive study of the *Volkswagenwerk* during the war offers telling confirmation. Construction of this *Volkswagen* plant, conceived during 1934 to 1937, had only been completed with the aid of the SS and its reservoir of extraordinarily cheap labor power, extracted from civilian deportees, prisoners of war, concentration camp inmates, and finally Hungarian Jews deported from Auschwitz, making foreign labor into 85.3 percent of the workforce in the main plant by 1945.[63] Forced laborers in the plant certainly suffered from the appalling atrocities Goldhagen detailed for the Lublin work camps. The racialized distinctions between Jews and other categories of forced labor (e.g., Poles and Soviet citizens, to name the next lowest in the hierarchy of exploitation) confirm what we know about the uniquely lethal and degrading treatment the Nazis always reserved for the Jews. But the racialized dehumanizing of the workers was only one dimension of the atrocities, if undoubtedly the most virulent; another came from the power relations structuring the labor process, whether managerially or on the shop floor, further radicalized by the ethnic enmities built into the social experience of working in the war economy. Likewise, Ferdinand Porsche, the real architect of the *Volkswagenwerk*, was an archetype of the self-constructed "apolitical" specialist, ostensibly pursuing the modernizing (and modernist) ethic of project-making and professional efficiency. Yet, Porsche built the company by cultivating political relations with the SS and other parts of the Nazi regime, by utilizing the machinery of racialized exploitation, and by creating an elaborate microcosm of the putative Nazi new order. No less than Johannes Pump and Anton Callesen – the SS heads of the Laagberg Concentration Camp servicing the *Volkswagen* plant, who exactly personified the sadistic killer-perpetrators Goldhagen brings to the fore – Porsche was also a principal author of the brutalities these workers had to endure.

That juxtaposition, between the successful businessman-engineer making his career (and his money) under the conditions the regime made available and the SS functionaries of systematized violence, enables an important recognition: by this time, living under the Third Reich afforded circumstances of professional advancement, obligatory service, and straightforward employment that neither implied nor required political identification with the regime's goals of a very explicit, programmatic or precise kind. To that degree Pump and Callesen need not have been "ideological warriors" or "warriors with a cause," just as Porsche needed no explicitly National Socialist loyalties to avow. Even where such Nazi ideals *could* be found, moreover, their translation into agency might be obscure and incomplete. Mark Roseman has rightly cautioned against seeing too straightforward a continuity between "ideas" and "actions" in that sense when seeking to understand an individual's motivations: "Though many key players brought with them values and ideals that helped spur their involvement in a racial war of extermination, most had to travel very far from their earlier selves to participate in genocide." Rather, "the relationship between perpetrators' convictions and their actions" was extremely "complicated and nonlinear."[64] As a "program" or an "agenda," Roseman argues, Nazi ideology was an unclear and unpredictable motivator.[65]

But to grapple with this question, we immediately need the *extended* understanding of ideology described earlier in this book – as being inscribed and embedded in cultural practices, institutional sites, and social relations, in what people did and the structured settings in which they did it, rather than just the ideas they consciously thought. In the course of his discussion Roseman oscillates between both meanings – between ideology as a specific set of ideas (a program, an agenda) and ideology as the process of handling one's relationship to the experienced world. By the time of Wannsee, he argues, "almost all of even the ideologically most committed had ... moved astonishingly far from where even just a few years earlier, they might have imagined they would be," from Wilhelm Stuckart ("the high-flying Nazi who represented the Interior Ministry") to Reinhart Heydrich and Adolf Eichmann.[66] But in that case, "ideology" was less about the programmatic agenda than about the journey; it was about *the process of managing or negotiating the distance*. Here Roseman calls upon Hitler's guiding authority in very much Kershaw's sense – "setting the tone, prescribing the boundaries, licensing every radical action, and spanning a rhetorical canopy that could shelter the most brutal of actions." This exertion of charismatic power, in a context of the Third Reich's fully realized prerogative state, provided the "structures and process" enabling radicalization to occur.[67] It was in the dynamics of practical translation, in all of the ingenuity, pragmatics, skillful maneuvering, appropriation of rhetoric, invoking of first principles, zealotry, and loyalism required by "working towards the *Führer*," that Nazi ideology – the production of Nazi subjects – could then do its work.

Once we move further away from the core institutions of the Nazi state – from the Reich Security Main Office (*Reichssicherheitshauptamt*, RSHA) and the other SS entities, for example, this extended notion of ideology becomes all the more key. Important here is the willingness, dating again from the mid 1980s, to see Nazi anti-Semitism as one strand of more elaborate race-based thinking in the early twentieth century. Empowered by Nazi governmentality after 1933, the exponents of anti-Semitic *Weltanschauung* captured the policy-making initiative for their own very particular and perverse epistemologies. In light of this approach, the place of anti-Semitism in the rise of the Nazi movement also shifts. Typified by Julius Streicher and his newspaper *Der Stürmer*, the Nazi Party's (NSDAP's) avowed anti-Semites were in the past often depicted as the bearers of a political extremism that appealed during the "movement phase" more to a certain strain of *völkisch* activism than to the electorate at large and for that reason tended to be played down in the pre-1933 agitation.[68] Viewed in this way, anti-Semitism under the Third Reich then seemed the ideological pathology of a cadre of manifest fanatics and borderline sociopaths whose ideas had somehow captured the imagination of a movement and could now use the dictatorship to seize free rein.

Under the new approach, in contrast, anti-Semitic thinking is linked to much wider patterns and syndromes of social Darwinist, eugenicist, and biologistic thought gaining currency in the 1900s. Drawing on conventionalized assumptions about racial difference widely diffused among Germany's professional, managerial, and administrative social layers, while resonating strongly with popular ideas of otherness that gave Jews an especially salient place, such scientistic thought could acquire public purchase. Anti-Semitism has been re-contextualized as a formation of ideas and attitudes particular to the conditions of societal change under modernity, as opposed to an assortment of prejudices persisting from less enlightened times deeper in the past. Accordingly, the contexts for the Third Reich's anti-Semitic laws underwent a profound shift. Once seen as integral to the larger project of designing a society to be organized around race, Nazi anti-Semitism reappears in a disturbingly scientistic and rationalizing guise – thus, no longer as an anti-modern, atavistic, and irrationalist refusal of civilized norms, but as a disturbing manifestation of the most hubristic potentialities of social engineering made imaginable by the progress of industrialization and the societal mobilizations of World War I. This broader context of race-related anti-Semitic thinking reflected aspirations on the right for the comprehensive redesigning of the social order, associated with the promise of technological, managerial, and scientific modernity.

This broadening of Nazi anti-Semitism takes two strong forms, one concerning the objects of Nazi racialism, the other the dynamics of implementation. *On the one hand*, research has focused on Nazism's other racialized enemies – not just the Sinti and Roma and other Eastern European subject nationalities, but also entire social categories such as Socialists and Communists, homosexuals, the mentally disabled, the infirm and incurably ill, the institutionalized elderly, multiple groups of the "socially incompetent" or "asocials" (vagrants and homeless, alcoholics, long-term unemployed, habitual petty offenders, hard-core criminals, prostitutes, sexually active teenaged girls, unwed mothers), to be followed after 1939 by Polish intellectuals, Soviet prisoners of war, "political commissars," and so forth. Stigmatizing these populations laid the ground for systematic extermination of the Jews in a double sense – both *discursively* by labeling such groups as "unworthy of life," and thereby preparing the comprehensive assaults on the Jews; and *practically* by the grisly process of experiment that began with the euthanasia program fully authorized in October 1939 (Operation T-4), the persecution of Sinti and Roma, and the mass murder of 2 million Soviet prisoners of war (POWs).

On the other hand, to understand this broader context of maltreatment, we have to grasp the eugenicist and related ideologies of social engineering pervading the medical, healthcare, criminological, and social policy-making professions long *before* the Nazis themselves came into power. As the new scholarship shows, processes of medicalization and racialization were well under way in the 1920s, involving a turn toward "biological politics" – in eugenics, population politics, welfare initiatives directed at women, family policies, criminology and penal reform, imagined projects of social engineering, and the deployment of science for social goals. From the early 1900s, anti-Semitic idioms were part of this, too, as social, cultural and political issues became systematically naturalized under the sign of race. Again, in these terms the ground for Nazi policies was being discursively laid – not in a narrow or literal sense of "linguistic" preparation, but by systems of practice and elaborate institutional machineries of knowledge production that over many years worked at demarcating deviant or "worthless" categories of people. In the process popular assumptions became restructured, changing the parameters for what an acceptable social policy could be.

This direction was encapsulated by Detlev Peukert's classic essay "The Genesis of the 'Final Solution' from the Spirit of Science," which re-periodized Nazism into a longer crisis of modernity dating from the early 1900s.[69] Similarly, Götz Aly and his collaborators produced dense documentation for the Third Reich's racialized social policies, the grandiose population planning behind the New Order, and the Holocaust's economic logic.[70] Together with Susanne Heim, Aly showed that the ideas and professional interests motivating the "pioneers" of the "Final Solution" were intimately related to the prior diffusion of a racialized paradigm of public policy and social administration.[71] As an ideological project, the Judeocide required not just the senior Nazi leadership, but an elaborate machinery of governmentality with an extensive reservoir of active social support. In one summary, "whilst real political decisions were taken within the secret inner spheres of the regime, both much of the initiative and the criteria for action came from key lobbying groups within the professional middle classes," involving "a wide measure of consensus among physicians, lawyers and bureaucrats."[72] One especially strong demonstration was Ulrich Herbert's biography of Werner Best, further amplified in Michael Wildt's account of the RHSA.[73] If in one dimension these core institutions clearly harbored a cohesive body of believers adhering programmatically to the Nazi outlook, then in another way their values and comportment were entirely consonant with a far broader sociology of professional ambition and goal-oriented drive toward career-making and personal accomplishment.

As wider research on the "racial state" shows, racially defined violence was not confined to the nationality frontier and the killing fields of the Eastern Front, but was endemic to the practice of the carceral universe inside Germany itself, including its correctional welfare and social policy complex, whose expansion rolled relentlessly outwards from 1935 to 1936 under the centralized control of Himmler's SS. As the camps expanded, with Sachsenhausen (1936), Buchenwald (1937), Flossenbürg, and Mauthausen (both 1938) joining the original Dachau (1933), along with Ravensbrück (1939) specifically for women, they filled less with the regime's political opponents than with those deemed harmful to the *Volksgemeinschaft* – that is, "anyone whose hereditary racial, moral, social, mental, or physical characteristics deviated from evolving Nazi definitions of the normal and desirable."[74] This was where the practice of the racial state became punitively concrete. The "pre-emptive designation of new categories of enemies on the grounds of their unfitness for membership in the Nazi community," effectively "the purging of the German social order after 1933," had resulted by 1943 in the committal to the camps of some 110,000 Germans, some two-thirds of them "asocials."[75] To cite a list drawn up by the Bavarian political police in August 1936, they included "beggars, vagabonds, gypsies, vagrants, work-shy individuals, idlers, prostitutes, grumblers, habitual drunkards, hooligans, traffic offenders, and so-called psychopaths and mental cases." As Jane Caplan summarizes: "The whole process can be understood as an immense net of regulation extended over Germany's criminal and 'deviant' populations and their transfer, whether from the streets or from penal and welfare institutions, to a few preferential sites of long-term confinement, at the head of which stood the concentration camps."[76]

In other words, the Third Reich's dehumanizing practices attacked an ever-expanding aggregation of "community aliens." Under Otto-Georg Thierack, the hardline veteran Nazi appointed Minister of Justice in August 1942, for example, over 20,000 state prisoners were transferred into the camps for "annihilation through labor," some two-thirds of whom perished. They included "racial" categories (Jews, Poles, Sinti and Roma), but also "asocials" convicted of criminal offenses who were considered "unreformable." Once in the camp system, these "asocials" were subject to every inhumanity wreaked on the Jews.[77] Wide sections of officialdom and the professions ("non-Nazi" as well as "Nazi") were responsible for this policy, with complex situational, bureaucratic, and ideological motivations. Thus, Himmler's assertion of dominance over the Third Reich's police and carceral complex had not only created an expanding institutional arena for the pursuit of his own ideas of racial renewal; it also opened the way for allied but differing projects of social discipline to be expedited too. The distinctively Nazi visions of social and racial engineering could be ruthlessly put into force, given the freeing of the state from any restraints after 1933, while longer-standing projects of social policing could finally be redeployed. As Caplan says, "The older paths of nineteenth-century authoritarian social discipline and Nazi political detention now merged into immense new projects of coercive bio-politics and intensive labor exploitation."[78] Once the Nazis had taken their ambitions into war, these purposes conjoined to still deadlier effect: the concentrationary policies, the designs for social and racial hygiene, the racially imagined reordering of European society, and the murderous intentions against the Jews could all now be realized. Under conditions of wartime, the synergies became genocidal.

Integrated histories

Holocaust historiography was long marked by disputes over the evidentiary superiority of written sources against testimony of victims and survivors, a difference already prefigured in the postwar trials of Nazis and other perpetrators. The case against Eichmann in Jerusalem in 1961, or the 22 defendants in the Frankfurt Auschwitz trials in 1963 to 1965, clearly rested on witness testimonies.[79] But even while foregrounding the value of *defendants'* evidence for purposes of self-incrimination, the Nuremberg trials themselves had deliberately avoided victim testimony in favor of the documentary record.[80] That discrimination persisted in the approach of historians thereafter, whether as historicist skepticism about the veracity of subjective memories or more consciously objectivist aversion against the emotionalism of survivors' accounts, linked to the myth-making propensities of so much Jewish writing. The classic occasion of this difference was an exchange between Saul Friedländer and Martin Broszat in 1987, prompted by Broszat's earlier article, "A Plea for the Historicization of National Socialism," to which Friedländer had taken exception, perceiving a disregard for a specifically Jewish historical standpoint.[81] Broszat had written: "the period still remains bound up with many and diverse monuments of mournful and accusatory memory, imbued with the painful sentiments of many individuals, in particular the Jews, who remain adamant in their insistence on a mythical form of this remembrance." In contrast, he argued, growing detachment could allow [West] German historians to replace the "demonological interpretation of National Socialism" with "historical explanation" of an appropriately "scholarly-scientific" kind.[82]

Friedländer's sensitivity to this particular comment now seems disproportionate, unlike his reservations about "distance" and "normalization," which raised serious epistemological and ethico-philosophical misgivings about Broszat's claims, while doubting pointedly whether West German historiography was quite as immune from myth-making as Broszat supposed.[83] At the same time, as the voluminous research of Nicolas Berg on the *Institut für Zeitgeschichte* (Institute of Contemporary History) in Munich shows, there is no question that Broszat and other structuralists of his generation marginalized the Jewish voices of Nazi persecution from their accounts, even to the extent of hampering the publication of research by Jewish outsider historians such as Hans-Günther Adler and Joseph Wulf.[84] But the complexities of accounting for Nazism beneath the West German intellectual-political climate of the 1950s and 1960s, which enabled certain lines of inquiry while impeding others, seem a likelier explanation for this syndrome than conscious apologetics or deliberate skewing of the historical record, although Broszat's personal history of concealment clearly lends itself to cautious psychoanalytic readings.[85] Moreover, even as the inhibition on conducting detailed biographical studies of Nazi perpetrators began falling away during the 1990s, the same interest was not yet extended to the minds and experience of the Jewish victims:

> … there are almost no studies by German historians that not only describe sympathetically and with regret the fate of the victims but exploit heuristically the victims' point of view; almost none that do not present and analyze events merely from the perspective of German policemen, bureaucrats, and officers; almost none from the standpoint of the Jewish councils and forced laborers, deported "gypsies," and inmates of the camps; almost none that break the perpetrators' interpretive monopoly that derived from the surviving documents.[86]

Such partiality of perspective, whose effects Friedländer found so pointedly inscribed in the terms of the Broszat exchange, remains persistently hard to overcome. German historians inside Germany itself are understandably fixated on the indigenous dynamics, asking how the Holocaust could have happened when and where it did. They examine primarily the conditions of responsibility for the event. But *that*, Herbert argues somewhat dubiously, is "an entirely different perspective" from the one that occurs to "an Israeli or Jewish historian. Despite all the internationalization of research, the question, 'What happened to my grandparents?' cannot be universalized easily, if at all."[87] The more probing focus on the perpetrators, in itself a huge gain, also only enhances older administrative perspectives, leaving the victims as "merely the targets of genocide and not as historical protagonists whose own thoughts, actions, and memories have a bearing on the event."[88] But by any ideal criteria, how can the virtues of an integrated perspective be contestable? How can any rounded understanding leave one side of the story out? As Friedländer says in the introduction to his own *magnum opus*: "The history of the Holocaust cannot be limited only to a recounting of German policies, decisions, and measures that led to the most systematic and sustained of genocides; it must also include the reactions (and at times the initiatives) of the surrounding world and the attitudes of the victims, for the fundamental reason that the events we call the Holocaust represent a totality defined by this very convergence of distinct elements."[89]

Friedländer's "integrated history" has perhaps five key elements. It means partly "a full, Europeanized history of the Holocaust" whose vision reaches beyond Germany itself to "the story of all the targeted Jewish cultures in Europe in a vortex of destruction," whose "continent-wide diversity and distance" are "radically negated as the Third Reich catapults its way eastward in 1941 and 1942, bringing millions more Jews (and POWs) under its control."[90] Secondly, it also crosses the boundaries separating scholarly historiography from other fields of knowledge – from politics, popular culture, journalism, other disciplines, and hybrid academic fields like Holocaust studies. A great deal of the impetus behind the remarkable flourishing of Holocaust-related historiography has come from these influences beyond the archive, the seminar room, and the precincts of history departments altogether. Indeed, the very ability of historians to recognize the Holocaust's centrality to German history, and even to the study of Nazism, has owed as much to the pressure of extraneous political, cultural, and intellectual forces during the last three decades, including journalism, testimony, memorializing, exhibits and museums, law suits, fictions, television, and film, as it has to the spontaneous trajectory of German historians if left purely to themselves. In that sense, history's perimeter fences are not so easily secured any more.[91]

Thirdly, Friedländer organized his account by what seemed a straightforwardly chronological framework, eschewing any conceptual or analytical signposting for the chapter and sub-chapter schema, but parceling the latter instead into ten roughly equal 60-page divisions in three roughly equal parts: "Terror (Fall 1939–Summer 1941)"; "Mass Murder (Summer 1941–Summer 1942)"; and "Shoah (Summer 1942–Spring 1945)." The logic of "an integrated history," he argues, determines this particular organization and writing strategy: it "imposes a return to a chronicle-like narration," one that "remains the only recourse after major interpretive concepts have been tried and found lacking."[92] His defense rests on the technical needs of a general history (the Holocaust) made up of so many complexities (geographically, institutionally, sociologically, ideologically, culturally, demographically) that their aggregation simply exceeds available analytical terms:

> We are dealing with events occurring in Germany, in every single country of occupied and satellite Europe, and well beyond. We are dealing with institutions and individual voices, with ideologies, religious traditions, etc. No general history of the Holocaust can do justice to this diversity of elements by presenting them as independently juxtaposed. Thus, analytical categories applicable to the study of the perpetrators and to the system of extermination

> have to be replaced by a succession of temporal frameworks, the only ones which can encompass perpetrators, victims, and surrounding society. For this reason and, furthermore, in order to follow the fate of individual Jews ... a chronological representation of the entire process becomes unavoidable.[93]

In effect, chapter by chapter, he builds a mobile (and moving) mosaic of converging simultaneities whose European-wide dispersal becomes rebound, seamlessly, into a single integrated narrative, in a forward movement heading for catastrophe.[94]

In constructing his narrative, fourthly, Friedländer recurs continuously to the ground of *Alltagsgeschichte* and the local spaces of the Jews' quotidian endangerment, occasional survival, and death. This allows him to accomplish two vital purposes for the type of general history he set out to write. On the one hand, the approach unsettles any account based on governmental sources and the administrative unfolding of the genocide alone, "fulfilling his requirements for a historical narrative that is fragmented, splintered, and fractured by the historian's voice." As Friedländer's text is constructed, it proceeds by "twists and turns," moving "ceaselessly between 'official' discourse, that is, Nazi documents, the victims, and the bystanders."[95] By bringing in "the Jewish dimension" in this way he issues a powerful rejoinder to Broszat's seemingly dismissive consignment of Jewish historiography on the Third Reich to mythologically inspired memory work. Strikingly, though, this validating of the micro-historical perspectives of local informants tacitly retracts Friedländer's earlier suspicions of *Alltagsgeschichte*, which in the exchange with Broszat he charged with a propensity for apologetics ("reinserting the Nazi phenomenon into normal historical narrative ... relativizing what still makes it appear as singular").[96] In fact, as argued in earlier chapters in this volume, the exponents of an everyday perspective have enabled some of the key gains in the study of Nazism and our grasp of its popular appeal. Friedländer is partially aware of this – one of Lüdtke's key essays is cited – but still keeps it at a distance. As he says: "The *Alltagsgeschichte* of German society has its necessary shadow: the *Alltagsgeschichte* of its victims."[97]

On the other hand, this new privileging of the everyday occurs deliberately by means of *witnessing* – that is, by utilizing "the unusually large number of diaries (and letters) written during the events and recovered over the following decades," coming from "Jews of all countries, all walks of life, all age groups, either living under direct German domination or within the wider sphere of persecution."[98] This is the final and most decisive element in Friedländer's integrated account – namely, the ethical imperative of the standpoint of the victims: "For it is their voices that reveal what was known and what *could* be known; theirs were the only voices that conveyed both the clarity of insight and total blindness of human beings confronted with an entirely new and utterly horrifying reality."[99] His use of the diaries forthrightly ratifies the gathering recognition that the voices of the victims demand to be heard; their testimony requires inclusion. In any purportedly integrated history, whose structure necessarily incorporates the decision-making processes and the machineries of implementation, they provide *the* essential counterpoint. Beyond this "testimonial value," moreover, Friedländer's recognition of "the individual voice" has a vital ethico-narrative purpose: "The victim's voice, suddenly arising in the course of the narration of these events, can, by its eloquence or its clumsiness, by the immediacy of the cry of terror, or, by the naivety of unfounded hope, tear through the fabric of the 'detached' and 'objective' historical rendition."[100]

Exemplary lives

If Saul Friedländer's integrated history brings Jewish subjects decisively into the main narrative, then a form of the old bifurcation nonetheless persists. Each of the other two general histories, those by Longerich and Browning, achieve their imposing completeness by bringing Hilberg's classic approach to the very highest level of synthesis. Gone is the excessively Berlin-centered and administrative standpoint, whose assumptions the new regionally focused scholarship has so markedly surpassed. Hilberg remained too convinced by the homogenizing impact of the Nazi program, giving excessive credence to its bureaucratic self-representation. Neither Browning nor Longerich remotely makes the same mistake. Browning, in particular, moves assuredly back and forth between the decision-makers in Berlin and the complexities of action in the field. But the basic architecture is recognizably the same. These are *German-historical* accounts. To be sure, the Holocaust – the Third Reich's primary anti-Semitism in its relation to genocide, imperial hubris, and all aspects of the racial state – has now moved to the very center of Nazism's history. But there is still no "Jewish dimension" in Friedländer's or Herbert's sense. They are not written from the standpoint of the victims. They have not integrated the multiplicities – the many diversities of population on a European plane, whether in large-scale or fragmentary forms. They lack Jewish subjects and Jewish stories, that primary element of the ground's eye view.

As early as 1957, Filip Friedman had urged getting away from a "Nazi-centric" approach to Jewish history during the war by adopting a "Judeo-centric" one instead.[101] The genealogies of recuperating Jewish experience are rightly associated with the reception of the Eichmann trial of 1961. Existing perceptions of Jewish passivity under the impact of the Nazi onslaught entered the realm of bitter public recrimination when Hannah Arendt implied that the Jews had colluded in their own destruction, especially via the Jewish Councils whom she described as outrightly collaborating. From the activity this controversy helped to ignite came the earliest monographs on particular ghettos, on aspects of Jewish resistance, and on the Jewish Councils, along with bodies of autobiography, some oral histories, and journalistic accounts of Jewish partisan activity, ghetto revolts, and rebellions in the camps.[102] Very quickly, the myth of Jewish fatalism ("like sheep to the slaughter") was laid to rest.

For current thinking about Jewish responses those older verdicts about "fatalism," "collaboration," or lack of resistance have long seemed naïve. Yisrael Gutman's history of the Warsaw Ghetto makes the circumstantial fetters on action abysmally clear. Whether material (smuggling, bribery, theft) or cultural (religious observance, educational provision, elaborate forms of welfare), actions were always about sustaining morale. Record-keeping, most famously in the Oneg Shabbat Archive inspired by Emmanuel Ringelblum, had that purpose too. Under Nazi rule *any* Jewish collectivism became what Gutman ascribes to the youth movement – namely, "a kind of existential enclave."[103] The Jews of Warsaw formed a comprehensive network of House Committees that delivered the ghetto's real associational fabric, underneath the *Judenrat*'s official governance and the larger public sector around the Jewish Social Assistance; they sustained an astonishing array of 47 underground newspapers across the political spectrum from early 1940 to late 1942; they built an elaborate system of bunkers that briefly frustrated the Nazis during the ghetto's final dissolution in May 1943. The youth movements generated the wartime energy, overcoming the paralysis of the older political generations while enunciating visions of the future. As Gutman says, the underground delivered "a consolidated and reliable nucleus" both for the Jewish Fighting Organisation and for the rallying of the "remnants" after the Liberation. Youth movements "played a decisive role in the struggle by keeping together a united cadre of people who maintained and cultivated social norms and values during a desperate time."[104] Their achievement, in maintaining contacts between the various ghettos, especially Warsaw and Vilna, the twin hubs of interwar Jewish culture, in securing arms and other supplies, in performing acts of sabotage, and in continuously regenerating political consciousness, was extraordinary.

A significant part of Israeli political culture had its origins along the Warsaw–Vilna axis.[105] Gutman also provides an appropriately nuanced account of the *Judenrat* under its leader Adam Czerniakow. As Trunk and others showed, the councils' behavior varied immensely. While leaderships very rarely sponsored armed resistance or flight outright (Minsk being an exception), "collaboration" was still rarer, with a huge range of responses in between.[106] Czerniakow inhabited this intermediate zone. Eschewing the "productivist" strategy of serving the German war effort, as pursued by Mordecai Chaim Rumkowski in Lodz, Jacob Gens in Vilna, and Ephraim Barash in Bialystok, he aimed for a buffer between the Nazis and the ghetto's interior life, preserving minimal autonomy by acceding to German demands. But any of the decisions taken – meeting Nazi demands to modify them, selecting some categories of people for deportation to protect others, distributing welfare to the ghetto poor rather than radically collectivizing resources – brought a heavy moral tax. Most of the protective devices, like the assignment of work papers or the inflation of the ghetto's public employment, meant discriminating against some to benefit others. Nor were the ghetto's ordinary inhabitants untouched by these dilemmas. The constraints on consistently observing basic rules of human decency, let alone any viable ethics of tolerance or social morality, were simply unimaginable. The very act of resistance penalized one's fellows rather than helping them. Chances of success were minimal, collective reprisals ferocious.

In light of monographs by Gutman and others, the predicament created for the Jews came to seem ever less tractable. Ordinary life under Nazi rules was so exceptional as to shatter the reliable assumptions of human interaction. Not only were rights, citizenship, and civic dignity taken away, access to careers and education closed, livelihoods destroyed, property seized, but the basic suppositions of living in society – neighborly coexistence and reciprocity, forms of mutuality, respect for opponents, friendship across differences, the kindness of strangers – no longer applied. As the studies of particular villages and regions, particular ghettoes and camps, particular lives, and particular journeys continue to heap up, categories of "resistance" and "collaboration" become ever harder to apply. Hilberg disavowed the former concept altogether, preferring the registers of "alleviation" and "compliance" for capturing the forms of individual and collective self-protection. Conversely, Yehuda Bauer, by now the doyen of an affirmative Jewish historiography, radically broadened what resistance might include. Simply "'keeping body and soul together' under circumstances of unimaginable privation and misery" was itself "one way of resisting the Nazis," he argued. Resistance became "any *group* action consciously taken in opposition to known or surmised laws, actions, or intentions directed against the Jews by the Germans and their supporters."[107] Primo Levi's "gray zone" has been one way of capturing this vicious indeterminacy; Lawrence Langer's "choiceless choices" became another.[108] In this understanding, human action and human response during the Holocaust was *always-already* defined by ambiguity and compromise; the exercise of agency was from the outset a soiled and damaged thing.

The resulting dilemmas may be engaged in many ways, some varying by discipline, some by philosophical inclination, others by historical methodology. One route has been highly abstract via combinations of critical theory, psychoanalysis, trauma theory, and aesthetics; via bio-political approaches associated with Michel Foucault and Giorgio Agemben; or via cultural histories emphasizing symbolic action.[109] For historians the commoner route has gone through various kinds of regional or local study, sometimes following an avowedly everyday-life analytic, more often simply delving very intensively downwards into the thickness of the local relations concerned, where the complexities can be encountered as what Raymond Williams called "specific and indissoluble real processes."[110] The insights come as often from a cumulative erudition, a finely textured feel for the particular context resting on careful and exhaustive reading and checking of all the accessible sources. Here, for example, is Browning's concluding reflection on his study of Starachowice:

> The Jews of Starachowice pursued strategies of survival through compliance and alleviation, in the form of labor and bribery, over resistance and flight. In this particular case, these choices not only seemed the last and best hope at the time, but they actually saved lives and allowed a remnant to survive. The precarious benefits of these policies were not equally shared, and those who benefited most were seldom individuals who stir our admiration. A few striking exceptions notwithstanding, persecution, exploitation, hunger, enslavement, and mass murder do not turn ordinary people into saints. My

history of the Starachowice Jews is one of horrific suffering, incredible endurance, and partial survival. But it cannot be a narrative of redemption and edification while remaining faithful to the evidence.[111]

In his pointillistic fashion, Friedländer eloquently prioritized accounts of this kind: "It is at the micro-level that the most basic and ongoing Jewish interaction with the forces acting in the implementation of the 'Final Solution' took place; it is at this micro-level that it mostly needs to be studied. And it is at the micro-level that documents abound."[112]

These potentials are brilliantly realized in Mark Roseman's account of the life of Marianne Ellenbogen (1923–1996), daughter to a prosperous Essen grain merchant Siegfried Strauss and his wife Regina, whose story – and Roseman's telling of it – captures the possibilities under discussion. Taking Friedländer's advocacy of fractured and multi-vocal narratives to heart, Roseman draws the reader into the very process through which his history came to be thought. He takes us directly inside the evidentiary and methodological dilemmas through which the historian arrives at the questions, sifts and refines them, tries them out, and brings them to interpretation, while patiently assembling the heterogeneous sources and knowledge (the "archive") that allows the history to be told – everything that usually precedes the writing and stays off the page. Roseman builds from a micro-history organized around an individual life to the largest questions of the history of the Holocaust and Third Reich, bringing them to a rare concreteness.[113]

The Strauss family history in many ways typified Jewish–German experience in the twentieth century. Observantly Jewish and ardently German, both sides of the family revealed the acculturation that was separating Germany's Jews from their co-religionists further to the east.[114] The Strauss twins Siegfried and Alfred built their grain and cattle-feed business after four years of military service in a war that also claimed the life of a younger brother, Richard. Of course, neither these patriotic credentials nor their social standing could protect the family from the Nazi onslaught. While various members managed to emigrate and some younger cousins escaped, Marianne's parents and younger brother Richard, her grandmother, her paternal uncles and aunts, and her mother's sister and husband were all deported to the East and killed. Marianne herself survived the Third Reich, married a British officer in Düsseldorf after the war, and lived in Liverpool until she died.

In these bare outlines the story rings familiar, appending a finely drawn miniature to the already well-known record – a microcosm of the general processes presented by the historiography of the past quarter-century, a vivid biographical counterpoint to studies of the Jews under Nazism. Yet, otherwise the story strikingly diverged. For one thing, the family was reprieved from deportation on 26 October 1941, dismissed from the Essen assembly-point at the last minute by the Gestapo and sent home.[115] "Snatched from the grave digger's spade," as Siegfried put it, they were protected by a hidden skein of relations running from the family banker, Friedrich W. Hammacher, to the *Abwehr*, the army's intelligence arm, which under Admiral Wilhelm Canaris and Major General Hans Oster was stealthfully obstructing Nazi policies from 1938 until mid 1943.[116] The *Abwehr* protected a small number of Jews, we now know, usually decorated veterans, by allowing them exit visas on pretext of using them as spies in the Americas. An intricate dance with the Gestapo ensued behind the scenes as the *Abwehr* sought to give the Strauss brothers time to organize their emigration. After excruciatingly tortuous negotiations with Gestapo, associated SS offices, tax authorities, the Currency Office, and other agencies, the family was finally approved to leave for Cuba in August 1943 only for the Gestapo abruptly to pull the rug. On 31 August, they were given two hours' notice. The future collapsed like a house of cards.[117]

These details are fascinating but sobering. The limited interconnections that survived Jewish ostracism between the Nuremberg Laws and deportation, even after the violence of *Reichskrystallnacht* and the outbreak of war, suggest both the persistence of non-compliance and its painfully prosaic scope. Any continuing intercourse between Jews and their fellow citizens oozed the ambivalence and compromised meanings that social historians from Broszat to Peukert have stressed. Any willingness to help was laden with self-interest, burdened by the hopelessly incommensurate exchanges imposed beneath the shadow of "Aryanization." Possessions committed by departing Jews to the safe keeping of "Aryan" friends or neighbors were often presumed to be permanent. Friendship circulated in a seller's market. Where a prior business relationship was involved, altruism and human sympathies easily "merged with legal opportunities for enrichment, which in turn merged with outright corruption on the part of the Gestapo and city officials."[118] As Roseman shows, family histories become excellent for opening such questions up.[119]

Roseman offers a patient but unsparing accounting of these ambiguities, which left the openings for ethical behavior under the Third Reich so fogged. Yet, he also finds extraordinary altruism. In late 1941 Marianne fell in love with Ernst Krombach (1921–1942), son of an Essen lawyer, whose family "belonged to the same assimilated, patriotic wing of the Essen Jewish community as the Strausses."[120] Wrenchingly, a few weeks after the couple became secretly engaged, the Krombachs were deported on 22 April 1942 to the transit camp of Izbica Lubielska, midway between Lublin and the newly opened killing center of Belzec.[121] As Roseman explains, the Essen deportees were stalled in Izbica for several months, temporarily saved by "a series of logistical hiccups in the killing machinery."[122] Remarkably, the two lovers stayed in contact, managing an intense if truncated correspondence through legal channels as late as August 1942, including cards sent by Ernst from the train journey during 22 to 24 April and over 100 small care packages Marianne scrounged together.

Astoundingly, Marianne found a direct link to the camp. Twenty-eight-year-old Christian Arras owned an Essen truck dealership doing military contract work. He knew the Strauss family, Ernst, and other Jews deported to Izbica, and went there at huge risk, offering to take letters and goods. On pretext of accompanying repaired army trucks, he reached Izbica on 19 August and bribed his way into the camp. He returned with a bundle of letters and Ernst's 18-page report for

Marianne on camp conditions, plus a "task list" of contacts and instructions. This document's unique qualities – the sole account of Izbica and a rare reporting of deportation written by a German Jew at the time – were matched by the startling incongruity of Arras's role: an unpolitical non-Jewish German, apparently patriotically loyal to the regime, certainly no dissident, volunteering to serve as a courier. In Marianne's memory he was also "SS," leaving his actions still less legible. But by patient corroboration, including interviews with Arras's widow and two Jewish witnesses, plus a diary in the Essen city archive, and the absence of a party or SS personnel file, Roseman reaches a firm conclusion: Arras was acting courageously out of human decency, "an unlikely hero"; "a good guy; he put his own life in jeopardy."[123]

Marianne's story becomes more extraordinary still. After losing contact with Ernst and learning of Izbica's virtual liquidation by December, her final efforts at tracing him were rebuffed by the Berlin Red Cross in April 1943, forcing her slowly to accept his loss.[124] After fresh deportations in June to July 1942, her own family's economic straits steadily deteriorated. Essen's Jewish remnant "were picked off one by one for deportation," until by July 1943 the Strausses became "probably the last full-Jewish family in the city, perhaps in the region."[125] On 31 August, absent the *Abwehr*'s protection, two Gestapo officials arrived with the deportation order. Marianne's father slipped her a wad of banknotes and she escaped. After a week at Essen police headquarters, her parents, brother, aunt, uncle, grandmother, and great-aunt were deported to Theresienstadt. Marianne went underground.

She was sheltered by an obscure Essen socialist network called the *Bund. Gemeinschaft für sozialistisches Leben* (The League. Community for Socialist Life), formed in 1924 around Artur Jacobs, a charismatic further education teacher, and his wife Dore, who taught dance and movement at the *Blockhaus*, the *Bund*'s Essen home opened in 1927. Disconnected from parties and informally based, the *Bund* joined a Marxist anti-capitalist critique to a Kantian conception of the ethical life: "Jacobs combined a belief in the historical mission of the proletariat with an intense concern for the moral choices that face individuals in their daily lives … The *Bund*'s aim was to create a socialist way of life that would incorporate the whole person – body, mind, and soul."[126] It survived 1933 by its charismatic organization, strict secrecy, and small size. Marianne met Jacobs through the Krombachs and after their deportation took solace in the *Bund*'s small clandestine subculture.[127] As the Strauss family prepared their *Abwehr*-expedited emigration, Jacobs let Marianne know that she could turn to the *Bund* in a crisis. On eluding the Gestapo on 31 August, she took refuge in the *Blockhaus*.[128]

She was protected by *Bund* members dispersed across northern Germany (Göttingen, Braunschweig, Remscheid, Mülheim, Burscheid), usually living openly under varying covers.[129] Frequent changes of refuge required hazardous train and tram journeys without valid papers at constant risk of exposure. For this life underground, whether the mundane practicalities of everyday survival or the solidarities of the *Bund*'s collective milieu, Roseman's guide was Marianne's diary, which opened extraordinary access to her inner life. Grounded by the quality of the

Bund's human relationships and passionately committed to philosophically mastering her fate, she based survival on a sovereign self-control. The diary reflected on the *Bund*'s "basic principles," reported her dreams, meditated on nature and landscape, probed the qualities of friendship, and mourned the loss of Ernst and her family. A remarkable document of interiority and courageous self-exploration, it recuperates an obscured cultural history of the 1930s, fully comparable to the often-celebrated aristocratic milieu of Adam von Trott and Helmut James von Moltke.[130]

With this meticulous reconstruction of one person's experience, Roseman suggests important directions for the future. The exceptional qualities of Marianne's story de-familiarize what we thought we knew – from the Strauss family's protection by the *Abwehr* and Marianne's clandestine links to Izbica to the revelations of the *Bund* and life underground. If exceptional, this story vividly illumines some of the Third Reich's shadowed corners. It takes us deep inside the arduousness of making a life under Nazi rule. It shows how perceptive and self-possessed individuals, committed to keeping the regime at bay, sought to manage the tensions that its demanding and intrusive everydayness imposed. The ethical dimensions of debates about conformity and *Resistenz* are most precisely engaged in such micro-historical ways.

Here Roseman shows the surprising "normality" of the life Marianne fashioned under Nazism – even while living on the run. Despite the Jews' expulsion from state schools in November 1938, education still provided escape: during 1939 to 1941 she enrolled in the Jewish Kindergarten Teachers College in Berlin and "*really* blossomed."[131] These widening horizons and the romance with Ernst became superimposed on the drama of separation from family, even as the downward slide of Jewish degradation quickened. But if the love relationship expanded voraciously into the psychic space of the final 18 months, bringing Marianne energy and direction, her general *joie de vivre* was equally plain. Immersing herself in the *Bund*'s collective ethos to the seeming effacement of any *Jewish* predicament bespoke the same earnest commitment to life as such. In reading this relationship with the *Bund*, Roseman returns several times to an idea of "passing." While underground, she managed three identities at once: for a few of the inner circle she was "a Jew on the run"; for other *Bund* members, "a politically endangered Aryan"; and for the world at large, "quite simply an ordinary German."[132] Here she precisely *refused* the fatefulness of the regime's racialized objectification, filling her diaries with abstract reflections on history and the philosophical problems of the present. The *Bund*'s holistic credo encouraged this belief in a future Germany capable of realizing the ideal of a generalized humanity, "[breaking] through the sense of isolation that characterized daily life in Nazi Germany."[133] In Roseman's view, "Marianne was 'passing' not only on the outside but also within her most intimate self. She refused to internalize the category 'Jew' which the Nazis imposed on her."[134] Inside the *Bund*'s self-protective milieu, simply denying the inevitability of the Nazis' racialized categories became the profoundest form of resistance.

If existentially this was a defeat of necessity by freedom, it came at a huge price: if Marianne survived, her fiancé and family did not. Roseman's book pivots around this drama:

> The escape was one of the ... most vivid and traumatic episodes of Marianne's life. The memory never really left her. Above all, it stood under the twin stars of liberation and betrayal. It was both a moment of decision when her survival was balanced on a knife edge and the moment when she abandoned her family, probably forever.[135]

With devastating irony, this act of self-preservation came amid acute disaffection. Following one conflict earlier in 1943, Marianne could find "nothing left to tie me to my parents." She longed for a break.[136] In this light, escaping had an unbearable allegorical charge. Adulthood under the best of circumstances requires putting some of the past away, extricating oneself from the wholeness of family and accepting its loss. In Marianne's case, this "normal challenge of emotionally disengaging from rather overbearing parents" was massively over-determined by the deadly logic of Jewish persecution under the Third Reich. Public and private merged into an unthinkable unity.

Roseman's reflections on this personal tragedy, in the dialectics of memory and history, provide the larger framing of this work. When Marianne emerged from hiding at the war's end, little of her past resurfaced. There were few contacts to any surviving family and friends. Though doggedly pursuing restitution claims during the 1950s, with all the usual demeaning results, she stayed unmoved by the Essen past. She discussed the wartime with none of her Liverpool family and friends. The *Bund* remained her one link. Finally re-entering the past in 1996, she did so from "a binding duty" to honor the *Bund*'s fellowship.[137] Yet, paradoxically, she had kept *everything*. Her Liverpool home hid a rich personal archive, including the wartime diaries, her love letters with Ernst and his Izbica report, together with the immediate postwar correspondence and all the documentation required by restitution. Gradually she released bits and pieces of this hoard, but it surfaced mostly after she died. Along with the other sources Roseman painstakingly massaged into existence, this archive not only grounded Marianne's spoken story, but also revealed memory's fallibility – not over fundamentals but over the significant detail, allowing an atrocity to be magnified or a conflict among friends effaced, and occasionally key elements to be changed. In engineering such adjustments, Marianne's memory negotiated the loss and guilt – guilt at survival, but also at her "sense of growing disconnection from the past." In this view, "the 'gesture' of reworking the past" was meant either "to try and keep it alive," or else "to impose some mastery on the moments that caused such pain."[138]

Roseman brilliantly vindicates the necessity of oral history. Time and again, he uses contemporary informants to revise or complete the "official" archive (like the Gestapo records). He found himself checking conventional documentation against the evidence of testimony as often as the other way round. The historian's knowledge materialized not by the presumed progression from research proposal via the archives to the printed page, but by the splendid serendipity of chance encounters, unexpected suggestions, and hidden connections. "This subcommunity of hidden knowledge!" Roseman exclaims after one of these surprises.[139] His trails constantly intersected with those of others – journalists, lawyers authenticating restitution claims, individuals seeking their severed pasts, museum and exhibition curators, other historians. He interweaves the story of his own progress through the vagaries of the multiple categories of documentation, gradually adding ever-richer layers of understanding from the moving margin of his knowledge. His ability to move back and forth between the telling of Marianne's story and the self-narrative of the unfolding of his own understanding produces a masterly meditation on the historian's craft.[140]

Conclusion

Some other current trends are powerfully widening the contexts for the Holocaust, mainly by creating much stronger comparative or transnational frames. *Nazism as a colonialism* is one source of such interest, as the preceding chapter sought to explore. The complex lines of continuity joining Hitler's visions of a drastically Germanized imperial East to both the abortive expansionism of 1917 to 1918 and the Wilhelmine-era *Weltpolitik* provide one way of resituating the "war against the Jews," along with the far richer array of antecedents and genealogies discussed in Chapter 5. That approach enlarges the terms in which Nazi anti-Semitism can be understood, whether by relating it to the other racial priorities of the European New Order or by considering the Jews among the other subjugated peoples defined as racial enemies deserving of exploitation and genocidal attack. Here the "Final Solution" becomes one element, if the most vital, among the larger purposes of planning and practice signified by *Generalplan Ost.* The Jews then become the most vulnerable among the nationalities thrown into severest endangerment once the Nazis began implementing their designs for resettlement, deportation, and general repopulating of the occupied territories. The genocidal rationalizing of the region's jumbled ethno-cultural geography marked out the Jews for special elimination, though always joined with more elaborate, racially theorized, demographic engineering. These insights begin with Aly and Heim; they are worked by Mazower and Baranowski into a new macro-historical framework; they are key for how Tooze describes Hitler's bid to seize Germany's place in the world order.[141] The analytics of colonialism also situate the Third Reich comparatively with the British and other early twentieth-century empires.[142]

Similarly, *comparative genocide studies* fundamentally recast the ground from which the Holocaust can be approached. Profoundly influenced by events in Bosnia and Rwanda in the mid 1990s, the default comparativism of new work compels a response from those working on the Judeocide. The sheer awfulness of intervening events cancels the ethical probity of insisting on the Holocaust's uniqueness – above all, with respect to Cambodia and Rwanda, but more broadly to the countless micro-political instances that never cease proliferating. A more specifically historicized argument stresses the European dominance since the last third of the nineteenth century of a type of national state whose capacities targeted minority subject populations once national security began defining the political agenda, particularly if territorial integrity became linked to exclusivist ethno-cultural solidarities. That geopolitical argument places the Judeocide in a larger history of state-sponsored episodes of organized violence, forced population transfers, and mass killing, driven by radical nationalist, racially motivated popular mobilization. Mark Levene, Donald Bloxham, Dirk Moses, and Dan Stone are key voices here.[143] The old "uniqueness" debate has been set aside, so that few scholars any longer hold such ground.[144] Contemporary events, combined with intensive revisiting of the Armenian case and a variety of colonial genocides, decisively complicate that earlier insistence.[145] Amid this work the German genocide of the Herero and Nama has been linked in direct continuity with the forms of Nazi rule in occupied Europe.[146] Applying the conceptual framework of colonialism to German expansionism during World War II seems increasingly non-controversial, especially for the East.[147]

These *comparative* or *transnational* aspects return us to the fully European quality of Friedländer's "integrated history of the Holocaust."[148] The latter functions not just on a *continental* plane, but also in a grasp of the *local*, where the victims' voices will alone be heard. A work that realizes this ideal is Browning's study of the Jews of Wierzbnik in central Poland, which tracks them through Nazi occupation, the formation and destruction of the ghetto, the various cycles of killings and atrocities, the creation of three slave labor camps in adjacent Starachowice, and the final transports to Birkenau.[149] Browning's book is a classic example of a regional or local study that brings together the experience of Jewish prisoners, Nazi authorities, and neighboring Poles. The sheer concreteness and density of its evidence and insights widen and complicate our understanding from the ground up. It provides an extraordinary micro-history in that sense. Against the skepticism and disregard of historians, lawyers, and public commentators, Browning's book also validates Friedländer's upholding of eyewitness testimony. Most of all, it compels us to acknowledge the "gray zone." In Starachowice, survival could not be calibrated by any reliable measure of "resistance" (armed, surreptitious, or spiritual) or even by less oppositional forms of self-protective agency. Instead, Browning argues, "We need a different vocabulary to describe their struggle for survival, and I would suggest words such as *ingenuity*, *resourcefulness*, *adaptability*, *perseverence*, and *endurance* as the most appropriate and accurate."[150]

These words are reminiscent of an aphorism of the Jewish Marxist and cultural critic Walter Benjamin, who in September 1940 killed himself on the border between France and Spain. In the seventh of Benjamin's *Theses on the Philosophy of History*, published in 1940, he describes the spoils of history falling to the rulers, who bear them in victory procession over the prostrate bodies of the defeated. Those spoils of history, its "cultural treasures," were forged in the "anonymous toil" of ordinary people: "There is no document of civilization which is not at the same time a document of barbarism," Benjamin says.[151] Yet, the goods of history are not the rulers' exclusive prerogative. They "make their presence felt" in other ways. "They manifest themselves in [the political struggle] as courage, humor, cunning, and fortitude. They have retroactive force and constantly call into question every victory, past and present, of the rulers."[152] Browning has described his reconstruction of the Starachowice story as not a redemptive history. I think this is wrong. Redemption comes not whole and complete, as closure or restoration, as a returning to grace. It comes as a kind of defiance, however cautious and bruised, as resources for struggle in Benjamin's sense – not necessarily, or even very frequently, in the name of politics (and perhaps hardly at all), but rather for the simpler possibility of trying to remake a life.

Abba Kovner, the poet and leader in the United Partisans' Organization (FPO) in the Vilna ghetto, told a story of one day going into an attic in the ghetto, where he found a tailor bent over his sewing machine. The tailor seemed to be sewing a long piece of paper, but without a thread. He asked the tailor what he was doing. Why was he sewing paper with no thread? The tailor answered: I am sewing to write the history of the Jewish people, and especially of the people today. There is no substance, only paper, and on it I am writing, but there is no thread. The most important of the accomplishments of recent historiography, perhaps, is that, finally, after many decades and in the spirit of Walter Benjamin, the stories are being threaded through the paper.[153]

Notes

1 *The Shorter Oxford Dictionary, Vol. I: A – Markworthy*, 3rd edn, Oxford: Oxford University Press, 1973, p975.

2 P. R. Mendes-Flohr and J. Reinharz (eds) *The Jew in the Modern World: A Documentary History*, New York: Oxford University Press, 1980, p482.

3 Born in Lvov, Friedman (1901–1960) wrote his doctoral dissertation in Vienna on the emancipation of the Galician Jews, *Die galizischen Juden im Kämpfe um ihre Gleichberechtigung (1848–1868)*, Frankfurt: Kauffmann Verlag, 1929. He taught in Lodz, Vilna, and Warsaw before the war, which he survived underground in Lvov. After liberation in 1944 he directed the Central Jewish Historical Commission for the newly formed Central Committee of Jews in Poland, gathering war crimes testimony and documentation. As such he produced the earliest studies, then served as head of education for the Joint Distribution Committee in Germany (1946–1948) before emigrating to New York. By the time Friedman's essays were posthumously collected, "Holocaust" was conventionally accepted. See F. Friedman, *Roads to Extinction: Essays on the Holocaust*, Philadelphia: Jewish Publication Society, 1980.

4 H. Arendt, *Eichmann in Jerusalem: A Report on the Banality of Evil*, rev. edn, New York: Penguin Books, 1977. For the fullness of the context: S. E. Aschheim (ed.) *Hannah Arendt in Jerusalem*, Berkeley: University of California Press, 2001; R. H. King and D. Stone (eds) *Hannah Arendt and the Uses of History: Imperialism, Nation, Race, and Genocide*, New York: Berghahn Books, 2007; A. D. Moses, "Genocide and Modernity," in D. Stone (ed.) *The Historiography of Genocide*, Houndmills: Palgrave Macmillan, 2010, pp156–93, esp. pp166–70. M. Marrus, *The Holocaust in History*, New York: Meridian, 1987, pp108–32, remains the best conspectus of this "Arendt moment."

5 For the concept of genocide and Raphael Lemkin's authorship, see A. Curthoys and J. Docker, "Defining Genocide," in Stone (ed.) *Historiography of Genocide*, pp10–13; M. McDonnell and A. D. Moses, "Raphael Lemkin as Historian of Genocide in the

Americas," *Journal of Genocide Research*, 2005, vol. 7, no. 4, pp501–29; D. Stone, "Raphael Lemkin on the Holocaust," ibid, pp539–50.

6 Dawidowicz, *The War Against the Jews*, pxxiv. See also Dawidowicz, *The Holocaust and the Historians*, Cambridge: Cambridge University Press, 1981, p10: "What underlies the attempt to deprive the Jews, as it were, of their terrible unique experience as a people marked for annihilation?"

7 Notable philosopher and Reform rabbi, Emil Fackenheim (1916–2003) had been imprisoned at Sachsenhausen after *Reichskristallnacht* before escaping to Britain in 1939. After internment in Canada, he trained in philosophy at University of Toronto, teaching there 1948 to 1984. By his own telling, Fackenheim experienced the Six Day War as an epiphany. He redefined himself as a "Holocaust theologian," freshly identifying with Zionism. He famously appended a "614th Commandment" to the 613 compiled by Maimonides: "The authentic Jew of today is forbidden to hand Hitler yet another, posthumous victory. [We are] commanded to survive as Jews, lest the Jewish people perish. We are commanded [to remember] the martyrs of the Holocaust, lest their memory perish. We are forbidden ... to deny or despair of God ... lest Judaism perish ... To abandon any of these imperatives, in response to Hitler's victory at Auschwitz, would be to hand him yet other, posthumous victories." He typifies the transition I am describing. In 1984 he emigrated to Israel. For the quotations, see Novick, *Holocaust in American Life*, pp199, 308, note 22. See also A. Gorman, "Whither the Broken Middle? Rose and Fackenheim on Mourning, Modernity, and the Holocaust," in Fine and Turner (eds) *Social Theory after the Holocaust*, pp47–70; M. Berenbaum, "Judaism," in P. Hayes and J.K. Roth (eds) *The Oxford Handbook of Holocaust Studies*, Oxford: Oxford University Press, 2010, pp607–19.

8 G. Steiner, *In Bluebeard's Castle: Some Notes Towards the Redefinition of Culture*, New Haven: Yale University Press, 1974; R. L. Rubenstein, *The Cunning of History: The Holocaust and the American Future*, New York: Harper and Row, 1975.

9 Y. Bauer, *The Holocaust in Historical Perspective*, Seattle: University of Washington Press, 1978, p31.

10 J. Robinson, "Holocaust," in *Encyclopaedia Judaica, Vol. 8: He-Ir*, Jerusalem: Keter Publishing House, 1972, pp827–905.

11 See *Jewish Resistance during the Holocaust: Proceedings of the Conference on Manifestations of Jewish Resistance, April 7–11, 1968*, Jerusalem: Yad Vashem, 1971.

12 Dedicated in 1993, the United States Holocaust Memorial Museum houses a large complex of exhibitionary, educational, outreach, commemorative, and research activity. See Novick, *Holocaust in American Life*, pp216–20, and for detail E. T. Linenthal, *Preserving Memory: The Struggle to Create America's Holocaust Museum*, New York: Columbia University Press, 1995. For the proceedings of the inaugural conference of the Center for Advanced Holocaust Studies, see M. Berenbaum and A. J. Peck (eds) *The Holocaust and History: The Known, the Unknown, the Disputed, and the Examined*, Bloomington: Indiana University Press, 1998.

13 Novick, *Holocaust in American Life*; T. Kushner, *The Holocaust and the Liberal Imagination: A Social and Cultural History*, Oxford: Blackwell, 1994; T. Segev, *The Seventh Million*, New York: Hill and Wang, 1993.

14 Novick, *Holocaust in American Life*, pp209–14; Y. Loshitzky (ed.) *Spielberg's Holocaust: Critical Perspectives on Schindler's List*, Bloomington: Indiana University Press, 1997. For the *Holocaust* reception in West Germany, see the *Special Issue* (the first of three on "Germans and Jews") of *New German Critique*, vol. 19, 1980, with contributions by J. Herf, A. S. Markovits and R. S. Hayden, S. Zielinski, M. Postone, and A. Huyssen. More generally, see Omer Bartov: "An Idiot's Tale: Memories and Histories of the Holocaust," and "Chambers of Horror: The Reordering of Murders Past," in Bartov, *Murder in Our Midst: The Holocaust, Industrial Killing, and Representation*, New York: Oxford University Press, 1996, pp89–113, and 153–86; and "Apocalyptic Visions," in Bartov, *Mirrors of Destruction: War, Genocide, and Modern Identity*, New York: Oxford University Press, 2000, pp143–212.

15 For the centrality of memory, see T. Judt, "From the House of the Dead: An Essay on Modern European Memory," in Judt, *Postwar: A History of Europe since 1945*, New York: Penguin, 2005, pp803–31; D. Stone, "Memory Wars in the 'New Europe'" in Stone (ed.) *The Oxford Handbook of Postwar European History*, Oxford: Oxford University Press, 2012, pp714–31. For Germany specifically: R. G. Moeller, *War Stories,* and A. D. Moses, *German Intellectuals and the Nazi Past*, Cambridge: Cambridge University Press, 2007.

16 G. A. Craig, *Germany 1866–1945*, Oxford: Oxford University Press, 1978, pp748–51. Craig's general European history textbook, *Europe Since 1815*, New York: Holt, Rinehart, and Winston, 1974, managed not to mention the Holocaust at all. See D. Diner, "Memory and Method: Variance in Holocaust Narrations," *Studies in Contemporary Jewry* XIII, Oxford: Oxford University Press, 1997, pp84–7, and for a book-by-book accounting, Dawidowicz, *Holocaust and the Historians*, pp22–67.

17 See Chapter 2 in this volume. Kershaw, *The Nazi Dictatorship*, pp80–107, remains the best guide. The framing of "intentionalism" *versus* "structuralism" was Tim Mason's at a conference of London's German Historical Institute at Windsor in 1979. See Mason, "Intention and Explanation: A Current Controversy about the Interpretation of National Socialism," ibid, pp23–40, reprinted in J. Caplan (ed.) *Nazism, Fascism, and the Working Class*, pp212–30.

18 Phrases taken from Dawidowicz, *War against the Jews*, pp193–208. Aside from Dawidowicz, see G. Fleming, *Hitler and the Final Solution*, Berkeley: University of California Press, 1984.

19 For Mommsen, see especially: "Hitler's Position in the Nazi System," and "The Realization of the Unthinkable," in Mommsen, *From Weimar to Auschwitz*, Princeton: Princeton University Press, 1991, pp163–88 and 73–125; "Soziale Motivation und Führer-Bindung des Nationalsozialismus," *Vierteljahrshefte für Zeitgeschichte*, vol. 18, 1970, pp392–409.

20 The best and most judicious accounting remains chapter five of Kershaw's *Nazi Dictatorship*, pp93–133.

21 See, above all, H. Mommsen, "Hannah Arendt and the Eichmann Trial," in Mommsen, *From Weimar to Auschwitz*, pp254–78, together with note 4 above.

22 R. Hilberg, *The Destruction of the European Jews*, Chicago: Ivan R. Dee, 1961, 2nd edn, 3 vols, New York: Holmes and Meier, 1985, 3rd edn, 3 vols, New Haven: Yale University Press, 2003. See also Hilberg, *Perpetrators, Victims, Bystanders: The Jewish Catastrophe 1933–1945*, New York: HarperPerennial, 1992, and his revealing autobiography, *The Politics of Memory: The Journey of a Holocaust Historian*, Chicago: Ivan R. Dee, 1996, esp. pp147–57 for his remarks about Arendt.

23 See C. R. Browning, "The Decision-Making Process," in D. Stone (ed.) *The Historiography of the Holocaust*, p174: "Clearly structure and process, not ideology and motivation, were at the center of Hilberg's work."

24 See, above all, Z. Bauman, *Modernity and the Holocaust*, Cambridge: Polity Press, 1989, and Peukert, "The Genesis of the 'Final Solution'," pp234–52.

25 For David Irving, see R. J. Evans, *Lying About Hitler: History, Holocaust, and the David Irving Trial*, New York: Basic Books, 2001; D. D. Guttenplan, *The Holocaust on Trial*, New York: Norton, 2001.

26 C. R. Browning, with J. Matthäus, *The Origins of the Final Solution: The Evolution of Nazi Jewish Policy, September 1939 to March 1942*, Lincoln: University of Nebraska Press, 2004; S. Friedländer, *The Years of Extermination*; Longerich, *Holocaust*. The introduction to Longerich's book, the extensively revised English edition of a work originally published in German, *Politik der Vernichtung: Eine Gesamtdarstellung der nationalsozialistischen Judenverfolgung*, Munich: Piper, 1998, subsequently relates the historiographical transformation since the early 1980s. See *Holocaust*, pp1–9. More than anyone, Browning held a place throughout the entire four decades of this accumulating scholarship for an empirically meticulous and ethically surefooted examination of the high-level decision-

making machinery in its relationship to events on the ground: *The Final Solution and the German Foreign Office: A Study of Referat D III of Abteilung Deutschland 1940–43*, New York: Holmes and Meier, 1978; *Fateful Months: Essays on the Emergence of the Final Solution*, New York: Holmes and Meier, 1985; *The Path to Genocide: Essays on Launching the Final Solution*, Cambridge: Cambridge University Press, 1992; *Ordinary Men*; *Nazi Policy, Jewish Labor, German Killers*, Cambridge: Cambridge University Press, 2000; *Collected Memories: Holocaust History and Postwar Testimony*, Madison: University of Wisconsin Press, 2003; *Remembering Survival*. For the general context of his work, see C. Wiese and P. Betts (eds) *Years of Persecution, Years of Extermination*.

27 Nothing better illustrates this than the bizarrely grandiose and unworkable, yet seriously conceived, fantasy of the "Madagascar Plan," actively explored between the end of May to autumn 1940 before being shelved. See Longerich, *Holocaust*, pp161–4, and Browning, *Origins*, pp81–9. For detail: M. Brechtken, *"Madagaskar für die Juden": Antisemitische Idee und politische Praxis*, Munich: Oldenbourg, 1997.

28 The blandly genocidal projections of the "Hunger Plan," the most shockingly murderous element in *Generalplan Ost* (General Plan East) as it materialized from summer 1941, make the genocidal readiness all the clearer. Projecting *30 million* deaths in the occupied East as an entailment of prioritizing Germany's own food needs helped to make the assault on the Jews appear practicable. See Kay, *Exploitation, Resettlement, Mass Murder*, esp. pp100–14, 120–39; Tooze, *The Wages of Destruction*, pp461–85; M. Ressler and S. Schleiermacher (eds) *Der Generalplan-Ost: Hauptlinien der nationalsozialistischen Planungs- und Vernichtungspolitik*, Berlin: Akadamie Verlag, 1993.

29 For critical orientation see Kershaw, *Hitler 1936–45*, pp459–95, along with "Improvised Genocide? The Emergence of the 'Final Solution' in the 'Warthegau'," and "Hitler's Role in the 'Final Solution'," in *Hitler, the Germans, and the Final Solution*, New Haven: Yale University Press, 2008, pp60–88 and 89–116. See also Evans, *Third Reich at War*, pp215–81; Wildt, *Uncompromising Generation*, pp217–326; Gerwarth, *Hitler's Hangman*, pp141–61, 178–217; Longerich, *Heinrich Himmler*, pp515–74; Browning, "Decision-Making Process," pp173–96. Two short books brilliantly summarize the arguments: M. Roseman, *The Wannsee Conference and the Final Solution: A Reconsideration*, New York: Metropolitan Books, 2002; Longerich, *Unwritten Order*. For a bold and judicious situating of the Holocaust in comparative genocide studies, see Bloxham, *The Final Solution*, pp131–258. Finally, Dan Stone provides a superb critical overview in "The Decision-Making Process in Context," in Stone, *Histories of the Holocaust*, Oxford: Oxford University Press, 2010, pp64–112.

30 Roseman, *Wannsee Conference*, p56.

31 See esp. Longerich, *Heinrich Himmler*, pp524–40. In this July to October period, Himmler did a "truly astounding amount of traveling" behind the lines. Thus "he did everything he could … to step up the mass executions of Jews in the Soviet Union … to the point of turning them into a comprehensive genocide." Ibid, p539.

32 Roseman, *Wannsee Conference*, p77.

33 Ibid, p66.

34 Longerich, *Unwritten Order*, p143.

35 Roseman, *Wannsee Conference*, p63.

36 The evidence here is discussed by T. Sandkühler, *"Endlösing" in Galizien: Der Judenmord in Ostpolen und die Rettungsinitiativen von Berthold Beitz, 1941–1944*, Bonn: Dietz, 1996, pp156–9; also Longerich, *Holocaust*, p284.

37 The general syntheses of Browning, Longerich, and Friedländer cited in note 26 above build on the research findings of a crucial constellation of regional studies. See note 64 in Chapter 3 of this volume. For commentary, see O. Bartov, "Seeking the Roots of Modern Genocide: On the Macro- and Micro-History of Mass Murder," in R. Gellately and B. Kiernan (eds) *The Specter of Genocide: Mass Murder in Historical Perspective*, Cambridge: Cambridge University Press, 2003, pp77–96.

38 See Epstein, *Model Nazi*, pp1–9.

39 Roseman, *Wannsee Conference*, p67.
40 Longerich, *Unwritten Order*, p151.
41 For Operation T-4 see note 41 in Chapter 2 of this volume.
42 Roseman, *Wannsee Conference*, p69.
43 Longerich, *Unwritten Order*, p151.
44 Longerich, *Holocaust*, p283.
45 Thus, Richard Breitman places the "fundamental decision to exterminate the Jews" in early 1941, after which "the Final Solution was just a matter of time – and timing." See his *Architect of Genocide* and "Plans for the Final Solution in Early 1941," *German Studies Review*, vol. 17, 1994, pp483–93. For a succinct rendition of debates over timing, see Browning, "Decision-Making Process."
46 Longerich, *The Unwritten Order*, p184.
47 For Browning ("Decision-Making Process," p188), the decisive point came "between 16 September and 25 October 1941" and that "Only in May 1942 … was the mass murder of Reich Jews fully and unequivocally underway," while earlier at the time of the invasion of the Soviet Union "the *implied genocide* in the future of Jews on Soviet territory was not yet the Final Solution for all Soviet Jewry, much less the other Jews of Europe." See Browning, *Nazi Policy, Jewish Workers, German Killers*, pp31, 55, 25. Christian Gerlach's placement of Hitler's decision in the second week of December 1941 in response to Pearl Harbor has not been persuasive. See Gerlach, "The Wannsee Conference, the Fate of the German Jews, and Hitler's Decision in Principle to Exterminate All European Jews," *Journal of Modern History*, vol. 70, 1998, pp759–812. Stone calls the search for the missing *Führerbefehl* (*Führer* command) aptly "a bogeyman of historical research." See Stone, "Decision-Making Process in Context," p67.
48 The last such moments accompanied A. J. Mayer's *Why Did the Heavens Not Darken? The "Final Solution" as History*, New York: Pantheon, 1989, and Goldhagen's *Hitler's Willing Executioners*, two works that subsumed interpretation into a tendentiously over-generalized argument about ideology tenuously related to the archives. See Browning, "The Holocaust as By-Product? A Critique of Arno Mayer," in *Path to Genocide*, pp77–85.
49 See, above all, D. Stone, *Constructing the Holocaust: A Study in Historiography*, London: Vallentine Mitchell, 2003. For the urtext in this genre, see S. Friedländer (ed.) *Probing the Limits of Representation: Nazism and the "Final Solution,"* Cambridge: Harvard University Press, 1992; also the writings of D. LaCapra, *Representing the Holocaust: History, Theory, Trauma*, Ithaca: Cornell University Press, 1994; *History and Memory after Auschwitz*, Ithaca: Cornell University Press, 1998; and *Writing History, Writing Trauma*, Baltimore: Johns Hopkins University Press, 2001; also I. Clendinnen, *Reading the Holocaust*, Cambridge: Cambridge University Press, 1999.
50 Cited by Stone, "Decision-Making Process in Context," p107. See Betts and Wiese (eds) *Years of Persecution, Years of Extermination.*
51 I. Kershaw, "Introduction," in Kershaw, *Hitler, the Germans, and the Final Solution*, p20. The original statement was made by Werner Willikens, State Secretary in the Ministry of Agriculture to a meeting of state agricultural representatives on 21 February 1934. See J. Noakes and G. Pridham (eds) *Nazism 1919–1945: A Documentary Reader. Vol. 2: State, Economy, and Society 1933–1939*, Exeter: University of Exeter, 1984, p207. See also Kershaw, "'Working towards the *Führer*': Reflections on the Nature of the Hitler Dictatorship," in *Hitler, the Germans, and the Final Solution*, pp29–48; A. McElligott and T. Kirk, "Editors' Introduction," in McElligott and Kirk (eds) *Working Towards the Führer. Essays in Honor of Sir Ian Kershaw*, Manchester: Manchester University Press, 2003, pp1–14.
52 Longerich, *Unwritten Order.*
53 Kershaw, "Introduction," p21, and "Hitler's Role in the 'Final Solution'."
54 D. Stone, "The Holocaust: Child of Modernity?" in Stone, *Histories of the Holocaust*, p127. Stone cites, in particular, D. Rebentisch, *Führerstaat und Verwaltung im Zweiten*

Weltkrieg: Verfassungsentwicklung und Verwaltungs politik 1939–1945, Stuttgart: Franz Steiner, 1989. The classic source for the concept is P. Hüttenberger, "Nationalsozialistische Polykratie." See also Caplan, *Government without Administration*, esp. ppvi–xii, pp260–338; Noakes, "Hitler and the Nazi State;" P. Hayes, "Polycracy and Policy in the Third Reich: The Case of the Economy," in Childers and Caplan (eds) *Reevaluating the Third Reich*, pp190–210.

55 For the conflicts over the *Deutsche Volksliste*, see Chapter 5 in this volume. For the disorders and efficiencies of Nazi administration using the example of the SS, see Stone, "Holocaust: Child of Modernity?" pp128–59; also Allen, *The Business of Genocide* and "A Bureaucratic Holocaust – Toward a New Consensus," in Feldman and Seibel (eds) *Networks of Nazi Persecution*, pp259–68.

56 Roseman, *Wannsee Conference*, pp79–86, 94–7. Also Stone's comment following Heinemann on inter-agency cooperation for racial purification policies in the East: "'polycracy' should not be understood as synonymous with chaos." See Stone, "Holocaust: Child of Modernity?" p132; I. Heinemann, "'Ethnic Resettlement' and Inter-Agency Cooperation in the Occupied Eastern Territories," in Feldman and Seibel (eds) *Networks of Nazi Persecution*, pp213–35.

57 See R. Hilberg, "German Railroads, Jewish Souls," *Society*, 1976, vol. 14, no. 1, pp520–56, and *Sonderzüge nach Auschwitz*, Mainz: Dumjahn, 1981; A. C. Mierzejewski, "A Public Enterprise in the Service of Mass Murder: The *Deutsche Reichsbahn* and the Holocaust," *Holocaust and Genocide Studies*, 2001, vol. 15, no. 1, pp33–46, and *The Most Valuable Asset of the Reich: A History of the German National Railway. Vol. 2: 1933–1945*, Chapel Hill: University of North Carolina Press, 2000.

58 Longerich, *Unwritten Order*, p151.

59 See now M. Fulbrook, *A Small Town Near Auschwitz: Ordinary Nazis and the Holocaust*, Oxford: Oxford University Press, 2012.

60 I have in mind less Bauman's *Modernity and the Holocaust* or work by Aly and Heim, than the registers in which Broszat and Mommsen tended to work. In some ways, Hilberg bridged from the latter to Bauman. He presented the Holocaust avowedly as an "administrative process." See Hilberg, *Destruction*, vol. 1, pp9, 62; Mommsen, *Beamtentum*; Broszat, *Hitler State*; C. R. Browning, "Bureaucracy and Mass Murder: The German Administrator's Comprehension of the Final Solution," in *Path to Genocide*, pp125–44; Aly and Heim, "The Economics of the Final Solution: A Case Study from the General Government," *Simon Wiesenthal Center Annual*, vol. 5, 1988, pp3–48, and *Architects of Annihilation*.

61 See note 37 above.

62 Herbert, *Hitler's Foreign Workers*; Herbert, "Labor and Extermination;" W. Gruner, *Jewish Forced Labor under the Nazis: Economic Needs and Racial Aims, 1938–1944*, Cambridge: Cambridge University Press, 2006.

63 Mommsen and Grieger, *Das Volkswagenwerk und seine Arbeiter*, p1027.

64 F. Biess and M. Roseman, "Introduction," in Biess, Roseman, and H. Schissler (eds) *Conflict, Catastrophe, and Continuity: Essays on Modern German History*, New York: Berghahn Books, 2007, p5, from the summary of Roseman's essay "Beyond Conviction?" pp83–103.

65 Ibid, p99.

66 Ibid, p95.

67 Ibid.

68 Playing down the impact of anti-Semitism as a primary motivator in the NSDAP's popular electoral appeal during 1928 to 1932 rested on a schematic distinction between "propaganda" and "mobilization," where the former implied the Nazis' programmatic ideology and the latter the range of social constituencies whose receptiveness enabled its appeal actually to work. The goal became "to comprehend the attractions of Nazism in terms of rational social and political choices of an electorate, and, rather than concentrating so heavily upon the output and content of propaganda, to evaluate a wide variety of responses to Nazi agitation." Very influential between circa 1975 and 1985,

the terms of this opposition mapped onto the dichotomous understanding of "ideology" and "social history" discussed in Chapters 2 and 3 in this volume. The now-classic commentary was I. Kershaw, "Ideology, Propaganda, and the Rise of the Nazi Party," in Stachura (ed.) *The Nazi Machtergreifung*, pp162–81, from which the quotation is taken (p170). See Kershaw's post-1933 companion essay, "How Effective Was Nazi Propaganda?" in D. Welch (ed.) *Nazi Propaganda*, London: Croom Helm, 1983, pp180–205, linking to *Popular Opinion and Political* and *The "Hitler Myth."*

69 See Peukert, "The Genesis of the 'Final Solution'."
70 The best introduction is now through Aly, "*Final Solution*." For a critical survey of the broader research context, Herbert (ed.) *National Socialist Extermination Policies*.
71 Aly and Heim, *Architects of Annihilation*.
72 N. Stargardt, "The Holocaust," in M. Fulbrook (ed.) *German History since 1800*, London: Arnold, 1997, p351. This essay is a fine rendition of approaches and research.
73 Herbert, *Best*; Wildt, *Uncompromising Generation*.
74 Caplan, "Introduction," in Herz, *The Women's Camp in Moringen*, p15.
75 Ibid, p15–16. For the transition from the targeting of political opponents to a racially driven system of eugenic selection, see Herbert, Orth, and Dieckmann (eds) *Nationalsozialistischen Konznetrationslager*, pp60–110; more generally, W. Ayaß, *"Asoziale"* and Gellately and Stoltzfus (eds) *Social Outsiders*.
76 Caplan, "Introduction," p16. For the general history of the camp system, see the references in note 110 in Chapter 2.
77 See N. Wachsmann, "'Annihilation through Labor': The Killing of State Prisoners in the Third Reich," *Journal of Modern History*, 1999, vol. 71, no. 3, 624–59.
78 Caplan, "Introduction," p44.
79 See H. Yablonka, *The State of Israel vs. Adolf Eichmann*, New York: Schocken, 2004; Pendas, *The Frankfurt Auschwitz Trial*.
80 Bloxham, *Genocide on Trial*.
81 The exchange plus the original article and Friedländer's published reply may be found in Baldwin (ed.) *Reworking the Past*, pp77–134. For the originals, see M. Broszat, "Plädoyer für eine Historisierung des Nationalsozialismus," *Merkur*, vol. 39, 1985, pp373–85; S. Friedländer, "Some Reflections on the Historicization of National Socialism," *Tel Aviv Jahrbuch für deutsche Geschichte*, vol. 16, 1987, pp310–24; Broszat and Friedländer, "Um die 'Historisierung des Nationalsozialismus.' Ein Briefwechsel," *Vierteljahrshefte für Zeitgeschichte*, vol. 36, 1988, pp339–72, translated as "A Controversy about the Historicization of National Socialism," *New German Critique*, vol. 44, 1988, pp81–126. See also Kershaw, "'Normality' and Genocide: The Problem of 'Historicization'," in *Hitler, the Germans, and the Final Solution*, pp282–302.
82 See Baldwin (ed.) *Reworking the Past*, pp106, 105.
83 As Broszat later clarified, this particular remark was far less generalized than Friedländer alleged, referring far more to just one tendency of Jewish-historical writing. In light of the intellectual climate represented by Emil Fackenheim, quoted at the beginning of this chapter, his description was not so far-fetched. As it happened, though, the ground of Israeli-based scholarship on Nazism was already shifting.
84 See N. Berg, *Der Holocaust und die westdeutsche Historiker: Erforschung und Erinnerung*, Göttingen: Wallstein, 2003, pp447–63; Berg, "The Holocaust and the West German Historians: Historical Research and Memory," in M. Zimmermann (ed.) *On Germans and Jews under the Nazi Regime: Essays by Three Generations of Historians*, Jerusalem: Hebrew University Magnes Press, 2006, pp85–103. But see also F. Bösch, "Versagen der Zeitgeschichtsforschung? Martin Broszat, die westdeutsche Geschichtswissenschaft und die Fernsehserie 'Holocaust'," *Zeithistorische Forschungen/Studies in Contemporary History, Online-Ausgabe*, 2009, vol. 6, no. 3, http://www.zeithistorische-forschungen.de/16126041-Boesch-3-2009.
85 While Broszat acknowledged his membership of the Hitler Youth, he never disclosed his own application for Nazi Party membership at the age of 18 in 1944.

86 U. Herbert, "Extermination Policy: New Answers and Questions about the History of the 'Holocaust' in German Historiography," in Herbert (ed.) *National Socialist Extermination Policies*, p171.
87 U. Herbert, "The Holocaust in German Historiography: Some Introductory Remarks," in Zimmermann (ed.) *On Germans and Jews*, p83. See also the discussion among Y. Weiss, U. Herbert, and S. Friedländer, in M. Brenner (ed.) *Jüdische Geschichtschreibung heute: Themen, Positionen, Kontroversen*, Munich: Beck, 2002, pp229–64.
88 O. Bartov, "Eastern Europe as the Site of Genocide," *Journal of Modern History*, 2008, vol. 80, no. 3, pp584–5.
89 Friedländer, *Years of Extermination*, pxv.
90 P. Betts and C. Wiese, "Introduction," *Years of Persecution, Years of Extermination*, p7.
91 See S. Friedländer, *Reflections of Nazism: An Essay on Kitsch and Death*, New York: Harper and Row, 1982.
92 S. Friedländer, "An Integrated History of the Holocaust: Possibilities and Challenges," in Wiese and Betts (eds) *Years of Persecution, Years of Extermination*, p25.
93 Ibid. Friedländer calls this method "simultaneous representation": "Only the succession of phases, each presenting the synchronicity of events both throughout occupied Europe and within each country can indicate, as mentioned, the interrelatedness and the very dimension of this history." Ibid, p24.
94 In light of Friedländer's own methodological-cum-philosophical credo, his stated commitment to the fracturing of orderly narrative progression and the importance of putting the historian's own voice into the text, there is obvious irony here. Against his own injunctions, Alon Confino observes, Friedländer has certainly produced an "overall interpretive framework," thereby delivering "a sort of total history (in a historiographical age that repudiates it) that 'penetrates all the nooks and crannies of European space'." See Confino, "Narrative Form and Historical Sensation: On Saul Friedländer's *Years of Extermination*," *History and Theory*, vol. 48, 2009, p203, quoting Friedländer, *Years of Extermination*, pxix. Dan Stone concurs: "the text is constructed masterfully, with a sure guiding hand, and the control of an apparently all-seeing narrator." Even while "resisting closure, offering multiple voices, and fracturing the narrative … Friedländer actually produces a text that is impressively coherent, carefully structured, and beautifully written. Precisely insofar as it succeeds in achieving its goals, the demand for an alternative history has actually produced the epitome of Holocaust historiography, since it appears to cover almost everything … and to have contained all this information within a narrative frame that is at once highly readable, controlled, and clearly argued. Even the intrusion of the historian's voice does not alienate, but provides a curious comfort, as one senses that one is in the hands of a sure guide." See D. Stone, "*Nazi Germany and the Jews* and the Future of Holocaust Historiography," in Wiese and Betts (eds) *Years of Persecution, Years of Extermination*, p347.
95 Ibid, p346.
96 For the quoted phrases, see S. Friedländer, "West Germany and the Burden of the Past: The Ongoing Debate," *Jerusalem Quarterly*, vol. 42, 1987, pp9–10.
97 S. Friedländer, "Trauma, Memory, and Transference," in G. H. Hartman (ed.) *Holocaust Remembrance: The Shapes of Memory*, Oxford: Blackwell, 1994, p262. See Lüdtke, "The Appeal of Exterminating 'Others'."
98 Friedländer, "An Integrated History," p23. See here A. Garbarini, *Numbered Days: Diaries and the Holocaust*, New Haven: Yale University Press, 2006.
99 Friedländer, *Years of Persecution*, p2.
100 Friedländer, "An Integrated History," p23. For a valuable tracking of the shifting historiographical treatment of victims' testimony between the immediate postwar years and the present, see T. Kushner, "Saul Friedländer, Holocaust Historiography, and the Use of Testimony," in Wiese and Betts (eds) *Years of Persecution, Years of Extermination*, pp67–79, along with D. Bloxham and Kushner, *The Holocaust: Critical Historical Approaches*, Manchester: Manchester University Press, 2005, pp16–60. Betts and Wiese,

"Introduction," p9, credit the reception of Victor Klemperer's diaries with inspiring much of the changed receptiveness to using first-person evidence. Two key works building on the latter are N. Stargardt, *Witnesses of War: Children's Lives under the Nazis*, London: Cape, 2007, and P. Fritzsche, *Life and Death in the Third Reich*, Cambridge: Harvard University Press, 2008. Important early texts from a mainly literary perspective were L. Langer, *Holocaust Testimonies: The Ruins of Memory*, New Haven: Yale University Press, 1991; S. Feldman and D. Laub, *Testimony: Crises of Witnessing in Literature, Psychoanalysis, and History*, New York: Routledge, 1992. See also D. Stone, "Holocaust Testimony and the Challenge to the Philosophy of History," in Stone, *History, Memory, and Mass Atrocity: Essays on the Holocaust and Genocide*, London: Valentine Mitchell, 2006, pp132–47; M. Fulbrook and U. Rublack, "In Relation: The 'Social Self' and Ego-Documents," *German History*, 2010, vol. 28, no. 3, pp263–72; N. Stargardt, "The Troubled Patriot: German *Innerlichkeit* in World War II," ibid, pp276–342; J. Wagner, "The Truth about Auschwitz: Prosecuting Auschwitz Crimes with the help of Survivor Testimony," ibid, pp343–57. For the Victor Klemperer diaries, see V. Klemperer, *I Shall Bear Witness: The Diaries of Victor Klemperer 1933–1941*, London: Weidenfeld and Nicolson, 1998, and *To the Bitter End: The Diaries of Victor Klemperer 1942–1945*, London: Weidenfeld and Nicolson, 1998.

101 See Friedman, *Roads to Extinction*, and note 3 above.

102 A major conference on Jewish resistance at Yad Vashem in April 1968 produced the foundational volume, *Jewish Resistance during the Holocaust*, followed by Reuben Ainsztein's remarkable compilation, *Jewish Resistance in Nazi-Occupied Eastern Europe: With a Historical Survey of the Jew as Fighter and Soldier in the Diaspora*, New York: Barnes and Noble, 1974. I. Trunk, *Judenrat: The Jewish Councils in Eastern Europe under Nazi Occupation*, London: Macmillan, 1972, Yiddish, 1970, was conceived as a direct rejoinder to Arendt, preceded in 1962 by his study of Lodz, translated as *Lodz Ghetto: A History*, Bloomington: Indiana University Press, 2008. Along with H. G. Adler's *Theresienstadt 1941–1945: Das Antlitz einer Zwangsgemeinschaft. Geschichte, Soziologie, Psychologie*, Tübingen: J. C. B. Mohr, 1960, this long remained the only scholarly monograph on a specific ghetto. It was then joined by Yitzhak Arad's account of Vilna, *Ghetto in Flames: The Struggle and Destruction of the Jews of Vilna in the Holocaust*, New York: Ktav Publishing House, 1982, Yiddish, 1980; and Yisrael Gutman's cognate history of *The Jews of Warsaw: Ghetto, Underground, Revolt*, Bloomington: Indiana University Press, 1982. Best historiographical guide is still M. Marrus, *The Holocaust in History*, New York: Meridian, 1987, pp108–55.

103 Gutman, *Jews of Warsaw*, p143.

104 Ibid, p144.

105 For these antecedents, see E. Mendesohn's authoritative *Zionism in Poland: The Formative Years, 1915–1926*, New Haven: Yale University Press, 1981.

106 For Minsk, see now B. Epstein, *The Minsk Ghetto 1941–1943: Jewish Resistance and Soviet Internationalism*, Berkeley: University of California Press, 2008.

107 Y. Bauer, *They Chose Life: Jewish Resistance in the Holocaust*, New York: American Jewish Committee, 1973, p33; the first statement is by Marrus, *Holocaust in History*, pp136–37, describing Bauer's views.

108 See especially Petropoulos and Roth (eds) *Gray Zones*; L. L. Langer, *Versions of Survival: The Holocaust and the Human Spirit*, Albany: State University of New York Press, 1982.

109 The best guide to this range of approaches is via the literature cited in note 49 above. The following provide a good place to start: Freidländer (ed.) *Probing the Limits of Representation*; D. LaCapra, "Trauma Studies: Its Critics and Vicissitudes," and "Approaching Limit Events: Siting Agamben," in LaCapra, *History in Transit*, pp106–43 and 144–94; D. Stone, "Georges Bataille and the Interpretation of the Holocaust," "Genocide and Transgression," and "Biopower and Modern Genocide," in Stone, *History, Memory, and Mass Atrocity*, pp69–93, 196–216, and 217–35; Stone, "The Holocaust: Child of Modernity?," in Stone, *Histories of the Holocaust*, pp113–59.

110 Williams, *Marxism and Literature*, p82.
111 C. R. Browing, "'Alleviation' and 'Compliance': The Survival Strategies of the Jewish Leadership in the Wierzbnik Ghetto and Starachowice Factory Slave Labor Camps," in Petropoulos and Roth (eds) *Gray Zones*, p34.
112 Friedländer, *Years of Extermination*, pxxiv.
113 M. Roseman, *A Past in Hiding: Memory and Survival in Nazi Germany*, New York: Metropolitan Books, 2000.
114 For the advantages of "acculturation" conceptually over "assimilation," see M. Kaplan, "Tradition and Transition. The Acculturation, Assimilation, and Integration of Jews in Imperial Germany. A Gender Analysis," *Leo Baeck Institute Year Book*, vol. 27, 1982, pp3–36.
115 For the decision to expel the German Jews as an element in the chronology of the "Final Solution," see Kershaw, *Nemesis*, pp472–87.
116 Roseman, *Past in Hiding*, p128.
117 Roseman's account of the *Abwehr*'s role can be found ibid, pp129–45 and pp250–3; also W. Meyer, *Unternehmen Sieben. Eine Rettungsaktion für vom Holocaust Bedrohte aus dem Amt Ausland/Abwehr im Oberkommando der Wehrmacht*, Frankfurt am Main: Hain, 1993.
118 Roseman, *Past in Hiding*, p137.
119 For details of the ethically compromised basis on which friends and neighbors aided the Strauss family, see ibid, pp137–8, 343. See Bajohr, *"Aryanization" in Hamburg*; Barkai, *From Boycott to Annihilation*; Bajohr, *Parvenüs und Profiteure.*
120 Roseman, *Past in Hiding*, p150.
121 Virtually nothing was previously known about the Izbica camp, which helped to feed the extermination camp at Belzec following the Wannsee conference in January 1942. See also M. Zimmermann, "Die Deportation der Juden aus Essen und dem Regierungsbezirk Düsseldorf," in U. Borsdorf and M. Jamin (eds) *Überleben im Krieg. Kriegserfahrungen in einer Industrieregion, 1939–1945*, Hamburg: Rohwolt, 1989, pp126–43.
122 Roseman, *Past in Hiding*, p211. See also Pohl, *Von der "Judenpolitik" zum Judenmord*, pp128–39; and for a rare eyewitness account of Izbica, T. T. Blatt, *From the Ashes of Sobibor. A Story of Survival*, Evanston: Northwestern University Press, 1997. This is a fine instance of Roseman's care in matching oral sources to the documentary record.
123 Roseman, *Past in Hiding*, p211. The first quote is Roseman's; the second is from his interview with Hanna Aron, daughter of the secretary in the Essen Jewish community offices. Arras was *not* in the SS but rather a non-commissioned officer in the Army in Poland, France, and Poland again, before receiving reserved occupational status. Survivor recollections often "blur German uniforms – whether the *Wehrmacht*, as in this case, or railway officials, or the police – into the evil, threatening outfit of the SS" (ibid, p210). For Arras, ibid, pp201–11, and Ernst's report from Izbica, ibid, pp186–97.
124 For details ibid, pp211–18.
125 Ibid, p243.
126 Ibid, pp232–3.
127 With Jewish exclusion from normal opportunities in 1933, Marianne was sent for dance classes with Dore Jacobs. She met Artur Jacobs at the Krombachs' apartment only the evening before Ernst's deportation. Ibid, p237.
128 The Essen *Bund* was little known until Roseman stumbled on its existence. Artur Jacobs's manuscript diary in the Essen city archive proved a key source. See also M. Grüter, "Der 'Bund für ein sozialistisches Leben': Seine Entwicklung in den 20er Jahren und seine Widerständigkeit unter dem Nationalsozialismus," Dissertation, University of Essen, 1988. See *Past in Hiding*, pp231–41, 264–338, 340–7, 360–3, 415–16.
129 Some of her protectors were unconnected with the *Bund*, including a distant cousin married to a non-Jew near Bremen, the sister of a former colleague in Barmen (also in a mixed marriage), and her aunt's former housekeeper in Wuppertal-Elberfeld. See ibid, p278 and, more generally pp272–92.

130 For example: K. von Klemperer (ed.) *A Noble Combat: The Letters of Sheila Grant Duff and Adam von Trott zu Soltz, 1932–1939*, Oxford: Oxford University Press, 1988; H. Bull (ed.) *The Challenge of the Third Reich: The Adam von Trott Memorial Lectures*, Oxford: Oxford Clarendon Press, 1986; B. Ruhm von Oppen (ed.) *Helmut James von Moltke. Letters to Freya: 1939–1945*, New York: Knopf, 1990; F. von Moltke, *Memories of Kreisau and the German Resistance*, Lincoln: University of Nebraska Press, 2005.

131 Roseman, *Past in Hiding*, p95.

132 Ibid, pp330–1.

133 "The diary is not a stream of consciousness or unmediated outpouring of emotion but a remarkably composed document. It was clearly influenced by a genre of reflective journal-keeping that sought to probe the essence of things, rather than record the day-to-day … The diary was also clearly a way or regaining balance, finding her feet, a deliberate counterweight to the fears of the day." See ibid, p329.

134 Ibid, p338.

135 Ibid, p260. The reworking of this and other incidents of loss in Marianne's memory during the intervening five decades becomes central to Roseman's reflections on the difficulties of mastering the past. In each case, the re-description altered part of the event without affecting either its human awfulness or the narrative's basic structure. Interpreting these slips required patiently measuring Marianne's initial recollections against all the available oral and documentary evidence, private and official, painstakingly assembled with the historian's true persistence and ingenuity.

136 Ibid, p242. When Marianne was summoned for Gestapo interrogation in November 1942, her parents checked her diary and letters for incriminating material in the event of a search. She was enraged at the violation of privacy, withdrew from them, and removed her belongings from the house. She recorded: "Unspoken and spoken accusations against the bad, cold daughter who shows her loved ones only ingratitude, egotism, and lack of trust. I am used to them and they affect me no more now than before" (ibid, also, for the following).

137 Ibid, pp418, 421.

138 Ibid, pp411–12.

139 Ibid, p209.

140 See Roseman, *Past in Hiding*, p10: "As in a detective story, I also felt my way, initially rather blindly, along an extending chain of witnesses. I found business contacts of Marianne's parents, distant relatives, ex–schoolmates, members of the *Bund*, and post-war friends. My search led me across Germany, Israel, the United States, and Argentina and brought me correspondents and contacts in Canada, Australia, France, Sweden, Poland, and the Czech Republic – a poignant reminder of the fate of German Jewry."

141 See Aly and Heim, *Architects of Annihilation*; Aly, *"Final Solution"*; Mazower, *Hitler's Empire*; Baranowski, *Nazi Imperialism*; Tooze, *Wages of Destruction*; also C. P. Kakel, *The American West and the Nazi East: A Comparative and Interpretive Perspective*, Houndmills: Palgrave Macmillan, 2011.

142 I have developed this argument more fully in G. Eley, "Empire by Land or Sea?" See also M. Davis, *Late Victorian Holocausts: El Niño Famines and the Making of the Third World*, London: Verso, 2002.

143 M. Levene, *Genocide in the Age of the Nation–State, Vol. 1: The Meaning of Genocide*, and *Vol. 2: The Rise of the West and the Coming of Genocide*, London: I. B. Tauris, 2005; D. Bloxham, *The Great Game of Genocide: Imperialism, Nationalism, and the Destruction of the Ottoman Armenians*, Oxford: Oxford University Press, 2005; Bloxham, *Final Solution*; A. D. Moses, "Genocide and Modernity," in Stone (ed.) *Historiography of Genocide*, pp156–93; Moses, "Holocaust and Genocide" and "Empire, Colony, Genocide: Keywords and the Philosophy of History," in Moses (ed.), *Empire, Colony, Genocide*, pp3–54; Moses and D. Stone (eds) *Colonialism and Genocide*; Stone (ed.) *Historiography of Genocide*; Stone, *History, Memory, and Mass Atrocity*; Stone, *Histories of the Holocaust*.

144 For a critique of the "uniqueness" perspective, see A. D. Moses, "Hannah Arendt, Imperialisms, and the Holocaust," in Langbehn and Salama (eds) *German Colonialism*, pp72–92.

145 Here see especially R. G. Suny, F. Möge Göçek, and N. Naimark (eds) *A Question of Genocide: Armenians and Turks at the End of the Ottoman Empire*, Oxford: Oxford University Press, 2011.

146 See J. Zimmerer, "The Birth of the *Ostland;*" J. Zimmerer and J. Zeller (eds) *Genocide in German South-West Africa: The Colonial War of 1904–1908 in Namibia and its Aftermath*, London: Merlin Press, 2008; Farber and Lower, "Colonialism and Genocide;" K. Kopp, *Wild East: Constructing Poland as Colonial Space*, Ann Arbor: University of Michigan Press, 2012, and "Arguing the Case for a Colonial Poland," in Langbehn and Salama (eds) *German Colonialism*, pp146–63. Especially helpful is M. P. Fitzpatrick, "The Pre-History of the Holocaust? The *Sonderweg* and the *Historikerstreit* Debates and the Abject Colonial Past," *Central European History*, 2008, vol. 41, no. 3, 477–503.

147 Degrees of consensus may easily be overstated. See, for instance, the "Review Forum" on Bloxham's *Final Solution*, with contributions by J. Matthäus, M. Shaw, O. Bartov, D. Bergen, and D. Bloxham, *Journal of Genocide Research*, 2011, vol. 13, no. 1–2, 107–52, especially the commentaries of Bartov (pp121–9) and Bergen (pp129–34).

148 It remains less than clear whether Friedlander is ready to forego the Holocaust's uniqueness. See Confino's astute discussion in "Narrative Form and Historical Sensation," p48; also Moses, "Redemptive Antisemitism and the Imperialist Imaginary," esp. pp234–5, 249.

149 Browning, *Remembering Survival.*

150 Ibid, p29, italics in the original.

151 W. Benjamin, "Theses on the Philosophy of History (Thesis VII)," in H. Arendt (ed.) *Illuminations*, London: Collins/Fontana, 1970, p258.

152 Ibid, (Thesis IV), pp256–7.

153 The story was Kovner's poetic embellishment of an actual encounter: "At one point, in the ghetto, he went to a cellar, and he saw there a tailor, and the man was actually sewing, but there was no material and no paper, there was simply nothing. And the tailor was working on the machine, and the machine had no needle, and no thread. And when Abba asked, thinking the tailor had gone out of his mind, the man answered, that he had no work, and the machine was useless, and he was pretending, just like the Jews were pretending that there was substance to their live in the ghetto, and that that was the core of the history of the Jews." Interview, "Yehuda Bauer, Historian of the Holocaust (Part 1)," *Online Dimensions: A Journal of Holocaust Studies*, 2004, vol. 18, no. 1, http://www.adl.org/education/dimensions_18_1/portrait.aspFor Kovner; see D. Porat, *The Fall of a Sparrow: The Life and Times of Abba Kovner*, Stanford: Stanford University Press, 2009.

7

WHERE ARE WE NOW WITH THEORIES OF FASCISM?

Times of emergency

"All history is contemporary history," wrote R. G. Collingwood in that oft-cited statement from *The Idea of History*, composed mainly in the late 1930s. He intended this "not in the ordinary sense of the word, where contemporary history means the history of the comparatively recent past, but in the stricter sense: the consciousness of one's own activity as one actually performs it." He continued: "History is thus the self-knowledge of the living mind. For even when the events which the historian studies are events that happened in the distant past, the condition of their being historically known is that they should vibrate in the historian's mind."[1] In Collingwood's understanding of the study of the past, "all history is the history of thought" recaptured by a process of critical imagining in an exercise of controlled and reconstructive empathy: the historian needs to "think over again for himself the thought whose expression he is trying to interpret." Historical knowledge is thus the "re-enactment in the historian's mind of the thought whose history he is studying."[2] Collingwood was here directly invoking what he called Benedetto Croce's "doctrine of the contemporaneity of history."[3] For Croce, the "past" only becomes written into "history" when animated by the needs and interests of "present life," when it resonates with some active concern akin to a "love affair" or "a danger that threatens me," or troubles some sense of "unhappiness" or "anxiety."[4] The *past* becomes *history* by vibrating in the "soul of the historian."[5] Every true history is "contemporary history," Croce insisted, "because, however remote in time events thus recounted may seem to be, the history in reality refers to present needs and present situations wherein those events vibrate."[6]

In both cases, Collingwood and Croce, the *presentism* of this stance was profoundly informed by the dangerousness of the early twentieth century, above all by the successive catastrophes of World War I and the advent of fascism. In Walter

Benjamin's words, and without over-literalizing the pertinence of the description, we might see ourselves as once again living through a "state of emergency."[7] "Truly, I live in dark times!" another contemporary, Bertolt Brecht, began one of his finest poems: "The person who laughs/Has simply not yet had/The terrible news."[8] In such times, an urgency is imparted to the historian's labors, one that sharpens our perspective, jolts the sensibility, changes what we are able to see. "The true image of the past," Benjamin wrote, is the one that "flits by," catches our attention, calls us to knowledge: "To articulate the past historically ... means to seize hold of a memory as it flashes up in a moment of danger."[9] The force of this aphorism is not to reduce history to a presentism of simplistic or exorbitant demands or to remove it from the historian's rules of knowledge. Rather, it sharpens the historian's sense of responsibility in exploring how and where those rules might fruitfully be applied. The urgency makes the historian's craftful expertise all the more vital rather than less. That expertise becomes the best guide to what the past might tell us and what not. The historian picks a trail carefully through history's landscape while surveying its resources and its ruins.

I have spent the entirety of my career worrying the problem of fascism. This is not the only set of questions I pursue. But it works as a persistent reminder, a recurring intention, a kind of default ground. My earliest work, *Reshaping the German Right*, was an attempt to understand what I called the conditions of possibility for a German fascism earlier in the twentieth century; *The Peculiarities of German History*, written concurrently, sought to disengage Germany's past from the deep-cultural teleology of catastrophic exceptionalism that in my view obscured the more relevant conjunctures of immediate crisis where Nazism actually began; soon after I wrote directly about theories of fascism *per se*.[10] In the meantime much has changed. When I first began thinking about the question it was barely two decades after fascism's defeat, marking more or less the same distance between the first Iraq War or the end of Communism and today. But the ease of the fascist analogy, usually to indict one's opponents, has not diminished. Nor has the gravity of the actually existing worlds of political conflict, political injustice, and collectively administered political violence. The new political circumstances of the twenty-first century make it urgently desirable to sort through the possible guidance that a concept of fascism might provide. I am moved by three impulses in that regard.

First, I would mention the pervasive racialization of European politics via the growth of a violently anti-immigrant and xenophobic Right, whose opponents have always reached easily for a language of anti-Nazi and anti-racist equivalence. This particular dynamic was already evident by the later 1970s but accelerated during the past two decades.[11] *Second*, there is another chain of equivalence in current political discourse linking *anti-Semitism*, *anti-Zionism*, and *radical Islamism* into a new polemical concoction of "Islamo-fascism," which equips its authors with an extraordinarily tendentious and self-serving equation.[12] In both these cases we need to sort through the necessary distinctions in historically grounded forms of analysis that might forefend against facile analogies.

A *third* impulse, deriving from the material ground of the divisiveness in the social worlds produced by contemporary capitalist restructuring rather than from these politically generated fields of adversarial discourse, involves the new politics of class formation and its associated institutional machineries of law, property, employment, residence, consumption, and mobility, whose effects reproduce and secure the now-prevailing patterns in the distribution of social inequality. Under conditions of neoliberalism and its impact upon the polities of the late capitalist countries – above all by the eviscerating of democratic citizenship in its historically realized forms – new extremes of social polarization are acquiring an ever-more dangerous anti-democratic edge. In circumstances of national emergency, to use the example of the United States – on the scale of 9/11 and its fallout, in the permanently embattled southwestern borderlands, or in the localized aftermath of Hurricane Katrina in New Orleans, itself the harbinger of similar and intensifying emergencies to come – these political dynamics easily threaten the kind of crisis where a politics *that begins to look like fascism* might coalesce. So it becomes important to examine the ways in which theories of fascism might help to bring these phenomena into focus.

The 1960s and 1970s: Sociologies of political backwardness

When scholarly discussion got seriously under way in the later 1960s, strongly driven by social scientists rather than historians, the accent fell heavily on forms of rule and the vagaries of comparative political development, with special attention to theories of mass society and latter-day versions of totalitarianism theory.[13] During this first period historians tended to see Nazism (less so Fascism in Italy) as a species of "anti-modernism," commonly addressed via the concept of the *Sonderweg* ("special path") that proposed Germany's fundamental difference from the "West."[14] By a second phase in the later 1970s and early 1980s, a different sociology was holding sway, stressing the study of social movements and deriving the rise of fascism from the social anger of the petty bourgeoisie and other displaced or damaged social categories suffering from the impact of a general societal crisis.[15] Convergently, by this time, a huge amount of monographic scholarship had also accumulated on both the German and Italian cases examining the social recruitment and social profile of the fascist movements concerned, including their relationship to particular social interests in town and country and their varying dynamics of mobilization. The emblematic text of that period was an enormous conference volume called *Who Were the Fascists?* (published in 1980), which brought together social historical research of the highest quality on a pan-European scale.[16] One consequence of these predominantly social-historical approaches – one might even say a necessary historiographical effect – was that, with very few exceptions, historians no longer took the ideology of fascism very seriously. This is the ground where the bulk of my discussion in this book has begun.

A salient feature of this older literature was a comparative developmentalism that in many respects continues to exert its influence. Here is one leading political scientist of a more recent generation, Sheri Berman, who sees fascism as a symptom of the degree to which "many of the habits, norms, and institutions that we now view as necessary to support a well-functioning democratic polity" failed to keep pace with the scale and forms of popular political mobilization in the early twentieth century.[17] A society's vulnerability to fascism under circumstances of crisis, the ground on which it might flourish, was created, in this view, by a deficit of civility, a lack of resilience in the institutional resources and collective self-organization of civil society, resulting from an insufficiently vigorous or decisive breakthrough to successful bourgeois modernity on a classical "Western" model.[18] The power of fascism's popular appeal is then to be explained by the failings of its opponents, not only of the socialist Left but also of liberalism, which "proved to have little to offer mass publics suffering from economic crisis, social dislocation, and cultural destabilization."[19]

In other words, the problem of fascism becomes re-described as a developmental syndrome of political backwardness and immaturity, an accumulation of deep-seated political incapacity, whether in its German or Italian variants.[20] This deep-historical perspective on *origins* postulated powerful linear continuities, showing how the interests of traditional élites and their pre-industrial, pre-modern mentalities could block the democratic modernizing of the political system, so that "authoritarian and anti-democratic structures in state and society" perdured.[21] The same argument from political backwardness then finds an experience of *successful* modernization in Britain, France, and the United States ("the West" of familiar parlance) that provides the measure of Germany's (and, by extension, Italy's) purportedly peculiar path.[22] On the one hand, the *Kaiserreich* was "authoritarian" in the generally agreed typology of nineteenth-century regimes. But on the other hand, authoritarianism's victory in shaping the Imperial German state is deemed an *exceptional* case, an abnormal interruption of a democratizing process that proceeded successfully elsewhere.

It is hard not to be impressed by the teleology holding this account together. For here "modernization" is avowedly abstracted from the present-day forms of liberal democracy in the post-1945 West. As such it is held to have been built into the structures of economic growth, a political accompaniment of the social values ("individual responsibility, risk-taking, the rational settlement of differences, tolerance, and the pursuit of individual and collective freedoms") that the rise of capitalism is supposed to have engendered.[23] Thus, not surprisingly, German historians have taken recourse to a vocabulary of "wrong turnings," "failures," "blockages," and "misdevelopment" or "mistaken development" in order to explain why German history diverged from the presumed model until after 1945. As Hans-Ulrich Wehler puts this, "any modern society attempting to be equal to the demands of constant social change" *logically requires* a constitutional framework of liberal democracy.[24] Conversely, the Imperial state's authoritarianism becomes the institutional expression of the "pre-industrial traditions" and their modernization-obstructing dominance over the pre-1914 political culture.

A radical disjunction is claimed in this way between "wealth" and "power," between the "modern" basis of the industrial capitalist economy and the "traditional" political arrangements that in Germany had never been swept away. Stability in the long run – the laying down of political culture capable of withstanding the later appeal and assaults of fascism – could only be ensured by developing more "modern" institutional arrangements for containing and handling social conflicts – that is, by "welfare-statist" and "parliamentary-democratic" replacements for "the rule of an authoritarian leadership and of privileged social groups centering around the pre-industrial elites of the aristocracy."[25] Otherwise, the inescapable dictates of power legitimation in the developed industrial economy could be satisfied only by artificial means of "secondary integration," which Wehler conceptualized systemically as "social imperialism," or the diversion outwards of social tensions into expansionist drives for imperialist accumulation. Between the modern economy and the backward state, accordingly, there arose destabilizing contradictions that were only bridgeable by manipulative techniques of rule, so long as the "real" solution of "modernizing" democratic reform was blocked. In this view, the unreformed Imperial state was incapable of reproducing itself other than by an escalating procession of crises, ending in the miscalculated risk of July 1914.[26]

This particular interpretation has always been structured by the need to explain Nazism: backwardness and traditionalism are found so easily in the *Kaiserreich*'s political culture because the difference of "1933" seems to require such clear divergence from the other long-range histories of the West. If Germany produced fascism, and the other capitalist societies hit by the world economic crisis did *not*, then deep historical peculiarities must surely have been in play. Hence the outcome of the crisis of Weimar, the *dénouement* of 1933, owed far more to those longstanding authoritarian handicaps than to the impact of capitalist crisis *per se*. "Prussian militarism … Junker cliques … veneration of the state by clergy and professoriat … preponderance of heavy industry in the political decision-making process" – *these* were the deciding factors.[27]

Fascism resulted from a blockage of modernization in that sense, from the failure of liberalism to vanquish the vectors of backwardness. The opening toward fascism came from the pathologies of an only partially bourgeois society. "In Germany there was no 'bourgeois dominance' based in successful industrial capitalism that tipped over into fascism," Wehler argues (caricaturing supposedly Marxist interpretations in all too familiar style), but rather its opposite – namely, "a deficit of civility [*Bürgerlichkeit*], of bourgeois parliamentarianism, and of firmly anchored bourgeois political culture." *That* was what "opened the way to the abyss."[28] Heinrich August Winkler agrees: "The reasons why democracy was liquidated in Germany in the course of the world economic crisis, and not in the other developed industrial societies, have less to do with the course of the crisis itself than with the different pre-industrial histories of these countries. The conditions for the rise of fascism have at least as much to do with feudalism and absolutism as with capitalism."[29]

In this way German history holds a key place in the literatures on comparative political development. It delivers the negative counter-case (the modernity *not* attained) against the liberal positivity of "the West." Early twentieth-century resistances against democracy, right-wing defense of privilege, coercive systems of authoritarian rule, recourse to violence, police repression, and attacks on civil liberties – everything out of keeping with an idealized construct of liberal democracy in the world since 1945 – become aligned on the "traditional" side of the backwardness *versus* modernity borderline. These were histories destined to be overcome, rather than problems or possibilities persisting inside the structures of modernity itself. *While* they persisted, in fact, they remained *ipso facto* evidence of a crisis-proneness that only fundamental liberalization could resolve. The pathologies of German history were modernity's absence. Thus, the failure of political modernization under the *Kaiserreich* before 1914 entailed a "permanent structural crisis" whose effects described a space where Nazism would eventually arise and succeed:

> Without a transformation of the social structure and the traditional power relationships, without social emancipation, modernization seems not to be possible ... The fatal consequences of the government politics through which the political predominance of the pre-industrial elites was to be maintained in the period of high industrialization were revealed quite clearly between 1914 and 1929, when these structures crumbled. By that time, the politics had helped create the dangerous conditions which smoothed the way for National Socialism.[30]

This claim, that the "powerful persistence of pre-industrial, pre-capitalist traditions" preempted the legitimacy of the Weimar Republic after 1918 and opened the way for the success of the Nazis, continues to shape perceptions of the German peculiarity.[31] As new research steadily accumulated during the 1980s and 1990s, though, the argument became significantly modified and sharpened, now stressing the expanding pre-1914 societal presence of the bourgeoisie, the growth of civility, and the greater diffusion of bourgeois values.[32] Wehler, in particular, has become more willing to acknowledge the degree to which bourgeois values permeated German society after unification and increasingly set the tone for German public life. He now distinguishes two primary domains of bourgeois success in that sense, involving values that began life sociologically during the late eighteenth and early nineteenth centuries inside a specifically bourgeois milieu, before then expanding to become universal social and cultural goods. He mentions first those "definite bourgeois organizational forms" that acquired generalized and normative validity and appeal, including most notably a particular model of the family, along with the *Verein* or voluntary association as the all-purpose medium of sociability, cultural exchange, and political action in a public sphere. Then, second, slipping imperceptibly from social history to the circulation of ideas, he sees "bourgeois norms and values" becoming culturally dominant – most decisively in the "system of law," but also in "the revolutionary principle of efficiency, orientation toward work, secularization, rationalization of thought and action, autonomy of the individual, individualism *per se*, and also the association of individuals for the purpose of clarifying their problems in public discussion."[33] This re-evaluation might be extended still further to the public culture and institutional arrangements of the new German Empire – to the legal and institutional infrastructure of the *Kaiserreich*, and to the growth and elaboration of public opinion via the modalities of an institutionally complex and legally guaranteed public sphere – while in the dynamically expanding late nineteenth-century capitalist economy, bourgeois values and accomplishments had their core domain.[34]

For the *Sonderweg* advocates, of course, it was always the *political* sphere in the stricter sense that revealed the German bourgeoisie's incapacity most clearly. If in the economy and civil society, even in the public sphere broadly understood, bourgeois achievements might be conceded, in other words, then in the state and political system (so goes the argument), the traditional élites remained just as entrenched as before. Even while allowing some revisions, Wehler and others reiterate the central argument about the backwardness in the *Kaiserreich*'s core political structures – monarchy, army, aristocratic privilege, Prussian predominance, more ambivalently the bureaucracy, but in general the institutionally secured primacy of the pre-industrial interests and élites – whose recalcitrance always impeded change, pre-empting the modernity that *was not* attained. After the recession of "vigorous bourgeois politics" since the 1870s, the bourgeoisie accommodated itself to subordinate positions (the argument runs), or at most to co-partnership with the old élites, moved not least by the challenge of the labor movement from below. Of the *combative* bourgeoisie needed for the breakthrough to modernity, present elsewhere in "bourgeois self-assurance, confidence in victory, deliverance from self-doubt, possession of political know-how, resistance to the new dangers from the right," there was no sign. To that degree, the master narrative of the *Sonderweg*, the deep structuralism of the account of the origins of Nazism, remains intact. The advance of the bourgeoisie halted at the gates of the political system. This was what separated German history in the nineteenth century from the successful modernizations of the West. The long-term meanings were immense. Nazism was "the bill for bourgeois conservatism and nationalism, for bourgeois timidity before the risky trial of strength, for the deficit of liberal-bourgeois political culture and successful bourgeois politics, and for the missing bourgeois stamp on state and society in general."[35]

German particularities: Modernity at the limit

Deconstructing these powerful identities of social and political history that organize our understandings of the German past, and dismantling the conceptual unities ascribed to "liberalism" and "bourgeoisie" is not easy because so many important beliefs of the post-1945 era are wrapped up in those assumptions. In this respect, the character of the Imperial German state between 1871 and 1914 offers one key site of critique. Why, for instance, should we assume that a state showing pronounced authoritarian features should express *ipso facto* the political rule of a landowning aristocracy and other pre-industrial élites? Why not explore the forms and limits of that state's adaptability during the societal transformations of Wilhelmine capitalism? The state transmuted under the latter's impact into an arena for reconciling and articulating a far wider range of dominant interests, which certainly encompassed the bourgeoisie in its various fractions. In that uneven, unfinished, and conflict-ridden process, it assembled a framework for the building of hegemony in its specifically late nineteenth-century German guise. Viewed in this way, the state of the *Kaiserreich* arguably proved just as adaptable as the states of Britain and France in discharging the tasks that "modern" states are called on to perform – securing the conditions of capitalist reproduction, doing the work of legitimation, organizing the unity of the dominant classes, mobilizing and holding the consent of the people. In that case, the "backward" or strictly reactionary elements may appear more isolated in the political system, the Constitution more flexible, and the "modernizing" forces more penetrative – making the "traditional" elements far less "traditional" – than most historians are ready to allow.[36]

Perhaps we should think again about what exactly the categories of the "traditional" and the "modern" might mean, whether in general or in the specific conjunctures of the *Kaiserreich*. In particular, the common equation between authoritarianism right-wing politics and imperialist foreign policies, on the one side, and "backwardness," archaism, and "pre-industrial traditions," on the other side, seems highly misleading. Precisely the most vigorous "modernizing" tendencies in the *Kaiserreich*, rather than the recalcitrantly "anti-modern" ones may have been the most pugnaciously consistent in pursuing imperialist and anti-democratic policies at home and abroad. If we replace the old "feudalization" thesis of an abject and supine bourgeoisie with a picture of bourgeois values cumulatively reshaping the Empire's cultural and institutional worlds, then other revisions can easily follow. The complexity now acknowledged in the Imperial polity and its relationship to the expanding dominance of bourgeois influences should lead us to discard the conceptual framework of the primacy of "pre-industrial traditions" *tout court*. Once we accept the irreducible contingency of political forms, and reject the premise that the societal predominance of a particular class carries the logical or law-like entailment of one type of state and political culture over another, we can approach the specificities of the *Kaiserreich* more constructively.

These thoughts are meant to clear some key ground. With its powerfully determinative reliance on deep-seated structural handicaps, producing a distinctive developmental pathology that marked German history off from the healthier trajectories of the West, the *Sonderweg* idea proposes its typologically conceived claims about German exceptionalism as a substitute for either *conjuncture* or *comparison* – where the one foregrounds the nature of the immediate fascism-producing crisis, the other a more carefully historicized set of contexts for seeing where Germany differed or converged. The *Sonderweg* approach makes it far harder to grasp World War I's overpowering effects. For the war brutalized contemporary sensibilities; it shook up and transformed the state–society relationship; it escalated the capacities for societal mobilization; it radicalized the dialectics of technology and violence; it pioneered the mass production of death. The *Sonderweg* approach also occludes the impact of the Russian Revolution, the wider revolutionary turbulence in Europe during 1917 to 1923, and the attendant polarizing of political options in authorizing the extremism that Nazism needed in order to thrive. The earlier conjunctures before 1914, whether in the Wilhelmine period opened by the 1890s or in the moment of German unification, also become diminished.[37]

If in some regards a more authoritarian state than the parliamentary polities in Britain, France, and Northwest Europe, with an official culture that appeared aggressively militaristic and a foreign policy restlessly expansionist, Germany's most visible characteristics in the European landscape of the time were its turbulent industrialism and modernizing drives. As contemporaries saw very well, the *Kaiserreich* was the most compelling example of a *modern state* yet in existence, a model of "national efficiency" sustained by the most dynamic capitalism in Europe. The Empire's accomplishments in science, technology, engineering, design, planning, architecture, and other applied fields, together with the strength of its cultural institutions and the growth of the public sphere, enable us to speak realistically of bourgeois predominance in society, anchored in the growing structural primacy of industrial production in the capitalist mode. Further, if the bourgeoisie was not the class directly and exclusively in charge of the state (but which nineteenth-century bourgeoisie, in that strong sense of collective political agency, ever *was*?), it increasingly dominated the social, institutional, and ideological arenas where politics and governance had perforce to be conducted – that is, by exercising hegemony in the Gramscian sense. The capacity of German society to generate so many authoritarian or "illiberal" symptoms before 1914, so many potentials for radical right-wing politics, was inseparable from its *modernities* in this sense – not as a reaction *against* the latter, but as extrusions from their leading edge.

So, in the end, German history *does* contain a pre-1914 dynamic whose complicated effects Nazism presupposed. Yet, this was not one deeply inscribed in the primacy of pre-industrial traditions descending from the early nineteenth century and before, driven by a set of oppositions and resistances to modernity, in a peculiarly German anti-modernism that idealized the past. Rather, this was a modernizing society profoundly fixed on its future. This real distinctiveness of Germany's national history can only be properly registered by abandoning the framework of German exceptionalism altogether – by acknowledging Germany's importance as an example of *successful* if conflict-ridden capitalist modernization. The *Kaiserreich* before 1914 was the opposite of a backward state equivalent to Tsarism or the underdeveloped European periphery. Envious of Imperial Germany's passage toward restlessly expanding industrial strength, contemporaries could see this completely. Both the internal conflicts of German society and its foreign expansionism were precisely an expression of its modernity, the effects of a modernizing society pressing against its limits. The subsequent possibility of Nazism is then to be grasped far more via the post-1918 crises of military defeat and revolutionary upheaval than through some deeper-rooted pathology of backwardness. "Normalizing"

German history in this way – by acknowledging the self-evident particularities, yet freeing them from exceptionalism's teleology – may be more disquieting. But it will take us much further in historical and political understanding.

Germany's fascism: Four theses

In my earlier treatment of fascism from 1983, I developed four strong responses to the *Sonderweg* approach, each of which still strike me as valid today.[38]

The *first* picks up the argument implied by the preceding paragraphs: the necessary crucible for fascist radicalization was the immediate conjuncture of violence, empire, and revolution surrounding World War I. How societies emerged from that conjuncture marked out the new space in which the varying fields of political conflict, the possible alignments, and the boundaries of feasible change could all unfold. Rather than any longer-term societal pathologies or deep-historical structures of political backwardness, in other words, it was the contrasting outcomes of the war and the associated political settlements that primarily enabled the opening toward fascism. For the radicalizing and strengthening of the right in Germany and Italy, also in Hungary and elsewhere in East-Central Europe, *this* was the decisive impetus.[39]

My *second* response concentrates on the specific nature of the immediate fascism-producing crisis. To become viable as a politics, fascism required an especially severe crisis of the state. Fascism prospered from an impairment of the state's capacity for doing the work of reproduction, whether in managing the economy or for maintaining cohesion in society. In Italy during 1920 to 1922, in Germany in 1930 to 1933, that paralysis encompassed the entire institutional machinery of politics, including the parliamentary and party-political frameworks of representation. On the one hand, sufficient cooperation could no longer be organized among the dominant classes and their key economic fractions using the given party-based arrangements. Parliamentary coalition-building became unbearably complicated, displacing politics into a process of factionalized maneuvering for influence over the executive. In the process the gap widened between a patently unrepresentative governmental practice, disastrously divorced from any popular legitimacy, and a febrile popular electorate, increasingly mobilized for action but with ever-diminishing practical effect. On the other hand, accordingly, the popular legitimacy of the same institutional framework passed into disarray. Amidst the severity of this crisis, continuing adjustment of the given institutional arrangements began to seem more and more futile. The appeal of more radical solutions beyond the bounds of the system consequently widened.[40] This way of formulating the problem, as the intersection of twin crises, a crisis of representation and a crisis of hegemony or popular consent, derived from the ideas of Nicos Poulantzas and their subsequent reworking through the reception of the thought of Antonio Gramsci.[41]

Third, it became vital to reinstate the importance of fascist ideology, not just as the critical dissection of fascist ideas in the programmatic and philosophical senses, as interpretive readings of the key texts, or as the analysis of the fascist outlook, but by studying the nature of the fascist popular appeal. In particular, the contested terrain of popular-democratic aspirations required careful investigation, for it was here that the socialist Left proved so lacking, the fascist Right most telling in the efficacy of their interventions. Where the Left kept aggressively to a class-corporate practice of proletarian self-defense, the fascists erupted violently but inventively into the arena and appropriated the larger populist potential. In this regard, fascism emerged as a new and audacious synthesis, one that combined radical authoritarianism, militarized activism, and the drive for a coercive state, professing a radical-nationalist, imperialist, and racialist creed, shaped by violent antipathy against liberals, democrats, and socialists. This outlook was not organized around a codified core of texts or ideas; it was never "a closed canonical apparatus" or a strongly and elaborately "articulated system of belief," although individuals could certainly be found who displayed such coherence and elaborate self-consciousness.[42] Rather, it formed a matrix of common dispositions, what Mussolini called a "common denominator," "a set of master tropes" ordered around "violence, war, nation, the sacred, and the abject."[43]

Finally, it was the direct and open recourse to unrestrained political violence – to repressive and coercive forms of rule, to guns rather than words, to beating up one's opponents rather than denouncing them from the speaker's platform – that ultimately distinguished fascism from its alternatives. Coercion or repression *per se* was not the decisive marker. The coercive resources of the state are always available for use, whether by routine application of the law for the protection of persons and property or the maintenance of law and order, or by curtailment of civil liberties under pressure of a national emergency, as during wartime or a general strike. Coercion in that sense is an entirely normal dimension of legally constituted governing authority, whether liberal, authoritarian, or democratic. Privately organized coercion was likewise common to the polities of societies undergoing capitalist development in the later nineteenth century: strike-breaking, vigilantism, economic paternalism, and servile labor, especially in the countryside, were all richly to be found.[44] Yet, precisely when measured against such precedents, fascist violence was shockingly new. In Germany this contrast was clear. The Anti-Socialist Law of 1878 to 1890, the harassment, deporting, and imprisonment of left-wing activists, the unleashing of police or troops against strikers and demonstrators – all these were one thing. But *terror*, first by means of a militarist and violently confrontational style of politics, then as a principle of state organization, was quite another.

To put it bluntly: *killing* socialists rather than just arguing with them, or at most legally and practically restricting their rights, amounted to the most radical of departures. The brutality of this break can hardly be exaggerated. Before 1914, attacks on democracy had unfolded only within normative legal and political contexts that were gradually bringing extra-democratic violence under significant constraint. The liberal-constitutionalist polities that became generalized all over Europe as a result of the 1860s made arbitrary authority potentially accountable to representative government, parliamentary oversight, and liberal systems of the rule of law. Moreover, as the European socialist parties gained in electoral strength and parliamentary influence from the 1890s they brought the older systems of repressive policing under further review. Although during the 1900s a fresh process of polarized contention could be seen gathering pace, this incremental strengthening of constitutional politics made it possible in much of Europe for political life to stabilize significantly on the given parliamentary terrain.[45] And it was *this* political culture of ritualized and respectful proceduralism that the massive disruption of World War I so badly disordered. *This* was the history of cumulative progressivism that fascists violently disavowed. It was the hard-won and patiently consolidated practical consensual ground of political civility that fascists in Italy and Germany elected so aggressively to desert.[46]

In each of these ways my preferred approach has been, broadly speaking, a contextual one, stressing the conjunctural decisiveness of World War I, the necessity of a political crisis in the cohesion and legitimacy of the liberal-parliamentary state, certain key ideological departures ordered around an aggressively expansionist and exclusionary nationalism, and the recourse of a radical-nationalist and anti-democratic new Right to shockingly unrestrained political violence. I argued, in summary, 25 years ago, that fascism was "best understood … as primarily a counter-revolutionary ideological project, constituting a new kind of popular coalition, in the specific circumstances of an interwar crisis. As such it provided the motivational impetus for specific categories of radicalized political actors in the immediate aftermath of the First World War, embittered by national humiliation, enraged by the advance of the Left." Rather than reaching for deep-cultural explanations or structural theories of political backwardness, I argued the benefits of "*theorizing fascism in terms of the crisis that produced it*."[47] This primary emphasis on the "*fascism-producing crisis*" is one I still very definitely uphold. But in the meantime certain perspectives need to be added.

Fascism then …

Since the early 1990s the historiography of fascism has fully participated in what we now commonly summarize as the cultural turn. The trend has moved from *social* histories toward *culturalist* approaches of various kinds: new intellectual histories of Nazism and Italian Fascism; critical re-readings of French fascist intellectuals; studies of fascist aesthetics and the fascist spectacle; major studies of cinema and film; monographic scholarship across the whole range of the arts; studies of fashion, consumption, and all aspects of popular culture; historical scholarship oriented toward everyday life; studies of sexuality; and so forth. Fascism is now approached far less as the consequence of societal crisis and political breakdown than via the symptomatology of a cultural crisis of modernity. From having been a species of "anti-modernism," it now re-emerges as an ultra-nationalist and "palingenetic" appropriation of modernist energies (Roger Griffin). The Marxist version of this shift has been from political theory and materialist sociology (Poulantzas, Frankfurt

School, Gramsci) to culture and aesthetics (Benjamin). A series of further discussions now also converge: the still proliferating literatures on the Holocaust, including a massive historiography that accepts the "racial state" as the Third Reich's defining reality; current interest in states of emergency and states of exception, coalescing around renderings of the thought of Hannah Arendt, Carl Schmitt, and Giorgio Agamben; the study of fascist aesthetics in their complicated and ambivalent relations to modernism. In responding to some of the implications, I will offer five briefly described theses.

1 Fascism was a modernism

The early twentieth-century intellectual Right's Janus-faced ambivalence when confronting aspects of the emergent social world of modernity has long been remarked: it embraced the new technologies of industrial expansion, the imperialist entailments of a powerful economy, and the new conditions of mass political action, even as it lamented the lost worlds of tradition. The many intellectual histories of the "conservative revolution" and Jeffrey Herf's concept of "reactionary modernism" remain the classic locations for such discussion.[48] Yet, while vehemently anti-liberal and anti-Bolshevik, bitterly opposed to the democratizing effects of the changes accompanying the end of the war, fascists were not "anti-modern" or "backward-looking" in any analytically sensible use of those terms. Nor was the outlook especially paradoxical. Its exponents were "modernist in the full temporal sense of affirming the temporality of the new." Their "image of the future [might] derive from the mythology of some lost origin or suppressed national essence, but its temporal dynamic [was] rigorously futural." What the conservative revolution wished to "conserve" had already been "lost (if, indeed, it ever existed, which is doubtful), and hence [had to] be created anew." Indeed, "the chance [now] present[ed] itself to fully realize this 'past' *for the first time*." Thus, "reactionary modernism" was not an unnatural coupling in which modernism and reaction became arbitrarily stitched together, but a dynamic and forward-moving synthesis. Amid the accelerated intensities of a general societal crisis, such right-wing forms of thought acquired their own "modernist temporality" once the destruction of the given forms of social authority had passed beyond a certain point. Under such conditions, the conservative revolution became a "novel, complex, but *integral* form of modernism in its own right."[49]

By now, a large and variegated range of literatures has accumulated around this insight: the works of Zeev Sternhell; Matthew Affron and Mark Antliff's *Fascist Visions*; an impressive cohort of people working on Italy, including Walter Adamson, Ruth Ben-Ghiat, Claudio Fogu, Emily Braun, Marla Stone, Richard Etlin, Jeffrey Schnapp, and others; a vast body of work on interwar Germany, particularly on architecture, design, and planning; and probably most insistently of all, the historian Roger Griffin, whose recent *Modernism and Fascism: The Sense of a Beginning under Mussolini and Hitler* fully codifies a long accumulating set of claims.[50] As Griffin says: "Fascism can thus be interpreted on one level as an intensely politicized form of the modernist revolt against decadence," which saw "culture as a site of total social regeneration." And:

> Fascism is a form of programmatic modernism that seeks to conquer political power in order to realize a totalizing vision of national or ethnic rebirth. Its ultimate end is to overcome the decadence that has destroyed a sense of communal belonging and drained modernity of meaning and transcendence and usher in a new era of cultural homogeneity and health.[51]

2 Germany was not Italy

The main impetus for current work on *fascism-in-general* is a certain consensus of intellectual history emphasizing the importance of a "fascist minimum" cohering around the cultural crisis of modernism generated by the Great War. The most vociferous voice here has certainly been Griffin's. Here is another of his summary statements: "Fascism is a political ideology whose mythic core in its various permutations is a palingenetic form of populist ultra-nationalism."[52] Now, Griffin has helped to show beyond doubt both the centrality of such ideas to the overall architecture of Nazi political belief and the far greater heterodoxy in the Third Reich's cultural sphere than previously thought. But the imposing weight of this textual evidence obscures a fundamental difference between the German and Italian cases. The cultural apparatuses of the Italian regime left far more autonomies and heterogeneous intellectual space than the coercive machineries of conformity under the Third Reich were ever likely to permit. Thus, on the one hand, the counter-revolutionary violence of 1920 to 1922 hoisted Mussolini into power extraordinarily quickly, whereas the Nazi Party (NSDAP) came to power only after building an elaborate popular movement across an entire decade. On the other hand, the Italian regime remained a work in progress until the mid 1930s, while the Third Reich began elaborating its state-institutional complex incredibly rapidly immediately after the seizure of power.

Whereas the Fascist state in Italy provided multifarious space for conservative intellectuals to remain active, epitomized perhaps by Giovanni Gentile, under the Third Reich such figures were either quickly extruded or began marking their partial and complicated distance, from Oswald Spengler, Stefan George, and Ernst Jünger to Ernst Niekisch, Mies van der Rohe, and Edgar Julius Jung. This difference has to compromise the persuasiveness and sufficiency of Griffin's "palingenetic" interpretation. If the circumstances of 1919 to 1922 during the Italian emergency allowed any manner of idealistic and utopian expectations to cluster around the openings toward a rejuvenated national future, in the Nazi case those more eclectic registers of fascist intellectuality were simply foreclosed. By the time the Nazi Party reached the precincts of power, the alignments and polarities of the possible had already been made brutally clear. Once the state-institutional machineries of the Third Reich were in place, the consequences of anti-Semitism and of the "racial state" were also ruthlessly consolidatory in that regard.

3 Fascism entailed an intensifying of modernist governmentality

By "modernist governmentality," here I mean the hubris of early twentieth-century medicalizing, welfarist, and social policy expertise, and the planning utopias that approached "populations as both the means and the goal of some emancipatory project."[53] I mean the new ways of constructing, imagining, visualizing, quantifying, regulating, policing, improving, reorganizing, comprehensively redesigning, and perhaps transforming "the social," the social sphere, or *society*. In this way, too, the old view of fascism as "anti-modernist" has been overturned. But if in the Italian case the critique has shown modernism's relation to fascism in *the arts, philosophy, literature, and aesthetics*, in Germany historians have turned to *bio-political perspectives*, or the eugenicist and related ideologies of social expertise pervading the medical, healthcare, criminological, and social policy professions. Processes of medicalization and racialization were already well under way during the Weimar Republic, involving eugenics, population politics, welfare initiatives directed at women, family policies, criminology and penal reform, imagined projects of social engineering, and the deployment of science for social goals. During the first three decades of the century, anti-Semitic idioms also figured within ever more ramified repertoires of biological politics, where social, cultural, and political issues were systematically naturalized under the sign of race. As Chapter 6 has suggested, these implications make Nazi anti-Semitism *less* the ideological pathology of a cadre of obviously sociopathic fanatics than part of a syndrome deeply embedded in conventionalized beliefs and practices endemic to Germany's professional, managerial, and administrative social layers. It was thus *the opposite of* an atavistic and irrationalist anti-modern refusal of civilized norms that drove Nazi interest in racial science. The latter expressed, instead, the most hubristic potentialities of social engineering, inspired by the promise of technological, managerial, and scientific modernity.

Once the bio-political complex merged with the hardening institutional capacities of the Nazi racial state, ambitions easily developed to redesign in its entirety the given social order. These aspects of the Third Reich's policies and practices are discussed extensively in several of the earlier chapters. At lower levels of ambition and intensity, with less radical penetration into either professions or state apparatuses, similar histories may be assembled in the Italian case, too.[54] On a transnationally European front, the varying relations of eugenicist thought to widely diffused anxieties about cultural dissolution, social degeneration, and demographic crises of the nation have also been attracting much historiographical attention.[55] Yet, while such discourses circulated universally across Europe, the Americas, the colonial world, and Japan, the particular virulence of the fascist versions should not be effaced. In advance of the seizure of power, the ground of bio-political intervention was in this sense being discursively laid. But for the *actually realized practice*, in the counting, marking, segregating, and eliminating of populations via the particular deployments of fascist governmentality, the aggressively centralist machinery of the fascists' prerogative state still had to be created.

4 Fascism learned how to colonize the everyday

Focusing on commercial entertainment cultures, the rhythms of everyday life, and the fascist politics of the spectacle, some recent work suggests that it was precisely the private economy of desire, organized around family, sex, friendship, recreation, and the body, that fascism proved so adept at mastering. It was likewise the same territory of dreaming and pleasure, sexuality and recreation that gave most of the Left significant trouble. Thus, film, for example, was often disparaged by socialist commentators as just a new source of escapism and corruption for a still-uneducated working class. According to one German left-socialist newspaper in 1919: "The path to the gambling dens of the big city begins in the dance halls and the cinemas ... Surrounded by superficial din and deadened in their souls, the misled section of the proletarian youth dances its way into depravity."[56] Labor movements lacked the political languages for appealing to the new generations of young working women, the shop-girls, hairdressers, typists, assembly-line workers, and cleaners. The Social Democrats' (SPD's) social policy expert, Marie Juchacz, attacked the "destructive" pleasures of "the young prettily dressed girls," who poured from the shops and businesses at the end of the working day.[57] Faced with the new leisure habits of the working-class young, socialists tended to moralize, invoking traditional working-class values against the frivolity of the new entertainments.

This proved extraordinarily shortsighted. The emergent apparatus of the "culture industry," from the razzmatazz of the cinema and the dance hall to the rise of spectator sports, the star-system, and the machineries of advertising and fashion, proved remarkably successful in servicing popular desires. As Ernst Bloch understood, moreover, fascism needed to be opposed not just as the instrument of anti-democratic terror, heedlessly brutal and distressingly effective though its violence may have been, but as an engine of political fantasy, too, which harnessed psychic needs and utopian longings the Left would neglect at their peril. If politics organized at the intersections of public and personal life, colonizing the imagination, shaping ordinary needs, and inscribing everyday transactions with its rules, then the same process also described a key space of possible negotiation. The fantasies produced in Hollywood were a bridge to ordinary desire. They described an imaginary space ready for occupation, whether the Left wanted to move there or not.[58]

5 Fascism was an imperialism

Finally, current work focuses most powerfully of all on fascist expansionism. I am thinking here of the widely shared view that not only the main thrust of Nazi ideology, but also the essential principle of the Third Reich's social system was the drive for war.[59] This has long been a commonplace of scholarship on Nazism, from Hans Mommsen and Tim Mason to Klaus Hildebrand, and from the new historiography of the Holocaust to the imposing consensus on the consequences of the "racial state." But in the German field there is now a growing body of work that seeks to define the Third Reich via the centrality of empire and colonialism, whether in relation to the fundamental drives of Hitler and his movement or to the compulsions shaping the racialized "New Order" they sought to create. For this new work the continuities linking the expansionism of the two World Wars can best be grasped by a common framework of colonialism. But the main problem here remains one of concretization – that is, what was the specific importance for fascism of the compulsion to empire? The conjunctural trauma of military humiliation and unrequited nationalist hopes from 1918 to 1919, together with the ultranationalist fixation on national rebirth, provide one way of doing this. But how *else* do we ground our understanding of the dynamics of expansionism in the fascist political imaginary? How important *exactly* was the imperialist drive for the emergence of fascism? As the new histories of the Nazi economy make compellingly clear, the drive for militarist expansion – the readiness to wager Germany's future on the gargantuan risk of a continental and tendentially global war – also rested on longer-term geopolitical compulsions of the early twentieth-century international system, themselves centering on the emergent primacy of the United States and concentrated structurally around the consequences of World War I.[60]

So this is where I currently stand. *On the one hand*, I reiterate the value of certain older theses about the conjunctural decisiveness of World War I, the determinative necessity of a particular kind of political crisis, and the shocking recourse to political violence, which converge to a strongly contextual explanation that also makes intelligible fascism's specific ideological qualities. *On the other hand*, we also need to add an emphasis on fascism's particular embrace of modernity; on the conjunctural determination of national particularities (Italy 1919 to 1922 *versus* Germany 1930 to 1934); on the particular intensities of fascist governmentality; on fascism's colonizing of the everyday; and on the dynamics of fascist expansionism.

... and now

How might this help us in the present? I began this chapter with some observations on the stakes of invoking a language of fascism today, usually in the form of pejoratives or polemical abuse, more occasionally as controlled historical citation. In that respect the first aid that history provides is differentiation: what is specific and different about the crisis of the present and the political forms it inspires? Once we historicize, what does the language of fascism enable us legitimately and efficaciously to see? What does it obscure? What does it illumine? What can we take from the histories of fascism in the form of theory? What might we learn from the generative contexts of a specifically fascist politics in the early twentieth century in the form of abstraction that can be useful for political understanding now?

In addressing these questions, we need to be as clear as possible that fascism is *first and foremost a type of politics, or a set of relations to politics*. That is what allows us to decontextualize, in the historian's sense of freeing the term from its immediate crucible of time and place (those particular crisis conjunctures of interwar Europe) and allowing the process of abstraction to give us the really useful knowledge we need for today. In that case, it becomes possible to argue the fundamentally generative consequences of the big violence and state/economy and state/society transformations of World War I *without* making those huge contingencies into something essential, not least because the equivalent impact of the war worked rather differently in another primary contemporaneous case, that of Japan. Likewise, if we limit fascism to a type of politics – the coercively nationalist recourse to political violence and exclusionary authoritarianism under worsening circumstances of governmental paralysis and democratic impasse – then we can explore the differing and particular ways in which this distinctive fascist relation to politics might be inscribed in our contemporary circumstances, too. If we accept that fascism should be theorized in terms of the crisis that produces it, to take another of my propositions – if the character of the immediately fascism-producing crisis is the best place to begin – then we have another helpful point of comparison to explore.

So what *is* the nature of the present crisis? Confining myself to the United States, and by extension to other parts of the late-capitalist world, and at the risk of reckless simplification, I want to suggest the following elements.

First, beginning in good Marxist fashion from the current transformations of economic life, I would foreground the still-unfolding consequences of fundamental capitalist restructuring. That would include deindustrialization; the dismantling of Western capitalism's historic manufacturing base; post-Fordist transition; the trans-nationalizing of labor markets and the re-proletarianizing of labor; a new regime of accumulation ordered around the mobility of capital and the spectacle of consumption; a regime of regulation ruthlessly validating private accumulation and the gutting of public goods; and the hypertrophied disorder of a deregulated financial sector whose dominance is severed (or freed) from any apparent mechanisms of accountability or relationship to productive investment. This first element – the fiscal crisis of late capitalism – has profound implications for the conduct of government, for the reliable stabilities of political order, for the organized distribution of state power, and for the practice of sovereignty.

Second, the entailment of late capitalist restructuring is a drastic and thorough-going process of class recomposition. Class formation in the United States is always highly regionalized, always porous to cross-border migrancy on a vast scale, always structured around race, always subject to extraordinarily effective mystification, always constructed into being something else. Yet, by any objective criteria, the working class of today – as a social category of wage-earners dependent for a livelihood on the sale or exchange of labor power – is larger, less secure, and less reliant on the collective solidarities of residence, workplace, associations, and organized political agency than ever before. Of course, even in the 1950s and 1960s the social citizenship of some workers (mainly skilled, male, white) – their job security, higher wages and greater benefits, access to healthcare and housing, expectation of pensions, limited recognitions under the law – always presupposed a much wider reservoir of cheap and disposable labor power (mobile, low-waged, insecure, unprotected), whether located inside the sovereign borders or in the neocolonial elsewhere. In those terms, the postwar experience of relatively humanized capitalism remained no less beholden to globalized systems of exploitation of natural resources, human materials, and grotesquely unequal terms of trade than the preceding era of imperialist expansion. Postwar gains were embedded in the privileged prosperity of a metropolitan boom whose very possibility rested on historically specific repertoires of extraction and exploitation operating on a world scale. But now even that relative working-class prosperity stands revealed as a finite and passing phenomenon. At ever-accelerating pace, the social relations of work have been transformed since the 1980s into the new low-waged, semi-legal, and deregulated labor market of a mainly service-based and transnationalized economy. This as-yet unstoppable story of the de-skilling, de-unionizing, de-benefiting, and de-nationalizing of labor via the rampant processes of metropolitan deindustrialization and global capitalist restructuring has comprehensively undermined the model of significant social improvement around which so much of postwar political culture became built.

Not the least of the changes under way since the 1970s is thus a *re-proletarianizing of labor*. From our vantage point now, the relative working-class prosperity of the postwar boom re-emerges as a highly contingent interlude in the life of a capitalist social formation whose ordering principles look very different over the fullest span of its history. From the mid 1970s, every element in the potentially democratizing architecture of a postwar political imaginary was brought under brutally effective political attack. By the 1990s, little remained of either the practices or the principles, let alone the material structures and institutional relations previously organizing the political common sense. The social contract associated with the New Deal and the Great Society was gone. Instead, the post-Communist era now brought compelling evidence of a radically stripped-down version of the labor contract. New forms of the exploitation of labor relentlessly accumulated around the expanding prevalence of minimum-wage, de-qualified and de-skilled, disorganized and deregulated, semi-legal, and migrant labor markets, in which livelihoods are systematically stripped of precisely those forms of security and organized protection that an earlier politics had sought, however inadequately, to instate. This decisive and maybe irreversible socio-political transition forms the second element of the crisis.

Third, we have a broken polity. Here I will confine myself to listing some symptoms: the atrophy of democratic practices at the level of the state, whether in the manifestly undemocratic arena of the legislature or the triangulated field linking Presidency, Congress, and Supreme Court; the continuous thinning-out of democratic proceduralism at all levels of the institutional polity and the conduct of elections; the growing curtailment of civil liberties and the growth of the carceral state; the entrenchment among the citizenry of a default presumption that government is defined irremediably by burdensomeness, corruption, incompetence, and non-accountability; and last but not least what I would call the widespread popular belief in the non-intelligibility of power, or the belief that power unfolds, and is exercised, in a distant place, behind closed doors and opaque glass, by conspiracies of élites who are beholden to no one and simply do not care. This constellation of popular political understandings produces a climate of what Lauren

Berlant calls "crisis ordinariness," in which the present acquires a "stretched-out" quality that "merges an intensified present with senses of the recent past and near future," so that the familiar "temporal compartmentalizations of an ordinariness that can be broadly taken for granted are themselves suspended," and the process that "shapes part of the consciousness of what's durable (predictable, reliable, tractable) about life in the ordinary" gets disrupted and lost. We live through a time in which major societal transformations have brutally disturbed the habituated practices and understandings of how lives could and should be expected and allowed to unfold, producing "a loss of trust in the historical future, threats to the sense of ongoingness in the durational present, and increased opacity within ordinary life." As Berlant says, the confidence in society as an attainable collective good suffers a sustained shock, so that the "ground for trust or solidarity" or "shared affective management" begins to seem non-recuperable. The present becomes experienced as a "disturbed field, rather than a normative world." "Survival" becomes a maze with no exit. Within the affective registers produced by the brokenness of the polity – cynical, dispiriting, rage-inducing – an impairment of publics and openness is the widening result. From the ground of such "crisis ordinariness" a confident and optimistic relation to the future becomes hard to produce. The future can no longer be grasped as historic or even as a future at all.[61]

Fourth, the global environmental catastrophe, and climate change in particular, now challenge the possibilities for effective and accountable governance at all these levels, exacerbating current transformations of economic life, the immiseration of the working class, and the brokenness of the polity, while hugely worsening international instability. Big climatic events and subtle environmental changes will stretch the resources of already disabled national states, even as they strain the cooperative capacities of societies divisively organized around widening social inequalities. The global effects of environmental deterioration – competition among nations for basic resources; struggles to contain economic migrancy and refugee populations fleeing endemic shortages, droughts, and floods; rivalries over resources for energy – are likely to reshape the language of national security ever less generously. Fortress mentalities, idioms of politics organized by anxiety, *gatedness* as the emerging social paradigm – these increasingly drive the authoritarian and violent tendencies of contemporary governmentality. This new dialectics of international conflict and societal crisis may well enable a politics that resembles fascism to coalesce.

In my own thinking about fascism, I have always insisted on the specific features of the immediately fascism-producing crisis as the best place to begin – paradigmatically in relation to the years 1917 to 1923 and 1929 to 1934 in Italy and Germany, but now also in relation to the bases of social and political life in the United States today. The most obvious difference between these two moments is the historic defeat of an older Left, or at least the loss of the conditions of possibility that enabled that Left to sustain a political presence that for a certain period of the mid twentieth century brought meaningful political effects. Concretely, there are no organized collective solidarities of comparable staying power, on that earlier model, any more. That loss has been produced systemically by each of the big processes described above whose impact cumulatively compose the present crisis: the fiscal crisis of late-capitalist restructuring; the recomposition of class; the breaking of the polity. In fact, the consequences of the transformations of the past three decades may have been so destructive that the political capacities for the organizing of democratic agency on a sufficiently large, sustained, and efficaciously collective scale may no longer be available. To be blunt: before 1922 in Italy and before 1933 in Germany could be found the strongest socialist and Communist parties under capitalism; but in 2012 in the United States there is … what?

In terms of the political climate capable of sustaining fascism, what strikes me here most is the difference between the deliriously future-obsessed collapsing of past and present into the untrammeled and affirmative violence of a drive for national renewal (this is the gist of Roger Griffin's particular formulations), in which futurity *per se* became one of the main drivers organizing a fascist political imaginary *between the wars*, and in contrast the kind of impasse Berlant finds *in the present*, whose registers of futurity seem so inveterately those of a paranoid and apocalyptic fear. Conducing to the fascist temptation is this collapse of publicness, civility, and the pluralist generosity in a common culture, the encroaching paralysis of any trustworthy relationship to a normative set of practices whose older habituations and guiding intuition used to be far more reliably democratic. *This* is what distinguishes the present. It contains a profoundly different order of crisis than the originary ones of the interwar, with a different set of state–society relations, different categories of political actors, different types of possible political agency, different forms and processes of publicness (of the possible ways of becoming public), and a different surrounding environment of capitalism, all of which have the effect of calling up a different set of coercively authoritarian political interventions and modalities than before. But if we theorize fascism as an exceptional set of relations to politics made feasible and compelling by the intensifying of a particular type of crisis, then we can surely deploy the same term.

To "seize hold of a memory as it flashes up in a moment of danger," for these purposes and in the spirit of Benjamin's injunction, means grasping the specificities of each of these two moments, 1917 to 1934 and 2001 to 2013. In that case, Benjamin's "true image of the past" becomes a montage: on the one hand, the counter-revolutionary projects of 1922 and 1933 and, on the other hand, the zones of exception materializing around Guantanamo, Katrina, and the borderlands of the Southwest.

Notes

1 See R. G. Collingwood, *The Idea of History*, Oxford: Oxford University Press, 1978.
2 R. G. Collingwood, *An Autobiography*, Oxford: Oxford University Press, 1970, pp107, 110–15.
3 Collingwood, *Idea of History*, p283.
4 B. Croce, "History and Chronicle," in H. Meyerhoff (ed.) *The Philosophy of History in our Time*, New York: Doubleday Anchor, 1959, pp45, 46.

5 Ibid, pp45, 55.

6 B. Croce, *History as the Story of Liberty*, London: George Allen and Unwin, 1941, p19. For excellent commentary, see A. Curthoys and J. Docker, *Is History Fiction?* Ann Arbor: University of Michigan Press, 2005, pp90–114.

7 Thesis VIII, Ibid, p259.

8 J. Willett and R. Mannheim (eds) *Bertolt Brecht: Poems*, London: Eyre Meuthen, 1976, p318.

9 W. Benjamin, "Theses on the Philosophy of History (Theses V and VI)." in *Illuminations*, ed. Hannah Arendt, London: Collins/Fontana, 1970, p257.

10 G. Eley, *Reshaping the German Right: Radical Nationalism and Political Change after Bismarck*, New Haven: Yale University Press, 1980; D. Blackbourn and G. Eley, *The Peculiarities of German History: Bourgeois Society and Politics in Nineteenth-Century Germany*, Oxford: Oxford University Press, 1984; Eley, "What Produces Fascism: 'Pre-Industrial Traditions' or a 'Crisis of the Capitalist State'?" *Politics and Society*, 1983, vol. 12, no. 1, 53–82, reprinted in Eley, *From Unification to Nazism: Reinterpreting the German Past* (London: George Allen and Unwin, 1986), pp254–82.

11 See, for instance, P. Hainsworth, *The Extreme Right in Western Europe*, London: Routledge, 2008; H.-G. Betz, "Against Globalization: Xenophobia, Identity Politics, and Exclusionary Populism in Western Europe," in L. Panitch and C. Leys (eds) *Socialist Register 2003*, New York: Monthly Review Press, 2003, pp195–213; P. H. Merkl and L. Weinberg (eds) *Right-Wing Extremism in the Twenty-First Century*, London: Routledge, 2003. For the wider ideological field, see G. Eley, "The Trouble with 'Race': Migrancy, Cultural Difference, and the Remaking of Europe," in R. Chin, H. Fehrenbach, G. Eley, and A. Grossmann, *After the Nazi Racial State: Democracy and Difference in Germany and Europe*, Ann Arbor: University of Michigan Press, 2009, pp137–81; and for the intellectual histories involved, R. J. Golsan (ed.) *Fascism's Return: Scandal, Revision, and Ideology since 1980*, Lincoln: University of Nebraska Press, 1998.

12 For a sampling of sympathetic usages, see N. Podhoretz, *World War IV: The Long Struggle Against Islamofascism*, New York: Vintage, 2008; C. Hitchens, "Defending Islamofascism," *Slate*, 22 October 2007, http://www.slate.com/articles/news_-and_politics/fighting_words/2007/10/defending_islamofascism.html (accessed 4 November 2012); W. Laqueur, "The Origins of Fascism: Islamic Fascism, Islamophobia, Antisemitism," OUPblog, http://blog.oup.com/2006/10/the_origins_of_2/ (accessed 4 November 2012). For valuable commentary, see A. D. Moses, "Paranoia and Partisanship: Genocide Studies, Holocaust Historiography, and the 'Apocalyptic Conjuncture'," *Historical Journal*, 2011, vol. 54, no. 2, pp553–83, esp. pp581–3.

13 Emblematic for the time: S. J. Woof (ed.) *European Fascism*, and *The Nature of Fascism*, London: Weidenfeld and Nicolson, 1968; G. Allardyce (ed.) *The Place of Fascism in European History*, Englewood Cliffs, NJ: Prentice-Hall, 1971; J. Linz, "Some Notes toward a Comparative Study of Fascism in Sociological Historical Perspective," in W. Laqueur (ed.) *Fascism: A Reader's Guide. Analyses, Interpretations, Bibliography*, London: Wildwood House, 1976, pp3–121, and Linz and A. Stepan (eds) *The Breakdown of Democratic Regimes: Europe*, Baltimore: Johns Hopkins University Press, 1978; G. Germani, *Authoritarianism, Fascism, and Populism*, New Brunswick, NJ: Transaction, 1978. B. Hagtvet, "The Theory of Mass Society and the Collapse of the Weimar Republic: A Reexamination," in S. U. Larsen, B. Hagtvet, and J.-P. Myklebust (eds) *Who Were the Fascists? Social Roots of European Fascism*, Bergen: Universitetsforlaget, 1980, pp66–117.

14 See G. Eley, "The British Model and the German Road: Rethinking the Course of German History before 1914," in Blackbourn and Eley, *Peculiarities of German History*, pp39–155.

15 Emblematically: A. Leppert-Fögen, *Die deklassierte Klasse. Studien zur Geschichte und Ideologie des Kleinbürgertums*, Frankfurt am Main: Fischer Tasschenbuch Verlag, 1974.

16 Larsen, Hagtvet, and Myklebust (eds) *Who Were the Fascists?*

17 S. Berman, "Three Faces of Fascism," *World Policy Journal*, Fall 2003, p96. See also Berman, "Civil Society and the Collapse of the Weimar Republic," *World Politics*, vol. 49, 1997, pp401–29, and *The Primacy of Politics: Social Democracy and the Making of Europe's Twentieth Century*, Cambridge: Cambridge University Press, 2006, pp125–51. For my own framework, see G. Eley, "Capitalist Stabilities: Future Deferred," Chapter 15, *Forging Democracy: The History of the Left in Europe, 1850–2000*, New York: Oxford University Press, 2002, pp235–48.

18 The fundamentals of this view were assembled via the postwar coalescence of what became modernization theory among the ascendant circles of Anglo-American social science and its adherents in the Federal Republic of Germany. The emblematic texts for German historians included F. Stern, *The Politics of Cultural Despair: A Study in the Rise of the Germanic Ideology*, Berkeley: University of California Press, 1961; R. Dahrendorf, *Society and Democracy in Germany*, London: Weidenfeld and Nicolson, 1968; B. Moore Jr., *Social Origins of Dictatorship and Democracy: Lord and Peasant in the Making of the Modern World*, Boston: Beacon Press, 1966. See also F. Stern, *The Failure of Illiberalism: Essays on the Political Culture of Modern Germany*, London: George Allen and Unwin, 1972. Foundational in West Germany were two essays by M. R. Lepsius, republished in Lepsius, *Demokratie in Deutschland. Soziologisch-historische Konstellationsanalysen. Ausgewählte Aufsätze*, Göttingen: Vandenhoeck und Ruprecht, 1993, pp25–50, 11–24. Imposingly codified by the writings of H.-U. Wehler and co-thinkers, this *Sonderweg* thesis stabilized for a while into a reigning orthodoxy among German historians. See especially H.-U. Wehler, *Das Deutsche Kaiserreich 1871–1918*, Göttingen: Vandenhoeck und Ruprecht, 1973, translated as *The German Empire 1871–1918*, Leamington Spa: Berg, 1985.

19 Berman, "Three Faces of Fascism," p96.

20 The useable core of this approach consists in a potential argument about convergent histories of state formation dating from the national unifications and constitution-making of the 1860s, with all of the complex trajectories unfolding inside those necessarily provisional political settlements. Yet whether "political backwardness" or "pre-industrial traditions" can provide sensible frameworks for theorizing these histories remains moot. Given the concurrences of state formation from the 1860s and later convergences between the 1920s and 1940s, Japan might also be integrated into this comparison. I have learned much in that regard from conversations with Julia Adeney Thomas and a workshop on "Fascisms Then and Now" at Notre Dame in October 2012, whose other Japan specialists were Mark Driscoll, Christopher Goto-Jones, and Rikki Kersten. See also notes 22, 37, and 39 below.

21 Dahrendorf, *Society and Democracy*, p15.

22 While these analytics lend themselves rather obviously to elsewhere (Latin America, China, Japan), opportunities remain surprisingly neglected. But see F. Finchelstein, *Transatlantic Fascism: Ideology, Violence, and the Sacred in Argentina and Italy, 1919–1940*, Durham: Duke University Press, 2010; A. Tansman (ed) *The Culture of Japanese Fascism*, Durham: Duke University Press, 2009. For analogous marshaling of a *Sonderweg* perspective for Japan, see two classic essays by M. Maruyama, "The Ideology and Dynamics of Japanese Fascism" (1947), and "Fascism – Some Problems: A Consideration of its Political Dynamics" (1952), in M. Maruyama, *Thought and Behavior in Modern Japanese Politics*, Oxford: Oxford University Press, 1969, pp1–24, and 157–77.

23 This is the inventory provided by J. Kocka in "Ursachen des Nationalsozialismus," *Aus Politik und Zeitgeschichte*, 21 June 1980, pp9–13.

24 H.-U. Wehler, "Industrial Growth and Early German Imperialism," in R. Owen and B. Sutcliffe (eds) *Studies in the Theory of Imperialism*, London: Longman, 1972, p84.

25 Ibid, p78. Wehler repeats the formulation in a later, slightly revised version of the essay, "Industrielles Wachstum und früher deutscher Imperialismus," in Wehler, *Aus der Geschichte lernen? Essays*, Munich: Beck, 1988, p261.

26 Wehler links this argument explicitly to Habermas's theory of legitimation. See especially, Wehler, *Bismarck und der Imperialismus*, p500; J. Habermas, *Legitimation Crisis.*

London: Heinemann, 1976; orig. German 1973, and "What Does a Crisis Mean Today? Legitimation Problems in Late Capitalism," *Social Research*, 1973, vol. 40, no. 4, pp643–67.

27 H.-U. Wehler, "30. Januar 1933 – ein halbes Jahrhundert danach," *Von Politik und Zeitgeschichte*, 29 January 1983, p53.

28 Ibid, p52.

29 H. A. Winkler, "Die 'neue Linke' und der deutschen Faschismus: Zur Kritik neomarxistischer Theeorien über den Nationalsozialismus," in Winkler, *Revolution, Staat, Faschismus: Zur Revision des Historischen Materialismus*, Göttingen: Vandenhoeck und Ruprecht, 1978, p83.

30 Wehler, "Industrielles Wachstum," p269.

31 The quoted phrase, which during the 1970s became the mantra of such discussions associated with the "Bielefeld view," is taken from Kocka, "Ursachen," pp9–13. Wehler and Kocka each taught for many years at the University of Bielefeld. For further explication, see Eley, "What Produces Fascism."

32 In German the same term, *bürgerlich*, carries both sociological and culturalist connotations, referring both to a particular social category or grouping and to the values and practices organizing a particular mode of social life and sociality (as in "bourgeois society"/"civil society"), often as a practical conflation or presumed simultaneity. Thus *Bürgerlichkeit* can signify both "civility" and "the culture of the bourgeoisie," just as *bürgerlich* describes either the characteristics of the bourgeois class or the faculties of a civil society. In the writings of the Bielefeld historians the conflation actively shapes the interpretive thrust: the *Bürgertum* as a social force is deemed the main driver in the creation of a civil society that could normatively secure the lasting and reliable victory of liberal-democratic values. Thus, in contrast with the other countries of the West in nineteenth-century Europe, Kocka argues, "German society ... was characterized by a special lack of *Bürgerlichkeit*, a deficit that continued to shape Germany's history into the twentieth century." See J. Kocka, "The European Pattern and the German Case," in Kocka and A. Mitchell (eds) *Bourgeois Society in Nineteenth-Century Europe*, Oxford: Berg, 1993, p3. Unlike the other terms (*Bürger, bürgerlich, Bürgertum*), revealingly, Kocka offers no translation for *Bürgerlichkeit*. See also J. Kocka, *Civil Society and Dictatorship in Modern German History*, Hanover, NH: University Press of New England, 2010. For helpful guidance: S.-L. Hoffmann, *Civil Society, 1750–1914*, Houndmills: Palgrave Macmillan, 2006; F. Trentmann (ed.) *Paradoxes of Civil Society: New Perspectives on Modern German and British History*, New York: Berghahn Books, 2000.

33 H.-U. Wehler, "Wie 'bürgerlich' war das Deutsche Kaiserreich?" in Wehler, *Aus der Geschichte lernen?*, pp204–5.

34 See also D. Blackbourn and R. J. Evans (eds) *The German Bourgeoisie: Essays on the Social History of the German Middle Class from the Late Eighteenth to the Early Twentieth Century*, London: Routledge, 1991.

35 Wehler, "Wie 'bürgerlich' war das Deutsche Kaiserreich?" pp216–17.

36 For the state, see, above all, G. Steinmetz, *Regulating the Social: The Welfare State and Local Politics in Imperial Germany*, Princeton: Princeton University Press, 1993, and "The Myth of an Autonomous State: Industrialists, Junkers, and Social Policy in Imperial Germany," in G. Eley (ed.) *Society, Culture, and the State in Germany, 1870–1930*, Ann Arbor: University of Michigan Press, 1996, pp257–318; G. Eley, "The British Model and the German Road," and "Liberalism, Europe, and the Bourgeoisie, 1860–1914," in Blackbourn and Evans (eds) *German Bourgeoisie*, pp75–90 and 293–317.

37 My discussion is focused strictly on the German case, but its argument about the difficulties of negotiating the political complexities created by a conflict-ridden process of capitalist modernization applies, in principle, to the Italian one too, particularly when the parallel histories of unification, state-making and imperialist expansion between the 1860s and 1914 are taken into account. The same framework, *mutatis mutandis*, may also fit the case of Japan. During 1914 to 1923 these cases then in some ways diverge: if

Germany was disastrously defeated by 1918, Italy was technically on the winning side, while Japan experienced directly no equivalent of the wartime carnage and home privations endured in the two European countries. On the other hand, in each of these cases the extremes of postwar humiliations in the peace settlements stoked radical-nationalist anger that proved crucial to the political momentum of the fascists. Beside the essays of Masao Maruyama cited in note 22 above, see S. Matsumoto, "Introduction," *Journal of Social Political Ideas in Japan*, 1966, vol. 4, no. 2, pp2–19; H. D. Harootunian, "Comment on Professor Matsumoto's Introduction," ibid, 1967, vol. 5, no. 2/3; F. R. Dickinson, *War and National Reinvention: Japan in the Great War, 1914–1919*, Cambridge: Harvard University Press, 1999; M. Metzler, *Letter of Empire: The International Gold Standard and the Crisis of Liberalism in Prewar Japan*, Berkeley: University of California Press, 2006; and esp. J. A. Thomas, *Reconfiguring Modernity: Concepts of Nature in Japanese Political Ideology*, Berkeley: University of California Press, 2001, pp1–31, 209–25.

38 Eley, "What Produces Fascism."

39 As already mentioned above, the strength of this emphasis on the crucible of the war complicates the inclusion of Japan. For the larger project of developing a concept of fascism on a global scale that might apply to Japan, one might say, the consequences of World War I in Germany and Italy represent an enormous definitional excess. If we make the big violence of the war essential to the understanding of fascism, then fascism becomes European and Japan falls out. Yet, acknowledging the war's salience for the production of fascism in Europe should not rule out the other criteria developed in the rest of my discussion following below – namely, the older theses about a severe crisis of the state, the importance of fascist ideology, and recourse to political violence, plus the five new ones about modernity, national particularities, governmentality, consumption, and imperialism.

40 This argument may be widened comparatively to the broader European context. Germany and Italy were the closest to each other, although the fascist potentials in *Germany* proceeded via two installments (1918–1923 and 1929–1933) whereas *Italy* required only one (1917–1922). *Spain* (with the successive crises of 1917–1923 and 1931–1936) and *Austria* (1927–1934) also come close, while *France* during the Popular Front (1934–1937) developed in a similar direction. Other European societies producing significant fascist movements between the wars – such as Hungary and Finland – also experienced the polarized political breakdown and associated left-wing insurgency after World War I.

41 N. Poulantzas, *Fascism and Dictatorship*, London: New Left Books, 1974; J. Caplan, "Theories of Fascism: Nicos Poulantzas as Historian," *History Workshop Journal*, vol. 3, 1977, pp83–100; E. Laclau, "Fascism and Ideology," in Laclau, *Politics and Ideology in Marxist Theory*, London: Verso, 1977, pp81–142. See D. Abraham, *The Collapse of the Weimar Republic: Political Economy and Crisis*, 2nd edn, New York: Homes and Meier, 1988, p287: "Could no bourgeois political force organize the political unity of the dominant economic fractions out of the diversity and fractiousness of their economic interests? Was no political unity available and no mass political support available within the Republic, despite the single-mindedness of the dominant classes' anti-socialism? Were the maintenance of capitalist economic relations and political democracy so antithetical in *this* conjuncture that abandonment and undermining of the Republic were self-evident necessities for the dominant classes?"

42 F. Finchelstein, "On Fascist Ideology," *Constellations*, vol. 15, no. 3, 2008, pp321, 322.

43 Ibid, p323.

44 The incidence of privately deployed coercion did not necessarily correlate with the strength of constitutional government or liberal systems of the rule of law. Such violence was far more prevalent, even structurally diffused, in the United States before 1914 than in Germany, for example. This particular contrast was most striking of all in those two societies' labor relations.

45 This is a generalization needing many qualifications. Thus, the strongest socialist parties, those achieving more than 25 percent of the popular vote in democratic elections before 1914, could be found in a central and northern European "social democratic core" (German-speaking Europe including the mixed German–Czech lands of Bohemia and Moravia, together with Scandinavia); the weaker parties were in Eastern and Southern Europe, where parliamentary systems remained less developed and repressive practices more extreme. Moreover, under the impact of industrial militancy and popular mobilizations affecting most of Europe during 1904 to 1907, centering around the 1905 Russian Revolution, the long-term pattern of parliamentary stabilization incipiently broke down. See Eley, *Forging Democracy*, pp62–118.

46 See especially M. R. Ebner, *Ordinary Violence in Mussolini's Italy*, Cambridge: Cambridge University Press, 2011; S. Reichardt, *Faschistische Kampfbünde. Gewalt und Gemeinschaft im italienischen Squadrismus und in der deutschen SA*, Weimar: Böhlau Verlag, 2002; M. Richards, *A Time of Silence: Civil War and the Culture of Repression in Franco's Spain, 1936–1945*, Cambridge: Cambridge University Press, 1998; A. A. Kallis, "Fascism, Violence, and Terror," in B. Bowden and M. T. Davis (eds) *Terror: From Tyrannicide to Terrorism* (St Lucia: University of Queensland Press, 2008), pp190–204; D. Woodley, *Fascism and Political Theory: Critical Perspectives on Fascist Ideology*, London: Routledge, 2010, pp105–31.

47 Eley, "What Produces Fascism," pp275, 277.

48 See J. Herf, *Reactionary Modernism: Politics, Culture, and Technology in Weimar and the Third Reich*, Cambridge: Cambridge University Press, 1984. This field of interpretation is engaged in chapter one. See the writings of Stefan Breuer: *Ordnungen der Ungleichheit. Die deutsche Rechte im Widerstreit ihrer Ideen 1871–1945*, Darmstadt: Wissenschaftliche Buchgesellschaft, 2001; *Anatomie der konservativen Revolution*, Darmstadt: Wissenschaftliche Buchgesellschaft, 1993; *Nationalismus und Faschismus: Frankreich, Italien und Deutschland im Vergleich*, Darmstadt: Wissenschaftliche Buchgesellschaft, 2005.

49 See P. Osborne, *The Politics of Time: Modernity and the Avant-Garde*, London: Verso, 1995, pp163–6.

50 Z. Sternhell, *The Birth of Fascist Ideology: From Cultural Rebellion to Political Revolution*, Princeton: Princeton University Press, 1994; M. Affron and M. Antliff (eds) *Fascist Visions: Art and Ideology in France and Italy*, Princeton: Princeton University Press, 1997; W. Adamson, *Avant-Garde Florence: From Modernism to Fascism*, Cambridge: Harvard University Press, 1993, and *Embattled Avant-Gardes: Modernism's Resistance to Commodity Culture in Europe*, Berkeley: University of California Press, 2007; R. Ben-Ghiat, *Fascist Modernities: Italy, 1922–1945*, Berkeley: University of California Press, 2004; C. Fogu, *The Historic Imaginary: Politics of History in Fascist Italy*, Toronto: University of Toronto Press, 2003; E. Braun, *Mario Sironi and Italian Modernism: Art and Politics under Fascism*, Cambridge: Cambridge University Press, 2000; M. S. Stone, *The Patron State: Culture and Politics in Fascist Italy*, Princeton: Princeton University Press, 1998; S. Falasca-Zamponi, *Fascist Spectacle: The Aesthetics of Power in Mussolini's Italy*, Berkeley: University of California Press, 1997; J. T. Schnapp, *Building Fascism, Communism, Liberal Democracy: Gaetano Ciocca – Architect, Inventor, Farmer, Writer, Engineer*, Stanford: Stanford University Press, 2003, and *Staging Fascism: 18BL and the Theater of Masses for Masses*, Stanford: Stanford University Press, 1996; R. A. Etlin (ed) *Art, Culture, and Media under the Third Reich*, Chicago: University of Chicago Press, 2002; R. Griffin, *Modernism and Fascism: The Sense of a Beginning under Mussolini and Hitler*, London: Palgrave Macmillan, 2007.

51 Griffin, *Modernism and Fascism*, pp181, 182.

52 Griffin, *The Nature of Fascism*, p26. See also Griffin, "The Primacy of Culture: The Current Growth (or Manufacture) of Consensus within Fascist Studies," *Journal of Contemporary History*, vol. 37, 2002, pp21–43.

53 See S. Kotkin, "Modern Times: The Soviet Union and the Interwar Conjuncture," *Kritika: Explorations in Russian and Eurasian History*, 2001, vol. 2, no. 1, pp111–64.

54 See M. S. Quine, *Italy's Social Revolution: Charity and Welfare from Liberalism to Fascism*, Houndmills: Palgrave Macmillan, 2002, and "The First-Wave Eugenic Revolution in Southern Europe: Science *sans frontières*," in A. Bashford and P. Levine (eds) *The Oxford Handbook of the History of Eugenics*, Oxford: Oxford University Press, 2010, pp377–97; A. Gillette, *Racial Theories in Fascist Italy*, London: Routledge, 2001; D. G. Horn, *Social Bodies: Science, Reproduction, and Italian Modernity*, Princeton: Princeton University Press, 1994.

55 See especially Bashford and Levine (eds) *Oxford Handbook*; M. Turda, *Modernism and Eugenics*, Houndmills: Palgrave Macmillan, 2010; Turda and P. J. Weindling (eds) *Blood and Homeland: Eugenics and Radical Nationalism in Central and Southeast Europe, 1900–1940,* Budapest: Central European University Press, 2007; M. Bucur, *Eugenics and Modernization in Interwar Romania*, Pittsburgh: University of Pittsburgh Press, 2002; R. Nye, "The Rise and Fall of the Eugenics Empire: Recent Perspectives on the Impact of Biomedical Thought in Modern Socity," *Historical Journal*, vol. 36, no. 3, 1993, pp687–700; A. Kallis, *Genocide and Fascism: The Eliminationist Drive in Fascist Europe*, New York: Routledge, 2009, pp48–84.

56 J. Wickham, "Working-Class Movement and Working-Class Life: Frankfurt am Main during the Weimar Republic," *Social History*, vol. 8, no. 3, 1983, p335.

57 Quoted from the discussion at the SPD's 1927 Kiel Congress, H. A. Winkler, *Der Schein der Normalität.Arbeiter und Arbeiterbewegung in der Weimarer Republik 1924 bis 1930*, Bonn: Dietz, 1985, pp353–5.

58 See E. Bloch, *Erbschaft dieser Zeit*, Frankfurt am Main: Suhrkamp, 1962. For the fascist politics of leisure, see especially: V. de Grazia, *The Culture of Consent: Mass Organization of Leisure in Fascist Italy*, Cambridge: Cambridge University Press, 1982; L. Passerini, *Fascism in Popular Memory: The Cultural Experience of the Turin Working Class*, Cambridge: Cambridge University Press, 1987.

59 For example, T. Mason, "The Legacy of 1918 for National Socialism," in A. J. Nicholls and E. Matthias (eds) *German Democracy and the Triumph of Hitler*, London: Macmillan, 1971, p218: "National Socialism appears as a radically new variant of the social imperialism of Bismarck and Wihelm II ... foreign expansion would legitimize not an inherited political and social system but an entirely new one." Mason's other works include: "Internal Crisis and War of Aggression, 1938–1939;" and "The Domestic Dynamics of Nazi Conquests: A Response to Critics," in J. Caplan (ed.) *Nazism, Fascism, and the Working Class*, Cambridge: Cambridge University Press, 1995, pp212–31, 295–322; "Domestic Crisis and War, 1939," in Caplan (ed.) *Social Policy*, pp294–330; "Debate: Germany, 'Domestic Crisis,' and War in 1939," with a Reply by Richard J. Overy, *Past and Present*, vol. 122, 1989, 205–40. A sense of the widely held more diffuse view of the Third Reich as "a regime inherently geared to war," can be gleaned from J. Noakes and G. Pridham (eds) *Nazism 1919–1945, vol. 3: Foreign Policy, War, and Racial Extermination. A Documentary Reader*, Exeter: University of Exeter Press, 1988, pp750–5 (here p751); I. Kershaw, *The Nazi Dictatorship*, pp134–60. See more specifically the writings of MacGregor Knox: "Conquest, Foreign and Domestic, in Fascist Italy and Nazi Germany," *Journal of Modern History*, vol. 56, 1984, pp1–57; "Expansionist Zeal, Fighting Power, and Staying Power in the Italian and German Dictatorships," in R. Bessel (ed) *Fascist Italy and Nazi Germany: Comparisons and Contrasts*, Cambridge: Cambridge University Press, 1996, pp113–33; *Common Destiny: Dictatorship, Foreign Policy, and War in Fascist Italy and Nazi Germany*, Cambridge: Cambridge University Press, 2000.

60 See, above all, A. Tooze, *The Wages of Destruction*. This largest of contexts defined by the evolving international system, going back to the 1850s and 1860s, accelerating through the two pre-war decades, and dramatically restructured via the wartime mobilizations and the terms of the postwar settlements, affords renewed opportunities for wider comparison, including not just Italy but Japan. For clarity on this matter I am indebted to Adam Tooze and discussions in the October 2012 Notre Dame Workshop mentioned in note 20 above.

61 L. Berlant, "Thinking about Feeling Historical," *Emotion, Space, and Society*, vol. 1, 2008, p5 (specific quotations from footnotes 8 and 12). See also Berlant, "Slow Death (Sovereignty, Obesity, Lateral Agency)," *Critical Inquiry*, vol. 33, no. 4, 2007, pp754–80, and "The Subject of True Feeling: Pain, Privacy, and Politics," in J. Dean (ed.) *Cultural Studies and Political Theory*, Ithaca: Cornell University Press, 2000, pp42–62. See now, above all, L. Berlant, *Cruel Optimism*, Durham: Duke University Press, 2011.

INDEX

abortion 98, 108, 125n35
aestheticization thesis 67, 209–10
aesthetics 7, 11n5, 44, 72, 178, 212
Africa 134
Agamben, Giorgio 209–10
agency 9, 11n13, 17, 41, 79, 168; collective agency 36–7, 206, 215; final solution 159; holocaust 178; suspension of ethical agency, 145–6; versus 'rule' 45–8; women 93–9, 103, 107, 112, 121–2
Allen, Michael Thad 76, 82, 140
Alltagsgeschichte (history of everyday life) 18, 38, 44–8, 171, 175, 213
Aly, Götz 43, 61, 68, 75, 77, 171, 184
Angrick, Andrej 76
anti-Semitism 6–7, 19, 30, 40, 170; core institutions 79, 136, 169; media 43, 73, 79; *völkisch* movement 6
apoliticism 1
architecture 44, 67, 71, 206, 210
Arendt, Hannah 79, 81, 156, 160, 176, 209–10
art and design 210
Ayçoberry, Pierre 28–36

Baltic States 69–72, 118, 120, 137–40
Baranowski, Shelley 71, 133, 184
Bauer, Yehuda 47, 157, 178
Bavaria Project 13, 17–18, 37
Beck, Ulrich: reflexive modernization 11n13
belonging 1, 73, 132
Benjamin, Walter 146, 185–6, 198–9, 209, 218; aestheticization of politics 4, 67, 209–10
Berg, Nicolas 173
Berlin 71
Berman, Sheri 201
Bessel, Richard 13
Best, Werner 43, 57n112, 76, 81–2, 143, 171
biological politics 18–19, 169; *see also* social engineering
Bismarck, Otto von 133–4
Blackbourn, David 142–3
Bloxham, Donald 47, 185
Boak, Helen 93–5
Bock, Gisela 95–9, 121
Böhme, Franz 163
Bolshevism 25–30, 36, 137, 139, 144, 164, 210
Bormann, Martin 24, 142
Bosnia 184
bourgeoisie: failings 1, 200; values 200–4
Boyer, Dominic 2
Braudel, Fernand 147
breach of civility vi, 74
Breuer, Stefan 5–10
Bridenthal, Renate 95
Britain 109, 134–5, 158, 206; liberalism 1, 5, 7; modernization 201, 205
Broszat, Martin 13–20, 29, 32, 60–1, 165, 172–5; Bavaria Project 13, 17–18, 37; *Resistenz* 44, 116; structuralism 159–60
Browning, Christopher 25–6, 47, 161–4, 176, 185
Bullock, Alan 22, 27
Burleigh, Michael 29–36, 61; criticism of 36–7; political religion 32–5; racial state 36, 43, 63, 75; violence 29–30

Cambodia 184–5
Canning, Kathleen 107–8
capitalist restructuring 11n13, 200, 215–18, 224n60
Caplan, Jane 171–2
Castoriadis, Cornelius 148
Catholic Centre Party 92
Catholic culture 125n39; women 92, 126n49
Central Europe 134, 136, 207
Chamberlain, Houston Stewart 3
'charismatic leadership' 27, 33–35, 67, 78–80, 165–9, 181
Chickering, Roger 5
Childers, Tom 13–14
Christianity 2, 32, 35, 76, 94, 109
Church 33, 75 *see also* organized religion
Churchill, Winston 24
cinema 67
citizen-consumer 106
citizenship 2–3, 106–7, 131, 136–7, 178, 200, 215; rights vii, 34
civic nationalism 3
civility 36, 119; collapse vi, 1, 74, 201–3, 218
class *see* social class
Claß, Heinrich 7, 136, 143
Cocks, Geoffrey 73
coercion 14, 16, 21, 28, 40–2, 91, 208; women 107
collaboration 30–1, 37–8, 46, 129n81, 158; elites 29; institutional 166; Jewish 176–8
Collingwood, Robin George 198–9
collusion 66, 122, 159–60, 176; institutional 37; women 95, 122
colonialism 6, 133–6, 140, 143–6, 184–5, 213–15; expansionist policies 119–22; racial superiority 27; *see also* expansionism
'committee of three' 23–4
common destiny 3
communal solidarity 3
communism 16–18, 170
complicity 14–15, 18, 21–2, 37, 91, 182; elites 15; Jewish 156; professional classes 159–60; societal complicity 64, 92, 167; women 122
concentration camps 28, 35, 38, 42, 52n41, 72, 171–2; knowledge of 43, 56n110; *see also* forced labor
conformity 14–18, 37–40, 60, 67, 91, 182; acquiescence 75, 102, 115
consent 14–17, 36–9, 42–8, 61, 74, 91, 205–7
conservative revolution 2, 6, 11n9
constructed ideal 3
consumerism 68–70, 72–4
continental integration 136
core institutions 75, 140, 169–71
Craig, Gordon 158–9
Cramer, Kevin 2
criminology 19, 170, 212
Croce, Benedetto 198–9
Crystal Night (*Reichskristallnacht*) 24, 26, 30, 40, 42
cultural belonging 132
cultural despair 37; working classes 17
'cultural' nationalism 3, 134–5
culturalism 19
cumulative radicalization 14, 16, 26–7, 32, 159, 161, 165; Nazism 159, 161; structuralism 24

DAF *see* Labor Front
Dahrendorf, Ralf 1
Daniel, Ute 103, 105, 106
Davis, Belinda 106–8
Dawidowicz, Lucy 157, 159
De Lagarde, Paul 3
democracy 28, 34–6, 158, 208; Nazi hostility 7; modernization 201–3
denunciations 38, 39–40; police reliance on 45
deportations 39–40, 45, 96, 133, 137, 161–3; gypsies 173; Hungarian Jews 167; Madagascar solution 25, 31, 189n27; Poles 25, 31, 77, 81, 119
Deutsche Volksliste (German Ethnic Register) 140, 166, 191n55
Dieckmann, Christoph 76
Diederichs, Eugen 3
division of society 43, 60, 70

Eastern Europe 77, 140; expansionist policies 117–20, 134
Eckart, Dietrich 32
economic crises and fascism, 201–2
Eichmann, Adolf 25, 76, 79, 85n26, 169; final solution 25; trial 172, 176
Ellenbogen, Marianne 179–84
ethnic cleansing 25, 137
ethnic fundamentalism 141
ethnic nationalism 3
ethnic resettlement 31; *see also* resettlement
eugenics 7, 19, 77, 169–70, 212; motherhood-eugenics discourse 96; social policy 108, 135, 137
European politics: radicalization 120, 162, 185, 199, 219n11

euthanasia 30–1, 35, 52n41, 106, 163–4, 170
Evans, Richard 36
everyday life history *(Alltagsgeschichte)* 18, 38, 44–8, 175, 213
expansionism 131–2, 184, 185, 200, 202, 213–14; Russia 139; women's involvement 117–20
extermination camps 163; *see also* concentration camps

Fackenheim, Emil 157, 187n7, 192n83
Falter, Jürgen 14
family policies 19, 30, 61, 100, 105, 212; *Volksgemeinschaft* 66–70
family values 6, 203
fascism 207, 209, 213, 214–18; anti-modernism 200–2; Germany 73, 82, 107, 199–200, 207–9, 211; imperialism 213–14; Islamo-fascism 199; Italy 158, 200; modernism 210–12; popular appeal 201, 207–8; workers 117
fascist radicalization 207
fertility 105
Fest, Joachim 22
final solution 15–16, 25–6, 28–31, 77, 158–67; origins 170–1, 188n26
First World War 4–10, 107, 214–15; disintegration of family values 105, 203; fascist radicalization 2, 19, 207; impact on Germany's imperialist ambitions 137–40; impact on Third Reich 33–4, 78–9, 107; impact on *völkisch* movement 10; women 108–9, 112; workforce 110, 112
Fischer, Conan 13
Fleming, Gerald 159
forced labor 38, 48, 132, 149n2, 167, 173; Siemans 114; *Volkswagenwerk* (Volkswagen factory) 167–8
foreign policy 22, 30, 135, 206
Forster, Albert 140, 145
Foucault, Michael 19, 178
four-year plan 101, 142
Fraenkel, Ernst 78, 90n82
France 72, 109, 134, 149n3, 205–6; German nationalism 2–7, liberalism 7; modernization 201; Vichy 158
Frank, Hans 142, 163
Freikorps 79, 138–9, 151n25
Friedlander, Henry 43, 61, 75
Friedländer, Saul 43, 161, 164; integrated history of the Holocaust 172–6, 185, 193n100
Friedman, Filip 156–7; Nazi-centric v Judeo-centric history 176
Fritsch, Theodor 8
Fritzsche, Peter 14

'Germanization' 120, 140, 142–3, 154n50, 184; Poland 118–119, 143; *völkisch* model 143
'Germanness' 118, 122, 131, 134
Galicia 163, 186n3
Gellately, Robert 38–44
genocide 15, 26, 77, 162–3, 185; Bosnia 184; Cambodia 184–5; individual collaboration 166–7; institutional collaboration 166; Rwanda 184; societal complicity 167; *see also* Jews, persecution
Gerlach, Christian 76, 190n47
German Ethnic Register *see Deutsche Volksliste*
German resistance 17, 18, 50n12, 55n90
German vulnerability to Nazism 1, 201, 207–8;
Gestapo 37–43, 80–1
global crises: environmental catastrophe 217
globalization 134
Globocnik, Odilo 118–9, 163, 165
Goebbels, Josef 4, 24–25, 32, 37, 78, 121; Propaganda Ministry 67
Goldhagen, Daniel 167–8
Göring 23, 78; Office of the four-year plan 142
Greiser, Arthur 144, 162–5
Grieger, Manfred 167
Griffin, Roger 209, 210–11, 218

Hamilton, Richard 14
Harvey, David 147
Harvey, Elizabeth 118–22
Haushofer, Karl 143
health 19, 94, 98, 110, 113–15; healthcare 61, 92, 170, 212, 215; public health 108–9, 111, 139, 162; women's reproductive health 38, 94–6, 108
Heim, Susanne 171, 184
Heinemann, Isabel 76–7
Herbert, Ulrich 43, 140, 167, 173, 176; biography of Werner Best 76, 82, 171; *Volksgemeinschaft* 61
Herf, Jeffrey 3, 210
Heydrich, Reinhard 25–7; ethnic resettlement 31, 144; final solution 53n51, persecution of Jews 80–1, 164; Reich Security Head Office 26
Hilberg, Raul 79, 160, 176, 178

Hildebrand, Klaus 16, 159, 213
Hillgruber, Andreas 16, 159
Himmler, Heinrich 4, 25, 27, 77–8, 171; anti-Semitism 30; *Deutsche Volksliste* 140; ethnic resettlement 31; final solution 53n51; genocide 162–4; Reich Commission for the Strengthening of Germandom 142–3; Supreme Chief of the German Police 80
Hitler Youth 43, 72, 91, 124n29
Hitler, Adolf 4, 22, 23–4, 27; anti-Bolshevick crusade 27, 30, 139; 'charismatic leadership' 27, 165; *Mein Kampf* 16, 159; *Reichstag* 'prophecy' 24–5, 165–6; Third Reich and 22–8; as a 'weak dictator' 24, 159
holocaust 19; comparative studies 184; cumulative radicalization 165; definition 156; deniers 161; historical context 156–86; integrated history 174–6, 185, 193–4n100; intentionalist analysis 159; public memory 158; structuralist analysis 159–60; 'uniqueness' 157; usage of term 156–7
homosexuality 35, 40, 170
Hugenberg, Alfred 7, 93
Hull, Isabel 2
Hüttenberger, Peter 32

identity 10, 108; bourgeois identity, 78; collective identity 62; national identity 106–8; political identity 106; women 97, 114–15
ideology v. social context 141
imaginary 45, 148–9; political imaginary 34–6, 213–18; social imaginary 148–9; spatial imaginary 133, 143–146; *Volksgemeinschaft* 74
imperialism 135, 201–2, 213–14; ambitions 207; drive for new order 131; National Socialism 136; social imperialism 202; *see also* expansionism
individual freedom 7
individual motivations 43, 203–4
industrialization 8–9, 73, 109–10, 170, 203
industrial labor markets 103; women 100
inequality 7, 61, 200
institutions: ethos and practice 140
integrated history 174–6, 185, 193–4n100
intentionalist approach 15–16; decision-making processes 160–1; fundamental beliefs 159; Hitler's grand design 159; intentionalist-structuralist controversy 24, 28, 77, 160–1
international competition 134–5
international conflict 135
Irving, David 161
Islamo-fascism 199
Italy 131, 134, 158; fascism 200–1, 207, 209, 211–14

Jamin, Mathilde 13
Jehovah's witnesses 35, 40
Jews 158; anti-Jewish policies 30, 161; collusion 176, 177–8; compliance 178–9; expulsion 73; genocide 15, 24–25, 26, 31, 161, 170; persecution of 21, 24–25, 40, 157, 172; racial distinction from other categories 167–8; resistance 157–8, 176–7, 178; *see also* anti-Semitism
July plot 17, 31, 34, 37, 50n12
Jünger, Ernst 4, 6, 79, 211

Kaiserreich 1–10, 19, 133, 139, 201–6
Kater, Michael 13
Keim, August 7
Keitel, Wilhelm 23
Kershaw, Ian 20, 27, 28, 44, 161–4; Bavaria Project 17; biography of Adolf Hitler 22–7; 'charismatic leadership' 165; compliance of the working classes 17–18; structuralism 24; *Volksgemeinschaft* 61–2
Koonz, Claudia 95–9, 121, 141
Koslov, Elissa Mailänder 46
Kraft durch Freude (KdF) *see* Strength through Joy
Kühne, Thomas 62–4

Labor Front 41, 65, 113, 115, 124n29
labor movements 16, 28, 50n15, 64–69, 204, 213
Lammers, Hans-Heinrich 23–4, 142
Lange, Friedrich 8
League of German Maidens 43, 91, 99
Lebensraum 36, 70–5, 95, 144, 146–9; *Mitteleuropa* 133–6, 138
Lefebvre, Henri 147
Lekan, Thomas 145–6
Lepsius, M. Rainer 1; milieu thesis 8
Levene, Mark 185
Ley, Robert 69, 71, 124n29
liberalism 204; rejection of 2; weakness 1–2, 201–2
Lohalm, Uwe 9–10
Longerich, Peter 76, 161–7, 176
Lower, Wendy 140

Lüders, Marie-Elizabeth 104–5
Lüdtke, Alf 18, 65–6, 102, 175; *Alltagsgeschichte* 45–8

Manoschek, Walter 76
marriage 99, 112, 116–17, 120, 195n129; family policies 43, 105, 108 *Volksgemeinschaft* 66, 85n28
Mason, Tim 16–19, 44, 60–1, 100; *Volksgemeinschaft* 61; women's role in Nazi society 94, 101–2
mass execution 39, 75, 114, 141, 163, 174; *see also* concentration camps; extermination camps; final solution; genocide; Jews
Mazower, Mark 133, 184
media 43–5; public memorializing 158, *see also* propaganda
medicalization 18, 170, 212
Mendes-Flohr, Paul 156
mentally disabled people 108, 137, 170–1
milieu thesis 1–2, 8
Ministry for the Occupied Eastern Territories 142
Mitteleuropa 134–6
modernity 7, 8, 9, 10, 204–7, 210; impact on family values 6; impact on religious values 6
modernization 8–10, 11n13, 201–4, 206, 220n18, 221n37 *see also* industrialization; technology
Möller, Horst 61
Mommsen, Hans 14, 15–20, 29, 32, 75, 160, 165; *Volksgemeinschaft* 61; *Volkswagenwerk* 167–8; *see also* cumulative radicalization
Moore, Barrington 1
Moses, Dick 148, 185
Mosse, George 1, 5, 63
motherhood 96, 101, 121, 125n44; *see also* family policies; family values; women
Mouton, Michelle 99

national belonging 1, 73; *Volksgemeinschaft* 141
National Socialism 4, 22, 36, 136–7, 172–3, 203; doctrinal message 67; German expansionist ambitions 139; social imaginary 148–9; social policy 66, 97; space 148–9; *Volksgemeinschaft* 66–7; *weltpolitik* 136; women 94, 97, 122n4, 125n44; worker welfare 71, 114
National Socialist Womanhood 43, 91
nationalism 2–10
nationhood 132–4
Nazi ideology 60, 75–83, 94, 141, 168–9; definition 75; drive to destroy Jewish presence 161; history of ideas 140; motherhood 96, 101; purity of the blood 94; use of rituals 4, 32, 44, 66–7, 77, 98, 209; vigor of the race 94; women 101
Nazi New Order 24–6, 31, 131, 142–3, 149; Eastern Europe 118–22; population planning 171; Third Reich 171; war against the Jews 157
Nazi party 13, 91, 93, 211; anti-Semitism 169, 191n68; jurisdictional powers 78; policy and practice 159
Nazism 4, 19, 164, 180; breach with the past 4; coercion v consent 14, 42, 43, 48; complicity 14; influence over women 102; Nazi sociology 13; police repression 14; use of rituals 4, 32, 44, 66–7, 77, 98, 209; spatial approach 132–3; war against the Jews 158
Nebe, Artur 82
Nelson, Robert 139–40
neoliberal transformations of capitalism 34, 200
Neumann, Franz 29, 78
Niethammer, Lutz 18
Nietzsche, Friedrich 3
Noakes, Jeremy 13
Nolan, Mary 22
Nuremberg trials 82, 85n26, 172

Oberwinder, Heinrich 8
Office of the four-year plan 142
Ohlendorf, Otto 82
oral histories, importance of 176, 183
organized religion, 33–4; *see also* Catholic culture; Christianity; Protestantism
organized violence *see* violence
Orth, Karin 76–77

penal reform 19, 170, 210
People's Welfare Organization 43, 98
persecution of the Jews 21, 24–25, 40, 157, 172; active participation of populace 43; *see also* Jews
Peukert, Detlev 20, 44–5; genesis of the 'final solution' 170–1
Poland, 25, 77, 81, 161–2, 172; Germanization policies 118–9, 143; settlement programs 117–19
police 14, 25–9, 38–41, 145, 166, 171; Gellately, Robert 38–41; Gestapo

37–40, 81, 56n104; Himmler 80–1, 172; Poland 163
political backwardness 200–4
political disorder 14, 22–3, 27, 100–1, 140; structuralism 159–60
political history 8–9; deconstruction of 204
political imaginary 213–18
political religion 3–4, 32–5, 36–7, 53n71
politics 199–200; political parties 41, 42, 92
polycracy 15, 24, 32, 165–166; polycratic disorder 81, 100, 140
population policy and planning 19, 171
Porsche, Ferdinand 168
post-conservatism 6–7; critique of modernity 8
post-Nazism 82
post-war normalization 82, 173
poverty and social policies 109
press *see* media
Proctor, Robert 20
propaganda 16, 20, 75, 113; cinema 67; Germanness 131; KdF 70; Labor Front 114; staged events 35, 44, 61, 66; women 94, 98
Propaganda Ministry 67, 73–4, 141
Protestantism 32–3
public policy 61, 105, 171

race 7, 19
racial hygiene 19, 77, 108, 114, 146, 172; reproductive health 38
racial state 36, 43, 60–1, 63, 140, 160; racially-defined violence 171
racialization 18, 36–8; European politics 199–200; medicalization and 170, 212
radical nationalism 6, 33, 76–9, 136; 143–5, 209; organized violence, 185; Wilhelmine Germany 136-40, women 116
rationalization: German Labor Front 113; modernization of the labor process 110; Siemens 110–117; women in the workplace 110–17
rationing 69, 103, 106
Ratzel, Friedrich 143
reactionary modernism 3–4, 145, 210
rearmament 72–3, 101; financial cost 69
reconciliation of nature and technology 4
Reese, Dagmar 99, 102, 116, 117, 121
reflexive modernization 11n13
Reich Chancellery 22, 142
Reich Commission for the Strengthening of Germandom 142
Reich Security Head Office (RSHA) 76–9; anti-Semitism 79; Nazi ideology 76–83, 169; Polish campaign 81
Reiche, Eric 13
Reichstage 'prophecy' 24, 165–6
Reinharz, Jehuda 156
Reismann-Grone, Theodor 143
religion 33–4; *see also* Catholic culture; Christianity; Protestantism
reporting *see* media; propaganda
resettlement 27, 31, 120, 133, 138, 184; ghettoization 161–2; Poland 117–19, 135, 142–4
Resistenz 17, 44, 50n12, 55n90, 116, 182; limiting effects 17
Riefenstahl, Leni 67
Riehl, Wilhelm Heinrich 3
rituals 4, 32, 44, 66–7, 77, 98, 209
Rohkramer, Thomas 2–5, 10
Roma 170–2
Roseman, Mark 162–3, 168–9; Ellenbogen, Marianne 179–84
Rosenberg, Alfred 4, 32, 142
Rößner, Hans 82
rule of law 28, 40
Russian empire 135, 137–8
Rwanda 184

Saarland 131
Sachse, Carola 111–17, 121
Safrian, Hans 76–7
Sandkühler, Thomas 76
Schellenberg, Walter 81
Schmiechen-Ackermann, Detlef 61
Schmitt, Carl 4, 80, 210
Schulz, Karl 82
secularization of society 33, 203; *see also* organized religion
Serbia 163
Sering, Max 143
Siemens 110–17
single communal faith 3–5, 10
Sinti 170, 172
Smith, Helmut 3
social administration 61, 171
social class 16, 215–16; class conflict 7, 16; shaping Nazism 20; *see also* bourgeoisie; working class
social Darwinism 7, 32, 134, 136, 169; Nazi expansionism 134; *see also* social engineering
social differentiation 21
social discipline 41, 44, 109, 172
social dissonance 8–9

social divisions 7, 43, 70, 71, 200, 217; Weimar 2, 39–41, 61
social engineering 19, 172; pre-Nazi 170–1
social history, deconstruction of 204
social imaginary 148–9
social inequality 200
social mobility 78–9
social order: remaking of 61
social policy 108, 109; company-based social provision 109–10; German Labor Front (DAF) 114–15; impact on women 109–10; rationalization 110–17; *see also* welfare policies
societal crisis 200, 209–10, 217
Sonderweg thesis 1–4, 7, 10, 11n5; anti-modernism 200; structuralism 204; *volkisch* movement 2
Soviet Union: invasion of 27, 141, 162; mass murder of Soviet Jews 162, 189n31
space 146–9
spatial expansionism 132–6
spatial imaginary 133, 143–146
special way *see Sonderweg* thesis
Speer, Albert 24, 67; reconstruction of Berlin 71
SS (*Schutz-Staffel*) 140; genocide 27, 161; Germanization 140; 'ideological warriors' 168; leadership 76, 78; Nazi ideology 140, 144, 169; post-war 82; practices 76, 78, 140;
Stahl, Friedrich Julius 3
Stalin, Joseph 24, 35
sterilization 95, 97–9, 108, 121, 126n46
Stern, Fritz 1–2
Stibbe, Matthew 93, 101; women 126n49
Stone, Dan 47, 162, 166, 185
Stormtroopers (SA) 13, 91
Strength through Joy (KdF) 72, 102; consumerism 70–1; egalitarianism 69–70; politicization of cultural practices 71; workplace welfare 65
structuralist approach 15, 14, 29; collusion of professionals 159; institutional Nazism 159; intentionalist-structuralist controversy 160–1; marginalizing the Jewish voice 173; practical complicity 159–60; societal responsibility 159–60; *sonderweg* 204
Sturmabteilung (SA) (stormtroopers) 13, 91
Sudetenland 131
Sweeney, Denis 46–7, 121

T-4 program 52n41, 164, 170
Taylor, Charles 148
technology 8, 36, 110, 145, 205–6
territorial integrity 132, 185
territorial revision 149n3
theories of fascism 198–218
Thierack, Otto-Georg 171
Third Reich 4, 13–14, 159; Hitler and 22–8; influence of WW1 78; *Kriegsjugendgeneration* 78–9; policing 14, 25–9, 38–48, 56n104, 163–6, 171–2; racial state 19, 36, 43, 60–3, 140, 160; relationship to women 94–100; *see also* Nazi ideology; Nazi New Order; Nazi party; Nazism
Tooze, Adam 69, 72–3, 184
totalitarianism 16, 28, 29, 35, 200; institutional cohesion 14
transnationalising of labor markets vi, 215–6
Treaty of Versailles 22, 133–6
Tröger, Annemarie 92

United States 29, 157–8, 214–8; modernization 200–1; as a world empire 72–3, 135
Utopia 2–4, 133, 165, 211–13; Heydrich 81; racial utopia 34–6

vacations 118; working classes 69–72
violence 28–9, 36, 48, 207, 208; destruction of the rule of law 40, 43, 208, 214–15; racially-defined violence 171
Volk und Raum 138
völkisch movement 2, 5–6, 144–145; anti-Semitism 6; 'blood and soil' 2, 6; Breuer, Stefan 5–10; Wilhelmine Germany 9–10
Volksgemeinschaft (national community) 17, 33, 59–63; coercion 43, 74, 145; missionaries 121–122; national belonging 141; popular consent to Nazi rule 61; social context v ideology 60–1, 63, 141; opponents of *Volksgemeinschaft* 171
Volkswagenwerk 167–8
von Liebert, Eduard 7
von Reventlow, Ernst 8
von Saldern, Adelheid 18

Wagener, Hermann 3
Wagner, Richard 3
Walkenhorst, Peter 136–7
Weber, Max 27–8, 78
Wehler, Hans-Ulrich 1, 201–4

Weimar Republic 2–10, 19, 74, 105; collapse 13, 202–3; division of society 43, 60–1; medicalization and racialization 212; welfare state 108, 110; women 92–6, 118
welfare policies 19, 108, 110; women 104–8; worker welfare 71, 114
Wiesen, Jonathan 73–4
Wildt, Michael 76–7, 140, 162, 171
Wilhelmine Germany 9; radical nationalism 136–40; *volkisch* movement 9–10; *volksgemeinschaft* 136; *weltpolitik* 184
Williams, Raymond 46, 65, 147, 178
Williamson, George 2
Winkler, Dörte 100
Winkler, Heinrich August 61
Wolf, Gerhard 140; Germanization 143
women 99, 117–21; complicity 95; employment 100–8; factory working 103; Hitler's accession and 92; home working 103; impact of Nazism 92; labor market 103; Siemens 110–17; support for the Nazi party 95, 107; *Volksgemeinschaft* 98, 99; welfare 104–8; women's history 18, 92; women's rights 92; women's votes 92
work 64–66; improvements in the workplace 65; women 100–8
working classes 16; coercion 16, 21; workers' underground resistance 18

Yad Vashem Conference (1968) 157, 194n102; Jewish resistance 157, 176